ART Connections

Arts Education for the 21st Century

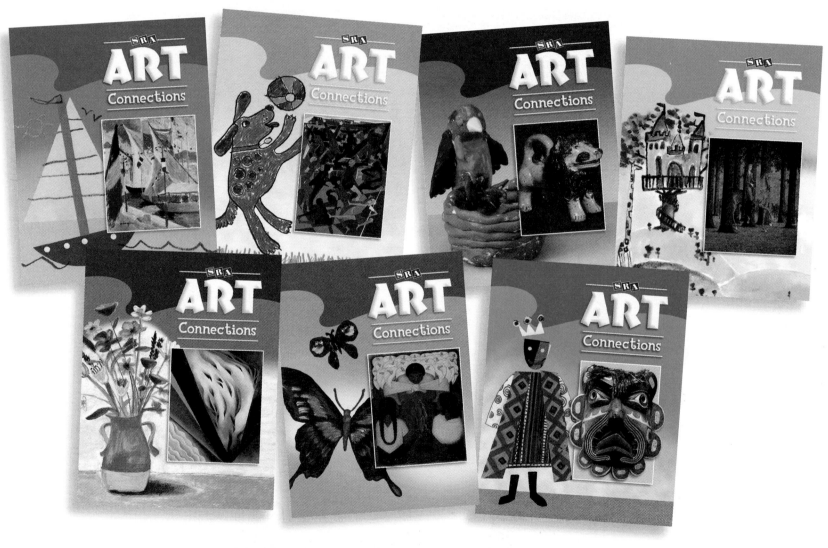

Culture   **Personal Expression**   **Creativity**

History   **Beauty**   **Critical Thinking**

Art encourages different ways of learning, knowing, and communicating.

i

All the Resources you Need for Great Art Teaching!

Art Connections provides everything teachers need to offer meaningful art education.

Student Edition K-6

Comprehensive student materials in two formats:

Student Edition

LEVEL 6

Big Book

LEVEL 6

Teacher Edition

Everything classroom and art teachers need to teach art effectively

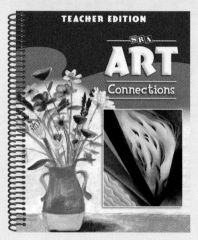

LEVEL 4

- Complete lesson plans to teach
  - elements and principles of art
  - art history and culture
  - art criticism
  - art production
- Art background
- Cross-curricular connections
- Program resources guide

Technology Components

e-Presentation for students and teachers

LEVEL K

e-Presentation offers the complete Student Edition as a presentation tool for teachers, complete with multimedia experiences, assessments, teacher materials, and a gallery of all artworks in the entire program.

This electronic gallery allows immediate access to all the artwork in the *Art Connections* program.

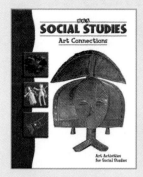
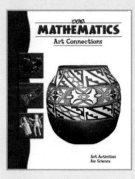
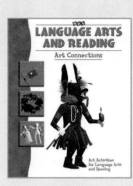

Cross-Curricular Art Connections include practical art projects for the classroom to help meet subject-area guidelines in

- Social Studies
- Mathematics
- Language Arts and Reading
- Science

LEVEL 3

Reading and Writing Test Preparation that reinforces art content

LEVEL 1

Home and After-School Connections for every unit, in English and Spanish

Professional Development Guide for both classroom teachers and art specialists

LEVEL 5

Assessment with tests in English and Spanish for every lesson

Art Around the World CD-ROM includes 150 works of art from the *Art Around the World Collection,* representing a variety of thought-provoking perspectives and activities.

The National Museum of Women in the Arts Collection CD-ROM dynamically explores the 200-print collection to introduce students to key women artists.

Enrich students' lives with exposure to the great masters and cultures of the world.

Fine-Art Resources

Transparencies Overhead transparency study prints for all lesson artwork allow for up-close examination.

LEVEL 5

Large Prints for each unit provide exemplary artwork to develop unit concepts.

LEVEL 2

LEVEL 1

Artist Profiles Pictures, background information, and profiles for every artist in the program provide valuable historical and cultural information at your fingertips.

Literature and Art Videos and DVD develop art connections to literature.

The Polar Express

Art Around the World 150-print resource explores the art of the world's cultures.

Artsource® Performing Arts Resource Package (Video and DVD) integrates the performing arts of dance, music, and theatre.

LEVEL 3

The National Museum of Women in the Arts Collection This 200-print resource provides famous artwork from famous women artists.

Theatre Arts Connections is a complete dramatic arts program that ties to **Art Connections**.

LEVEL 4

Elements and Principles of Art Teaching Resources

Elements of Art poster reinforces line, shape, color, value, form, space, and texture.

Principles of Art poster develops concepts of rhythm, balance, movement, harmony, variety, emphasis, and unity.

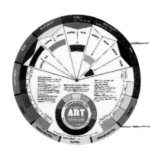

Use the **Color Wheel** to explore color concepts.

Flash Cards provide a quick review of the elements and principles of art.

Build a foundation in the elements and principles of art.

36 Lessons at every grade level develop the elements and principles of art in six-lesson units.

◀ Rembrandt van Rijn.
Portrait of Rembrandt.

◀ Frida Kahlo.
Frida y Diego Rivera.

Unit 5

Space, Proportion, and Distortion

Artists use accurate proportions to
realistically depict people and objects.

Copley painted this realistic portrait of the Pepperell family
in 1778. The Pepperell family lived in New England until
about the time of the American Revolution, when they
moved to England. At about the same time, Sir William
Pepperell lost most of his wealth. Notice that Copley used
correct proportions to make the painting realistic.

△ **John Singleton Copley.**
(American).
*Sir William Pepperell
and His Family.* 1778.

Oil on canvas. 90 × 108 inches
(228.6 × 274.32 cm.). North
Carolina Museum of Art, Raleigh,
North Carolina.

Artists use space in paintings to give the
appearance of depth on a flat surface.

▶ How do you think John Singleton
Copley created space in *Sir William
Pepperell and His Family?*

▶ Which objects in the painting look
closer to you? Which objects look
farther away?

Artists use accurate **proportions** to
show people or things realistically.

▶ Do you think the people in Copley's
painting look like they have been
painted with accurate proportions?
Explain.

In This Unit you will learn about
different ways that artists show size
and placement. Here are the topics you
will study:
▶ Foreground, middle ground, and
background
▶ Perspective techniques
▶ Point of view
▶ Face proportion
▶ Body proportions
▶ Distortion

Unit Openers introduce students to unit concepts and master artists.

(Master Artist Profile)

John Singleton Copley

(1738–1815)

John Singleton Copley was a popular
portrait painter during the eighteenth
century. When he was seventeen years
old he created a portrait of George
Washington. In his attempt to capture
details and to make his subjects appear
natural, Copley sometimes required
fifteen or sixteen sittings for a single
portrait. Copley moved to England
during the American Revolution and
did not return to America.

154 Unit 5   Unit 5 155   **LEVEL 4**

Unit Wrap-Ups review concepts, explore Art Museums or Art Careers and allow students to experience Artsource® connections to dance, theatre, and music.

Wrapping Up Unit 5

Space, Proportion, and Distortion

△ **Jacob Lawrence.** (American). *Study for
the Munich Olympic Games Poster.* 1971.

Gouache on paper. 35⅞ × 27 inches (90.17 × 68.58 cm.).
Seattle Art Museum, Seattle, Washington.

180 Unit 5

Wrapping Up Unit 5

Space, Proportion, and Distortion, continued

Show What You Know

🔲 Art Criticism Critical Thinking

Describe **What do you see?**
During this step you will collect information about
the subject of the work.
▶ How many people do you see? What kinds of facial
expressions do they have?
▶ What are the people doing? What are they wearing?
▶ What is the setting?

Analyze **How is this work organized?**
Think about how the artist used the elements and
principles of art.
▶ Which people or objects look closest to you?
Which look farthest away?
▶ What is in the foreground, the middle ground, and
the background?
▶ Where do you see a part of someone's body that
overlaps and covers part of another person or object?
▶ What is the point of view of this painting?
▶ Where do you see distortion?

Interpret **What is the artist trying to say?**
Use the clues you discovered during your analysis to
find the message the artist is trying to show.
▶ Which runner do you think will win the race? Why?
▶ What is the mood of this painting?
▶ What sounds would you hear if you could go into
the painting?

Decide **What do you think about the work?**
Use all the information you have gathered to decide
whether this is a successful work of art.
▶ Is the work successful because it is realistic,
because it is well-organized, or because it has a
strong message?

VISIT A MUSEUM
The Smithsonian

Space and Proportion in Music

...born in Cuba.
...ld he moved to
...eard harp music.
...from his friend
...master harpist.
..., but eventually
...fe to the harp.

...make a simple

...nd. Vibration is
...nsation caused in
...of air. You can hear
...a string tightly
...ck the string.

...tch rubber bands
...re that rubber
...knesses.

...e if you get
...ls. The thickness,
...e strings will

...thicknesses of
...igher or lower

△ Ortiz. "Joropo Azul."

🔲 Art Criticism

Describe Describe how you
made your instrument.

Analyze What did you do to get
a higher or lower tone or pitch?

Interpret What did you feel as
you created an instrument and
heard the sounds it made?

Decide Were you able to get a
satisfying musical sound from
your simple instrument?

Unit 5 183

Unit 5 181   **LEVEL 4**

vi

Integrate the four disciplines of art into every lesson for well-rounded exposure to all the dimensions of art.

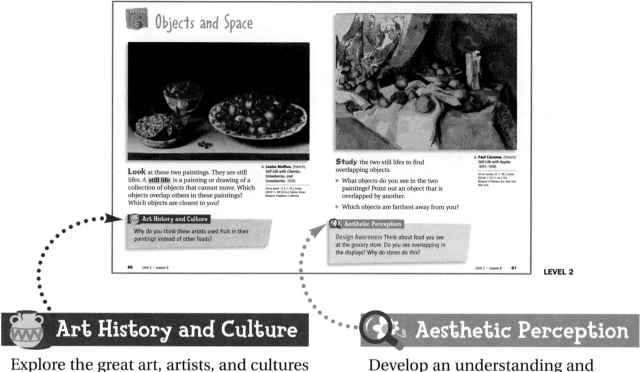

Art History and Culture

Explore the great art, artists, and cultures of the world.

Aesthetic Perception

Develop an understanding and appreciation for art.

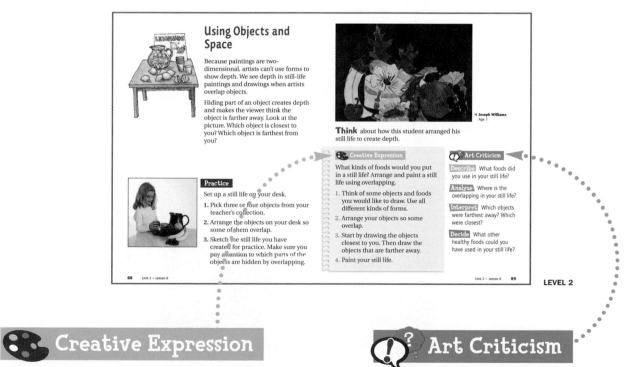

Creative Expression

Encounter a broad range of art media in a variety of hands-on art activities that give students an avenue for self-expression and self-esteem.

Art Criticism

Enrich critical-thinking skills as students learn about the elements and principles of art by examining their own and others' artwork.

ART Connections

Add dimension to all subjects with meaningful art connections.

Connect Art to Mathematics, Social Studies, Science, Language Arts and Reading.

History
Develop historical understanding as students explore art history and culture in every lesson.

LEVEL 1

LEVEL 2

Reading and Writing Test Preparation
Use art content, information about artists, art concepts, and art history to practice reading and writing skills in every unit.

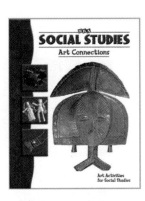

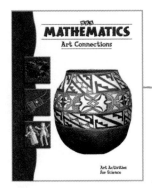

Cross-Curricular Art Connections
These books provide a wealth of exciting art activities designed specifically to support subject-area studies in Science, Mathematics, Social Studies, Language Arts and Reading as they reinforce art concepts.

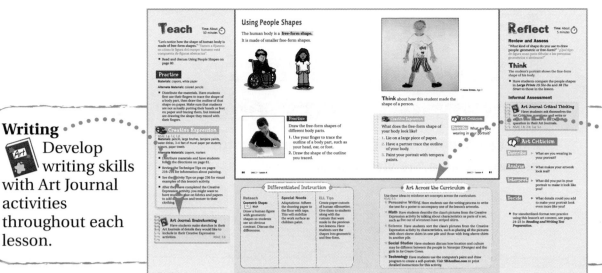

LEVEL 1

Writing
Develop writing skills with Art Journal activities throughout each lesson.

Cross-Curricular Ideas
Show students how artwork and concepts relate to science, mathematics, social studies, reading/language arts, and technology in every lesson.

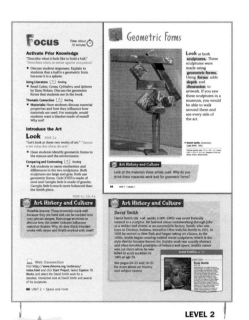

LEVEL 2

LEVEL 4

LEVEL 3

Cross-Curricular Integration
Integrate language arts and reading, math, science, and social studies concepts naturally as students work through each art lesson.

Vocabulary Development
Key vocabulary terms are highlighted, defined, and reviewed to develop the language of art.

Literature Integration
Integrate literature with Illustrator Profiles and Literature and Art video experiences at the beginning of every unit.

Research has shown that incorporating the arts into core curriculum areas in a way that actively involves students in the learning process produces "significant positive effects on student achievement, motivation, and engagement in learning, and notable changes in classroom practices" ("Different Ways of Knowing: 1991-94 National Longitudinal Study Final Report" in Schools, Communities, and the Arts: A Research Compendium).

Integrate all the Performing Arts for a complete Art education.

Expose children to music, dance, and theatre as they explore the visual arts.

Music

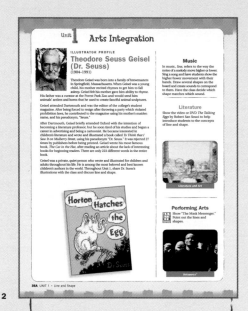

LEVEL 2

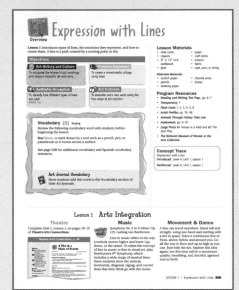

LEVEL 5

Music Connections
in every Unit Opener translate the visual arts elements and principles into music.

Music Experiences
in every lesson from Macmillan/McGraw-Hill's *Spotlight on Music* expand creativity and develop music appreciation.

Artsource®
music performances on video and DVD explore the elements and principles of art through the performing arts.

LEVEL 4

Artsource®
dance performances on video and DVD explore the elements and principles of art through the performing arts.

LEVEL 3

Artsource®
theatre performances on video and DVD explore the elements and principles of art through the performing arts.

LEVEL 5

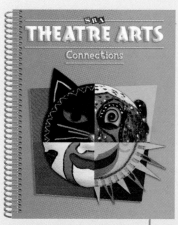

LEVEL 3

Theatre Arts Connections for grades K–6 lessons explore the elements and principles of theatre arts as students develop the elements and principles of visual arts.

Case studies have indicated that students perceive "that the arts facilitate their personal and social development." It also appears that to gain the full benefit of arts education, students should be exposed to all of the arts, including fine arts, dance, theatre, and music ("Arts Education in Secondary School: Effects and Effectiveness" in <u>Critical Links</u>, p. 76).

Meet Today's Standards for Art Education.

Art Connections exceeds the national standards for art education.

National Standards for Arts Education

Content Standard #1:

Understanding and applying media, techniques, and processes

The Creative Expression activity in every lesson of *Art Connections* develops understanding and experience with a wide variety of media, techniques, and processes. Practice activities in every lesson focus specifically on techniques.

Content Standard #2:

Using knowledge of structures and functions

Art Connections develops the elements and principles of art in every grade level, K–6. Units and lessons are organized to explore the elements and principles in exemplary art and then to practice techniques and create works of art that employ specific structures and functions of art.

Content Standard #3:

Choosing and evaluating a range of subject matter, symbols, and ideas

Art Connections introduces students to subject matter and symbols at the beginning of every grade level and then uses that knowledge throughout every lesson in the Aesthetic Perception questions and Creative Expression activities as students explore content to develop meaning in artwork.

Ali M. Forbes. Age 7.

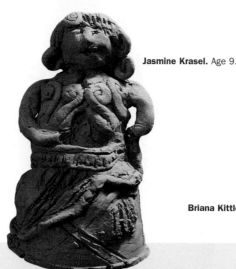
Jasmine Krasel. Age 9.

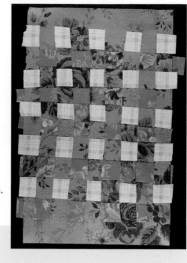
Briana Kittle. Age 6.

Content Standard #4:

Understanding the visual arts in relation to history and cultures

Every lesson in *Art Connections* has a specific objective related to the understanding of art history and culture. These objectives are met as students analyze and interpret exemplary artwork and develop their own artwork.

Content Standard #5:

Reflecting upon and assessing the characteristics and merits of one's own work and the work of others

The four steps of art criticism are explored in every lesson throughout the program as students analyze their own artwork and the work of others.

Content Standard #6:

Making connections between visual arts and other disciplines

Theatre, Dance, and Music are integrated into every unit of *Art Connections*. The elements and principles of visual art are translated into Dance, Theater, and Music through the Artsource® lessons and experiences. In addition, *Theatre Arts Connections* lessons and Music connections throughout the program develop a comprehensive understanding of the connections between visual arts and the performing arts.

Cross-curricular connections are built into every lesson through teaching strategies and ideas that integrate language arts and reading, math, science, and social studies concepts. Art Projects for each of the different subject areas are also included in the program.

Let the experts bring the best practices to your classroom.

Rosalind Ragans, Ph.D., Senior Author

Artist, Associate Professor Emerita

Georgia Southern University

Authors

Willis "Bing" Davis

Artist, Art Consultant

Associate Professor Emeritus,

Central State University, Ohio

Tina Farrell

Assisstant Superintendant, Curriculum and Instruction

Clear Creek Independent School District, Texas

Jane Rhoades Hudak, Ph.D.

Professor of Art

Georgia Southern University

Gloria McCoy

Former President, Texas Art Education Association

K–12 Art Director

Spring Branch Independent School District, Texas

Bunyan Morris

Art Teacher

Effingham County School System

Springfield, Georgia

Nan Yoshida

Art Education Consultant

Los Angeles, California

Contributors

Jackie Ellet

Elementary Art Teacher

Duncan Creek Elementary School

Georgia

Artsource® Music, Dance, and Theatre Lessons

Education Division

The Music Center of Los Angeles County

National Museum of Women in the Arts Collection

National Museum of Women in the Arts

Washington, D.C.

Your Fine-Arts Partner for K–12 Art, Theatre, Dance and Music

McGraw-Hill offers textbook programs to build, support, and extend an enriching fine-arts curriculum from kindergarten through high school.

**Senior Author
Rosalind Ragans**

Start with Art SRA

SRA/McGraw-Hill presents *Art Connections* for Grades K–6. *Art Connections* builds the foundations of the elements and principles of art across the grade levels as the program integrates art history and culture, aesthetic perception, creative expression in art production, and art criticism into every lesson.

Art Connections also develops strong cross-curricular connections and integrates the arts with literature, *Theatre Arts Connections* lessons, *Artsource®* experiences, and integrated music selections from Macmillan/McGraw-Hill's *Spotlight on Music*.

**Author
Rosalind Ragans
and Gene Mittler**

Integrate with Art Glencoe

Glencoe/McGraw-Hill offers comprehensive middle and high school art programs that encourage students to make art a part of their lifelong learning. All Glencoe art programs interweave the elements and principles of art to help students build perceptual skills, promote creative expression, explore historical and cultural heritage, and evaluate artwork.

- Introduce students to the many themes artists express.
- Explore the media, techniques, and processes of art.
- Understand the historical and cultural contexts of art.

**Author
Rosalind Ragans**

ArtTalk offers high school students opportunities to perceive, create, appreciate, and evaluate art as it develops the elements and principles of art.

Motivate with Music Macmillan McGraw-Hill

Macmillan/McGraw-Hill's *Spotlight on Music* offers an exiting and comprehensive exposure to music foundations and appreciation.

Sing with Style Glencoe

Glencoe/McGraw-Hill introduces *Experiencing Choral Music* for Grades 6–12. This multilevel choral music program includes instruction in the basic skills of vocal production and music literacy, and provides expertly recorded music selections in many different styles and from various periods of history.

Connections

Getting Started
The very basics...

Here are some tips for Getting Started with Art Connections.

Before School Begins

❶ Explore the components you have (student materials, **Overhead Transparencies**, **Large Prints**, and so on). Consider uses and alternative uses for each of the components.

❷ Plan your year.
  - Consider how often you meet with students.
  - Decide how many lessons you can present.
  - Examine your curriculum requirements.
  - Select the lessons that best meet your curriculum requirements.

❸ Organize art materials.
  - Identify the *Creative Expression* activities you will have students develop.
  - Determine how you will budget materials to last the entire year.
  - Compile a list of materials and order them.
  - Arrange classroom space to store materials.

❹ Arrange classroom space to create and store student artwork.

The First Day of School

❶ Give an overview of your expectations, objectives, and what you want students to accomplish.

❷ Introduce the artroom to students. Show them where things are kept.

❸ Establish and communicate:
  - rules for behavior.
  - rules for handling art materials.
  - rules for cleaning up.

❹ Begin the **Art Connections** introductory lessons, including *What Is Art?*, *About Art Criticism*, *About Aesthetic Perception*, and *About Art History and Culture*.

Planning a Lesson

❶ Review the lesson in the *Teacher's Edition*, including lesson objectives, in-text questions, *Practice*, and *Creative Expression* activities.

❷ Assemble program components, such as **Transparencies, Large Prints,** and the **Big Book**.

❸ Make any copies of activities or assessments that will be needed for the lesson.

❹ Assemble art materials.

❺ Determine how you will assess the lesson.

TEACHER EDITION

SRA ART Connections

Level K

Authors

Rosalind Ragans, Ph.D., Senior Author

Willis "Bing" Davis   Jane Rhoades Hudak, Ph.D.   Bunyan Morris
Tina Farrell   Gloria McCoy   Nan Yoshida

Contributing Author

Jackie Ellett

ART
SOURCE
ARTSOURCE

Education Division
The Music Center of Los Angeles County

SRA

Columbus, OH

The McGraw·Hill Companies

Authors

Senior Author
Dr. Rosalind Ragans, Ph.D.
Associate Professor Emerita
Georgia Southern University

Willis "Bing" Davis
Associate Professor Emeritus
Central State University - Ohio
President & Founder of SHANGO:
The Center for the Study of
African American
Art & Culture

Tina Farrell
Assistant Superintendent,
Curriculum and Instruction
Clear Creek Independent School
District,
League City, Texas

Jane Rhoades Hudak, Ph.D.
Professor of Art
Georgia Southern University

Gloria McCoy
Former President,
Texas Art Education Association
Spring Branch Independent
School District, Texas

Bunyan Morris
Art Teacher
Effingham County School System,
Springfield, Georgia

Nan Yoshida
Art Education Consultant
Retired Art Supervisor,
Los Angeles Unified School
District
Los Angeles, California

Photo Credit **Cover,** Henri Charles Manguin, *Port Saint Tropez, le 14 Juillet.* The Museum of Fine Arts, Houston, Texas. Photograph ©The Bridgeman Art Library. ©Artist Rights Society (ARS), New York/ADAGP, Paris.

SRAonline.com

Send all inquiries to:
SRA/McGraw-Hill
8787 Orion Place
Columbus, OH 43240-4027

Printed in the United States of America.

ISBN 0-07-600390-6

2 3 4 5 6 7 8 9 BCM 10 09 08 07 06

Contributors

Contributing Author
Jackie Ellett, Ed.S
Elementary Art Teacher
Duncan Creek Elementary School
Hoschton, Georgia

Contributing Writer
Lynda Kerr, NBCT
Ed. D. Candidate, Art Teacher
Henry County, Georgia

 Artsource® Music, Dance, Theatre Lessons
Mark Slavkin, Vice President
for Education
The Music Center of Los Angeles County
Michael Solomon, Managing Director
Music Center Education Division
Melinda Williams, Concept Originator and
Project Director
Susan Cambigue-Tracey, Project Coordinator
and Writer
Madeleine Dahm, Movement and Dance
Connection Writer
Keith Wyffels, Staff Assistance
Maureen Erbe, Logo Design

Music Connections
Kathy Mitchell
Music Teacher
Eagan, Minnesota

More about Aesthetics
Richard W. Burrows, Executive Director
Institute for Arts Education
San Diego, California

Art History
Gene A. Mittler, Ph.D.
Professor Emeritus
Texas Tech University

Resources for Students with Disabilities
Mandy Yeager
Ph.D. Candidate
The University of North Texas
Denton, Texas

Brain-Based Learning in the Arts
Jamye Ivey
K-12 Art Supervisor
Dougherty County School System, Georgia

Safe Use of Art Materials
Mary Ann Boykin

Director, The Art School for Children and
Young Adults
University of Houston–Clear Lake
Houston, Texas

Integrating the Four Art Forms
Susan Cambigue-Tracey
The Music Center of Los Angeles County

Using Writing to Enhance Your Art Curriculum
Mary Lazzari, EdS
Elementary Art Teacher
Clarke County School District
Athens, Georgia

Museum Education
Marilyn J. S. Goodman
Director of Education
Solomon R. Guggenheim Museum
New York, New York

Displaying Student Artwork
Jackie Ellett
Duncan Creek Elementary School
Hoschton, Georgia

Student Activities

Cassie Appleby
Glen Oaks Elementary School
McKinney, Texas

Maureen Banks
Kester Magnet School
Van Nuys, California

Christina Barnes
Webb Bridge Middle School
Alpharetta, Georgia

Beth Benning
Willis Jepson Middle School
Vacaville, California

Chad Buice
Craig Elementary School
Snellville, Georgia

Beverly Broughton
Gwinn Oaks Elementary School
Snellville, Georgia

Missy Burgess
Jefferson Elementary School
Jefferson, Georgia

Marcy Cincotta-Smith
Benefield Elementary School
Lawrenceville, Georgia

Joanne Cox
Kittredge Magnet School
Atlanta, Georgia

Carolyn Y. Craine
McCracken County Schools
Paducah, Kentucky

Jackie Ellett
Duncan Creek Elementary School
Hoschton, Georgia

Tracie Flynn
Home School
Rushville, Indiana

Phyllis Glenn
Malcom Bridge Elementary
Bogart, Georgia

Dallas Gillespie
Dacula Middle School
Dacula, Georgia

Dr. Donald Gruber
Clinton Junior High School
Clinton, Illinois

Karen Heid
Rock Springs Elementary School
Lawrenceville, Georgia

Alisa Hyde
Southwest Elementary
Savannah, Georgia

Kie Johnson
Oconee Primary School
Watkinsville, Georgia

Sallie Keith, NBCT
West Side Magnet School
LaGrange, Georgia

Letha Kelly
Grayson Elementary School
Grayson, Georgia

Diana Kimura
Amestoy Elementary School
Gardena, California

Desiree LaOrange
Barkley Elementary School
Fort Campbell, Kentucky

Deborah Lackey-Wilson
Roswell North Elementary
Roswell, Georgia

Dawn Laird
Goforth Elementary School
Clear Creek, Texas

Mary Lazzari
Timothy Road Elementary School
Athens, Georgia

Michelle Leonard
Webb Bridge Middle School
Alpharetta, Georgia

Lynn Ludlam
Spring Branch ISD
Houston, Texas

Mark Mitchell
Fort Daniel Elementary School
Dacula, Georgia

Martha Moore
Freeman's Mill Elementary School
Dacula, Georgia

Connie Niedenthal
Rushville Elementary
Rushville, Indiana

Barbara Patisaul
Oconee County Elementary School
Watkinsville, Georgia

Elizabeth Paulos-Krasle
Social Circle Elementary
Social Circle, Georgia

Jane Pinneau
Rocky Branch Elementary School
Watkinsville, Georgia

Marilyn Polin
Cutler Ridge Middle School
Miami, Florida

Michael Ramsey
Graves County Schools
Mayfield, Kentucky

Rosemarie Sells
Social Circle Elementary
Social Circle, Georgia

Jean Neelen-Siegel
Baldwin School
Alhambra, California

Debra Smith
McIntosh County School System
Darien, Georgia

Patricia Spencer
Harmony Elementary School
Buford, Georgia

Melanie Stokes
Smiley Elementary School
Ludowici, Georgia

Rosanne Stutts
Davidson Fine Arts School
Augusta, Georgia

Fran Sullivan
South Jackson Elementary School
Athens, Georgia

Kathy Valentine
Home School
Burkburnett, Texas

Debi West
Rock Springs Elementary School
Lawrenceville, Georgia

Sherry White
Bauerschlag Elementary School
League City, Texas

Patricia Wiesen
Cutler Ridge Middle School
Miami, Florida

Deayna Woodruff
Loveland Middle School
Loveland, Ohio

Gil Young
El Rodeo School
Beverly Hills, California

Larry A. Young
Dacula Elementary School
Dacula, Georgia

Table of Contents

▲ **Katsushika Hokusai.** *The Great Wave Off Kanagawa.*

Unit 1 Line

➥ indicates Core Lessons   **5**

Reading Comprehension Skills and Strategies

➊ Vocabulary, Comparing and Contrasting, Adjectives and Adverbs

➋ Vocabulary, Discussing the Selection, Adjectives and Adverbs

➌ Vocabulary, Identifying Details, Comparing and Contrasting

➍ Vocabulary, Drawing Conclusions, Adjectives and Adverbs

➎ Vocabulary, Comparing and Contrasting, Cause and Effect

➏ Making Inferences, Adjectives and Adverbs, Vocabulary

◄ **Grant Wood.**
American Gothic.

Unit 2 Shape

6   ◗◆ indicates Core Lessons

Reading Comprehension Skills and Strategies

❶ Comparing and Contrasting, Adjectives and
   Adverbs, Vocabulary
❷ Classify and Categorize, Vocabulary,
   Adjectives and Adverbs

❸ Discussing the Selection, Comparing and
   Contrasting, Making Inferences
❹ Comparing and Contrasting, Classify and
   Categorize, Vocabulary

❺ Main Idea and Details, Comparing and
   Contrasting, Vocabulary
❻ Drawing Conclusions, Main Idea and Details,
   Vocabulary

◄ **Henri Matisse.**
*Woman in a
Purple Coat.*

Unit 3 Color

➦ indicates Core Lessons   **7**

Reading Comprehension Skills and Strategies

❶ Discussing the Selection, Vocabulary, Adjectives and Adverbs

❷ Main Idea, Adjectives and Adverbs, Comparing and Contrasting

❸ Main Idea and Details, Adjectives and Adverbs, Vocabulary

❹ Comparing and Contrasting, Adjectives and Adverbs, Vocabulary

❺ Main Idea and Details, Making Inferences, Cause and Effect

❻ Comparing and Contrasting, Adjectives and Adverbs, Vocabulary

◀ **Allan Houser.**
Earth Song.

Unit 4 Space and Form

8

●◆ indicates Core Lessons

Reading Comprehension Skills and Strategies

❶ Visualizing, Adjectives and Adverbs, Vocabulary
❷ Making Inferences, Adjectives and Adverbs, Vocabulary

❸ Comparing and Contrasting, Finding Details, Vocabulary
❹ Making Inferences, Adjectives and Adverbs, Vocabulary

❺ Identifying Details, Drawing Conclusions, Vocabulary
❻ Making Inferences, Adjectives and Adverbs, Vocabulary

◀ **Beau Dick.**
Urban Raven/
Urban Indian
Transformation
Mask.

Unit 5 Texture

◆ indicates Core Lessons

9

Reading Comprehension Skills and Strategies

❶ Drawing Conclusions, Adjectives and Adverbs, Vocabulary

❷ Making Inferences, Adjectives and Adverbs, Vocabulary

❸ Identifying Details, Adjectives and Adverbs, Vocabulary

❹ Drawing Conclusions, Adjectives and Adverbs, Vocabulary

❺ Making Inferences, Adjectives and Adverbs, Vocabulary

❻ Main Idea and Details, Adjectives and Adverbs, Vocabulary

▲ **Maria Martinez.** *Two Black-on-Black Pots.*

Unit 6 Principles of Art

10

❖ indicates Core Lessons

Reading Comprehension Skills and Strategies
❶ Drawing Conclusions, Adjectives and Adverbs, Vocabulary
❷ Vocabulary, Adjectives and Adverbs
❸ Main Idea and Details, Drawing Conclusions, Vocabulary
❹ Drawing Conclusions, Adjectives and Adverbs, Vocabulary
❺ Main Idea and Details, Comparing and Contrasting, Vocabulary
❻ Main Idea and Details, Adjectives and Adverbs, Vocabulary

Technique Tips

Activity Tips

11

Overview

The purpose of these pages is to open students' minds to the idea that visual arts include many components and take many forms. The arts satisfy the human needs for display, celebration, personal expression, and communication. We use the visual arts to enhance our innermost feelings and to communicate ideas. Art is made by people. Even people who are not professional artists can enjoy the creative process.

Activating Prior Knowledge

- Ask students what they think art is. Encourage creative, divergent thinking. In visual art, there are many answers to a question.

Questions to Discuss

- Have students look at the images on pages 12 and 13 and name the things that are visual art. Then ask the following questions.
    - ▶ Which of these things could you hold in your hands?
    - ▶ Which one could you walk inside?
    - ▶ Which ones would you hang on a wall?
    - ▶ Which ones could you wear?
- Encourage students to think about things they have at home that fit the categories on these pages. The building they live in is architecture. They have dishes and other containers. Many of them have things hanging on the walls to enhance their visual environments. A few may have sculpture in the home. Many will have seen sculpture in and around public buildings.

What Is Art?

Art is . . .

Painting

▲ **Georgia O'Keeffe.** (American). *Autumn Leaves—Lake George.* 1924.

Oil on canvas. Columbus Museum of Art, Columbus, Ohio.

Drawing

▲ **Leonardo da Vinci.** (Italian). *Self Portrait.* 1514.

Red chalk, Royal Library, Turin, Italy.

Sculpture

▲ **Artist Unknown.** (Italy). *Camillus.* A.D. 41–54.

Bronze. $46\frac{7}{8}$ inches high (119.08 cm.). The Metropolitan Museum of Art, New York, New York.

Architecture

▲ **Artist Unknown.** (India). *Taj Mahal.* 1638–1648.

Marble. 240 feet tall (73.15 meters). Agra, India.

Printmaking

▲ **Katsushika Hokusai.** (Japanese). *Kirifuri Waterfall on Mt. Kurokami in Shimotsuke Province.* c. 1833–1834.
....
Color woodblock print. 15 9/16 × 10 3/8 inches (38.9 × 26.3 cm.). Honolulu Academy of Arts, Honolulu, Hawaii.

Pottery

▲ **Harrison Mc Intosh.** (American). *Stoneware Vase #661.* 1966.
....
Glazed stoneware. 15 1/4 × 13 inches (38.74 × 33.02 cm.). Renwick Gallery, Smithsonian American Art Museum, Washington, D.C.

Weaving

▲ **Artist Unknown.** (Ashanti Peoples, Ghana). *Kente Cloth.*
....
Museum of International Folk Art, Santa Fe, New Mexico.

Clothing

◄ **Artist Unknown.** (American). *Arapaho Man's Shirt.* c. 1890.
....
Buckskin and feathers. 37 inches (93.68 cm.) long. Buffalo Bill Historical Center, Cody, Wyoming.

Art is created by people.

Using the Credit Line

The credit line is a list of important facts about the work of art that appears below or next to the work. For example, you can help students understand the size of an artwork and how it relates to their own size. Most credit lines contain the following information.

- Name of the artist.
- Title of the work. This always appears in italics. If the word *detail* follows the title, it means that the image is part of a larger work of art.
- Year the work was created. A *c* before the date indicates that the piece was made around the year given.
- Medium used by the artist.
- Size of the work. The first number is the height, the second is the width, and a third number indicates depth for three-dimensional works.
- Location of the work. This tells the museum, gallery, or collection in which the work is housed.

Art Studios, Galleries, and Museums

Works of art are created in **studios.** A studio is an artist's workplace, much like a classroom is a studio for students. Almost everything an artist needs to create an artwork will be found in his or her studio. It is possible for people to visit artist studios, but an invitation from the artist is usually required.

Art galleries are private businesses where art dealers display and sell works of art. Art galleries are typically open to the public and the works of art may be viewed even if the patrons do not intend to buy anything.

A **museum** is a public or private building where valuable and important works of art are cared for and displayed for the public to view. *Curators* are people who supervise the museum and organize exhibitions. *Docents* are special tour directors who help explain the art to visitors.

Overview

These pages introduce students to the three components that define a work of art: the subject, the composition, and the content.

Subject

The subject is the image that the viewer can easily identify in a work of art. The subject may be one person or many people. It may be a thing. It can be an event, such as a party. In recent years, some artists have chosen to create nonobjective art. This is art that has no recognizable subject matter. In this type of art, the elements of art become the subject.

Composition

The composition is the way the principles of art are used to organize the elements of art. Notice the patterns the artist used in *Classic Serape Style Wearing Blanket.*

Content

The content is the message the work communicates to the viewer. The message may be an idea, such as family unity, or an emotion or feeling, such as joy or loneliness. If the work of art is functional, such as *Classic Serape Style Wearing Blanket,* then the function is the meaning. Does the work of art look like it could perform the function it is supposed to?

What Is Art?

Every work of art has three parts.

Subject

This is the object you see in the artwork.

Composition

This is how the artwork is organized.

Content

This is what the artwork means.

▲ **W.H. Brown.** (American). *Bareback Riders.* 1886.
Oil on cardboard mounted on wood. 18½ × 24½ inches (46.99 × 61.60 cm.). National Gallery of Art, Washington, D.C.

What is the subject of this artwork?

▲ **Artist Unknown.** (Native American, Navajo). *Classic Serape Style Wearing Blanket.* 1875.
Plied cotton and Saxony wool. $73\frac{1}{2} \times 47$ inches (186.69 × 119.38 cm.). Utah Museum of Fine Arts, University of Utah, Salt Lake City, Utah.

How is this work organized?

▲ **Jacob Lawrence.** (American). *Children at Play.* 1947.
Tempera on Masonite panel. 20 × 24 inches (50.8 × 60.96 cm.). Georgia Museum of Art, University of Georgia, Athens, Georgia.

What does this artwork mean?

■ Ask students what is the first thing they look for when they look at a work of art. Students may say they look at color, size, or what it's about. Some may say they look for the feeling or message they get from it. Give students time to explore this question. It will provide a good context for the discussion on these pages.

Questions to Discuss

■ Read with students the text on pages 14 and 15. Share with them some of the information above. Encourage students to think about their responses during the Activating Prior Knowledge discussion as they look at these images and think about the information you have shared with them.

▶ Read the questions, and discuss the answers. The subject of *Bareback Riders* is two circus riders on a horse. *Classic Serape Style Wearing Blanket* is organized in rows of pattern. *Children at Play,* like all artwork, will mean different things to different people. Possible answers include the joy of friendship and playing together and so on.

Overview

In art, *subject* means something an artist has depicted or represented in an artwork. For example, the subject matter of Claude Monet's painting of trees is called a landscape. Some subject matter, like Monet's landscape, is easy to identify. Others are more difficult because the artwork may be symbolic or nonobjective. Artists create works of art on a variety of subjects: the natural world, literature, religion, the constructed world, history, and so on. These pages deal with several of the most common subject-matter topics—people, objects, everyday life, stories, things outside, colors and shapes, and things that have a deeper meaning.

Talk with students about each subject-matter topic description below. Encourage them to look for examples of different subject matter in the lessons. By helping them to look at each subject in greater detail and by asking thoughtful questions, your students will begin to develop an understanding for differences among subject matter in art.

Nonobjective

Sometimes artwork is nonobjective. It does not have an identifiable subject matter—no familiar subjects are shown. People respond to the way the artwork has been organized and designed. Nonobjective art focuses specifically on the elements and principles of art: line, shape, color, and so on.

▶ **Question:** The artwork does not use a subject we can identify. What are some of the lines, shapes, and colors you see in this picture?

Subject Matter

Artists make art about many subjects. Name the subjects you see on these pages.

Colors and Shapes

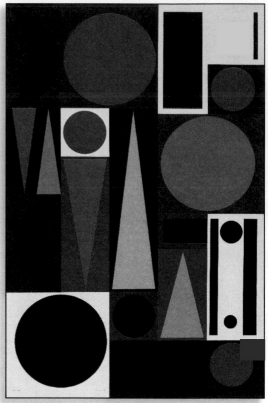

▲ **Auguste Herbin.** (French). *Composition on the Word "Vie" 2.* 1950.

Oil on canvas. $57\frac{1}{2} \times 38\frac{1}{4}$ inches (146.05 × 97.16 cm.). Museum of Modern Art, New York, New York.

Things Outside

▲ **Claude Monet.** (French). *The Four Trees.* 1891.

Oil on canvas. 32¼ × 32⅛ inches (81.92 × 81.58 cm.). The Metropolitan Museum of Art, New York, New York.

Landscape

This area includes the natural world—plants, animals, or other things outside. The suffix *scape* means "a view of." For example, a *cityscape* is buildings and city life seen in an artwork. A *seascape* is a scene of the sea.

▶ **Question:** What objects do you see in this landscape?

Genre

In art, the term *genre* is used to indicate subjects that have to do with ordinary people engaged in everyday activities.

▶ **Question:** What everyday activities are these people doing?

What Is Art?

Everyday Life

▲ **Carmen Lomas Garza.** (American). *Naranjas (Oranges)*.
Gouache. 20 × 14 inches (50.8 × 35.56 cm.). Collection of Mr. and Mrs. Ira Schneider, Scottsdale, Arizona.

A Story

▲ **Artist Unknown.** (Hmong Peoples, Asia). *Hmong Story Cloth.*
Cotton. 18 × 18 inches (45.72 × 45.72 cm.). Private collection.

A Story

A story is an account of an incident from a real person's life, a historic event, or from a myth, legend, or other piece of symbolic literature.

▶ **Question:** What story do you think is being told in this artwork?

Portrait

This category includes portraits, self-portraits, and group portraits. Portraits are one of the oldest subjects in art history. An artist tries to present both an accurate depiction and other aspects of a person's character in a portrait.

▶ **Question:** What do you think the artist is telling us about these people?

What Is Art?

People

▲ **Isabel Bishop.** (American). *Ice Cream Cones.* 1942.
Oil and egg tempera on fiberboard. 33⅞ x 20 inches (86.04 x 50.8 cm.).
Museum of Fine Arts, Boston, Massachusetts.

Objects

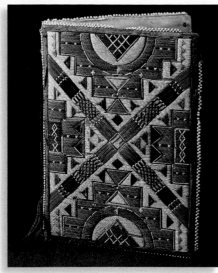

▲ **Artist Unknown.** (Mi'kmaq People, Nova Scotia, Canada). *Letter Holder or Book Cover.*
....
Birch bark decorated with porcupine quills, glass beads, and silk. 10¼ × 14½ inches (26.04 × 36.83 cm.). Museum of International Folk Art, Santa Fe, New Mexico.

Things with a Deeper Meaning

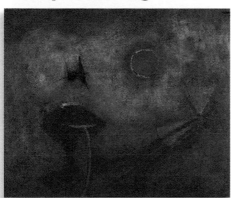

▲ **Rufino Tamayo.** (Mexican). *Toast to the Sun.* 1956.
....
Oil on canvas. 31½ x 39 inches (80 x 99 cm.). Wichita Art Museum, Wichita, Kansas.

Objects

Sometimes works of art are functional. Pottery, baskets, architecture, teapots, and furniture are just a few examples of artwork that is functional.

▶ **Question:** What do you think this work was used for?

Things with a Deeper Meaning

Sometimes works of art contain symbols—visual signs of something invisible. For example, a dove can be a symbol of peace, or an hourglass may represent the passing of time. Symbols represent a broader idea or sometimes have a secret meaning. Sometimes the title of a work can give you clues to its meaning.

▶ **Question:** What do you think this artwork means?

Overview

Each language has its own system of words and rules of grammar. To learn a new language, you need to learn new words and a new set of rules for putting the words together. The language of visual art also has its own system. The words of the language are the **elements** of art. They are the basic visual symbols in the language of art. Just as there are basic kinds of words such as nouns, verbs, adjectives, and adverbs, there are basic kinds of art elements. These are line, shape, color, value, space, form, and texture. These elements are the visual building blocks that the artist puts together to create a work of art. No matter what materials are used, the artwork will contain all of the visual elements. Sometimes one element will be more important than the others.

Visual images are organized according to rules. In language, these are the rules of grammar. In visual art, the rules for organizing the elements of art are called the **principles** of art. These principles include pattern, rhythm, balance, emphasis, harmony, variety, and unity.

Activating Prior Knowledge

- Ask students what they think of when they hear each of the following words: *line, shape, color.* Encourage them to look around the classroom for examples.

Questions to Discuss

- Have students examine the images on pages 22 and 23. Ask them what they can tell about each photo. What stands out in each image? How does each image help explain the element or principle?

Elements of Art

Art talks with . . .

Line

Shape

Form

Space

Color

Value

Texture

Principles of Art

Pattern

Rhythm

Balance

Emphasis

Harmony

Variety

Unity

What Is Art? **23**

The Language of Art

The elements and principles of art are the concepts or ideas that artists use to organize their artwork. Artists use a variety of media and materials to make art. *Media* are types of art such as photography, watercolor, and so on. *Materials* are the things used to make the art, such as markers, paint, paper, clay, fabric, wood, metal, or glass.

There are specific techniques and processes that artists use to manipulate the materials. For example, the proper way to hold a brush to create a thin line with watercolor paint is a specific technique unique to watercolor painting. The process of creating a finished watercolor painting consists of many interwoven steps such as thinking about what to paint, sketching several ideas, deciding which elements and principles will enhance the work, choosing the best sketch, deciding which watercolor techniques to use, and finally producing the finished work.

Special techniques and procedures are used with each material. You will need to learn different techniques and follow different procedures for modeling clay than you will for creating paper sculpture. Drawing with crayons requires different techniques and procedures from drawing with oil pastels or chalk. Using the computer to make original art requires that you learn how to use specific computer hardware and software.

Overview

Art history is the record of art from the past to the present. By looking at art from the past, we learn what the people who lived before us were like—their feelings and beliefs, clothes, food, houses, and how they viewed the world around them.

Questions to Discuss:

Knowledge

▶ Who created the artwork?

▶ When was the artwork created?

▶ What is the artwork's title?

▶ Have you ever seen an artwork like this? Where?

Comprehension

▶ Is this artwork useful? How is it used?

▶ Compare this artwork with another artwork from a similar time. How are the works of art alike and different?

▶ What interests you most about this artwork?

Application

▶ What types of materials were used to create this artwork?

▶ Demonstrate how the artwork was created.

▶ Explain how this artwork could have a different use today.

Analysis

▶ What are the main lines, shapes, and colors in this artwork?

▶ Compare this painting with another painting in this book. How are they alike? How are they different?

▶ What does this artwork mean?

About Art

▲ **Mary Cassatt.** (American). *Susan Comforting the Baby.* 1881.
Oil on canvas. 25⅝ x 39⅜ inches (65.1 x 100 cm.). Museum of Fine Arts, Houston, Texas.

 **Art History and Culture**

Look at the painting.

▶ How are the people dressed?

▶ What are they doing?

▶ What can you learn about the artist?

Synthesis

▶ How many titles can you create for this artwork? Name them.

▶ Name a person you would like to give this artwork to as a gift. Why?

Evaluation

▶ Do you think this artwork is interesting? Why?

▶ Summarize this artwork's unique qualities.

What to Do

■ Help students find out more about the life and times of Mary Cassatt. Students may dress up as the artist and tell the artist's story to classmates.

■ Show students a work by another artist who lived at the same time as Cassatt. Have pairs of students role-play a discussion between the two artists talking about their work.

■ Have students work in groups to act out this painting. They should act out what happened before, during, and after the moment shown in the painting.

Overview

Aesthetic Perception

Aesthetic perception encourages students to make choices rather than give "right answers." By understanding the process of aesthetic perception, students can see something from a new perspective and ultimately realize that art is all around them.

Journal writing is an integral part of aesthetic perception. It is an ongoing record of what a student does, notices, and thinks. Journals track the evolution of thoughts and experiences over time. Through this recorded journey, the student has the ability to reflect on where one has been and where one is going. Dictating or drawing thoughts and questions intensifies each student's life experiences.

Guidelines for Aesthetic Perception

Students like to know what is important about a work of art and what was important to the artist. They are fascinated with information, questions, and descriptions. There are some guiding principles in the development of aesthetic perception at this level that can profoundly influence teaching practice.

1. All aesthetic perception actively involves the learner.

2. All aesthetic perception involves reflection.

3. The works of art have substance. Their tools and a working vocabulary are vital to empower the learner.

4. Aesthetic perception is a process based upon examination of the artist's choices and the choices in response made by the viewer.

5. All responses are valid. Right and wrong are irrelevant issues when viewing works of art.

6. All works of art relate to each other, and each relates to all other areas of life.

About Art

▲ **Mary Cassatt.** (American). *Susan Comforting the Baby.* 1881.
Oil on canvas. 25⅝ x 39⅜ inches (65.1 x 100 cm.). Museum of Fine Arts, Houston, Texas.

⊗ Aesthetic Perception

Look
▶ Look at the work of art.
What do you see?

Look Inside
▶ Pretend you are Susan.
Tell a story about this work of art.

Look Outside
▶ What does this work make you feel?

▶ What will you remember about this
work of art?

Questions to Discuss
▶ What is happening in this work of art?

▶ What is this work of art about?

▶ What is your favorite part of this work of
art?

▶ What is most important in this artwork?

▶ What happened just before and just after
in this work of art?

▶ If you were in this work of art, what would
you be doing?

▶ What have you learned about the work of
art?

▶ What does the artist want you to know or
think about in this work of art?

▶ How do you feel about the work of art?

▶ What will you remember about this work
of art?

Things to Do
▪ Draw yourself into the work of art.

▪ Draw what you can't see in the work of art.

▪ Act out or show the story in the work of
art.

▪ Role-play an interview with the artist
about how the work of art was made.

Overview

Art Criticism

Art criticism is an organized system for looking at and talking about art. The purpose of art criticism is to get the viewer involved in a perception process that delays judgment until all aspects of the image have been studied. Learning art criticism also gives each viewer the confidence to discuss a work of art without worrying what other people might think.

Describe **What do I see?**

During this step, the viewer lists all the obvious things in the artwork. Objectivity is important.

Questions to Discuss

▶ List and describe everything you see in the artwork. Answers may include: In the center of the work is a very young child sitting in a stroller. One hand is clutching her head and the other is reaching toward the viewer. The child is wearing a white dress with a ruffled collar. Susan is leaning close to the child so that her face is touching the baby's face. One arm is around the baby's back. Her hair is pulled into a knot (and so on).

Analyze **How is the work organized?**

During this step the viewer examines how the elements and principles of art are used in the artwork.

Questions to Discuss

▶ Describe the elements of art you see. Where do you see lines? What shapes can you find? What colors do you see? Answers may include: **Line**—We see lines of brush strokes all over. There are vertical lines on the wall and the shutters. **Shape**—Susan, the child, the stroller, the bird, and the plants are free-form shapes. The shutters are rectangles. **Color**—Most of the colors look dull brown and gray. The faces look very red. There are spots of red in the dull green plants (and so on).

▶ How has the artist used the principles of design? Answers may include: **Emphasis**—The area of emphasis seems to be the two faces (and so on).

▲ **Mary Cassatt.** (American). *Susan Comforting the Baby.* 1881.
Oil on canvas. 25⅝ x 39⅜ inches (65.1 x 100 cm.). Museum of Fine Arts, Houston, Texas.

 **Art Criticism**

Describe

▶ List the people and things you see.

Analyze

▶ What lines, shapes, colors, and textures do you see?

▶ What part stands out?

Interpret

▶ What is happening? What is the artist telling you about Susan and the baby?

Decide

▶ Have you ever seen another artwork like this?

More About Aesthetic Judging

You can use art criticism to make aesthetic judgments about functional objects such as cars or shoes. Follow the first two steps (**Describe** and **Analyze**) as described. During **Interpret,** consider the purpose of the object as its meaning. (Does a pitcher look like it will pour liquid without spilling?) As you **Decide,** consider whether the object works when it is used. (If a chair is not comfortable to sit in, it is not functioning properly and is not successful as a chair.)

Interpret What is the artist saying to me?

During interpretation, viewers will make inferences about the message in the work of art. Each interpretation can be different because each is based upon the feelings and life experiences of the viewer.

Questions to Discuss

▶ What is the artist trying to tell us about these people and their lives? Answers will vary. Some students will think Susan is the mother. Even if she isn't, it is obvious she cares for the child. The child may have awoken from a bad dream, or she may be reaching for a toy that fell.

Decide

This is when the viewer decides whether or not the work is successful. There are two levels of judgment to be made. The first is personal: do you like the work?

The second level is also subjective, but it uses aesthetic theories to help the viewer decide whether the work is successful. More than one theory may be used to judge a work.

▪ Some critics think that the most important thing about a work of art is the realistic presentation of the subject matter. This aesthetic theory is called **imitationalism** or **realism.**

▪ Other critics think that composition is the most important fact in a work of art. This aesthetic theory, called **formalism** or **composition,** emphasizes the design qualities and the arrangement of the elements of art using the principles of art.

▪ Some critics claim that no object should be considered art if it fails to arouse an emotional response in the viewer. **Emotionalism** or **expressionism** is a theory concerned with the content or the meaning of the work of art.

Questions to Discuss

▶ Have you seen another artwork that looks like this? Answers will vary.

▶ Have you seen any works of art in this book that show adults and children relating to each other?

Overview

Creative Expression

The creative process, like the writing process or the scientific method, is an organized approach to creative problem solving that can be used by professional artists and students alike. Throughout *Art Connections,* the Creative Expression activities are presented as problems to be solved. Remind students of the steps in the creative process as they work on the activities.

Get an idea.

- Inspiration can come from many places. In the *Art Connections* Creative Expression activities, the idea comes from the activity instructions. Professional artists may get ideas from a client who has commissioned a piece of art from nature, from a historical event, from everyday life, or from the available media and materials.

- Try the following to help students when they have trouble getting an idea.

1. As a class, brainstorm about where to get ideas for artwork: works by other artists, personal experiences, stories students have read, and so on.

2. Encourage students to write ideas in the Ideas section of their Art Journals. Remind students that they can make notes for ideas anytime, not just in art class.

3. Pair students who are having trouble thinking of ideas with students who have many ideas. One student can model getting ideas for the other student.

Plan your work.

- Once students have an idea, they must decide the best way to execute that idea. Would a two-dimensional or three-dimensional artwork best convey the idea that students are trying to show? Should students use watercolor or pencil?

Make a sketch.

- Just like professional writers, professional artists do not make a perfect work on the first try. They may make several sketches, evaluate those sketches, and revise them before deciding on a final vision for the artwork.

- Encourage students to make sketches in the Ideas section of their Art Journals.

About Art

▲ **Mary Cassatt.** (American). *Susan Comforting the Baby.* 1881.
Oil on canvas. $25\frac{5}{8}$ x $39\frac{3}{8}$ inches (65.1 x 100 cm.). Museum of Fine Arts, Houston, Texas.

 **Creative Expression**

How can you make art?

1. Get an idea.
2. Plan your work.
3. Make a sketch.
4. Use the media.
5. Share your final work.

Use the media.

- In this stage of the creative process, students make their artwork based on their plans. Encourage students to practice using unfamiliar media, and to try out new techniques on a small practice piece before using those techniques on their artwork.

- Even during this stage of the process, students may get new ideas. Encourage them to be flexible.

Share your final work.

- Art is meant to be shared with and viewed by others. Encourage students to share their artwork with family or friends, display it in the classroom, or display it in the school display area. This is also a good time for students to self-evaluate their work using the four steps of art criticism.

More About Art Journals

- Art Journals are a wonderful way to work through ideas. At the beginning of the school year, help students set up an Art Journal. This can be a spiral notebook or a three-ring binder with pages for writing and sketching. The Art Journal will be divided into sections for Concepts, Ideas, Critical Thinking (Art Criticism), and Vocabulary.

1. Encourage students to use the Concepts section of their journals for summarizing unit and lesson concepts, writing questions they have, and listing other things they want to learn. Younger students may dictate or draw their thoughts.

2. Students can use the Ideas section of their Art Journals for brainstorming, organizing, planning, and sketching. Remind students that they can write ideas in their journals any time; they do not need to wait until a designated time in art class.

3. Students can use the Critical Thinking section of their journals to self-evaluate their work using the four steps of Art Criticism. In *Art Connections* students are asked to self-evaluate after each Creative Expression activity. This can be a valuable tool to help students review art concepts and get ideas for their next work. Younger students may dictate their thoughts.

4. Encourage students to use the Vocabulary section of their Art Journals to record unfamiliar words, summarize or explain definitions, and so on. Developing vocabulary is an important step in being able to think about and communicate about art.

Overview

Elementary teachers are responsible for the safety of their students. Specific guidelines have been established by the Center for Safety in the Arts, and these guidelines should be followed to ensure that both students and teachers use art materials safely. Following are some general tips for using art materials safely. For more detailed information, see "Safe Use of Art Materials" on page T12 of this book.

Safe Art Materials

- Use only water-soluble AP- or CP-designated markers. Never use permanent or scented markers.

- Use only dustless chalk.

- Make sure that crayons have the AP or CP label to ensure that they do not contain lead.

- When using tempera paint, use only liquid tempera, not powdered tempera. Do not use any spray paints or fixatives.

- Use only water-soluble printers' inks.

- Use pencils to carve into soft surfaces for printing blocks. Do not use mat knives or other sharp instruments.

- Do not allow young children to use sharp scissors; blunt points are safe.

- Do not use rubber cement unless it bears the AP or CP label. Do not use solvent-based glues.

Safety

- ► Use art materials only on your artwork.
- ► Keep art materials out of your mouth, eyes, and ears.
- ► Use only safety scissors. Keep your fingers away from the blades.

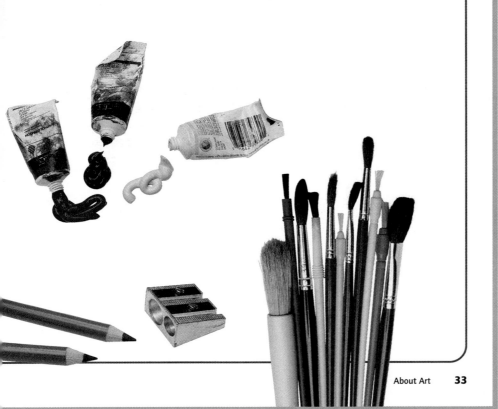

- ▶ Wash your hands after using the art materials.
- ▶ Wear an art shirt or smock to protect your clothes.
- ▶ Always follow your teacher's directions.

General Safety Precautions for Art

- ■ Read the labels on all materials used in the art room. Look carefully for the AP/CP labels. If these are not present, be suspicious. Imported art materials should be looked upon with extreme caution. Other countries have not developed the rigid safety codes adopted by the United States.

- ■ Do not accept or use old art materials that may have been left in the school or donated by some well-meaning adult. If the materials do not bear the current safety codes, toss them out.

- ■ Never allow food or drink in the room where art activities are being conducted. Dust and even fibers float freely in the air and can readily contaminate food or drink.

- ■ Practice cleanliness. Have children wash their hands thoroughly with soap after using art materials.

- ■ Use absolutely no permanent markers or solvent-based materials in the art room. If a material stains the clothes or hands and does not clean up with simple soap and water, it is not appropriate or safe for young children to use.

- ■ Use plastic containers for washing paintbrushes; glass is dangerous in the hands of young children.

- ■ Paper cutters should not be used by elementary school children. The paper cutter should be kept out of the students' reach, and left in a locked position always with the blade turned to the wall.

- ■ Do not use commercial dyes around children; use vegetable or natural dyes (flowers, teas, onion skins).

- ■ Do not allow children in a room where a kiln is firing; both the heat and the fumes are dangerous.

Unit 1 Planning Guide

	Lesson Title	Suggested Pacing	Creative Expression Activity
Lesson 1	**Thick and Thin Lines**	45 minutes	Create a design using thick and thin lines.
Lesson 2	**Lines Can Make Calm Pictures**	45 minutes	Create a calm landscape using vertical and horizontal lines.
Lesson 3	**Lines Can Make Busy Pictures**	45 minutes	Create an image that looks exciting by using diagonal and zigzag lines.
Lesson 4	**Curved Lines**	45 minutes	Create a drawing that shows movement by using curvy lines.
Lesson 5	**Smooth and Rough Lines**	45 minutes	Create a drawing using smooth and rough lines.
Lesson 6	**Broken Lines**	45 minutes	Create a paper mosaic collage using broken lines.
ARTSOURCE	**Lines in Dance**	35 minutes	Create a variety of lines by using motions and body positions.

Materials	Program Resources	Fine Art Resources	Literature Resources
1" easel brushes and small brushes (#6 or #8), liquid tempera paints, 12" × 18" white paper, newspaper, palettes, water dishes, paper towels	*Reading and Writing Test Preparation*, pp. 6-7 *Flash Cards*, 1-6 *Assessment*, pp. 9-10 *Home and After-School Connections*, pp. 7-10	*Transparency*, 1 *Artist Profiles*, pp. 46, 64 *Animals Through History Time Line* *Large Prints*, 1 and 2 *The National Museum of Women in the Arts Collection*	*The Magic of Spider Woman* by Lois Duncan
9" × 12" blue construction paper, 9" × 12" paper in various colors, glue	*Reading and Writing Test Preparation*, pp. 8-9 *Flash Cards*, 1 and 2 *Assessment*, pp. 11-12	*Transparency*, 2 *Artist Profiles*, pp. 17, 29 *Large Print*, 2 *Art Around the World*	*The Seashore Book* by Charlotte Zolotow
computer, paint program, printer with paper	*Reading and Writing Test Preparation*, pp. 10-11 *Flash Cards*, 3 and 5 *Assessment*, pp. 13-14	*Transparency*, 3 *Artist Profiles*, pp. 5, 39 *Animals Through History Time Line* *Large Print*, 1 *Art Around the World*	*The 100th Day of School* by Angela Shelf Medearis
12" × 18" colored paper, oil pastels, tissue or paper towels	*Reading and Writing Test Preparation*, pp. 12-13 *Flash Cards*, 4 and 6 *Assessment*, pp. 15-16	*Transparency*, 4 *Artist Profiles*, pp. 4, 18 *Large Prints*, 1 and 2 *Art Around the World*	*Feel the Wind* by Arthur Dorros
12" × 18" white paper, jumbo crayons	*Reading and Writing Test Preparation*, pp. 14-15 *Flash Cards*, 1-6 *Assessment*, pp. 17-18	*Transparency*, 5 *Artist Profiles*, pp. 8, 44 *Animals Through History Time Line* *Large Prints*, 1 and 2 *Women in the Arts Collection*	*Ginger* by Charlotte Voake and *The Cat in the Hat* by Dr. Seuss
construction paper precut into 4" × 1/2" strips, 9" × 12" paper for background (contrasting color from strips), glue or glue sticks, pencils	*Reading and Writing Test Preparation*, pp. 16-17 *Flash Cards*, 1-6 *Assessment*, pp. 19-20	*Transparency*, 6 *Artist Profiles*, pp. 6, 48 *Animals Through History Time Line* *Large Prints*, 1 and 2 *Women in the Arts Collection*	*One Windy Wednesday* by Phyllis Root
"Impressions #2" performed by Bella Lewitzky and Lewitzky Dance Company			

1 Line

Lesson 1: **Line Quality** is the thickness or thinness of a line.

Lesson 2: **Line Direction** is the path that a line takes as it is made with a moving tool. A **vertical line** moves up and down and a **horizontal line** moves side to side.

Lesson 3: **Diagonal (slanted) lines** move at an angle, from corner to corner. **Zigzag lines** are diagonal lines that connect.

Lesson 4: A **curved line** bends and changes direction slowly.

Lesson 5: Artists use **line texture** to show how things feel if touched. A **rough line** is uneven. A **smooth line** is even.

Lesson 6: **Broken lines** are lines with spaces between them.

Introduce Unit Concepts

"A line is a mark made when a tool, like a crayon or marker, is moved across a surface, such as a piece of paper." "Una línea es una marca hecha cuando una herramienta como un creyon o un marcador, se mueve a través de una superficie como una hoja de papel".

Line

■ Explain that if an artist moves his or her hand in different directions, he or she will make different types of lines.

■ Have students practice making lines quickly and slowly, watching their hands as they move across the paper.

■ Make a path of scrap papers on the floor. Then have students move in a line across the papers as they pick them up.

Cross-Curricular Projects

■ See the *Language Arts and Reading, Mathematics, Science,* and *Social Studies Art Connections* books for activities that further develop line concepts.

Line

Artists use lines to create their works of art.

▲ **Katsushika Hokusai.** (Japanese). *The Great Wave Off Kanagawa.* 1831–1833.

Polychrome woodblock print. $10\frac{1}{8} \times 14\frac{15}{16}$ inches (25.72 × 37.95 cm.). The Metropolitan Museum of Art, New York, New York.

34 Unit 1

Fine Art Prints

Display *Large Prints 1 Interior with Egyptian Curtain* and *2 Cat and Kittens.* Refer to the prints throughout the unit as students learn about lines.

Large Print 1

Large Print 2

Artists use many types of lines.

▶ Can you find some different kinds of lines?

In This Unit you will:

▶ learn about lines.

▶ see how artists use lines to make their works of art.

▶ use lines in your artwork.

Self-Portrait.

Katsushika Hokusai

(1760–1849)

Katsushika Hokusai

▶ was a Japanese artist.

▶ created prints.

▶ made landscapes.

Unit 1   **35**

🏺 Art History and Culture

Katsushika Hokusai

Katsushika Hokusai (kät´sū´ shē kä hō´ kū sī) (1760–1849) lived most of his life in Edo (now called Tokyo). He studied wood block engraving at an early age, and at eighteen became a pupil of the Ukiyo-e master Katsukawa Shunsho. Ukiyo-e prints are landscapes and scenes of everyday life. His artistic output was tremendous, estimated at some 30,000 prints, sketches, and paintings.

See pages 16–21 and 24–25 for more about subject matter and art history.

Artist Profiles, p. 18

◀ Artist Profile ▶
Katsushika Hokusai
1760–1849
Katsushika Hokusai (kät sōō´ shē kä hō´ kōō sī) was born in the city that is now Tokyo. He changed his name more than 30 times. No one knows why. When his home became dirty, he moved. He lived in 93 different places! Hokusai supported himself by illustrating comic books, greeting cards, and novels. During his lifetime he had two wives and seven children.

Hokusai was not interested in money. To pay his bills he would hand over an envelope of money he had received for a painting. Sometimes it was enough, and sometimes it wasn't. When he was broke, he bought art supplies after dark, hoping avoid people he owed. Hokusai painted

Examine the Artwork

"Artists use lines to show us the shapes and details of things." "Los artistas usan las líneas para mostrarnos las figuras y los detalles de las cosas".

▪ Have students look at Katsushika Hokusai's *The Great Wave Off Kanagawa.* Ask them to describe what they see in the artwork.

▪ Define the different kinds of lines. Then have students answer the question on page 35 pertaining to lines in Hokusai's artwork.

▶ Thick and thin lines—The thick black lines inside the great wave give it strength. The small scale of the boat was drawn with thin, delicate lines.

▶ Vertical and horizontal lines—The lines of the rectangle in the top left corner.

▶ Curved lines—The long, curved lines of the waves flow from left to right giving us the feeling that the waves are moving. The short, curved lines on parts of the waves convey the froth of the water.

▶ Diagonal lines—The lines on the sides of the mountain. The slanted line on the front of the boat in the foreground.

▶ Textured lines—The texture of rough water is shown by using repeated curved lines at the tip of the wave.

▶ Broken lines—Note the broken lines of the waves' spray that make our eyes move around the ocean.

Unit Pretest

T Display *Transparency 43* as a pretest. Answers: 1. A, 2. B, 3. B.

Home Connection

▪ See *Home and After-School Connections* for family newsletters and activities for this unit.

ILLUSTRATOR PROFILE
Beatrix Potter
(1866–1943)

Beatrix Potter was the daughter of a wealthy London family. Her brother was sent away to school, so her childhood was quite lonely. Potter entertained herself by drawing creatures that she kept as pets, such as rabbits and mice. Later she began writing story-letters about these animals for her young friends.

One boy received a letter containing *The Tale of Peter Rabbit*. He liked the story so much that Potter decided to make it into a book and publish it. This self-published version was then discovered by the publishing house of Frederick Warne and Company and printed as a commercial edition. *The Tale of Peter Rabbit* became tremendously popular. Potter was subsequently asked to write additional books for the publisher.

While studying Unit 1, share Potter's illustrations with the class and discuss the use of line in her works of art. Ask students to identify the different kinds of lines Potter used in her illustrations.

Music

Line in music refers to the way a melody moves higher or lower. Sing a song and have the children show the higher/lower melodic movement with their hands. Draw lines in several shapes on the board. Then create sound corresponding to the direction implied by one of the lines. Have the class decide which line matches the sounds.

Literature

Watch the video or DVD *Saint George and the Dragon* by Margaret Hodges to explore how artists use lines.

Literature and Art

Performing Arts

ART SOURCE Show *Impressions #2*. Point out how the dancers create a variety of lines with their motions and body positions.

Artsource®

Lesson 1 Overview

Thick and Thin Lines

Lesson 1 introduces line quality. One kind of line quality is the thickness or thinness of a line. **Thick** and **thin lines** are covered in this lesson.

Objectives

 **Art History and Culture**

To recognize that Native American culture is famous for its weaving tradition

 Creative Expression

To create a design using thick and thin lines

 Aesthetic Perception

To distinguish between thick and thin lines in Native American woven blankets and the environment

 Art Criticism

To evaluate one's own work using the four steps of art criticism

Vocabulary ⭐ Reading

Review the following vocabulary words with students before beginning the lesson.

thick line línea gruesa—a line that is wide

thin line línea fina—a line that is narrow

See page 59B for additional vocabulary and Spanish vocabulary resources.

Art Journal: Vocabulary

Have students add these words to the Vocabulary section of their Art Journals.

Lesson Materials

- 1" easel brushes and small brushes (#6 or #8)
- liquid tempera paints (use a single color or the primary colors)
- 12" × 18" white paper, newspaper
- palettes, water dishes, paper towels

Alternate Materials:

- resources from the library/museum: books, weavings, pictures of Navajo weavers, a loom, dye stuffs, blankets with lines on them
- Print images from the Navajo weaving photo tour at **www.museum education.org.**
- crayons or markers

Program Resources

- *Reading and Writing Test Prep.,* pp. 6–7
- *Transparency 1*
- *Flash Cards 1–6*
- *Artist Profiles,* pp. 46, 64
- *Animals Through History Time Line*
- *Assessment,* pp. 9–10
- *Large Prints 1 Interior with Egyptian Curtain* and *2 Cat and Kittens*
- *The National Museum of Women in the Arts Collection*

Concept Trace

Line Quality
Introduced: Level K, Unit 1, Lesson 1

Reinforced: Level 1, Unit 1, Lesson 1

Lesson 1 Arts Integration

Theatre

Complete Unit 1, Lesson 1, on pages 18–19 of the *Theatre Arts Connections* book.

Theatre Arts Connections, p. 18

Objectives
- **Perception** To identify that actions happen in an order
- **Creative Expression** To show the actions of a story by playing a theatre game
- **History and Culture** To learn about early storytellers using chant
- **Criticism** To informally evaluate one's own work

Materials
- Copies of "Plot and Story" Warm-Up, p. 19
- Journals or drawing paper

Vocabulary
chant
pantomime

1 Plot and Story

Focus Time: About 10 minutes

"In this lesson we will play Theatre Games with movement to show what happens in a story." (See page T5 for more about Theatre Games.)

Activate Prior Knowledge
▶ Hand out the **"Plot and Story" Warm-Up.**
▶ Have students complete the last picture. Discuss what happens first in the story, what happens second, and what happens last. Ask individual students to tell the story based upon the pictures.

Teach Time: About 15 minutes

Prepare Have students sit in a circle around you.
▶ **Lead** Sing "The Farmer in the Dell." Tell students that this song tells a story.
▶ Sing the first verse of "The Farmer in the Dell." Create a movement in the center of the circle to represent the farmer.
▶ Wave your hand as a cue and have the group ask, "Then what (The farmer takes a wife.) Guide a student to the center of the circle to represent the wife. *Continue*

Music

 Sing *Miss Mary Mack.* There are four short phrases (sentences) to each verse of the song. Describe the melodic direction of each phrase as upward; each melodic line the same. Play the game: On "Miss" pat legs, on "Ma" cross hands to opposite shoulders, on "-ry" clap own hands, on "Mack, Mack, Mack" clap partner's hands directly across from you on each word. The direction of the game's action is also upward. Design a blanket with only upward strokes.

Movement & Dance

Have students spread out and find personal space to work in. Using the body, they explore creating wide shapes and narrow shapes. Students select one wide shape and one narrow shape and take four counts for each one. Have half the class watch as the other half performs their wide and narrow shapes.

Time: About 10 minutes

Activate Prior Knowledge

"Do you have a favorite blanket?" "¿Tienes una cobija favorita?"

- Discuss the use of the blanket and encourage students to tell how they think it was made.

Using Literature ☆ Reading

- Read *The Magic of Spider Woman* by Lois Duncan, illustrated by Shonto Begay.

Thematic Connection ☆ Social Studies

- **Native Americans:** Discuss the history of the Navajo as one of the first peoples to settle in the United States.

Introduce the Art

Look

"This blanket was woven by a Native American artist." "Esta cobija fue tejida por un artista nativo americano".

- Ask students what *Native American* means.

- Have students describe the lines they see in the blankets.

Comparing and Contrasting ☆ Reading

- Tell students that Navajo artists get ideas for line designs from nature.

Identify Customs and Traditions ☆ Social Studies

- Explain that weaving is the art of joining yarns and fibers to make a large piece of cloth like a blanket.

Adjectives and Adverbs ☆ Language Arts

- List on a chart the adjectives and adverbs students use to describe the fine art.

 Art History and Culture

Share information from the Art History and Culture sections with students. Ask students to name things they have seen in nature that look like lines on the Native American blankets. Possible answers: mountains, rivers, trees, icicles, hills, valleys, and paths.

National Standards for Arts Education in Visual Arts (NSAE) 3.a; 3.b; 4.a

💻 **Web Connection**

Visit **www.umfa.utah.edu** for more information about the *Classic Serape Style Wearing Blanket* at the Utah Museum of Fine Arts.

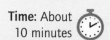 **Lesson 1** Thick and Thin Lines

Look at the Native American blankets. The artists used thick and thin lines in their blankets.

◄ **Artist Unknown.** (Native American, Navajo). *Classic Serape Style Wearing Blanket.* 1875.

Plied cotton and Saxony wool. $73\frac{1}{2} \times 47$ inches (186.69 × 119.38 cm.). Utah Museum of Fine Arts, University of Utah, Salt Lake City, Utah.

 Art History and Culture

Native American artists get ideas from nature. What things have you seen in nature that look like the lines on the blankets?

 Art History and Culture

Navajo Weavers

Native Americans are famous for making woven blankets. Many Navajo weavers use a back-strap loom to weave. This is a portable loom that is attached to the weaver's back and to a stable item, such as a tree or frame when used. Standing looms are also frequently used.

See pages 16–21 and 24–25 for more about subject matter and art history.

Artist Profiles, p. 64

Artist Profile

Classic Serape-Style Wearing Blanket

The Navajo lived in the American Southwest and called themselves *Dineh*, "the people of the earth." In the early 1800s, the Navajo were a powerful and warring tribe. In 1863, they were defeated and forced to relocate to Fort Sumner, where they signed a peace treaty. The Navajo became traders and raised sheep. The wool trade was important for the development of Navajo weaving, an art the Navajo learned from the Pueblo tribe.

◄ **Artist unknown** (Native American, Navajo). [United States]. *Classic Serape-Style Wearing...*

Study both works of art.

▶ Where do you see thick lines?

▶ Where do you see thin lines?

▲ **Sylvia Long.** (American).
Illustration from *Ten Little Rabbits,*
by Virginia Grossman. ©1991.
....
Pen, ink, and watercolor. Chronicle Books,
San Francisco, California.

 Aesthetic Perception

Design Awareness Find thick and thin lines on the walls and floor of the classroom.

Art History and Culture

Sylvia Long

Sylvia Long (sil´ vē ə lông) (1948–) learned about Native American culture from her grandfather, who worked on a reservation when he was young. Long gained first-hand experience when she lived on a reservation in Wyoming where her husband worked as a doctor. *Ten Little Rabbits* was Sylvia Long's first children's book. Long prefers drawing animals rather than people and spends a lot of time outdoors studying her subjects before drawing them.

See pages 16–21 and 24–25 for more about subject matter and art history.

Artist Profiles, p. 46

◆ Artist Profile ◆
Sylvia Long
b. 1948
Sylvia Long (sil´ vē ə lông) illustrates children's books and has earned many awards and honors from organizations such as the American Library Association and the American Booksellers Association. Born in New York, Long graduated from the Maryland Institute of Art and Arizona State University. She has widely exhibited her work for more than 20 years. She began her career as a children's book illustrator in 1991 with *Ten Little Rabbits.* This first book received enthusiastic reviews from children and parents alike, and marked the start of a large readership. Long lives in Arizona with her husband and sons.

Study

▶ *Classic Serape Style Wearing Blanket* has diamond patterns that are made with thick red lines. The three horizontal straight lines are made up of thick diagonal lines. *Ten Little Rabbits* has thick lines on the blanket that the rabbit in the foreground is wearing.

▶ *Classic Serape Style Wearing Blanket* has thin lines in the zigzags at the top and bottom of the blanket, as well as broken horizontal thin lines through the middle of the blanket. The three horizontal straight lines have a thin, red horizontal line in them. *Ten Little Rabbits* has thin horizontal and zigzag lines on the blanket the two rabbits are holding.

■ For more examples of utilitarian art, see *The National Museum of Women in the Arts Collection.*

Art Journal: Concept
Have students draw a picture in their Art Journals of what they think thick and thin lines look like.

Aesthetic Perception

Design Awareness Discuss thick and thin lines that can be found on the walls and floor of the classroom. Floor tiles and the alphabet display might create thick lines. Seams between floor tiles or lines on the board might create thin lines. Encourage students to find as many examples as they can.

Developing Visual Literacy Invite students to share any personal experiences that contribute to their understanding of the works of art. For example, have any of them seen mountains or land like what is shown in *Ten Little Rabbits?* Are the lines on the blankets similar to the lines they saw in nature?   NSAE 3.a; 5.b

NSAE 5.a; 5.c

 Web Connection
Visit **www.sylvia-long.com/** to find out more about Sylvia Long and study her portfolio.

Time: About 30 minutes

"Let's make thick and thin lines." *"Formemos líneas gruesas y finas".*

- Demonstrate a thin line by having several students form a single-file line.

Practice

- Have the students create thick and thin lines by following the steps on page 38.
- Ask which line is wide and which is narrow. Which line has more people?

Creative Expression

Materials: 1" easel brushes, #6 or #8 brushes, liquid tempera paints (use a single color or the primary colors), 12" × 18" white paper, newspaper, palettes, water dishes, paper towels

Alternate Materials: resources from the library/ museum: books, weavings, pictures of Navajo weavers, a loom, dye stuffs, blankets with lines on them. Print images from the Navajo weaving photo tour at **www.museum education.org.**, crayons or markers

- "What kind of design would you make on a blanket using thick and thin lines?" *"¿Qué tiop de diseño harían en una cobija usando lineas gruesas y fínas?"*

- Have students decide which brush will make a thick line and which one will make a thin line and use both kinds of lines to create their designs.

- Distribute the materials and have students follow the directions on page 39.

- See pages 216–218 for additional information and tips for using a paintbrush and tempera paint.

- See the Activity Tips on page 232 for visual examples of this lesson's activity.

NSAE 1.a; 1.c

Art Journal: Brainstorming

Identify Physical Characteristics of Places

⭐ Social Studies

Have students brainstorm ideas for items found in nature that they could represent in their designs. Have students draw these items in their Art Journals. Discuss how these items can be drawn in the Creative Expression activity using thick and thin lines.

Using Thick and Thin Lines

A **thick line** is wide.

A **thin line** is narrow.

Practice

1. Stand and line up with some classmates. Form a thin line.
2. Next form a thick line with your classmates.

Differentiated Instruction

Reteach
Have students draw lines using a thick, blunt crayon and a thin, pointed crayon so that they can immediately see the difference in lines.

Special Needs
For students who have difficulty grasping small paintbrushes, use tape or a rubber band to attach a foam rubber cylinder around the brush for the student to grasp.

ELL Tips
Draw thick and thin lines on the board using different colors. Ask each student to go to the board and pick out either a thin or thick line. Show students the *Classic Serape Style Wearing Blanket* and have them pick out the thick and thin lines.

◄ **Kristina Jimenez.** Age 5.

Think about the kinds of lines you see in the student's artwork.

 Creative Expression

How would you use thick and thin lines to make a design?

1. Think about thick and thin lines.
2. Create a blanket for yourself with different lines.

 **Art Criticism**

Describe How many thick lines did you paint? Thin lines?

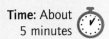

Reflect

Time: About 5 minutes

Review and Assess

"Which kind of line is wide, a thick line or a thin line?" "¿Qué tipo de línea es ancha, una línea gruesa o una línea fina?"

Think

Discuss the student art question. The student used mostly thick lines with some thin yellow lines.

- Use *Large Prints 1* Interior with Egyptian Curtain and *2 Cat and Kittens* to compare the thick and thin lines in them to those found in the works of art for this lesson.

Informal Assessment

Art Journal: Critical Thinking
Have students answer the Describe question by writing the numbers in their Art Journals.

 **Art Criticism**

Have students ask themselves the following questions.

Describe ► How many thick lines did you paint? How many thin lines did you paint?

Analyze ► Which lines stand out on your paper, the thick ones or the thin ones?

Interpret ► What does your blanket design remind you of that is found in nature?

Decide ► What do you like best about your painting?

NSAE 2.b; 5.a; 5.c

- For standardized-format test practice using this lesson's art content, see pages 6–7 in *Reading and Writing Test Preparation*.

Art Across the Curriculum

Use these simple ideas to reinforce art concepts across the curriculum.

★ **Descriptive Writing** Read *The Legend of the Loom: A Navajo Legend,* told by Sarah Natani, illustrated by Baje Whitethorne. Study the illustrations. Have students draw a picture of things in nature that could be the inspiration for a Navajo blanket.

★ **Math** Read *Ten Little Rabbits* by Virginia Grossman and Sylvia Long. Count the rabbits in the illustrations.

★ **Science** Study natural dyes like those that are used to create the color in Native American woven blankets such as fresh berries, spinach leaves, and carrot tops.

★ **Social Studies** The Navajo live in Arizona and New Mexico. Learn about geographical features of the desert. Have students draw a desert landscape.

★ **Technology** Using a paint program, have students create a geometric design with thick or thin lines. Visit **SRAonline.com** to print detailed instructions for this activity.

Thick and Thin Lines

Extra! For the Art Specialist

Time: About 30 minutes

Focus

Use *Transparency 1* and the *Large Prints 1 Interior with Egyptian Curtain* and *2 Cat and Kittens* to introduce students to thick and thin lines. Demonstrate thick and thin lines by drawing on the board or overhead.

Teach

Have students make tiny blankets by gluing thick and thin fibers and ribbons to pieces of fabric.

Reflect

Have students use the four steps of art criticism to evaluate their work. Did they effectively design a blanket using both thick and thin lines?

Alternate Activity

Materials:
- 10" square pieces of stiff fabric, such as burlap or cotton
- ribbons and yarns of various widths cut 10" in length
- glue
- craft sticks

1. Show students the ribbons and yarn fibers and ask students to identify them as thick or thin lines.

2. Have students choose thick and thin ribbons and yarn fibers to glue on their blanket designs.

3. Encourage students to draw a line of glue on their fabric and then use craft sticks to press the ribbons and yarn fibers into the line of glue.
   NSAE 1.c

Research in Art Education

One study showed that when students study art forms from minority cultures, this instruction seems to be "effective in diminishing students' stereotypical attitudes and perceptions toward a minority culture." The arts can help teachers become "catalysts for cultural understanding and respect" ("North American Indian Music Instruction: Influences upon Attitudes, Cultural Perceptions, and Achievement" in *Schools, Communities, and the Arts: A Research Compendium*). As students learn about Native American weaving in this lesson, encourage their questions about Native American culture. Continue to study the culture through books, videos, or guest speakers.

Assessment

Use the following rubric to evaluate the artwork students make in the Creative Expression activity and to assess students' understanding of thick and thin lines.

Have students complete page 9 or 10 in their *Assessment* books.

	Art History and Culture	Aesthetic Perception	Creative Expression	Art Criticism
3 POINTS	The student demonstrates understanding that Native American culture is known for its weaving tradition.	The student accurately distinguishes between thick and thin lines.	The student's painting clearly illustrates thick and thin lines.	The student thoughtfully and honestly evaluates his or her own work using the four steps of art criticism.
2 POINTS	The student's understanding that the Native American culture is known for its weaving tradition is weak or incomplete.	The student shows emerging awareness of thick and thin lines, but cannot consistently identify them.	The student's painting shows some awareness of thick and thin lines.	The student attempts to evaluate his or her own work, but shows an incomplete understanding of evaluation criteria.
1 POINT	The student cannot demonstrate understanding that Native American culture is known for its weaving tradition.	The student cannot identify thick and thin lines.	The student's painting shows no understanding of thick and thin lines.	The student makes no attempt to evaluate his or her own artwork.

Assessment, p. 9

Name _____ Date _____

Thick and Thin Lines

Lesson 1 UNIT 1

| 1 | 2 |
| 3 | 4 |

For the teacher: Use the following prompts for this activity.
1. Using a crayon, draw a thin line in box 1.
2. Draw a thick line in box 2.
3. Draw thick and thin lines in box 3.
4. Draw something you see in the room that has thick or thin lines in box 4.

Level K   Unit 1 • An Introduction to Line   9

 **Lesson 2 Overview**

Lines Can Make Calm Pictures

Lesson 2 introduces line direction. Line direction is the path that a line takes as it is made with a moving tool. A **vertical line** moves up and down and a **horizontal line** moves side to side.

Objectives

 Art History and Culture

To understand that artists from different times and places use calm lines in their paintings

 Creative Expression

To create a calm landscape using vertical and horizontal lines

 Aesthetic Perception

To identify vertical and horizontal lines in nature and fine art

Art Criticism

To evaluate one's own work using the four steps of art criticism

Vocabulary 🖈 Reading

Review the following vocabulary words with students before beginning the lesson.

vertical line línea vertical—a straight line that moves up and down

horizontal line línea horizontal—a straight line that moves side to side

See page 59B for additional vocabulary and Spanish vocabulary resources.

 Art Journal: Vocabulary

Have students add these words to the Vocabulary section of their Art Journals.

Lesson Materials

- 9" × 12" blue construction paper
- 9" × 12" construction paper in various colors
- glue

Alternate Materials:
- any drawing media

Program Resources
- *Reading and Writing Test Prep.*, pp. 8–9
- *Transparency 2*
- *Flash Cards 1* and *2*
- *Artist Profiles*, pp. 17, 29
- *Assessment*, pp. 11–12
- *Large Print 2* Cat and Kittens
- *Art Around the World Collection*

Concept Trace
Line Direction
Introduced: Level K, Unit 1, Lesson 2

Reinforced: Level 1, Unit 1, Lesson 2

Lesson 2 Arts Integration

Theatre
Complete Unit 1, Lesson 2 on pages 20–21 of the *Theatre Arts Connections* book.

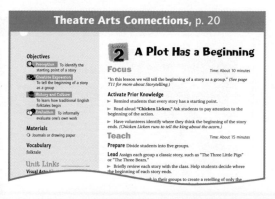

Music
 Listen to *The Swan*, from *The Carnival of the Animals*, by Camille Saint-Seans. The melody is smooth; there are no large leaps or jumps. This small melodic range is combined with a slow beat and some long, held-out notes to suggest the image of a swan swimming gracefully. The sound of the cello adds to the sense of calm. Use scarves to move in space to the music and/or make your art with this as background music.

Movement & Dance
Identify horizontal and vertical lines in the classroom. Working with a partner, students create a horizontal and vertical line together. Now explore how each of the lines might move. Example: To move a vertical line you might explore moving up and down. To move a horizontal line you might explore moving side to side. Take eight counts to transition to partner's position and repeat.

 **ocus**

Time: About 10 minutes

Activate Prior Knowledge

"What do you like about being outside?"
"¿Qué les gusta de estar afuera?"

■ Encourage students to discuss the things they see and do outside.

Using Literature ⭐ Reading

■ Read *The Seashore Book* by Charlotte Zolotow. Have students find examples of vertical and horizontal lines in the paintings by Wendell Minor.

Thematic Connection ⭐ Science

■ **Outside:** Identify that heat causes change, such as ice melting. Observe and chart the weather conditions outside for several days. Note changes that occur due to increased heat.

Introduce the Art

Look

"What is happening in these paintings?"
"¿Qué pasa en estas pinturas?"

■ Lead students in a discussion about the lack of activity in the paintings.

■ Ask students to identify the parts of the paintings that look calm. Why do they look calm?

Discussing the Selection ⭐ Reading

■ Have students describe the lines they see in the paintings. Ask them to identify the vertical and horizontal lines.

■ Explain that although the artists lived at different times and painted in different styles, both used vertical and horizontal lines to show calmness in their paintings.

Adjectives and Adverbs ⭐ Language Arts

■ List on a chart the adjectives and adverbs students use to describe the fine art.

NSAE 3.a; 4.a

🏺 Art History and Culture

Share information from the Art History and Culture sections with students. Encourage students to describe how light outside can look different.
NSAE 3.a; 3.b

💻 **Web Connection**
Search The Metropolitan Museum of Art Web site at **www.metmuseum.org/home.asp** to view works of art by Claude Monet.

Lines Can Make Calm Pictures

◀ **Claude Monet.** (French). *The Four Trees.* 1891.
....
Oil on canvas. $32\frac{1}{4} \times 32\frac{1}{8}$ inches (81.92 × 81.58 cm.). The Metropolitan Museum of Art, New York, New York.

Look at these works of art. Artists use **vertical** and **horizontal lines** to make art look calm.

🏺 Art History and Culture

Some artists, such as Monet, like to paint outside. They show how the natural light looks in their paintings.

🏺 Art History and Culture

Claude Monet

Claude Monet (klōd mō nā´) (1840–1926) painted numerous paintings of poplars late in the impressionist period. Impressionists preferred to paint outdoors so they could capture the effects of natural light and weather on their subjects. Monet often painted the same subject in a series, such as his *Poplars,* to show the same subject in different light, weather, and even seasons.

See pages 16–21 and 24–25 for more about subject matter and art history.

Artist Profiles, p. 29

◆ Artist Profile ◆
Claude Monet
1840–1926
Claude Monet (klōd mō nā´) did not want to be a painter as a young man in France. He was already well paid for drawing caricatures of tourists. Painter Eugene Boudin saw talent in Monet's exaggerated drawings and encouraged him to paint. Although artists were "supposed" to paint in studios, Boudin urged Monet to paint outside in the open air. There Monet learned to capture his first impressions on canvas. He recorded these impressions during a long and productive life. His greatest wish was to "mingle more closely with nature."

▲ **David Hockney.** (British).
American Collectors. 1968.
·······························
Acrylic on canvas. 63⅞ × 120 inches
(213.4 × 304.8 cm). The Art Institute
of Chicago, Chicago, Illinois.

Study both works of art.

▶ Where do you see vertical lines?

▶ Where do you see horizontal lines?

Aesthetic Perception

Seeing Like an Artist Where do you see
vertical and horizontal lines outside?

Art History and Culture

David Hockney

David Hockney (dā´ vəd häk´ nē) (1937–   ) is often considered to
be a pop artist. Pop art began in England in the 1950s and caught
on in the United States in the 1960s. Many artists considered the
trend in art at this time to be too pretentious and wanted to bring
art back to everyday, or "popular," life. Pop art explores images
common to consumer culture, such as advertisements, product
packaging, celebrities, and comic strips. Labeling Hockney as a pop
artist might not be entirely accurate, and Hockney himself has
rejected the title. Although
his most publicized work is
his pop art, he explores
various painting styles,
photography, and theatre set
design.

See pages 16–21 and 24–25
for more about subject
matter and art history.

Artist Profiles, p. 17

◆ Artist Profile ◆
David Hockney
b. 1937

David Hockney (dā´ vəd häk´ nē) was born
in 1937 into a working class family in the
northern industrial section of Bradford,
England. By the time he was 11, he had
decided to become an artist. At 16, he
attended the Bradford School of Art, and
went on to study at the Royal College of Art.
In 1961, he made his first trip to the United
States. The brightness and light of California
was a sharp contrast from the rain and fog
of England. He was impressed by the sense
of space in the sprawling city of Los Angeles,
and moved permanently to the United
States in 1978 to become part of the
California art scene.

Study

▶ The tree trunks in *The Four Trees* were
created with vertical lines. In *American
Collectors,* vertical lines can be seen on the
window blinds, the outline of the windows,
the broad maroon lines between the sets of
windows, the tree trunk, the sides of the
rectangular stones in the sculpture by the
man, and the back of the man's pants.

▶ Horizontal lines run through the tile
flooring, the roofline, and the gray shadow
below the windows. In *The Four Trees,* the
shrubbery along the bank of the water
forms a horizontal line.

■ For more examples of art from Europe, see
the *Art Around the World Collection.*

Art Journal: Concept
Have students draw a picture in
their Art Journals of what they think
horizontal and vertical lines look like.

Aesthetic Perception

Seeing Like an Artist Have students look
outside to find examples of vertical and
horizontal lines. Answers will vary but might
include: tree trunks, flower stems, bars on
playground equipment, lines painted on
playground pavement, grass blades, grout
lines between bricks of the building, lines
painted on the street, and flag poles.

Developing Visual Literacy Have students sit
outside and observe their surroundings. Find
objects that are still and calm. Locate the
vertical and horizontal lines in those objects.

Web Connection
Visit **www.artic.edu/aic/** for more information
about David Hockney and the Art Institute of
Chicago Museum.

 **each**

"Let's practice making vertical and horizontal lines." "Practiquemos cómo hacer líneas verticales y horizontales".

■ Draw a vertical and horizontal line on the board.

Practice

Materials: None

■ Ask students to watch as you draw vertical and horizontal lines on the board.

■ Have the students draw vertical and horizontal lines by following the steps on page 42.

Creative Expression

Materials: 9" × 12" blue construction paper, 9" × 12" construction paper in various colors, glue

Alternate Materials: any drawing media

"What are some objects you see outside?" "¿Cuáles son algunos de los objetos que ven afuera?"

■ See the Activity Tips on page 232 for visual examples of this lesson's activity.

■ Tearing the paper with the grain will make straight lines. Tearing against the grain will create short, irregular pieces.

■ Distribute the materials and have the students follow the directions on page 43.

■ Have students arrange the horizontal lines first to make the ground.

■ Then arrange the vertical lines to make trees, grass, flower stems, and so on.

■ Students can use smaller pieces of paper to make clouds, leaves, bushes, and flowers.

■ Once the arrangement is in place, have students glue it to the paper.

NSAE 1.a; 1.c

Art Journal: Brainstorming
Talk about what the students see in nature that they could show in their landscapes. Have students draw these items in their Art Journals.

Using Vertical and Horizontal Lines

Vertical lines move up and down.

Horizontal lines move from side to side.

Practice

1. Use your finger to draw a vertical line in the air.

2. Now draw a horizontal line in the air.

Differentiated Instruction

Reteach
Have students stand to model vertical lines. Have a few students lie down head to toe to represent a horizontal line. Then have students practice drawing vertical and horizontal lines.

Special Needs
Students who have difficulty tearing paper can use pre-cut or torn paper to create their landscape.

ELL Tips
Draw a vertical line on the board and ask students to say the word *vertical*. Have students trace a vertical line in the air. Repeat with a horizontal line. Then randomly draw vertical and horizontal lines on the board. As students trace the lines in the air, ask them to identify the line types.

◄ **Thomas Lazzari.**
Age 5.

Think about where vertical and horizontal lines are used in this student's work.

 Creative Expression

How can you make a picture look calm?

1. Tear the paper into short and long pieces.
2. Place the pieces on the page to make a calm landscape.
3. Glue the pieces to the page.

 Art Criticism

Interpret What appears to be standing still in your picture?

Art Across the Curriculum

Use these simple ideas to reinforce art concepts across the curriculum.

★ **Persuasive Writing** Show students some magazine advertisements. Discuss the purpose of an advertisement. Have students draw a picture of a quiet place to visit for a vacation advertisement.

★ **Math** Use vertical or horizontal lines to divide pictures of whole parts into halves. For example, have students draw a vertical line through the middle of a picture of a pizza to make halves.

★ **Science** Identify the five senses and recognize which senses can be used while observing nature.

★ **Social Studies** Identify customs associated with national holidays that are experienced outdoors, such as fireworks and parades.

★ **Technology** Show students how to use the line tool in a paint program to create straight vertical and horizontal lines. Visit **SRAonline.com** to print detailed instructions for this activity.

Reflect

Time: About 5 minutes

Review and Assess

"What kinds of lines help make your artwork look calm?" "¿Qué tipos de líneas ayudan a hacer que sus obras de artes parezcan calmadas?"

Think

Discuss the student art question. The tree trunks are vertical lines. The ground is a horizontal line.

■ Use *Large Print 2 Cat and Kittens* to practice identifying vertical and horizontal lines.

Informal Assessment

Art Journal: Critical Thinking
Have students answer the Interpret question in their Art Journals by drawing a picture.

 **Art Criticism**

Have students ask themselves the following questions.

Describe ► Where did you use vertical lines? Horizontal lines?

Analyze ► Does your landscape look calm? Why or why not?

Interpret ► What appears to be standing still in your picture?

Decide ► Are you satisfied with your artwork? What would you change if you did this project again?

NSAE 2.b; 5.a; 5.c

■ For standardized-format test practice using this lesson's art content, see pages 8–9 in *Reading and Writing Test Preparation*.

Lines Can Make Calm Pictures

Extra! For the Art Specialist

Time: About 30 minutes

Focus

Focus *Use Transparency 2* and the *Large Print 2 Cat and Kittens* to introduce students to vertical and horizontal lines.

Teach

Have students make a torn paper collage and use markers to fill the paper with details.

Reflect

Have students use the four steps of art criticism to evaluate their work. Did they effectively create a collage using calm lines? Did they use both vertical and horizontal lines? Did they add details with markers?

Alternate Activity

Materials:
- 9" × 12" paper (white and assorted colors)
- glue
- markers

1. Have students make the torn paper collage as directed in the Creative Expression activity on page 42.

2. Discuss other things that they could draw into their designs such as birds and birds' nests, little animals, people, flowers, leaves, grass, and sky. Have students fill the paper with objects drawn with markers.
   NSAE 1.a; 1.c

Research in Art Education

It has been shown that "elementary [art] programs establish a foundation in the arts for all students, not just for those in specialized programs or those who choose an arts course of study in high school." Providing consistent, quality instruction in the arts in elementary school also ensures that students have the time to foster skills in the arts. Many of these skills take time to develop *(Gaining the Arts Advantage: Lessons from School Districts that Value Arts Education)*. For this reason, skills are often repeated throughout *Art Connections*. Line direction is introduced in this lesson and reinforced in the next two lessons.

Assessment

Use the following rubric to evaluate the artwork students make in the Creative Expression activity and to assess students' understanding of vertical and horizontal lines.

Have students complete page 11 or 12 in their *Assessment* books.

	Art History and Culture	Aesthetic Perception	Creative Expression	Art Criticism
3 POINTS	The student demonstrates understanding that artists from different times and places can use calm lines in their paintings.	The student accurately identifies vertical and horizontal lines in nature and fine art.	The student's landscape clearly illustrates vertical and horizontal lines.	The student thoughtfully and honestly evaluates his or her own work using the four steps of art criticism.
2 POINTS	The student's understanding that artists from different times and places can use calm lines in their paintings is weak or incomplete.	The student shows emerging awareness of vertical and horizontal lines, but cannot consistently identify them.	The student's landscape shows some awareness of vertical and horizontal lines.	The student attempts to evaluate his or her own work, but shows an incomplete understanding of evaluation criteria.
1 POINT	The student does not understand that artists from different times and places can use calm lines in their paintings.	The student cannot identify vertical or horizontal lines in nature or fine art.	The student's landscape shows no understanding of vertical and horizontal lines.	The student makes no attempt to evaluate his or her own artwork.

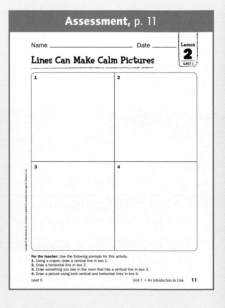

Assessment, p. 11

Name _____ Date _____
Lesson 2 UNIT 1

Lines Can Make Calm Pictures

For the teacher: Use the following prompts for this activity.
1. Using a crayon, draw a vertical line in box 1.
2. Draw a horizontal line in box 2.
3. Draw something you see in the room that has a vertical line in box 3.
4. Draw a picture using both vertical and horizontal lines in box 4.

Level K   Unit 1 • An Introduction to Line   11

Lesson 3 Overview

Lines Can Make Busy Pictures

Lesson 3 continues the study of line direction, the path a line takes as it is made with a moving tool. **Diagonal lines** move at an angle. **Zigzag lines** are diagonal lines that connect.

Objectives

 Art History and Culture

To learn that artists from different places use diagonal and zigzag lines to make exciting works of art

 Creative Expression

To create an image that looks exciting by using diagonal and zigzag lines

 Aesthetic Perception

To identify diagonal and zigzag lines in art and the environment

Art Criticism

To evaluate one's own work using the four steps of art criticism

Vocabulary ⭐ Reading

Review the following vocabulary words with students before beginning the lesson.

diagonal line línea diagonal— a slanted line; a line that moves at an angle

zigzag line línea en zigzag—diagonal lines that connect

See page 59B for additional vocabulary and Spanish vocabulary resources.

Art Journal: Vocabulary

 Have students add these words to the Vocabulary section of their Art Journals.

Lesson Materials

- computer
- paint program
- printer with paper

Alternate Materials:
- markers, pencils
- dustless chalk
- crayons or oil pastels
- 12″ × 18″ white or light colored paper

Program Resources

- *Reading and Writing Test Prep.*, pp. 10–11
- *Transparency 3*
- *Flash Cards 3* and *5*
- *Artist Profiles*, pp. 5, 39
- *Animals Through History Time Line*
- *Assessment*, pp. 13–14
- *Large Print 1 Interior with Egyptian Curtain*
- *Art Around the World Collection*

Concept Trace
Line Direction
Introduced: Level K, Unit 1, Lesson 2

Reinforced: Level 1, Unit 1, Lesson 3

Lesson 3 Arts Integration

Theatre

Complete Unit 1, Lesson 3 on pages 22–23 of the *Theatre Arts Connections* book.

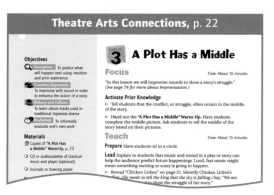

Music

Listen to *Circus Music* from *The Red Pony*, by Aaron Copeland. Imagine this music as the background music to the act in the painting by W. H. Brown. Raise your hand when the actors take their bows. Can you think of any other tricks ponies would do? How about clowns?

Movement & Dance

Using masking tape, create a wide zigzag line on the floor that goes from one diagonal to another. Students form a line and travel down the zigzag pathway using different locomotor movements and making sharp changes of direction. Example: Walk, gallop, hop. Which of these locomotor movements is the most effective on a zigzag pathway?

Focus

Time: About 10 minutes

Activate Prior Knowledge

"Have you ever been to a circus parade or seen one on television?" "¿Alguna vez han ido a un circo o han visto alguno por televisión?"

- Encourage students to discuss circus events, animals, and costumes.

Using Literature [★] Reading

- Read *The 100th Day of School* by Angela Shelf Medearis, illustrated by Joan Holub. Find straight, slanted, and curved lines in the illustrations. Then try to find similar lines in your classroom.

Thematic Connection [★] Social Studies

- **Cooperation** Discuss how the people in *Bareback Riders* have to cooperate in order to perform successfully. Have students identify ways they cooperate.

Introduce the Art

Look

"This painting about the circus was created by a folk artist—an artist who is self-taught." "Esta pintura acerca del circo la creó un artista popular, o sea, un artista que es autodidacta".

Identifying Details [★] Reading

- Have students describe what they see in the painting.

- Have students interpret what they see. Who or what seems to be moving in the picture? How can you tell?

- Have students draw the lines of the horse's legs in the air and name the kind of lines. Repeat with the legs of the acrobats.

Adjectives and Adverbs [★] Language Arts

List on a chart the adjectives and adverbs students use to describe the fine art.

NSAE 4.a

 Art History and Culture

Share information from the Art History and Culture sections with students. Schoenhut created a variety of wooden toys as well as dolls, dollhouses, and blocks.

🖥 **Web Connection**

Visit **www.nga.gov/kids/kids.htm** for more art activities for children.

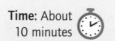

Lines Can Make Busy Pictures

▲ **W. H. Brown.** (American). *Bareback Riders.* 1886.

Oil on cardboard mounted on wood.
18½ × 24¼ inches (46.99 × 61.60 cm).
National Gallery of Art, Washington, D.C.

Look at the artwork on these pages. Both works of art look busy.

 Art History and Culture

Artists create art for many reasons. The artist made *Humpty Dumpty Circus* so it could be used as a toy.

 Art History and Culture

W. H. Brown

William Henry Brown (wil´ yəm hen´ rē broun) (active 1886–1887) was a folk artist. Folk artists are self-taught—they have not received any formal schooling in art, unlike fine artists. Not much is known about W.H. Brown or his work because he was not "famous." He taught himself to paint because he enjoyed it.

See pages 16–21 and 24–25 for more about subject matter and art history.

Artist Profiles, p. 5

◆ Artist Profile ◆

W. H. Brown
active 1886–1887

W. H. Brown (broun) was a folk artist who painted and signed an isolated group of four paintings. The few facts known about Brown came from the inscription of "Binghamton, New York" on three of the paintings. Directories for the city of Binghamton list five W.H. Browns as living in the town between 1885 and 1887. Among the professions of these W. H. Browns were carpenter, machine agent, shoemaker, shopkeeper, and laborer. The painter of *Bareback Riders* was likely one of these tradesmen.

▲ **W. H. Brown.** (American). *Bareback Riders.* 1886.

▲ *Schoenhut's Humpty Dumpty Circus.*
....
Toy Sculpture. Children's Museum of Indianapolis, Indiana.

Study both pictures.

▶ Where are diagonal lines?

▶ Where are zigzag lines?

🔍 Aesthetic Perception

Seeing Like an Artist Can you find diagonal and zigzag lines around you?

🏺 Art History and Culture

Albert Schoenhut

Albert Schoenhut (al´ bert shōn´ hət) and his company, A. Schoenhut Company, American Toymakers, manufactured wooden toys in Philadelphia from about 1872 to the early 1930s, when the Great Depression hit. He learned his craft from his native country of Germany, where wooden toy making has a long history. German craftspeople specialized in intricately carved and painted wooden dolls, farm animals, and Noah's Ark animals.

See pages 16–21 and 24–25 for more about subject matter and art history.

Artist Profiles, p. 39

● Artist Profile ●
Albert Schoenhut
Albert Schoenhut (al bert shōn hōōt) came to the United States from Germany in the 1860s. A child from a German toy-making family, Schoenhut founded his own toy company in Philadelphia, Pennsylvania, and he produced his first toy in 1872. Albert Schoenhut Company American Toymakers became known as a high-quality wooden toy manufacturer and continued to produce toys until 1935.

▲ **A. Schoenhut Co. American Toymakers.** (United States). *Humpty Dumpty Circus.* c. 1930. Toy Sculpture. Children's Museum of Indianapolis, Indiana.

About the Media

Study

▶ Diagonal lines in *Bareback Riders*—the bottom of the banners; both acrobats' legs and arms; the horse's legs; the trim around the clown's neck, arm, and thighs.

▶ Diagonal lines in *Schoenhut's Humpty Dumpty Circus*—the pole the man on the ladder is carrying; the upright leg of the clown who is lying down.

▶ Zigzag lines in *Bareback Riders*—the fabric around the collar, waistband, and tops of the legs on the clown in the left foreground; the flags hanging from the wooden posts.

▶ Zigzag lines in *Schoenhut's Humpty Dumpty Circus*—the design on the pedestal on which the elephant has placed one foot; the green line on the fabric on the elephant in the right foreground.

■ For more examples of art from North America, see the **Art Around the World Collection.**

📕 Art Journal: Concept

Have students draw a picture in their Art Journals of what they think diagonal and zigzag lines look like.

🔍 Aesthetic Perception

Design Awareness Ask students to find diagonal and zigzag lines within the classroom. Continue looking for these lines in other areas of the school, such as the library, playground, and cafeteria. Does one kind of line seem to be more common than the others? NSAE 3.a; 3.b

Developing Visual Literacy
Comparing and Contrasting ⭐ Reading
Ask students to bring a toy to class. Have them compare and contrast their toys to *Schoenhut's Humpty Dumpty Circus.*

💻 Web Connection

Visit the Web site for the Children's Museum of Indianapolis at **www.childrensmuseum.org/ circus/schoenhut.htm** to find out more about Albert Schoenhut and *Humpty Dumpty Circus.*

Teach

Time: About 30 minutes

"Let's take turns role-playing circus performers." "Túrnense para hacer el papel de los artistas de un circo".

- Demonstrate the activity by taking a turn at role-playing. For example, you could pretend to walk on a tight rope. Have the students guess what you are doing.

Practice

Materials: No materials are needed.

- Have students demonstrate line direction by following the steps on page 46.
- Help students analyze the lines that the performers create as they move their bodies, arms, and legs.

Creative Expression

Materials: computer, paint program, printer with paper

Alternate Materials: markers, pencils, dustless chalk, crayons, or oil pastels, and paper

"What would you like to do if you could be in a circus?" "¿Qué les gustaría hacer si pudieran estar en un circo?"

- Assist students in opening a paint program on the computer.
- Review how to use the various tools in the paint program.
- See the Activity Tips on page 233 for visual examples of this lesson's activity.
- Have the students follow the directions on page 47.
- Print the students' work when finished.

NSAE 1.a; 1.c

Art Journal: Brainstorming

Visualizing ⭐ Reading

Have students think about what different people and animals do in a circus. Ask students to close their eyes and visualize a clown performing. Have students sketch in their Art Journals some of the different things clowns do. Ask students what kinds of lines they used to draw their clowns.

Using Diagonal and Zigzag Lines

Lines move in different directions.

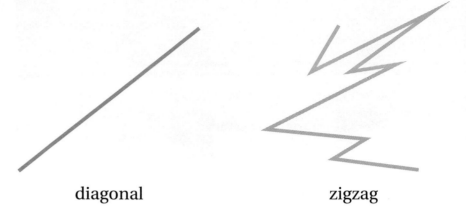

diagonal   zigzag

Practice

1. Pretend you are a circus performer.
2. Ask classmates to guess what you are doing.

Differentiated Instruction

Reteach
Have students role-play line movement (diagonal and zigzag) in a game of Simon Says.

Special Needs
Some students with developmental disabilities may need extra practice making zigzag and diagonal lines before creating their clown drawings. Have students create these lines using chenille stems as another means of reinforcing these concepts.

ELL Tips
Draw each kind of line. Say the name of each line as you draw it and have students repeat the name. Then write the word next to the line. Invite students to the board to identify each kind of line.

Think about how this artist used diagonal and zigzag lines.

◀ **Grayson Hulett.**
Age 5.

 Creative Expression

What lines do you see on a clown?

1. Use the shape and pencil tools to draw a clown.
2. Make the hair by drawing zigzag lines.
3. Decorate the costume with diagonal lines.

 **Art Criticism**

Decide Can you draw your picture using only diagonal lines?

Unit 1 • Lesson 3　**47**

● **Art Across the Curriculum** ●

Use these simple ideas to reinforce art concepts across the curriculum.

★ **Narrative Writing** Have students draw a picture to tell a story about what they would do if they had a job in the circus.

★ **Math** Look at shapes and discuss the different kinds of lines that make up shapes.

★ **Science** Observe plants and animals in nature. Identify different kinds of lines in nature.

★ **Social Studies** Learn about rules for safety. List some safety rules for the acrobats in *Bareback Riders*.

★ **Technology** Use the paintbrush tool in a paint program to practice making diagonal and zigzag lines. Visit **SRAonline.com** to print detailed instructions for this activity.

 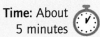　Time: About 5 minutes

Review and Assess

"In what directions do lines move?" "¿En cuáles direcciones se mueven las líneas?"

Think

Discuss the student art question. The artist used zigzag lines to draw the hair and diagonal lines to decorate the tie.

■ Use *Large Print 1 Interior with Egyptian Curtain* to compare the diagonal and zigzag lines in them to those found in the artwork for this lesson.

Informal Assessment

Art Journal: Critical Thinking
Have students answer the Decide question in their Art Journals. First have them draw a horizontal line to divide the page in half. In the top half have students draw a picture that shows movement. In the bottom half have students draw something standing still.

 **Art Criticism**

Have students ask themselves the following questions.

Describe ▶ What are you showing in your drawing?

Analyze ▶ Identify and describe the different lines you used to draw your picture.

Interpret ▶ What people, animals, and objects appear to be moving? Tell about the people's movements. What appears to be standing still?

Decide ▶ Could you draw your picture using only diagonal lines? Why or why not?

NSAE 2.b; 5.a; 5.c

■ For standardized-format test practice using this lesson's art content, see pages 10–11 in *Reading and Writing Test Preparation.*

LESSON 3 • Lines Can Make Busy Pictures　**47**

Lines Can Make Busy Pictures

Extra! For the Art Specialist

Time: About 30 minutes

Focus

Use *Transparency 3* and *Large Print 1 Interior with Egyptian Curtain* to introduce students to different kinds of lines.

Teach

Discuss the activities of a circus, such as clowns on bikes, dancing horses, and acrobats on high wires. Ask students how they could use busy lines to make a busy picture. Demonstrate on the board how you can turn a stiff, calm clown into an active clown by slanting its body using diagonal lines. (Erase your drawing before the students begin their own drawings.)

Reflect

Have students use the four steps of art criticism to evaluate their work. Were they effective in making their circus picture look busy by using diagonal and zigzag lines?

Alternate Activity

Materials:
- 12″ × 18″ white paper
- crayons

1. Invite students to take turns acting out circus activities.

2. Have students draw circus pictures using lots of diagonal and zigzag lines to make the pictures look busy.
   NSAE 1.a; 1.c

Research in Art Education

Schools with rich in-school art programs tend to have a more positive atmosphere—children at these schools are "more likely than children in low-arts schools to have a good rapport with their teachers." This holds true across socio-economic lines ("Learning In and Through the Arts: Curriculum Implications" in *Champions of Change*, p. 41). This positive atmosphere is highly conducive to the organization and cooperation needed when using and sharing art materials.

Assessment

Use the following rubric to evaluate the artwork students make in the Creative Expression activity and to assess students' understanding of diagonal and zigzag lines.

Have students complete page 13 or 14 in their *Assessment* books.

	Art History and Culture	Aesthetic Perception	Creative Expression	Art Criticism
3 POINTS	The student recognizes that artists from different places use diagonal and zigzag lines to make exciting works of art.	The student accurately identifies and physically mimics diagonal and zigzag lines in his or her environment.	The student's drawing clearly illustrates diagonal and zigzag lines.	The student thoughtfully and honestly evaluates his or her own work using the four steps of art criticism.
2 POINTS	The student's recognition that artists from different places use diagonal and zigzag lines to make exciting works of art is weak or incomplete.	The student shows emerging awareness of diagonal and zigzag lines, but cannot consistently identify them.	The student's drawing shows some awareness of diagonal and zigzag lines.	The student attempts to evaluate his or her own work, but shows an incomplete understanding of evaluation criteria.
1 POINT	The student does not recognize that artists from different places use diagonal and zigzag lines to make exciting works of art.	The student cannot identify diagonal and zigzag lines.	The student's drawing shows no understanding of diagonal and zigzag lines.	The student makes no attempt to evaluate his or her own artwork.

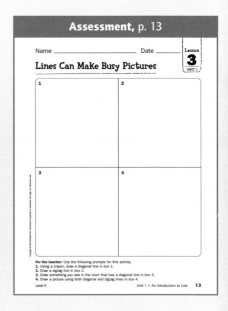

Assessment, p. 13

Name _____ Date _____

Lesson **3** UNIT 1

Lines Can Make Busy Pictures

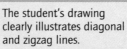

For the teacher: Use the following prompts for this activity.
1. Using a crayon, draw a diagonal line in box 1.
2. Draw a zigzag line in box 2.
3. Draw something you see in the room that has a diagonal line in box 3.
4. Draw a picture using both diagonal and zigzag lines in box 4.

Level K

Unit 1 • An Introduction to Line **13**

◀ **Katsushika Hokusai.** (Japanese). *Boy Juggling Shells.* Edo period.
••••••••••••••••••••
Album leaf, ink, and color on paper. 13 5/16 × 9 1/2 inches (33.81 × 24.13 cm.). The Metropolitan Museum of Art, New York, New York.

Study the pictures.

▶ What things look like they are moving?

▶ Where do you see curved lines?

Aesthetic Perception

Seeing Like an Artist Trace in the air one thing that you see in one of the pictures.

Study

▶ The young girl's skirt in *The Fly* and the shells in *Boy Juggling Shells* appear to be moving.

▶ In *The Fly* the tree branches, people's arms, and land are drawn with curved lines. In *Boy Juggling Shells* the balls and boy's fingers have curved lines.

■ For more examples of art from Asia, see the *Art Around the World Collection.*

Art Journal: Concept

Have students draw a picture in their Art Journals of what they think a curvy line looks like.

Aesthetic Perception

Seeing Line an Artist Have students look around and mentally select one thing they see. Tell the students to trace the object in the air and notice the kinds of lines they make as they trace the object.

Developing Visual Literacy Discuss how the people are playing in *The Fly* and *Boy Juggling Shells.* Ask students what they like to do when they play and if they would enjoy the activities they see in the fine art.

Art History and Culture

Katsushika Hokusai

Katsushika Hokusai (kät sū´shē kä hō´kū sī) (1760–1849) was a Japanese artist born in Edo (now called Tokyo). Hokusai made thousands of drawings, prints, and paintings during the Edo Period (1603–1867). He is best known for his many prints of Mount Fuji.

See pages 16–21 and 24–25 for more about subject matter and art history.

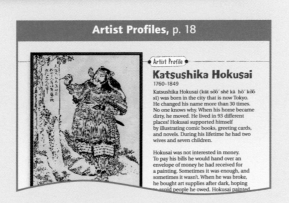

Artist Profiles, p. 18

● Artist Profile ●

Katsushika Hokusai
1760-1849

Katsushika Hokusai (kät sōō´ shē kä hō´kōō sī) was born in the city that is now Tokyo. He changed his name more than 30 times. No one knows why. When his home became dirty, he moved. He lived in 93 different places! Hokusai supported himself by illustrating comic books, greeting cards, and novels. During his lifetime he had two wives and seven children.

Hokusai was not interested in money. To pay his bills he would hand over an envelope of money he had received for a painting. Sometimes it was enough, and sometimes it wasn't. When he was broke, he bought art supplies after dark, hoping to avoid people he owed. Hokusai painted

Web Connection

Find out more about Katsushika Hokusai and other Japanese artists. Visit the Web site for the Tokyo National Museum at **www.tnm.jp/scripts/Index.en.idc.**

 each

Time: About 30 minutes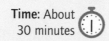

"Let's take turns role-playing some movements until I call "freeze." *"Túrnense para representar algunos movimientos hasta que yo diga 'paralizados'"*.

- Model role-playing a movement, such as swimming. Say "freeze" and stop your motion at that time.

- Ask students to describe the direction of your body, arms, and legs.

Practice

Materials: No materials are needed.

- Have the students demonstrate lines that show movement by following the steps on page 50.

- Have students run in place, throw a ball, hop, and jump.

- After calling "freeze," discuss the line direction of the students' bodies, arms, and legs.

 Creative Expression

Materials: oil pastels; 12" × 18" colored paper; tissue or paper towels

Alternate Materials: any drawing media

"What is the most fun for you to play on the playground?" *"¿Qué juego les es más divertido para jugar en el patio de recreo?"*

- Conduct a discussion that helps students think about playground activities.

- See the Technique Tip on page 216 for information on using oil pastels.

- Encourage students to be aware of how curved lines and diagonal lines show things moving.

- Distribute the materials and have the students follow the directions on page 51.

- See the Activity Tips on page 233 for visual examples of this lesson's activity.

NSAE 1.a; 1.c

 Art Journal: Brainstorming
Have students sketch a playground activity in their Art Journals.

50 UNIT 1 • Line

Using Curved Lines to Show Movement

Curved lines show things moving.

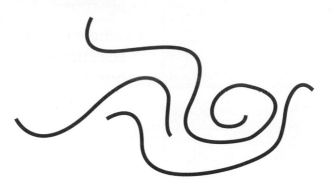

Practice

1. Listen as the teacher calls out a movement.

2. Keep making the movement until the teacher says "freeze."

50   Unit 1 • Lesson 4

Differentiated Instruction

Reteach
Have students pose in different positions, and then outline their bodies on mural paper. Help students identify the lines that express the movement they were making.

Special Needs
Reinforce the objective of this activity by having students act out some of the movements they use in their favorite playground game.

ELL Tips
Have each student go up to the picture and point to things that they see as "moving." Have the students role-play the movement. When students perform these movements, have them describe the movements in a sentence, such as "Heath is running" or "Jen is moving."

◄ **Tiffany Palmer.**
Age 5.

Think about how this student artist made things look like they are moving.

 **Creative Expression**

How would you show yourself moving in a picture?

1. Think of your favorite game to play on the playground.
2. Draw a picture of yourself playing.
3. Use curved and diagonal lines to show things moving.

 **Art Criticism**

Analyze Name the different kinds of lines you used to create your drawing.

Unit 1 • Lesson 4   **51**

Art Across the Curriculum

Use these simple ideas to reinforce art concepts across the curriculum.

★ **Poetry Writing** Have students draw pictures of two things that rhyme. Help students write the rhyming words below their pictures.

★ **Math** Count objects in the fine art, such as the number of shells in *Boy Juggling Shells* and the number of people or trees in *The Fly*.

★ **Science** Recognize animals and insects that live in groups or communities, noting how the people in *The Fly* live in a community.

★ **Social Studies** Use terms such as *over, under, near, far, left,* and *right* to describe locations of objects and people in the fine art.

★ **Technology** Use a paint program to draw a picture of yourself playing. Visit **SRAonline.com** to print detailed instructions for this activity.

 **Time:** About 5 minutes

Review and Assess

"What kind of lines make things look like they are moving? Like they are standing still?"
"¿Qué tipos de líneas hacen que las cosas parezcan estar en movimiento? ¿Cuáles las hacen parecer que están inmóviles?"

Think

Discuss the student art question. The clouds appear to be moving. The diagonal lines on the legs make it look like she is running.

■ Use the **Large Prints 1** *Interior with Egyptian Curtain* and **2** *Cat and Kittens* to provide more examples of lines that show things moving or standing still.

Informal Assessment

Art Journal: Critical Thinking
Have students answer the Analyze question in their Art Journals by drawing the different kinds of lines they used in the Creative Expression activity.

 **Art Criticism**

Have students ask themselves the following questions.

Describe ▶ What are you and your friends doing?

Analyze ▶ Name the different kinds of lines you used to create your drawing.

Interpret ▶ How did you show that you and your friends are happy and having fun?

Decide ▶ Give your drawing a name. Why did you choose this name?

NSAE 2.b; 5.a; 5.c

■ For standardized-format test practice using this lesson's art content, see pages 12–13 in **Reading and Writing Test Preparation.**

Curved Lines

Extra! For the Art Specialist

Time: About 30 minutes

Focus

Use **Transparency 4** and **Large Prints 1** *Interior with Egyptian Curtain* and **2** *Cat and Kittens* to identify lines that show motion. Place a clear transparency over the art transparency and trace these lines.

Teach

Have students create the oil pastel drawing from the Creative Expression activity on page 50. Then demonstrate how to use watercolor paints to create a watercolor resist effect on oil pastels.

Reflect

Have students use the four steps of art criticism to evaluate their work. Were they successful in using watercolor paints to create a watercolor resist effect? Did they use curved lines to show movement?

Alternate Activity

Materials:
- oil pastels
- 12" × 18" white drawing paper
- watercolor paints
- soft brushes
- water containers

After the students have made their playground drawings with oil pastels (see page 50), have them use watercolor paints in the resist method to add ground and sky to their paintings.

NSAE 1.a; 1.c

Research in Art Education

One case study showed that students who were "learning disabled and who were 'reluctant' readers" were better able to engage in reading when the creation and analysis of visual art was incorporated in their discussions of stories. This suggests that combining visual art with reading may help certain readers ("Reading *Is* Seeing: Using Visual Response to Improve the Literary Reading of Reluctant Readers" in *Critical Links*, p. 144). Remind students that *The Fly* helps tell the story of what William Blake has written in his poem.

Assessment

Use the following rubric to evaluate the artwork students make in the Creative Expression activity and to assess students' understanding of lines that show movement.

Have students complete page 15 or 16 in their *Assessment* books.

	Art History and Culture	Aesthetic Perception	Creative Expression	Art Criticism
3 POINTS	The student recognizes that *The Fly* illustrates the story in the poem.	The student accurately describes the lines that arms, legs, and bodies make as they move.	The student's drawing clearly illustrates lines that show movement.	The student thoughtfully and honestly evaluates his or her own work using the four steps of art criticism.
2 POINTS	The student's recognition of *The Fly* as a story illustration is weak or incomplete.	The student shows emerging awareness of lines that show movement, but cannot consistently identify them.	The student's drawing shows some awareness of lines that show movement.	The student attempts to evaluate his or her own work, but shows an incomplete understanding of evaluation criteria.
1 POINT	The student does not recognize that *The Fly* illustrates the story in the poem.	The student cannot identify lines that show movement.	The student's drawing shows no understanding of lines that show movement.	The student makes no attempt to evaluate his or her own artwork.

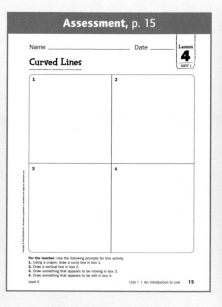

Assessment, p. 15

Name _____ Date _____

Lesson **4** UNIT 1

Curved Lines

1	2
3	4

For the teacher: Use the following prompts for this activity.
1. Using a crayon, draw a curvy line in box 1.
2. Draw a vertical line in box 2.
3. Draw something that appears to be moving in box 3.
4. Draw something that appears to be still in box 4.

Level K   Unit 1 • An Introduction to Line   15

 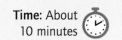

Focus

Time: About 10 minutes

Activate Prior Knowledge

"What games do you play at recess?" "Qué juegos juegan en el recreo?"

- Encourage students to talk about games they play. Have a few volunteers demonstrate a movement from one of those games.

Using Literature ⭐ Reading

Read *Feel the Wind* written and illustrated by Arthur Dorros. Have students find things that are moving and things that are standing still in the illustrations. Ask what kinds of lines were used to show movement.

Thematic Connection

Sports/Games: Discuss different games and sports that the students play. Identify the games/sports in the fine art in the lesson.

Introduce the Art

Look

"The first painting illustrates a poem."
"La pintura ilustra el poema".

- Explain that the artist, William Blake, used different lines to tell a story.

- Have students look at the fine art in their books and point to the lines that show things moving.

- Ask students what kinds of lines were used to show that something is moving.

Drawing Conclusions ⭐ Reading

- Ask students to study Blake's picture and tell what they think the poem might be about.

Adjectives and Adverbs ⭐ Language Arts

- List on a chart the adjectives and adverbs students use to describe the fine art.

🏺 Art History and Culture

Share information from the Art History and Culture sections with students. Encourage students to describe the story that is taking place in each painting. Answers will vary, but should include mention of the people in the picture as well as descriptions of where they are and what they are doing.
NSAE 4.a

💻 Web Connection

Visit **www.blakearchive.org/** to learn more about William Blake's art and poetry. [NOTE: This site is for teacher use only.]

Curved Lines

Look at the pictures. These artists used curved lines to show things moving.

◀ **William Blake.** (British). *The Fly* from *Songs of Innocence and of Experience.* c. 1825.
Color-printed relief etching. 6 3/16 in. × 5 9/16 inches (15.7 × 14.1 cm.). The Metropolitan Museum of Art, New York, New York.

🏺 Art History and Culture

Sometimes works of art tell a story. What story do you think is being told in each picture?

🏺 Art History and Culture

William Blake

The poems by William Blake (wil´ yəm blāk) (1757–1827) in *Songs of Innocence and Experience* express how the world is viewed throughout different stages of life, from our first stage of childhood innocence to the maturity that comes with experience. *Songs of Innocence* was published in 1789, followed by *Songs of Experience* in 1794.

See pages 16–21 and 24–25 for more about subject matter and art history.

Artist Profiles, p. 4

Artist Profile

William Blake
1757–1827

William Blake (wil´ yam blāk) was raised in a poor household. He received little formal schooling, but was able to enjoy works of classic literature. After witnessing his brother's death from tuberculosis, Blake remarked that he saw his brother's soul "ascend heavenward, clapping its hands for joy." His view of spirituality led him to meet London psychics, visionaries, and other writers and intellectuals.

Blake divided his time between composing and engraving illustrated poetry, and survived on his earnings as a contract engraver. Blake had very strong political opinions, and in 1803 he was charged with high treason. He was forced to move back

 **Lesson 4 Overview** Curved Lines

Lesson 4 introduces lines that show people and objects moving or standing still.

Objectives

 Art History and Culture

To recognize that William Blake's *The Fly* illustrates the story that is told in the poem

Creative Expression

To create a drawing that shows movement by using curvy lines

Aesthetic Perception

To observe and describe the lines that arms, legs, and bodies make as they move

Art Criticism

To evaluate one's own work using the four steps of art criticism

Vocabulary Reading

Review the following vocabulary word with students before beginning the lesson.

line línea—a mark made by moving a tool such as a pencil, pen, or crayon across a surface

See page 59B for additional vocabulary and Spanish vocabulary resources.

 Art Journal: Vocabulary

Have students add this word to the Vocabulary section of their Art Journals.

Lesson Materials
- oil pastels
- tissue or paper towels
- 12" × 18" colored paper

Alternate Materials:
- any drawing media

Program Resources
- *Reading and Writing Test Prep.*, pp. 12–13
- *Transparency 4*
- *Flash Cards 4* and *6*
- *Artist Profiles,* pp. 4, 18
- *Assessment,* pp. 15–16
- *Large Prints 1* Interior with Egyptian Curtain and *2* Cat and Kittens
- *Art Around the World Collection*

Concept Trace
Lines that Show Movement
Introduced: Level K, Unit 1, Lesson 4

Reinforced: Level 1, Unit 1, Lesson 4

Lesson 4 Arts Integration

Theatre

Complete Unit 1, Lesson 4 on pages 24–25 of the *Theatre Arts Connections* book.

Theatre Arts Connections, p. 24

Music

Upward and downward melodies can suggest movement in our bodies. Listen to *Tuileries* from *Pictures at an Exhibition,* by Modest Mussorgsky. What animals are suggested by these brisk, flitting, high melodies? Use your own "wings" to move to the music.

Movement & Dance

Work with everyday actions to create lines that are curved, round or arched. Exaggerate each action.

Examples: Explore the action of throwing an object (arched).
Explore the action of catching a beach ball (rounded).
Explore the action of diving into water (curved).

Smooth and Rough Lines

Lesson 5 introduces line texture. Line texture is the way an artist uses lines to show how things might feel if touched. A **rough line** is uneven. A **smooth line** is even. Visual line texture is covered in this lesson.

Objectives

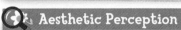

Art History and Culture
To understand that artists create works of art about different themes, pets being one of them

Creative Expression
To create a drawing using smooth and rough lines

Aesthetic Perception

To locate smooth and rough lines in their artwork and in their environment

Art Criticism
To evaluate one's own work using the four steps of art criticism

Vocabulary ⭐ Reading
Review the following vocabulary words with students before beginning the lesson.

smooth suave—having an even surface, free from irregularities

rough áspera—having an irregular surface that is uneven and bumpy

See page 59B for additional vocabulary and Spanish vocabulary resources.

Art Journal: Vocabulary
Have students add these words to the Vocabulary section of their Art Journals.

Lesson Materials
- 12" × 18" white paper
- jumbo crayons
- crayon remnants
- scrap paper

Alternate Materials:
- images of cats
- changeable markers
- oil pastels

Program Resources
- *Reading and Writing Test Prep.,* pp. 14–15
- *Transparency 5*
- *Flash Cards 1–6*
- *Artist Profiles,* pp. 8, 44
- *Animals Through History Time Line*
- *Assessment,* pp. 17–18
- *Large Prints 1* Interior with Egyptian Curtain and *2* Cat and Kittens
- *The National Museum of Women in the Arts Collection*

Concept Trace
Line Texture
Introduced: Level K, Unit 1, Lesson 5

Reinforced: Level K, Unit 5, Lesson 2

Lesson 5 Arts Integration

Theatre
Complete Unit 1, Lesson 5 on pages 26–27 of the *Theatre Arts Connections* book.

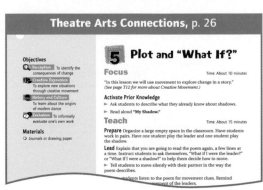

Music

Listen to *Persons with Long Ears,* from *The Carnival of the Animals,* by Camille Saint-Saen. Show the huge leaps with your hands. Even though the melody is to suggest the song of the donkey, what actions could we imagine the donkey making? Compare this piece to *The Swan* and find the smooth and rough lines.

Movement & Dance
Explore different ways to reach and stretch various parts of the body. Identify one particular stretch and teach it to the class. Take a full four counts to complete the stretch, keeping the flow of energy smooth and continuous. Repeat, still using four counts but this time break up the flow of energy with jagged staccato movements.

Focus

Time: About 10 minutes

Activate Prior Knowledge

"When you touch a cat, how does it feel? When you touch dirt, how does it feel?"

"Cuando tocan un gato, ¿cómo se siente? Cuando tocan tierra, ¿cómo se siente?"

- Encourage students to explore the concept of smooth and rough textures.

Using Literature ⭐ Reading

- Students can find smooth and rough lines in the animal illustrations in *Ginger* by Charlotte Voake or *The Cat in the Hat* by Dr. Seuss.

Thematic Connection ⭐ Science

- **Animals:** Have students name different types of animals and tell whether the animals would feel smooth or rough when touched.

Introduce the Art

Look

"If you could touch the cats, how would they feel?" *"Si pudieran tocar los gatos, ¿cómo se sentirían?"*

Comparing and Contrasting ⭐ Reading

- Have students compare and contrast the cats in the two paintings.

- What kinds of lines were used to paint the cat in *L'Hiver: Chat Sur un Coussin*?

- What kinds of lines are in Currier and Ives' *My Little White Kittens into Mischief*?

Cause and Effect ⭐ Reading

- Ask students why they think the artists used different kinds of lines to paint their cats.

- Explain that artists often use their family members and pets as the subject matter in their artwork.

🏺 Art History and Culture

Share information from the Art History and culture sections with students. Ask students to name other animals that artists might show in their works of art. Possible answers include: dog, horse, bird, fish, and other animals commonly kept as pets.

💻 **Web Connection**
Explore the *Just for Fun* section at www.metmuseum.org/explore/index.asp.

Smooth and Rough Lines

▲ **Theophile-Alexandre Steinlen.** (Swiss/French). *L'Hiver: Chat sur un Coussin (Winter: Cat on a Cushion).* 1909.

Color lithograph. 20 × 24 inches (50.8 × 60.96 cm.). The Metropolitan Museum of Art, New York, New York.

Look at the pictures of the cats. Do you see how the cats look different? Some lines look smooth and some look rough.

🏺 Art History and Culture

Steinlen often showed his own cats in his art.

🏺 Art History and Culture

Theophile-Alexandre Steinlen

Theophile-Alexandre Steinlen (thē´ ō fĭl ä lek sän´ dr stīn´ lən) (1859–1923) was often inspired by daily life and frequently used his family and cats in his posters. He may be best known for his study of cats, as they were featured in some of his most famous works. Artists throughout the centuries have been fascinated by the mysterious qualities of the cat. Throughout history, cats have been the symbol of various things, such as motherhood and a good harvest. Artists create images of cats that may convey fantasy, whimsy, sly humor, power, or pure happiness.

See pages 16–21 and 24–25 for more about subject matter and art history.

Artist Profiles, p. 44

▸ Artist Profile ◂
Théophile-Alexandre Steinlen
1859-1923

Théophile-Alexandre Steinlen (thē´ ō fĭl ä lek sän´ dr stīn´ lan) was born in Lausanne, Switzerland. In 1882 he moved to Paris and soon became part of a group of artists in Montmartre. Steinlen created politically charged drawings for socialist newspapers as well as art for posters and advertisements. He is best known for his involvement in the art nouveau movement.

◂ **Pieter Dupont.** (Netherlands). *Théophile-Alexandre Steinlen.* 1901.

▲ **Currier and Ives.**
(American). *My
Little White Kittens
into Mischief.* 1865.
....
Hand-colored lithograph.
8¼ × 12½ inches
(20.96 × 31.75 cm.). The
Metropolitan Museum of
Art, New York, New York.

Study both works of art.

▶ Where do you see smooth lines?

▶ Where do you see rough lines?

Aesthetic Perception

Design Awareness Look around the room. Find
something that looks smooth.

Art History and Culture

Currier and Ives

The firm of Currier and Ives was in operation as a lithography shop
from 1834–1907. Numerous employees, including artists, colorists,
lithographers, and stone grinders, worked together to produce
more than a million prints of more than 7500 different titles. The
prints were popular in part because of their inexpensive price, but
also because of the variety of subject matter. Prints were available
in nearly any category the public might desire, including sports,
humor, hunting, religion, politics and disaster scenes.

See pages 16–21 and 24–25
for more about subject
matter and art history.

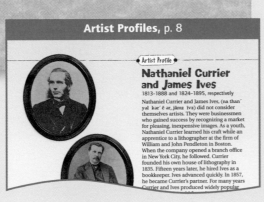

Artist Profiles, p. 8

◀ Artist Profile ▶

**Nathaniel Currier
and James Ives**
1813–1888 and 1824–1895, respectively
Nathaniel Currier and James Ives, (na than´
yal kar´ē ər, jāmz īvz) did not consider
themselves artists. They were businessmen
who gained success by recognizing a market
for pleasing, inexpensive images. As a youth,
Nathaniel Currier learned his craft while an
apprentice to a lithographer at the firm of
William and John Pendleton in Boston.
When the company opened a branch office
in New York City, he followed. Currier
founded his own house of lithography in
1835. Fifteen years later, he hired Ives as a
bookkeeper. Ives advanced quickly. In 1857,
he became Currier's partner. For many years
Currier and Ives produced widely popular

Study

▶ *L'Hiver: Chat Sur un Coussin* has smooth
lines outlining the body of the cat and
around the cat's eyes. The top edge of the
table in *My Little White Kittens into
Mischief* looks smooth.

▶ *L'Hiver: Chat Sur un Coussin* has rough
lines on the red cushion. The stripes on
the cat's body and hair in its ears look
rough. The side edge of the table in *My
Little White Kittens into Mischief* looks
rough. The hair on the cats is also rough,
especially on their backs and tails.

■ For more examples of genre art, see *The
National Museum of Women in the Arts
Collection.*

Art Journal: Concept
Have students draw a picture in
their Art Journals of what they think
smooth and rough lines look like.

Aesthetic Perception

Design Awareness Have students look around
the room to find objects that look smooth.
Ask them to explain how they know the
object would feel smooth. How are the
smooth objects alike?
NSAE 3.a; 3.b
Developing Visual Literacy
Predicting ⭐ Reading
Think about the cats and their personalities
in each painting. Imagine what the cats are
thinking. What do you think the cats are
going to do next?

 Web Connection
Visit **www.currierandives.com/** to learn more about
Currier and Ives.

 **Teach**

"Let's practice making smooth and rough lines." *"Practiquemos haciendo líneas suaves y ásperas"*.

▪ Use a jumbo crayon to demonstrate drawing a smooth line on scrap paper. Then demonstrate drawing a rough line by using the side of the tip or the bottom of the crayon, or by using a small crayon remnant and dragging it on its side across the paper.

Practice

Materials: Jumbo crayons, crayon remnants, and scrap paper

Alternate Materials: Images of cats, changeable markers, oil pastels

▪ Have the students create smooth and rough lines by following the steps on page 54.

Creative Expression

Materials: 12" × 18" white paper, jumbo crayons

Alternate Materials: images of cats, dogs, and other pets

"Imagine you own a pet. What would it look like? Would it be rough, smooth, or both?" *"Imagínense que tienen un gato. ¿Cómo sería? ¿Sería áspero, suave o ambos?"*

▪ See the Technique Tips on page 214 for tips on drawing with crayons.

▪ Distribute the materials and have the students follow the directions on page 55.

▪ See the Activity Tips on page 234 for visual examples of this lesson's activity.

NSAE 1.a; 1.c

 Art Journal: Brainstorming

Have students sketch some images of cats in their Art Journals. Have them choose the one they like best to draw again in the Creative Expression activity.

Using Smooth and Rough Lines

Lines can make things look **smooth.**

Lines can look **rough.**

Practice

1. Draw a smooth line on your paper.
2. Draw a rough line on your paper.

Differentiated Instruction

Reteach

Have students draw lines on a smooth surface and on a rough surface using a crayon. Ask students which line looks smooth and which line looks rough.

Special Needs

If students have difficulty holding drawing media, use a styrofoam ball that can fit in the palm of the hand as a holder. Pencils (for making thin lines) and big crayons (for making thick lines) can be alternately stuck in the ball.

ELL Tips

Show students examples of smooth and rough fabrics. Let students feel each fabric and say "smooth" or "rough" as they touch each one. Show students how some things outside the classroom appear to be smooth and other things appear to be rough.

▲ **Hillary Lawrence.**
Age 5.

Think about where you see smooth and rough lines in this picture.

Creative Expression

What kind of pet do you like?

1. Think about different types of pets.
2. Draw a pet using smooth and rough lines.

Art Criticism

Analyze Where are the smooth lines? Where are the rough lines?

❖ Art Across the Curriculum ❖

Use these simple ideas to reinforce art concepts across the curriculum.

★ **Persuasive Writing** Ask students how they would convince their parents to let them have a pet. Have students draw a picture to show how they would take care of this pet.

★ **Math** Use time to measure and compare the length of activities. Have students study the two cats in the fine art in this lesson. Ask which work of art they think took longer to complete and why.

★ **Science** Identify objects from outside that feel rough and smooth. Have students draw one rough and one smooth object that they found outside.

★ **Social Studies** Learn more about responsibility. Discuss what is involved in taking care of a cat or other pet.

★ **Technology** Draw a picture of a pet in a paint program. Experiment with different tools to create rough and smooth lines. Visit **SRAonline.com** to print detailed instructions for this activity.

 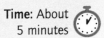 **R**eflect Time: About 5 minutes ⏱

Review and Assess

"How is a smooth line different from a **rough** line?" "¿En qué se diferencia una línea suave de una áspera?"

Think

Discuss the student art question. The artist used smooth lines for the outline of the rabbit and rough lines to create fur.

■ Use *Large Prints 1 Interior with Egyptian Curtain* and *2 Cat and Kittens* to compare the rough and smooth lines in them to those found in the artwork for this lesson.

Informal Assessment

Art Journal: Critical Thinking
Have students answer the Analyze question by pointing to their art and showing which lines are smooth and which lines are rough. Ask students to sketch two cat tails in their Art Journals— one that is rough and one that is smooth.

Art Criticism

Have students ask themselves the following questions.

Describe ▶ What did you draw in your picture?

Analyze ▶ Where are the smooth lines? Where are the rough lines?

Interpret ▶ Give your picture a name. Tell why you chose that name.

Decide ▶ Do you think that using smooth and rough lines makes your drawing more interesting? Why?

NSAE 2.b; 5.a; 5.c

■ For standardized-format test practice using this lesson's art content, see pages 14–15 in *Reading and Writing Test Preparation.*

Smooth and Rough Lines

Extra! For the Art Specialist

Time: About 30 minutes

Focus

Use *Transparency 5* and *Large Prints 1 Interior with Egyptian Curtain* and *2 Cat and Kittens* to demonstrate how artists use different lines to show how things feel. Ask students to tell which painting they like best and why, using appropriate vocabulary.

Teach

The students will create a line design using vertical, horizontal, diagonal, zigzag, curved, rough, and smooth lines.

Reflect

Have students use the four steps of art criticism to evaluate their work. Did they effectively create smooth and rough lines using the rubbing plates? Did they make lines of different lengths and widths?

Alternate Activity

Materials:
- crayons and pieces of unwrapped crayons
- texture rubbing plates
- scrap paper
- 12" × 18" white paper

1. Have the students feel the surface of the rubbing plates to feel how bumpy they are.

2. To see how the texture plates affect the lines, have students draw lines on scrap paper held on top of a rubbing plate.

3. Call out a line type such as vertical or horizontal. The students should draw this type of line somewhere on their papers as either a rough or smooth line. Lines can be of varying lengths and widths. (Make wide lines with the sides of broken crayons.)

NSAE 1.a; 1.c

Research in Art Education

Research has shown that assessing knowledge through a combination of drawing and writing can lead to higher scores for content knowledge. This applied to native English speakers and limited English speakers alike. This suggests "that drawing may be one way to reveal what students know but cannot put into words" ("The Arts, Language, and Knowing: An Experimental Study of the Potential of the Visual Arts for Assessing Academic Learning by Language Minority Students" in *Critical Links*, p. 141). In *Art Connections* lessons, students will answer questions in their Art Journals by drawing pictures. Encourage students to tell you about what they have drawn.

Assessment

Use the following rubric to evaluate the artwork students make in the Creative Expression activity and to assess students' understanding of smooth and rough lines.

Have students complete page 17 or 18 in their *Assessment* books.

	Art History and Culture	Aesthetic Perception	Creative Expression	Art Criticism
3 POINTS	The student recognizes that artists create works of art about different themes.	The student accurately locates smooth and rough lines in his or her artwork and the environment.	The student's drawing clearly illustrates smooth and rough lines.	The student thoughtfully and honestly evaluates his or her own work using the four steps of art criticism.
2 POINTS	The student's recognition that artists create works of art about different themes is weak or incomplete.	The student shows emerging awareness of smooth and rough lines, but cannot consistently identify them.	The student's drawing shows some awareness of smooth and rough lines.	The student attempts to evaluate his or her own work, but shows an incomplete understanding of evaluation criteria.
1 POINT	The student does not recognize that artists create works of art about different themes.	The student cannot identify smooth and rough lines.	The student's drawing shows no understanding of smooth and rough lines.	The student makes no attempt to evaluate his or her own artwork.

Assessment, p. 17

Name _____ Date _____

Lesson 5 UNIT 1

Smooth and Rough Lines

1	2
3	4

For the teacher: Use the following prompts for this activity.
1. Using a crayon or pencil, draw a smooth line in box 1.
2. Draw a rough line in box 2.
3. Draw a picture of something that looks smooth in box 3.
4. Draw a picture of something that looks rough in box 4.

Level K   Unit 1 • An Introduction to Line   17

Lesson 6 Broken Lines

Overview

Lesson 6 introduces broken lines. **Broken lines** are lines with spaces between them.

Objectives

 Art History and Culture

To recognize mosaics as a complex art form

 Aesthetic Perception

To locate broken lines in their environment

Creative Expression

To create a paper mosaic collage using broken lines

Art Criticism

To evaluate one's own work using the four steps of art criticism

Vocabulary Reading

Review the following vocabulary words with students before beginning the lesson.

solid line línea continua—a continuous line

broken line línea entrecortada—a line that is separated into smaller pieces with spaces between each piece

See page 59B for additional vocabulary and Spanish vocabulary resources.

Art Journal: Vocabulary

Have students add these words to the Vocabulary section of their Art Journals.

Lesson Materials

- construction paper, precut into 4" × $\frac{1}{2}$" strips
- 9" × 12" paper for background (contrasting color from strips)
- glue or glue sticks
- pencils
- paper clips

Alternate Materials:
- any drawing media

Program Resources

- *Reading and Writing Test Prep.*, pp. 16–17
- *Transparency 6*
- *Flash Cards 1–6*
- *Artist Profiles*, pp. 6, 48
- *Animals Through History Time Line*
- *Assessment*, pp. 19–20
- *Large Prints 1* Interior with Egyptian Curtain and *2 Cat and Kittens*
- *The National Museum of Women in the Arts Collection*

Concept Trace
Broken Lines
Introduced: Level K, Unit 1, Lesson 6

Reinforced: Level 1, Unit 1, Lesson 1

Lesson 6 Arts Integration

Theatre

Complete Unit 1, Lesson 6 on pages 28–33 of the *Theatre Arts Connections* book.

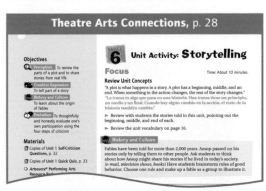

Music

 Sing the first phrase of *Twinkle Twinkle Little Star* without taking a breath. Were you completely smooth? Without changing the speed, sing it again with each word so short and cut off that there are spaces between them. This broken style is used in *Shake My Sillies Out*. Does it suggest a mood?

Movement & Dance

Take masking tape and place small dots on the floor. Place twice as many dots as there are students. Each student finds a dot to stand on and explores moving from one dot to another, without stepping in the space between. Explore stretching, reaching, and jumping movements. Call out when it is time for each action so all students are moving with the same idea.

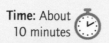

Focus

Activate Prior Knowledge

"I'm going to draw a line on the board called a broken line. Where have you seen a line like this?" "Voy a trazar una línea en el pizarrón llamada línea entrecortada. ¿Dónde han visto una línea como ésta?"

- Draw a broken line on the board.

- Lead students to think about places where a broken line is used. Board games, the dividing line on a street.

Using Literature Reading

- Read *One Windy Wednesday* by Phyllis Root, illustrated by Helen Craig. Have students find the broken lines in the illustrations.

Thematic Connection
Making Inferences Science

- **Weather/Seasons:** Name the four seasons and identify characteristics of each season. Discuss why Marc Chagall might have chosen the name *The Four Seasons* for his sculpture.

Introduce the Art

Look

"One kind of art that has broken lines is a mosaic." "Un tipo de arte que tiene líneas entrecortadas es un mosaico".

- Explain that a broken line looks like someone has taken a pair of scissors and cut a line into small pieces.

- Ask students to look at the pictures of mosaics in their books and find a broken line that outlines the shape of something.

- Discuss mosaics as an art form. Ask students to tell where they have seen a mosaic before.

Art History and Culture

Share information from the Art History and Culture sections with students. Mosaics are made of small pieces of paper, stone, tile, or glass and are usually set in plaster or concrete.

Web Connection

Visit **www.metmuseum.org/explore/Tiffany/ menu.html** for more information about Louis Comfort Tiffany.

Broken Lines

Look at both works of art. This type of artwork is called a **mosaic.** Artists use small pieces of glass or stone to make broken lines in mosaics.

◄ **Louis Comfort Tiffany.** (American). *Garden Landscape and Fountain.* c. 1905–1915.

Favrile-glass mosaic, cement. Landscape: 8 feet 7½ inches × 9 feet 6 inches (2.63 × 2.90 meters). Fountain and base: 24 × 77 × 61¾ inches (60.96 × 195.58 × 156.85 cm.).

Art History and Culture

Artists have been making mosaics for thousands of years. They are usually made on floors or walls.

Art History and Culture

Louis Comfort Tiffany

Louis Comfort Tiffany (loo´ əs kəm´ fərt ti´ fə nē) (1848–1933) experimented with many forms of art including painting, interior design, and decorative arts. He was fascinated with colored glass and became well known for creating lamps. Tiffany extended his work with glass by creating mosaics like *Garden Landscape and Fountain.* Rather than use only squares of colored glass, Tiffany cut the glass into shapes that conformed to the design he was creating.

See pages 16–21 and 24–25 for more about subject matter and art history.

Artist Profiles, p. 48

Artist Profile

Louis C. Tiffany
1848–1933

Louis Comfort Tiffany (loo´ əs kom´ fərt ti´ fə nē) was born in New York City. Charles Lewis, his father, was the founder of a notable silver and jewelry company. Tiffany did not become involved in this company but instead studied with the painter George Innes. After studying glassmaking, Tiffany worked as an interior designer for Louis C. Tiffany and Associated Artists for several years, and then went on to found Tiffany Furnaces in 1892, followed by Tiffany Studios in 1902. He experimented with new kinds of glass, designing lamps and stained-glass windows, as well as furniture, ceramics, and jewelry. In 1919 he set up a foundation to support artists.

▲ **Marc Chagall.** (Russian).
The Four Seasons. 1974.
··
Ceramic mosaic. 70 × 10 × 14 feet
(21.34 × 3.05 × 4.27 meters). First
National Bank Plaza, Chicago, Illinois.

Study both works of art.

▶ Find a broken line.

▶ Trace it with your finger.

Aesthetic Perception

Seeing Like an Artist Make broken lines with
your finger in the air.

Study

▶ The swans and wall around the pond in
Garden Landscape and Fountain are
outlined by broken lines.

▶ Observe as students point out broken lines
in *The Four Seasons,* such as outlines of
the flower.

■ For more examples of landscapes, see *The
National Museum of Women in the Arts
Collection.*

Art Journal: Concept

Have students draw a picture in
their Art Journals of what they think a
broken line looks like.

Aesthetic Perception

Seeing Like an Artist Ask students to use
their fingers to draw broken lines in the air.

Developing Visual Literacy Ask students to
describe what they see in *The Four Seasons*
and give examples of similar objects they
have seen, such as birds, musical
instruments, people, the sun, and buildings.
Ask students why they think Chagall used
those images in his mosaic.
NSAE 4.a

Art History and Culture

Marc Chagall

Marc Chagall (märk shə gäl´) (1887–1985) was born in Vitsyebsk, a
small town in Russia. He studied art in Saint Petersburg and then in
Paris. After the Russian Revolution he returned to his hometown to
become the director of the Art Academy of Vitsyebsk. In 1919
Chagall became art director of the Moscow Jewish State Theater,
where he painted murals in the lobby and created sets for the
shows. In 1923 he returned to France where he lived most of the
remainder of his life. Chagall was influenced by French cubism and
Russian expressionism.

See pages 16–21 and 24–25
for more about subject
matter and art history.

Artist Profiles, p. 6

◆ Artist Profile ◆
Marc Chagall
1887–1985
Marc Chagall (mark sha gäl´) was born in
a small town in Russia, Vitebsk, which is
now part of Belarus. He studied art in Saint
Petersburg and then in Paris, France. After
the Russian revolution he served as the
director of the art academy in his
hometown. From 1919 to 1922, Chagall was
the art director of the Moscow Jewish State
Theater. He painted murals in the theater
lobby and created sets for the shows. In
1923, he moved to France. He spent most
of the rest of his life there, except for a brief
period of residence in the United States
from 1941 to 1948.

Web Connection
Discover other art on display in Chicago at
the Art Institute of Chicago Museum at
www.artic.edu/aic/collections/index.html.

Teach

Time: About 30 minutes

"Let's make a solid line and a broken line with paper clips." "Hagamos una línea continua y una línea entrecortada con sujetapapeles".

- Draw a solid line and a broken line on the board.

Practice

Materials: paper clips

- Have the students demonstrate solid and broken lines by following the steps on page 58.

Creative Expression

Materials: construction paper, precut into 4" × $\frac{1}{2}$" strips; 9" × 12" paper for background (contrasting color from strips); glue or glue sticks; pencils

Alternate Materials: any drawing media

"Let's use broken lines to create an animal mosaic." "Usemos líneas entrecortadas para crear un mosaico con el diseño de un animal".

- Lead a discussion about different kinds of animals.

- Display the **Animals Through History Time Line.**

- See the Technique Tips on pages 221–222 for information on using scissors and glue.

- See the Activity Tips on page 234 for visual examples of this lesson's activity.

- Show students how to cut the paper strips into squares.

- Model placing one dot of glue on each square and positioning the colored-paper "tile" on the paper to form the animal outline, being sure to leave a small space between squares.

- Distribute the materials and have the students follow the directions on page 59.

NSAE 1.a; 1.c

Art Journal: Brainstorming

Have students decide on a favorite animal and draw it in their Art Journals.

Using Broken Lines

Lines with spaces between them are **broken lines.** A mosaic has broken lines. See the spaces between the tiles.

Practice

1. Make a solid line with paper clips.
2. Make a broken line with paper clips.

Differentiated Instruction

Reteach
Making Connections

⭐ Reading

Have several students make a solid line by joining hands with their arms outstretched. Then have them release hands and rest their arms at their sides to create a broken line. Create similar lines with classroom materials such as erasers.

Special Needs

Some students may need more direction in completing this project. Some may experience more success if allowed to lightly draw their animal on the paper prior to gluing shapes down.

ELL Tips

Bring in a cracked or crazed piece of ceramic. Have each student feel a broken line. Draw a simple outline of a dog or cat using broken lines.

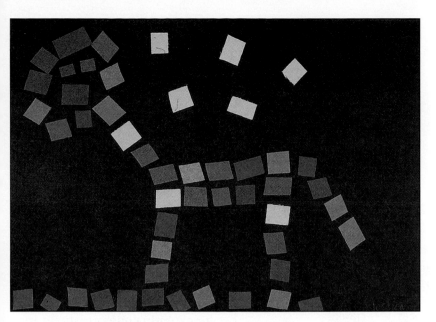

▲ **Jessica M. Hopkins.**
Age 5.

Think about how this student artist used broken lines to make her picture.

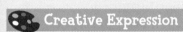 **Creative Expression**

How would you make a picture with broken lines?

1. Cut paper strips into small squares.
2. Glue them to the paper to form an outline of an animal.

 **Art Criticism**

Decide Do you like the colors you used?

Art Across the Curriculum

Use these simple ideas to reinforce art concepts across the curriculum.

★ **Expository Writing** Have students draw several pictures to show the sequential steps for cleaning up after creating a work of art.

★ **Math** Identify the geometric shapes found in the fine art examples in this lesson.

★ **Science** Distinguish between items that are living and non-living. Identify living things in the fine art, such as animals and plants.

★ **Social Studies** Understand time sequence vocabulary, such as *before*, *after*, and *long ago*. Recognize that a lot of art (like *Large Print 2 Cat and Kittens*) was created long ago.

★ **Technology** Use the square tool in a paint program to create broken lines. Visit **SRAonline.com** to print detailed instructions for this activity.

 **R**eflect 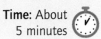 Time: About 5 minutes

Review and Assess

"What is a broken line?" "¿Qué es una línea entrecortada?"

Think

Discuss the student art question. Broken lines appear in the outline of the horse's head, its neck, back, tail, and legs, and on the ground.

■ Compare and contrast the lines in *Large Prints 1 Interior with Egyptian Curtain* and *2 Cat and Kittens* to the broken lines in the mosaic.

Informal Assessment

Art Journal: Critical Thinking
Write *yes* and *no* on the board. Have students answer the Decide question by writing *yes* or *no* in their Art Journals.

 **Art Criticism**

Have students ask themselves the following questions.

Describe ► What animal did you create? What is the animal doing?

Analyze ► Does the broken line outline the shape of the animal?

Interpret ► Does the animal look happy? Sad? Brave? Scared?

Decide ► Do you like the colors you used? Why did you choose those colors?

NSAE 2.b; 5.a; 5.c

■ For standardized-format test practice using this lesson's art content, see pages 16–17 in *Reading and Writing Test Preparation*.

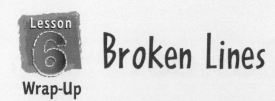

Lesson 6 Wrap-Up

Broken Lines

Extra! For the Art Specialist

Time: About 30 minutes

Focus

Display **Transparency 6** and **Large Prints 1** *Interior with Egyptian Curtain* and **2** *Cat and Kittens*. Ask students to look for broken lines in the art.

Teach

Have students make broken lines with beans to create an animal mosaic.

Reflect

Have students use the four steps of art criticism to evaluate their work. Did they effectively create a mosaic by using beans to make broken lines?

Alternate Activity

Materials:

- large dried beans such as lima or kidney beans (small items like dried peas are too difficult to hold)
- tacky glue
- 10″ squares of colored posterboard or tagboard
- crayons

1. Brainstorm types of animals.

2. Have students use crayons to draw a large animal on the posterboard so that it touches the edges of the board.

3. Then have students put one dot of glue on a bean and place it on the line. Students should continue until the broken line of beans is complete around the outline of the animal.

NSAE 1.a; 1.c

Research in Art Education

"The elementary classroom offers an environment that can foster creativity, independence, self-awareness, self-expression, and an understanding of the visual world. Education through art can provide opportunities for exploring one's creativity, for communicating ideas, and enabling students to express themselves through the use of materials, processes, and tools" (Andra Nyman, "Cultural Content, Identity, and Program Development: Approaches to Art Education for Elementary Educators," in *Contemporary Issues in Art Education,* edited by Y. Gaudelius and P. Speirs, 61–69. New Jersey: Prentice Hall, 2002).

Assessment

Use the following rubric to evaluate the artwork students make in the Creative Expression activity and to assess students' understanding of broken lines.

Have students complete page 19 or 20 in their **Assessment** books.

	Art History and Culture	Aesthetic Perception	Creative Expression	Art Criticism
3 POINTS	The student recognizes mosaics as a complex art form.	The student accurately locates broken lines in the environment.	The student's mosaic clearly illustrates broken lines.	The student thoughtfully and honestly evaluates his or her own work using the four steps of art criticism.
2 POINTS	The student's recognition of mosaics as a complex art form is weak or incomplete.	The student shows emerging awareness of broken lines, but cannot consistently identify them.	The student's mosaic shows some awareness of broken lines.	The student attempts to evaluate his or her own work, but shows an incomplete understanding of evaluation criteria.
1 POINT	The student does not recognize mosaics as a complex art form.	The student cannot identify broken lines.	The student's mosaic shows no understanding of broken lines.	The student makes no attempt to evaluate his or her own artwork.

Assessment, p. 19

Name _____ Date _____

Lesson **6** UNIT 1

Broken Lines

For the teacher: Use the following prompts for this activity.
1. Using a crayon or pencil, draw a solid line in box 1.
2. Draw a broken line in box 2.

Level K   Unit 1 • An Introduction to Line   **19**

broken line—a line that is separated into smaller pieces with spaces between each piece **línea entrecortada**—una línea que es separada en pequeños fragmentos con espacios entre cada uno

diagonal line—a slanted line; a line that moves at an angle **línea diagonal**—una línea oblícua; un línea que se mueve en un ángulo

horizontal line—a straight line that moves side to side **línea horizontal**—una línea recta que se mueve de lado a lado

line—a mark made by moving a tool such as a pencil, pen, or crayon across a surface **línea**—una marca hecha moviendo una herramienta como un lápiz, bolígrafo o creyon a través de una superficie

rough—having an irregular surface that is uneven and bumpy **áspera**—tener una superficie irregular que es desigual y con baches

smooth—having an even surface, free from irregularities **suave**—tener una superficie regular, libre de irregularidades

solid line—a continuous line **línea continua**—una línea continua

thick line—a line that is wide **línea gruesa**—una línea que es ancha

thin line—a line that is narrow **línea fina**—una línea que es estrecha

vertical line—a straight line that moves up and down **línea vertical**—una línea recta que se mueve hacia arriba y abajo

zigzag line—diagonal lines that connect **línea en zigzag**—líneas diagonales que se conectan

Vocabulary Practice

T Display *Transparency 37* to review unit vocabulary words.

Answering Questions ⭐ Vocabulary
Ask students questions using the vocabulary words. Encourage students to use the vocabulary words in their answers. For example: Do you see a horizontal line on the board? Yes, the tray at the bottom of the board is a horizontal line.

Definitions: Demonstrate Meanings ⭐ Vocabulary
Display *Large Print 1* *Interior with Egyptian Curtain*. Have volunteers select a vocabulary word, such as *thick line*, and explain how it is shown in the artwork.

Visualization Strategies ⭐ Vocabulary
Allow students to identify different kinds of lines throughout the classroom. Have students label these lines with sentence strips displaying the vocabulary terms.

Art Criticism

Critical Thinking Art Criticism is an organized system for looking at and talking about art. You can criticize art without being an expert. The purpose of art criticism is to get the viewer involved in a perception process that delays judgment until all aspects of the artwork have been studied.

- See pages 28–29 for more about art criticism.

Describe

▶ Ask students to describe what they see in this painting. Possible answers include: a dock, sailboats, sails, masts, water, colorful flags, a mountain in the distance, and sky with white clouds.

Analyze

▶ Discuss with students the kinds of lines used in Manguin's painting. Possible answers include: thick lines—on the dock, the post on the dock, and the roof of the closest boat; thin lines—on the flag poles and the yellow masts; straight lines—on the flag poles, the masts, and the posts holding up the roof of the closest boat; diagonal lines—on the dock, the yellow flagpole on the closest boat, the red, white, and blue flags, the small triangular flags at the top of the sails, and the sails; curved lines—on the bows of the boats, the flag on the left and the flag near the center, the sails, and the mountain; rough lines—on the flagpoles, and on the rope that holds the flags in front of the violet sail.

Wrapping Up Unit 1

Introduction to Line

▲ **Henri-Charles Manguin.** (French).
Port Saint Tropez, le 14 Juillet. 1905.
Oil on canvas. 24$\frac{1}{2}$ × 19$\frac{3}{4}$ inches (62.23 × 50.17 cm).
The Museum of Fine Arts, Houston, Houston, Texas.

60 Unit 1

Art History and Culture

Henri-Charles Manguin

Henri-Charles Manguin (än rē′ shärl män gan′) (1874–1949) was a French painter who was best known for his landscapes. Manguin was considered a *fauve*, which is French for "wild beast." Fauvists painted with "wild" colors, contrary to the style that was popular in the early 1900s.

See pages 16–21 and 24–25 for more about subject matter and art history.

Artist Profiles, p. 25

> **Artist Profile**
>
> **Henri-Charles Manguin**
> 1874–1949
>
> Henri-Charles Manguin (än rē′ shärl män gan′) was born in Paris and grew up in a wealthy family. His father died when Manguin was six and his mother lavished supportive attention on him. At 15 he decided to quit his formal education and devote all of his time to painting. A jovial member of the fauvist painters, Manguin was respected by his peers and earned a reputation as a painter of luxuriant and joyful compositions. His wife, Jeanne, encouraged him to paint and was the subject of many of his works.

 **Art Criticism** Critical Thinking

Describe
▶ Tell what you see in this painting.

Analyze
▶ What kinds of lines do you see in the painting?

Interpret
▶ Do the lines in this painting make it look busy or calm?

Decide
▶ Would you like to see this painting hanging in your school? Why or why not?

Interpret

▶ Ask students to explain whether the lines in the painting make it look busy or calm. Possible answer: The diagonal and curved lines make it look busy.

▶ Ask students if this looks like a place they would want to be. Answers will vary.

▶ Discuss with students: If you could go into this painting, what would you hear and smell? Answers will vary. Some might say they would hear music, the waves lapping, or the flags flapping in the wind. They might feel the spray of water or the push of the wind. One might smell salt water or fish on the dock.

▶ Ask students why they think so many flags are flying in the painting. Possible answers: It is a holiday, festival, or party.

Decide

▶ Ask students if they would like to see this painting hanging in their school, and explain why or why not. Answers will vary.

NSAE 5.a; 5.c

Art Journal: Writing
Have students draw a picture in their Art Journals to answer the Analyze Aesthetic Perception question. Discuss the other questions aloud.

 ## Aesthetic Perception

Critical Thinking Have students study pictures of various kinds of boats. How do these boats compare with *Port Saint Tropez, le 14 Juillet*?

Describe ▶ Point to and name the kinds of lines you see on the boats.

Analyze ▶ Are any of these lines the same as the lines you saw in *Port Saint Tropez, le 14 Juillet*?

Interpret ▶ What do you think it would be like to ride in one of the boats in *Port Saint Tropez, le 14 Juillet*?

Decide ▶ Would you like to ride on one of the boats?
▶ Why or why not?

"Artists use different kinds of lines in their works of art." "Los artistas usan diferentes tipos de líneas en sus obras de arte".

T Review unit vocabulary with students using *Transparency 37*.

► Review the different line qualities, directions, and characteristics in the student lessons.

► Have students name the types of lines they would use to draw various objects in their classroom.

Art Journal: Writing

Read the questions on page 62 to students. Have students write their answers in their Art Journals or on a separate sheet of paper. Answers: 1. B, 2. A, 3. B.

T For further assessment, have students complete the unit test on *Transparency 43*.

LET'S VISIT A MUSEUM
The Museum of Fine Arts, Houston

LEARN ABOUT MUSEUMS

► The art collection at The Museum of Fine Arts in Houston, Texas, contains over 27,000 works of art. Renaissance, baroque, impressionist, post-impressionist, and African gold art highlight the museum's outstanding collection.

► For information about visiting a museum, see the Museum Guide from *The National Museum of Women in the Arts Collection.*

"Every child is an artist. The problem is how to remain an artist once you grow up."
—Pablo Picasso

Wrapping Up Unit 1

Introduction to Line, continued

Show What You Know

Answer these questions on a sheet of paper.

❶ Which of these lines is thick?

A. _____

B. ▬▬▬▬▬▬

❷ Which of these lines looks calm?

A.　　　　　　B.

❸ Which of these lines is broken?

A. ▬▬▬▬▬▬

B. ▬ ▬ ▬ ▬ ▬ ▬ ▬

62　Unit 1

Unit Assessment Options

Aesthetic Perception

Practice

Encourage students to identify the various types of lines they see around them.

Creative Expression

Student Portfolio

Have students review all the artwork they have created during this unit and select the pieces they wish to put into their portfolios. Have students share their portfolios with classmates and comment constructively about the art.　NSAE 5.a; 5.c

Art Criticism

Activity

Have students select their favorite work of art from the unit. Guide students through study of their selected work using the four steps of art criticism. (See pages 28–29 for more about Art Criticism.)

LET'S VISIT A MUSEUM
The Museum of Fine Arts, Houston

This museum is in Houston, Texas. It is the largest art museum in the Southwest.

Lines in Dance

Bella Lewitzky creates dances. Her dancers make curved, straight, and slanted lines with their bodies.

What to Do Make lines with your body.

1. Look at the painting. Name the kinds of lines you see.

2. Move your body to show each kind of line.

▲ **Vincent van Gogh.** (Dutch)
The Starry Night. 1889.
....
Oil on canvas. $28\frac{3}{4} \times 36\frac{1}{4}$ inches (73.03 × 92.71 cm.).
Museum of Modern Art. New York, New York.

▲ **Lewitzky Dance Company.**
"Impressions #2"

 Art Criticism

 What lines did you show with your body?

 ## Art History and Culture

Dance Choreography

A choreographer creates dances. Choreographer Bella Lewitzky brought images by artist Vincent van Gogh into the studio for her dancers to explore improvisationally. When she found ideas she liked, she organized them into dances. Her father, a painter, helped her develop a "graphic eye" that she used to translate line from paintings into dance.

 # Lines in Dance

Objective: To create a variety of lines by using motions and body positions

Materials: *Impressions #2* (Vincent van Gogh) performed by Bella Lewitzky and Lewitzky Dance Company. Running time: 3:27

Focus
Time: About 10 minutes

- Read and discuss the information on page 63.

- Have students brainstorm the types of lines they see in *The Starry Night.* Write these words on the board.

Art History and Culture

- Have students discover the kinds of lines they can create with their bodies while exploring contemporary American dance.

Teach
Time: About 20 minutes

Aesthetic Perception

- Ask students to describe what they see in Van Gogh's painting *The Starry Night.*

Creative Expression

- Have students stand in an open space. Call out words you listed on the board. Ask students to express these words using their bodies.

- **Informal Assessment** Comment positively on their interpretations of the various types of lines.

Reflect
Time: About 5 minutes

Art Criticism

- Have students draw a picture in their Art Journals to answer the Describe Art Criticism question on page 63. Discuss the following questions:

Analyze ▶ Were your movements wide or narrow?

Interpret ▶ How was moving in a curved line different from moving in a zigzag line?

Decide ▶ How well did you show the different types of lines in movement?

Unit 2 Planning Guide

	Lesson Title	Suggested Pacing	Creative Expression Activity
Lesson 1	**Shape**	45 minutes	Create an imaginary creature.
Lesson 2	Geometric Shapes	45 minutes	Create a design using geometric shapes.
Lesson 3	**Free-Form Shapes**	45 minutes	Create leaf prints with free-form shapes.
Lesson 4	**More About Shapes**	45 minutes	Create a drawing of a house, using geometric and free-form shapes.
Lesson 5	**Body Shapes**	45 minutes	Create a self-portrait using body shapes.
Lesson 6	**The Shape of People**	45 minutes	Create a family portrait using different-sized body shapes.
ART SOURCE	**Shape in Dance**	35 minutes	Create a variety of sizes and types of circle shapes through body design and motion.

Materials	Program Resources	Fine Art Resources	Literature Resources
computer, paint program, printer with paper	*Reading and Writing Test Preparation,* pp. 18–19 *Flash Cards,* 7–11 *Assessment,* pp. 21–22 *Home and After-School Connections,* pp. 11–14	*Transparency,* 7 *Artist Profiles,* pp. 28, 41 *Large Prints,* 3 and 4 *The National Museum of Women in the Arts Collection*	*Paul Bunyan* by Steven Kellogg
3" paper squares of assorted colored construction paper, 10" × 10" squares of background paper, glue, scissors, jar lids, pencils	*Reading and Writing Test Preparation,* pp. 20–21 *Flash Cards,* 7, 9, 10 and 11 *Assessment,* pp. 23–24	*Transparency,* 8 *Artist Profiles,* pp. 16, 47 *Large Prints,* 3 and 4 *The National Museum of Women in the Arts Collection*	*Color Zoo* by Lois Ehlert
collection of real leaves, 12" × 18" white paper, water soluble printing ink, brayer and inking plate, newspapers to cover inking area of table	*Reading and Writing Test Preparation,* pp. 22–23 *Flash Card,* 8 *Assessment,* pp. 25–26	*Transparency,* 9 *Artist Profiles,* pp. 32, 53 *Large Prints,* 3 and 4 *Art Around the World*	*The Wind Blew* by Pat Hutchins
12" × 18" paper (light-colored), write-over markers	*Reading and Writing Test Preparation,* pp. 24–25 *Flash Cards,* 7–11 *Assessment,* pp. 27–28	*Transparency,* 10 *Artist Profiles,* pp. 7, 42 *Large Prints,* 3 and 4 *The National Museum of Women in the Arts Collection*	*Billy and the Big New School* by Catherine and Lawrence Anholt
12" × 18" paper, markers, large mirror	*Reading and Writing Test Preparation,* pp. 26–27 *Flash Cards,* 8 and 18 *Assessment,* pp. 29–30	*Transparency,* 11 *Artist Profiles,* pp. 22, 23 *Large Prints,* 3 and 4 *The National Museum of Women in the Arts Collection*	*My Friends* by Taro Gomi
12" × 18" drawing paper, markers (multicultural colors), patterned papers or wall paper samples, glue sticks	*Reading and Writing Test Preparation,* pp. 28–29 *Flash Cards,* 8 and 18 *Assessment,* pp. 31–32	*Transparency,* 12 *Artist Profiles,* pp. 3, 38 *Large Prints,* 3 *The National Museum of Women in the Arts Collection*	*Jojo's Flying Side Kick* by Brian Pinkney
"Suite of Appalachian Music and Dance" performed by the AMAN International Folk Ensemble			

Unit Overview

2 Shape

Lesson 1: **Shape** is a flat, two-dimensional area that is defined by its outline.

Lesson 2: **Geometric shapes** are precise shapes. Simple geometric shapes are circles, squares, triangles, and rectangles.

Lesson 3: **Free-form shapes** are all shapes that are not geometric. People, animals, plants, and objects are examples of free-form shapes.

Lesson 4: **Geometric and free-form shapes** are everywhere. Students distinguish between these shapes.

Lesson 5: **Body shapes** are free-form shapes.

Lesson 6: **Various sizes of body shapes** are studied in this lesson.

Introduce Unit Concepts

"Different shapes tell us different messages. You can often recognize an object by its shape." "Los diferentes tipos de figuras nos dan distintos mensajes. A menudo pueden reconocer un objecto por su figura".

Shape
- Have students use a piece of yarn to trace around the outside edges of an object. Encourage them to identify that the yarn line has begun and ended in the same place.

- Encourage students to investigate the shapes of outdoor objects.

- Have students play a sorting game of geometric and free-form shapes. Let them sort objects or pictures into one of these categories.

Cross-Curricular Projects
- See the **Language Arts and Reading, Mathematics, Science,** and **Social Studies Art Connections** books for activities that further develop line concepts.

Shape

Artists use many kinds of shapes in their artwork.

▲ **Grant Wood.** (American). *American Gothic.* 1930.

Oil on beaverboard. 29¼ × 24½ inches (74.3 × 62.4 cm.). The Art Institute of Chicago, Chicago, Illinois.

64 Unit 2

Fine Art Prints

Display **Large Prints 3** *Le Gourmet* and **4** *Fruit Displayed on a Stand.* Refer to the prints throughout the unit as students learn about shape.

Large Print 3

Large Print 4

Artists use big **shapes** and small **shapes.**

▶ Use your finger to trace shapes you see in the painting.

▶ How are the shapes different?

In This Unit you will:
▶ learn about shapes.
▶ practice using shapes in your artwork.

Return from Bohemia.

Grant Wood
(1892–1942)

▶ was an American artist.

▶ created paintings of farm people and country scenes.

Unit 2   **65**

Examine the Artwork

"Let's find shapes in this family portrait."
"Vamos a buscar figuras en este retrato familiar".

■ Have students study Wood's *American Gothic* and describe what they see.

■ Have students answer the questions pertaining to shapes on page 65.

▶ Students might trace **geometric shapes**—the rectangular shape of the house; rectangles in the windows; triangular-shaped roof; the circular shape of the man's eyeglasses, or **free-form shapes**—the people; the plants and trees; the pitchfork.

▶ Some of the shapes are big and some are small. The shapes are made with different kinds of lines (straight, curved, diagonal, horizontal, vertical). Students might recognize that some of the shapes are geometric and some are free-form.

Unit Pretest

T Display *Transparency 44* as a pretest. Answers: 1.B; 2.A; 3.A

Home Connection

See *Home and After-School Connections* for family newsletters and activities for this unit.

Art History and Culture

Grant Wood

Grant Wood (grant wud) (1892–1942) painted many landscapes from his hometown in Stone City, Iowa. This small Midwestern city celebrates the artist's life and work every year during the Grant Wood Festival. A regionalist, Wood painted idealistic scenes and events that were typical of the area in which he lived. He used such a difficult procedure that he could finish only two paintings a year. According to Wood, some of his greatest inspirations came to him while milking cows.

See pages 16–21 and 24–25 for more about subject matter and art history.

Artist Profiles, p. 54

◀ Artist Profile ▶
Grant Wood
1892-1942

Grant Wood (grant wŏŏd) was born in Iowa and lived there most of his life. His father died when Wood was ten years old. When he was 14 he won third prize in a national Crayola contest by coloring a leaf. He studied drawing and design after high school. As a soldier in World War I, he designed artillery camouflage. After the war, Wood taught art in several high schools and studied art during multiple trips to Europe. In 1927, he retired from teaching high school to paint full-time. Later he served as the Iowa director of the Public Works Art Project. He taught at the University of Iowa and lectured across the nation.

ILLUSTRATOR PROFILE
Tana Hoban
(c. 1917–   )

Tana Hoban's parents emigrated from Russia to Philadelphia, where the author and illustrator was born. At her father's encouragement, Hoban took art classes as a young girl, and, while she was often the youngest student in the class, her paintings invariably attracted attention and praise.

Hoban continued to pursue painting at the Moore College of Art in Philadelphia, from which she graduated in 1938. Following a year spent painting in Europe on a fellowship, Hoban returned to Philadelphia, where she was employed as a freelance artist. In 1939 Hoban married Edward Gallob, who gave Hoban a gift that would alter the course of her artistic career: her first camera.

In 1946 Hoban put painting on hold to develop her career as a photographer, and she quickly earned recognition for her outstanding work. By 1950 Hoban already had photographs on permanent display in New York's Museum of Modern Art.

Hoban had a keen interest in child development, and children were often the subjects of her work. She merged her skills and interests in 1970, when she produced her first picture book for children, *Shapes and Things*. Hoban went on to publish more than 50 books for young children, characterized by stunning photographs and basic concepts, such as shapes, opposites, and numbers.

While studying Unit 2, share Hoban's illustrations with the class and discuss the use of shape in her works of art. Ask students to identify the different kinds of shapes Hoban used in her illustrations.

Music

Shape has no one single meaning in music. It can refer to the movement of a melodic line or the way a musical phrase is "shaped" by a performer through gradual changes in volume. In addition, the shape of an instrument contributes greatly to its beauty and tone.

Literature

Watch the video or DVD *Free Fall* by David Wiesner to see wonderful examples of free-form shapes.

Literature and Art

Performing Arts

Show *Suite of Appalachian Music and Dance.* Have students identify the shapes created by the dancers as they move.

Artsource®

Lesson 1 · Shape
Overview

Lesson 1 introduces shape. Shape is a flat, two-dimensional area that is defined by its outline.

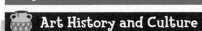
Objectives

 Art History and Culture

To observe that artists use imagination to create works of art

 Creative Expression

To create a drawing using shapes

 **Aesthetic Perception**

To recognize that lines outline shapes

Art Criticism

To evaluate one's own work using the four steps of art criticism

Vocabulary Reading

Review the following vocabulary words with students before beginning the lesson.

shape figura—a two-dimensional area that is defined in some way. While a form has depth, a shape has only height and width.

outline contorno—a line that shows or creates the outer edges of a shape

See page 89B for additional vocabulary and Spanish vocabulary resources.

 Art Journal: Vocabulary

Have students add these words to the Vocabulary section of their Art Journals.

Lesson Materials
- computer
- paint program
- printer with paper

Alternate Materials
- crayons or markers
- white or light-colored paper

Program Resources
- *Reading and Writing Test Prep.,* pp. 18–19
- *Transparency 7*
- *Flash Cards 7–11*
- *Artist Profiles,* pp. 28, 41
- *Assessment,* pp. 21–22
- *Large Prints 3 Le Gourmet* and *4 Fruit Displayed on a Stand*
- *The National Museum of Women in the Arts Collection*

Concept Trace
Shape
Introduced: Level K, Unit 2, Lesson 1
Reinforced: Level 1, Unit 2, Lesson 1

Lesson 1 Arts Integration

Theatre
Complete Unit 2, Lesson 1 on pages 36–37 of *Theatre Arts Connections.*

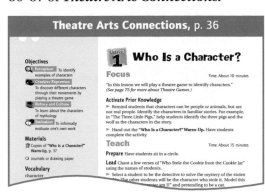

Music
 Collect several classroom instruments. Draw their shapes in a list on the board. As you sing the song *Johnny Works with One Hammer,* go down the list and change on each verse. Do it again with two shapes for every verse.

Movement & Dance
Explore creating the shapes of familiar objects using the body. Work on the floor. Each shape should be in contrast to the one before; for example, banana, pencil, pumpkin, starfish, and table. Identify the type of lines that are being used to create each shape, how the size of each shape varies, and how each shape might move.

Focus

Activate Prior Knowledge

"What kinds of imaginary creatures have you seen on television?" "¿Qué tipos de criaturas imaginarias han visto en la televisión?"

- Invite students to share experiences.

- Discuss using imagination to explore things out of the ordinary.

Using Literature ⭐ Reading

- Read *Paul Bunyan*, retold and illustrated by Steven Kellogg. Ask students to identify examples of imagination in the story.

Thematic Connection ⭐ Reading

- **Imagination:** Read *Jabberwocky* by Lewis Carroll or *There's a Nightmare in My Closet* by Mercer Mayer to the class. Focus on the element of imagination in each story. Encourage students to tell the class about other stories they have heard about imaginary creatures.

Introduce the Art

Look

"This picture is about imaginary creatures." "Esta pintura trata de criaturas imaginarias".

- Describe what the creatures are doing.

Comparing and Contrasting ⭐ Reading

- How are the creatures the same? How are they different?

- Explain to students that artists use imaginary shapes in artwork.

Adjectives and Adverbs ⭐ Language Arts

- List on a chart the adjectives and adverbs students use to describe the fine art.

National Standards for Arts Education in Visual Arts 3.a

🏺 Art History and Culture

Share information from the Art History and Culture sections with students. Ask students how the imaginary creatures in the fine art are alike and different. Possible answers: They all have eyes, arms, legs, noses, and hands. They all look like cartoons.

💻 Web Connection

To learn more about children's book authors and illustrators, visit the Children's Book Council Web site at **www.cbcbooks.org/html/aboutauthors.html.**

Shape

Look at the works of art on these pages. Artists use **outlines** to help us see the **shape** of objects.

▲ **Graeme Base.**
(Australian). Scene from *Jabberwocky* © Graeme Base, 1987.
••••••••••••••••••••••
Harry N. Abrams, Inc.
New York, New York.

🏺 Art History and Culture

Both of these artists created imaginary creatures. How are they alike and different?

🏺 Art History and Culture

Graeme Base

Children's book author and illustrator Graeme Base (gram bās) (1958–) was born in England, but moved with his family to Australia when he was eight. After studying graphic design in college, he worked in advertising before trying his hand at book illustration.

Base prefers to write his own stories instead of illustrating books written by other people, so he can change the words to better fit the pictures. The first book that he wrote and illustrated, *My Grandma Lived in Gooligulch*, was published in 1983.

Base may spend from two to three years working on the illustrations for a single book. His favorite page from *Animalia*, the Horrible Hairy Hogs, took two months.

See pages 16–21 and 24–25 for more about subject matter and art history.

Artist Profiles, p. 41

⇒ Artist Profile ⇒
Graeme Base
b. 1958

Graeme Base (gram bās) was born in Amersham, England. He moved to Australia when he was eight years old. He writes and illustrates children's books. He draws things from his childhood, things around him, and things from his imagination. He loves animals, and wildlife is often represented in his work. Base likes to write his own stories so that he can change the words around as he makes the drawings. He thinks of picture books as a way to teach children.

◄ **Mercer Mayer.**
(American). Scene
from *There's a*
Nightmare in My
Closet. 1976.

Dial Books for Young
Readers, A Member of
Penguin Group (USA) Inc.,
New York, New York.

Study the pictures.

▶ What shapes do you see in the
pictures?

 Aesthetic Perception

Seeing Like an Artist Use your finger to trace
a line around something near you. What shape
did you make?

 Art History and Culture

Mercer Mayer

Mercer Mayer (mər´sər mā´ ər) (1943–   ) has illustrated more than
300 books since he began his career as a children's book
author/illustrator in 1966. Mayer's most popular books are the
Little Critter series which he began writing in 1976. He has also
created illustrations for books by many other authors. Mayer enjoys
the challenge of creating his story illustrations digitally.

See pages 16–21 and 24–25 for more about subject matter and art
history.

Artist Profiles, p. 28

Study

▶ Answers will vary since types of shapes
have not yet been discussed in depth.
Students may describe familiar shapes,
such as circles on the dresser, squares at
the top of the door frame, a rectangle on
the door, and circles or ovals for the
creatures' eyes.

■ For more examples of narrative art, see
The National Museum of Women in the
Arts Collection.

Art Journal: Concept
Have students draw a picture of
what they think an outline of a shape
looks like.

 Aesthetic Perception

Seeing Like an Artist Encourage students to
look all around them and trace many objects
with their fingers. Discuss the types of
shapes they traced. How are they the same?
How are they different?

Developing Visual Literacy Study the faces of
the creatures in the pictures. How do the
artists help us know how the creatures are
feeling?

 Web Connection
Learn more about Mercer Mayer and his books by
visiting **www.littlecritter.com/**.

# Teach

Time: About 30 minutes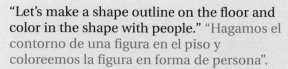

"Let's make a shape outline on the floor and color in the shape with people." *"Hagamos el contorno de una figura en el piso y coloreemos la figura en forma de persona".*

- Demonstrate creating a shape by drawing the outline of a shape on the floor with yarn.

Practice

Materials: Yarn

- Create the outline of a shape on the floor with yarn. Narrate as you create the shape: "I'm going to close my shape by touching the ends of the yarn together."

- Invite some or all of the students to step inside the outline.

- Explain that the outline is like a fence to hold them inside the shape.

- Have the students create new shapes as directed in step 2 on page 68.

Creative Expression

Materials: computer, paint program, printer with paper

Alternate Materials: crayons or markers on white or light-colored paper

- Help students open a paint program on the computer.

- Encourage students to use a variety of drawing and shape tools to draw an imaginary creature.

- Have students use the fill tools to add color to the creature.

- Then have students use a thick black line to trace around the outside shape of the creature.

- See the Activity Tips on page 235 for visual examples of this lesson's activity.

NSAE 1.a; 1.c

Art Journal: Brainstorming

Have students brainstorm ideas for imaginary creatures and draw these items in their Art Journals. Discuss how the creatures can be drawn in the Creative Expression activity using lines to outline the bodies.

Using Shape

The line around the edge of a **shape** is the **outline.**

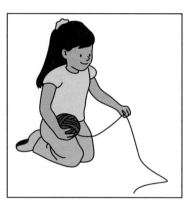

Practice

1. Step inside the outline your teacher creates on the floor.

2. Take turns making new shape outlines with the yarn.

Differentiated Instruction

Reteach
Use a piece of string or yarn to show the concept of two ends meeting or joining together to form a shape.

Special Needs
Before students begin drawing their imaginary creature, have students look at a larger image of the lesson artwork and trace the outline with their fingers.

ELL Tips
Display a ball, a small can, and a pencil, and label each object. Then on the board, draw the outline shape of each object. Ask students to trace the outline shapes on the board.

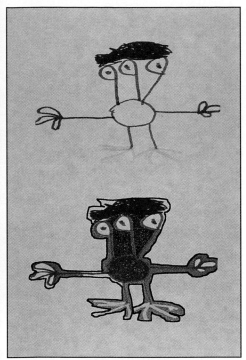

Think about the shapes you see in this student's work.

◄ **Seth Paulson.** Age 6.

Creative Expression

What kinds of shapes do imaginary creatures have?

1. Think about the different imaginary creatures you have seen in books.
2. Draw an imaginary creature of your own.

 **Art Criticism**

Interpret Is your picture funny or scary? What makes you think that?

Art Across the Curriculum

Use these simple ideas to reinforce art concepts across the curriculum.

★ **Descriptive Writing** Have students draw a picture that describes what might happen during a wild rumpus.

★ **Math** Count the hands and feet in the picture from *Jabberwocky*.

★ **Science** Discuss the five senses. Identify which body parts the monsters would use to see, hear, touch, taste, and smell.

★ **Social Studies** Study the environments shown in the pictures. Identify familiar outdoor characteristics seen in *Jabberwocky* (trees and plants) and familiar bedroom characteristics shown in *There's a Nightmare in My Closet* (closet, furniture, and toys).

★ **Technology** Use a paint program to draw an imaginary creature. Visit **SRAonline.com** to print detailed instructions for this activity.

Reflect

 Time: About 5 minutes

Review and Assess

"How do you outline the shape of something?" "¿Cómo hacen el contorno de algo?"

Think

Discuss the student art question. He used round shapes for the eyes and body and small oval shapes for the fingers.

■ Identify lines that outline shapes in **Large Prints 3** *Le Gourmet* and **4** *Fruit Displayed on a Stand*.

Informal Assessment

Art Journal: Critical Thinking
Have students answer the Interpret question by drawing a picture in their Art Journals.

 **Art Criticism**

Have students ask themselves the following questions.

Describe ► What is your imaginary creature doing?

Analyze ► How many shapes did you create? Did you draw lines that meet to create new shapes?

Interpret ► Is your picture funny or scary? What makes you think that?

Decide ► What do you like best about using different shapes to make an imaginary picture?

NSAE 2.b; 5.a; 5.c

■ For standardized-format test practice using this lesson's art content, see pages 18–19 in *Reading and Writing Test Preparation*.

Lesson 1 Shape
Wrap-Up

Extra! For the Art Specialist
Time: About 30 minutes

Focus

Use **Transparency 7** and **Large Prints 3** *Le Gourmet* and **4** *Fruit Displayed on a Stand* as you discuss how the artists used line to make shapes. Trace your finger around each shape. Describe the lines that make each shape.

Teach

Have students use shape stencils to create a drawing of a creature.

Reflect

Have students use the four steps of art criticism to evaluate their work. Did they use the shape stencils effectively to create a drawing of a creature?

Alternate Activity

Materials:
- 10" × 12" white drawing paper
- pencils, markers
- cardboard geometric stencils in various sizes

1. Have the children describe the different shapes they see in the creatures illustrated in *Jabberwocky* and *There's a Nightmare in My Closet.*

2. Hold up cardboard stencils of the shapes the students name. Demonstrate how to place the stencils on paper and trace around them.

3. Direct the students to draw a creature using the stencils. Have students color the shapes with markers and add lines for texture. Then have students draw the environment where their creatures live.

NSAE 1.a; 1.c

Research in Art Education

There is a link between "arts education and creative thinking, academic self-concept, and school climate" ("Learning in and Through the Arts: The Question of Transfer" in *Critical Links*, p. 66). Students in schools with quality arts programs tend to use more creativity, take more risks, and view themselves as academically competent. Creativity is fostered in this lesson as students create imaginary creatures.

Assessment
Use the following rubric to evaluate the artwork students make in the Creative Expression activity and to assess students' understanding of shape.

Have students complete page 21 or 22 in their *Assessment* books.

	Art History and Culture	Aesthetic Perception	Creative Expression	Art Criticism
3 POINTS	The student observes that artists use imagination and identifies such use in fine art.	The student accurately recognizes that lines outline shapes.	The student's drawing clearly illustrates lines that outline shapes.	The student thoughtfully and honestly evaluates his or her own work using the four steps of art criticism.
2 POINTS	The student observes that artists use imagination and can sometimes identify such use in fine art.	The student shows emerging awareness that lines outline shapes.	The student's drawing shows some awareness of lines that outline shapes.	The student attempts to evaluate his or her own work, but shows an incomplete understanding of evaluation criteria.
1 POINT	The student does not understand that artists use imagination and cannot identify such use in fine art.	The student does not recognize that lines outline shapes.	The student's drawing shows no understanding of lines that outline shapes.	The student does not attempt to evaluate his or her own artwork.

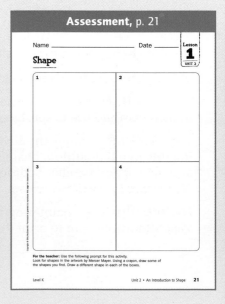

Assessment, p. 21

Name _____ Date _____

Lesson **1** UNIT 2

Shape

For the teacher: Use the following prompt for this activity. Look for shapes in the artwork by Mercer Mayer. Using a crayon, draw some of the shapes you find. Draw a different shape in each of the boxes.

Level K   Unit 2 • An Introduction to Shape   21

Lesson 2 Geometric Shapes

Overview

Lesson 2 introduces geometric shapes. Geometric shapes are precise shapes that can be described using mathematical formulas and are recognized by their names. Simple geometric shapes are circles, squares, triangles, and rectangles.

Objectives

 Art History and Culture

To recognize that artists use geometric shapes to create works of art

 Creative Expression

To create a design using geometric shapes

 Aesthetic Perception

To identify geometric shapes by name and locate them in the artwork

Art Criticism

To evaluate one's own work using the four steps of art criticism

Vocabulary Reading

Review the following vocabulary words with students before beginning the lesson.

geometric shape figura geométrica—a mathematical shape, such as a circle, square, rectangle, or triangle

The following words appear as art on student page 72 and in the student glossary.

circle círculo, **square** cuadrado, **triangle** triángulo, **rectangle** rectángulo

See page 89B for additional vocabulary and Spanish vocabulary resources.

 Art Journal: Vocabulary

Have students add these words to the Vocabulary section of their Art Journals.

Lesson Materials

- 3" paper squares of assorted colored construction paper
- 10" × 10" squares of background paper
- glue, scissors, jar lids, and pencils
- 12" × 18" light-colored paper
- crayons or markers

Alternate Materials

- crayons or markers instead of paper and glue for Creative Expression activity

Program Resources

- *Reading and Writing Test Prep.*, pp. 20–21
- *Transparency 8*
- *Flash Cards 7, 9, 10* and *11*
- *Artist Profiles*, pp. 16, 47
- *Assessment*, pp. 23–24
- *Large Prints 3 Le Gourmet* and *4 Fruit Displayed on a Stand*
- *The National Museum of Women in the Arts Collection*

Concept Trace

Geometric Shapes
Introduced: Level K, Unit 2, Lesson 2

Reinforced: Level 1, Unit 2, Lesson 2

Lesson 2 Arts Integration

Theatre

Complete Unit 2, Lesson 2 on pages 38–39 of *Theatre Arts Connections.*

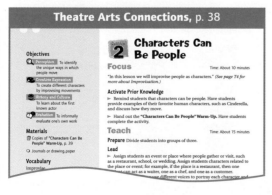

Music

 Borrow a poster of orchestral instruments from the library or music teacher. As you name each one, find the geometric shapes within each. Can you find the circle in the French horn, the rectangle in the violin, a triangle, and so on?

Movement & Dance

Work in groups of four to create the following geometric shapes: circle, square, and rectangle. Students can explore creating each shape on two different levels, on the floor and standing. Now see if the whole class can work together to create each of these shapes. Make a giant circle, square, and rectangle by working together.

 **ocus**

Activate Prior Knowledge

"Have you ever seen a design like the one in this book?" "¿Alguna vez han visto un diseño como el que está en este libro?"

■ Discuss how the design was made from many shapes and colors.

Using Literature ☆ Reading

■ Have students identify geometric shapes in the animal pictures in *Color Zoo* by Lois Ehlert.

Thematic Connection ☆ Math

■ **Shapes:** Have students create patterns with geometric shapes.

Introduce the Art

Look

"Many shapes are repeated in this design. Let's look at it closely." "Muchas figuras se repiten en este diseño. Vamos a observarlo detalladamente".

Geometry ☆ Math

■ Have students name the shapes in the design.

Classify and Categorize ☆ Reading

■ Focus on one shape at a time, such as a circle. Have students point to examples of that shape in the picture.

■ What colors were used? Find shapes that have the same color.

■ Share and discuss information from ***Artist Profiles*** pages 16 and 47 with students.

Adjectives and Adverbs ☆ Language Arts

■ List on a chart the adjectives and adverbs students use to describe the fine art.

NSAE 4.a

Art History and Culture

Share information from the Art History and Culture sections with students. Ask students to point to geometric shapes they see in the works of art. Possible answers: Herbin's work has circles, squares, triangles, rectangles, semi-circles, and arcs. Thiebaud's work has a circle (plate), triangle (pie), and rectangles (glass case). The short sides on the case might be mentioned as squares.

💻 Web Connection

Visit **www.moma.org/** for more information about The Museum of Modern Art.

Geometric Shapes

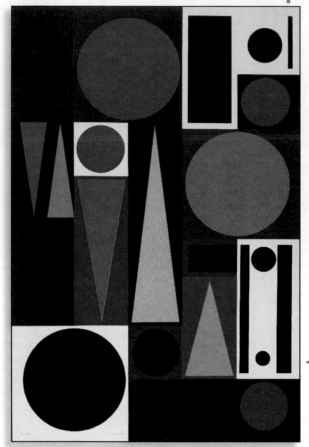

Look at the shapes in these works of art. They are **geometric shapes.**

◀ **Auguste Herbin.** (French). *Composition on the Word "Vie" 2.* 1950.
••••••••••••••••••••••••
Oil on canvas. $57\frac{1}{2} \times 38\frac{1}{4}$ inches (146.05 × 97.16 cm). Museum of Modern Art, New York, New York.

🏺 Art History and Culture

Some works of art have shapes and designs instead of everyday objects like people or places.

🏺 Art History and Culture

Auguste Herbin

Auguste Herbin (ō gōōst´ âr´ ban) (1882–1960) first painted still lifes and landscapes, but his interest later turned to shapes and colors, which he explored by creating cubist and abstract paintings. Herbin developed a code-like system for painting geometric shapes in which the shapes represented letters and the arrangement of the shapes created words.

See pages 16–21 and 24–25 for more about subject matter and art history.

Artist Profiles, p. 16

Artist Profile
Auguste Herbin
1882–1960
Auguste Herbin (ō gōōst´ âr´ ban) was born in France and studied at the École des Beaux-Arts. Later he went to other countries to paint. In Italy, he noticed how different kinds of light changed the way things look. From then on he tried to ignore little details and paint only the main part of his subject. Herbin was enthusiastic and curious and loved his work. During the last years of his life Herbin created tapestry designs.

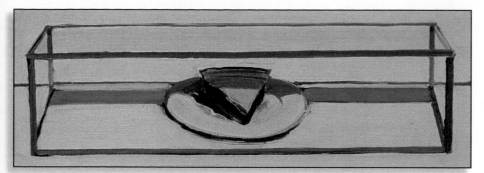

▲ **Wayne Thiebaud.** (American).
Caged Pie. 1962.
Oil on canvas. $20\frac{1}{8} \times 28\frac{1}{8}$ inches
(51.11 × 71.43 cm.). San Diego Museum
of Art, San Diego, California.

Study the pictures.

▶ Do you know the names of any of
the geometric shapes you see?

🔍 **Aesthetic Perception**

Design Awareness Look at your clothes.
Do you see a ■, a ▲, a ●, or a ▬ ?

Study

▶ Possible answers: circle, square, triangle,
and rectangle. Students might also
mention semi-circle or half circle. The
short sides on the pie case might be
named as squares.

■ For more examples of abstract/
nonobjective art, see *The National
Museum of Women in the Arts Collection.*

Art Journal: Concept
Have students draw in their Art
Journals a picture of what they think are
geometric shapes.

🔍 **Aesthetic Perception**

Design Awareness Geometric shapes are
often used in clothing designs. Ask students
to identify the geometric shapes they see on
the clothes of their classmates.

Developing Visual Literacy Ask students why
they think the artist painted *Caged Pie.* Have
they ever seen pie or other foods in a case?
Where?

Art History and Culture

Wayne Thiebaud

American artist Wayne Thiebaud (wān tē´ bō) (1920–) began his
career as a cartoonist but is known more for his excellence in
teaching and his still life paintings of everyday objects. Baked
goods, such as pies and cakes, often are the subject matter of
Thiebaud's paintings. Although he is often considered a pop artist,
Thiebaud considers himself a realist. His most recent work is more
simplified and abstract and often focuses on the urban landscapes
of San Francisco.

See pages 16–21 and 24–25
for more about subject
matter and art history.

Artist Profiles, p. 47

Artist Profile
Wayne Thiebaud
b. 1920

Wayne Thiebaud (wān tē´ bō), one of
California's most famous contemporary
painters, has earned as many awards for
excellence in teaching as he has for his
painting and printmaking. He became
interested in drawing in high school and
later worked as a freelance cartoonist and
illustrator. He continued his artwork during
his military service in the U.S. Air Force
during World War II. He drew cartoons
for the military base newspaper. In 1949
Thiebaud decided to become a painter.
His first one-person show in New York City
was praised by the critics. At that time his
subjects were mass-produced consumer
goods, particularly junk food, and he was
mistakenly classified with the pop artists

💻 **Web Connection**
Visit **www.sdmart.org/** to learn about the San
Diego Museum of Art.

 **each**

Time: About 30 minutes

"Let's find some geometric shapes around us." "Vamos a buscar algunas figuras geométricas a nuestro alrededor".

- Model by pointing out a geometric shape you found in the classroom or by looking out the classroom window.

Practice

Materials: 12" × 18" light-colored paper, crayons, or markers

- Assign each student a partner.

- Have the students identify geometric shapes as directed on page 72.

- Ask students to look around the classroom and out the window to find different geometric shapes.

- Have students take turns drawing the shapes they found.

- Ask students to study the shapes they drew and decide which kind of shape they saw most often.

Creative Expression

Materials: 3" squares of assorted colored construction paper, 10" × 10" squares of background paper, glue, scissors, jar lids, pencils

Alternate Materials: crayons or markers instead of paper and glue

- For the Creative Expression activity, students will draw and cut their own shapes. Some students might need shape templates to trace. Some might need precut shapes.

- See pages 221–222 in Technique Tips for information and tips about scissors and glue.

- Distribute the materials and have the students follow the directions on page 73.

- See the Activity Tips on page 235 for visual examples of this lesson's activity.

NSAE 1.c

Art Journal: Brainstorming

Ask students to think about which geometric shape(s) they like best and why. Have students draw their favorite geometric shapes in their Art Journals.

Using Geometric Shapes

Geometric shapes have names.

circle

square

triangle

rectangle

Practice

1. Take turns with your partner. Find circles, squares, triangles, and rectangles around you.

2. Draw the shapes you find on your paper. Which shape do you see the most?

Differentiated Instruction

Reteach
Use everyday objects to create geometric shapes. Arrange pencils into squares, rectangles, and triangles. Shape a rubber band or yarn into a circle.

Special Needs
Students who have difficulty cutting may benefit from the use of adaptive scissors for this lesson activity. Students with severe disabilities who may not be able to cut and glue are fully capable of making choices and expressing preferences in art making.

ELL Tips
Display paper cutouts or two-dimensional shapes of a circle, square, triangle, and rectangle. Label each one. Say the names of the shapes. Ask students to handle the shapes and repeat the name of each. Then say the name of a shape and let volunteers pick up the appropriate shape.

Think about the kinds of geometric shapes this student used.

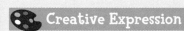◀ **Jeb Smith.** Age 5.

 Creative Expression

What are your favorite geometric shapes?

1. Cut out some shapes.
2. Choose the ones you like best and glue them on the paper.

 Art Criticism

Describe How many different geometric shapes did you use? What are the names of the geometric shapes you used?

◉ Art Across the Curriculum ◉

Use these simple ideas to reinforce art concepts across the curriculum.

★ **Persuasive Writing** Have students draw a picture of something they would do to persuade their parents or guardians to give them dessert.

★ **Math** Have students use language such as *over, under, above,* and *below* to describe the location of shapes in the fine art. The yellow triangle is above the black circle. As one student says the statement, the other students find the shapes the student is referring to.

★ **Science** Discuss the five senses. Identify which senses can be used when eating a real piece of pie.

★ **Social Studies** Draw a picture that shows one person helping another, such as an adult helping a child make a pie.

★ **Technology** Use the shape tools in a paint program to create a design of geometric shapes. Visit **SRAonline.com** to print detailed instructions for this activity.

 **Time:** About 5 minutes

Review and Assess

"What are the names of the geometric shapes you learned about?" "¿Cuáles son los nombres de las figures geométricas de las que aprendieron?"

Think

Discuss the student art question. He used rectangles for the train cars, circles for the wheels and sign, squares for windows and triangles for parts of the engine.

■ Identify geometric shapes in *Large Prints 3 Le Gourmet* and *4 Fruit Displayed on a Stand.*

Informal Assessment

Art Journal: Critical Thinking
Have students answer the Describe question in their Art Journals. Students can refer to page 72 for help with the names of the shapes. If writing the names is too difficult, have students draw the shapes they used and color them appropriately.

Art Criticism

Have students ask themselves the following questions.

Describe ▶ How many different geometric shapes did you use? What are the names of the geometric shapes you used? What colors did you use?

Analyze ▶ Did you repeat any shapes?

Interpret ▶ How does your arrangement of shapes make you feel?

Decide ▶ Which shapes do you like best in your arrangement?

NSAE 2.b; 5.a; 5.c

■ For standardized-format test practice using this lesson's art content, see pages 20–21 in *Reading and Writing Test Preparation.*

Geometric Shapes

Extra! For the Art Specialist

Time: About 30 minutes

Focus

Use *Transparency 8* and *Large Prints 3* Le *Gourmet* and *4 Fruit Displayed on a Stand* as you discuss how the artist used geometric shapes. How many geometric shapes can you name? Point to your favorite shape.

Teach

Ask students to think about geometric shapes and create a print of their favorite shape.

Reflect

Have students use the four steps of art criticism to evaluate their work. Did they effectively create a print of their favorite shape?

Alternate Activity

Materials:

- 12" × 18" white paper
- sponges in various geometric shapes
- shallow tray or plate to hold paint
- tempera paint

1. Ask students to describe their favorite shapes and name things around them that are these shapes.

2. Show examples of shaped objects the students will use for printing.

3. Demonstrate how to apply paint to the object and make a print.

4. Instruct students to create a print with their favorite shape.

NSAE 1.c

Research
in Art Education

A pilot project evaluating the effects of arts education showed that "when students spend additional time in arts programs their performance in other school subjects does *not* decline." Teachers do not need to be afraid that devoting class time to arts education will hurt students' studies in other areas ("The Arts in the Basic Curriculum Project: Looking at the Past and Preparing for the Future" in *Critical Links,* p. 90). In addition, art concepts can often be taught across the curriculum, reinforcing both art and other subject areas.

Assessment

Use the following rubric to evaluate the artwork students make in the Creative Expression activity and to assess students' understanding of geometric shapes.

Have students complete page 23 or 24 in their *Assessment* books.

	Art History and Culture	Aesthetic Perception	Creative Expression	Art Criticism
3 POINTS	The student recognizes that artists use geometric shapes to create art and can identify these shapes in fine art.	The student accurately identifies geometric shapes by name and locates them in fine art.	The student's design clearly illustrates geometric shapes.	The student thoughtfully and honestly evaluates his or her own work using the four steps of art criticism.
2 POINTS	The student shows emerging awareness that artists use geometric shapes to create art and can identify some shapes in fine art.	The student shows emerging awareness of geometric shapes.	The student's design shows some awareness of geometric shapes.	The student attempts to evaluate his or her own work, but shows an incomplete understanding of evaluation criteria.
1 POINT	The student cannot recognize that artists use geometric shapes to create art and cannot identify these shapes in fine art.	The student cannot identify geometric shapes by name or locate them in fine art.	The student's design shows no understanding of geometric shapes.	The student does not attempt to evaluate his or her own artwork.

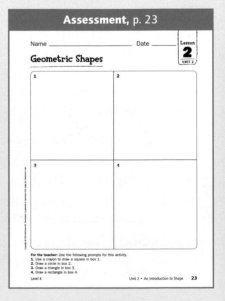

Assessment, p. 23

Name _____ Date _____

Lesson 2 UNIT 2

Geometric Shapes

1	2
3	**4**

For the teacher: Use the following prompts for this activity.
1. Use a crayon to draw a square in box 1.
2. Draw a circle in box 2.
3. Draw a triangle in box 3.
4. Draw a rectangle in box 4.

Level K   Unit 2 • An Introduction to Shape   **23**

Free-Form Shapes

Lesson 3 introduces free-form shapes. Free-form shapes are all shapes that are not geometric. People, animals, plants, and objects are examples of free-form shapes.

Objectives

Art History and Culture

To recognize illustrators as artists

Creative Expression

To create leaf prints with free-form shapes

Aesthetic Perception

To locate free-form shapes in the works of art and in students' environment

Art Criticism

To evaluate one's own work using the four steps of art criticism

Vocabulary Reading

Review the following vocabulary word with students before beginning the lesson.

free-form shape figura abstracta—an irregular and uneven shape whose outline is curved, angular, or both.

See page 89B for additional vocabulary and Spanish vocabulary resources.

Art Journal: Vocabulary

Have students add this word to the Vocabulary section of their Art Journals.

Lesson Materials

- collection of real leaves
- 12" × 18" white paper
- water soluble printing ink
- brayer and inking plate
- newspapers to cover inking area of table
- various large free-form shapes that can be held up for the class to see (such as a jacket, large leaf, or banana)

Alternate Materials

- crayons and watercolors (Make crayon rubbings of leaves and fill shapes with watercolors.)

Program Resources

- *Reading and Writing Test Prep.*, pp. 22–23
- *Transparency 9*
- *Flash Card 8*
- *Artist Profiles*, pp. 32, 53
- *Assessment*, pp. 25–26
- *Large Prints 3* Le Gourmet and *4 Fruit Displayed on a Stand*
- *Art Around the World Collection*

Concept Trace

Free-Form Shapes
Introduced: Level K, Unit 2, Lesson 3

Reinforced: Level K, Unit 2, Lessons 4, 5, and 6
Level 1, Unit 2, Lesson 3

Lesson 3 Arts Integration

Theatre

Complete Unit 2, Lesson 3 on pages 40–41 of *Theatre Arts Connections.*

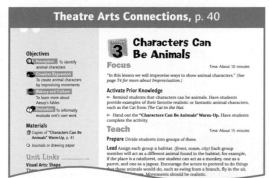

Music

 Vocal exploration can take our voice high, low, heavy, light, soft, and loud. Using your voice on "oo," describe a leaf falling to the ground. Some students may have slower leaves than others may. Draw a free-form shape on the board. Trace the shape with your finger and sing "ah" to show the ups and downs and curlicues.

Movement & Dance

Students walk in the space, weaving in and around each other to the beat of a drum or other percussive instrument. When the drum stops, call out an action or descriptive word to be interpreted by the students in a shape. Examples are: twisted, open, closed, jagged, reaching, and curved. Challenge students to explore more than one movement shape for each word.

Focus

Time: About 10 minutes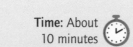

Activate Prior Knowledge

"What are some shapes and colors of leaves you have seen?" "¿Cuáles son algunas de las formas y colores de las hojas que ustedes han observado?"

- Have students draw leaf shapes in the air. Show students leaves you have brought to class. Explain that these shapes are not geometric shapes but are called free-form or organic shapes.

Using Literature ⭐ Reading

Read *The Wind Blew* by Pat Hutchins. Have students identify free-form shapes in the illustrations.

Thematic Connection ⭐ Science

- **Wind:** Observe changes in the weather, including the wind. Have students note windy days on a calendar by drawing blowing leaves.

NSAE 3.a; 3.b

Introduce the Art

Look

"Let's look at the free-form shapes in this illustration." "Miremos las figuras abstractas de esta ilustración".

Discussing the Selection ⭐ Reading

- Discuss the illustration and what students think the story is about.

Comparing and Contrasting ⭐ Reading

- Discuss how these free-form shapes are alike and how they are different from geometric shapes. Free-form shapes are irregular and uneven. Geometric shapes are even and precise.

Making Inferences ⭐ Reading

- Ask students how they think the boy feels. He could be excited, amazed, or scared.

NSAE 4.a

🏺 Art History and Culture

Share information from the Art History and Culture sections with students. Ask students if an illustrator is an artist. Yes, illustrators are artists because they create art. Their art is displayed in a book.

💻 Web Connection

Learn more about shape and other art elements at **www.sanford-artedventures.com/study/g_shape.html.**

Free-Form Shapes

▲ **David Wiesner.** (American). *Free Fall.* 1988.
••••••••••••••••••
Illustration. Courtesy of Lothrop, Lee, and Shepard Books.

Look at the different shapes in these works of art. Shapes that are not geometric are called **free-form shapes.**

🏺 Art History and Culture

People who draw or paint pictures for books are called illustrators. Their art helps tell stories.

🏺 Art History and Culture

David Wiesner

David Wiesner (dā´ vəd wēz´ nər) (1956–) began his career by illustrating textbooks. Later, he began writing and illustrating picture books. He won a Caldecott medal for his picture book *Tuesday.* His wordless picture book *Free Fall,* from which the artwork in this lesson is taken, is a Caldecott honor book.

See pages 16–21 and 24–25 for more about subject matter and art history.

Artist Profiles, p. 53

› Artist Profile ‹
David Wiesner
b. 1956

David Wiesner (dā´ vəd wēs´ nər) was born into a New Jersey family that encouraged his creativity. His art career began when he was five or six years old and he began watching reruns of an old television show called *You Are an Artist.* This show and books by the show's star gave Wiesner his first lessons in using perspective, light, and scale. In high school he wrote and filmed a story about a vampire who got the best of some bullies. After earning a degree in art, Wiesner illustrated textbooks. He also began to combine his ability to tell stories with his artistic skills, an area in which he has been very successful. He won a Caldecott Medal and other recognition for *Tuesday,* his almost wordless story about flying frogs.

◄ **Georgia O'Keeffe.** (American). *Autumn Leaves—Lake George.* 1924.

Oil on canvas. Columbus Museum of Art, Columbus, Ohio.

Study the pictures.

▶ Point to the shapes in these pictures that are not geometric shapes.

Aesthetic Perception

Seeing Like an Artist Name a free-form shape you see. Trace the shape with your finger.

Art History and Culture

Georgia O'Keeffe

Georgia O'Keeffe (jôr´ jə ō kēf´) (1887–1986) is best known for her paintings of natural forms, such as animal skulls, shells, bleached bones, and close-ups of flowers. She also painted landscapes, often of the desert in New Mexico where she spent much of the second half of her life. O'Keeffe was married to the famous American photographer Alfred Stieglitz and appeared in many of his photographs. Stieglitz did much to promote O'Keeffe's career by organizing exhibitions of her work in many galleries.

See pages 16–21 and 24–25 for more about subject matter and art history.

Artist Profiles, p. 32

Artist Profile
Georgia O'Keeffe
1887–1986

Georgia O'Keeffe (jōr´ jə ō kēf´) was born in Sun Prairie, Wisconsin. At the age of ten she began taking private art lessons, but the thing she liked most was experimenting with art at home. By 13, she had decided to become an artist. She trained under experts and won many prizes for her art. For years she challenged the art world with her unique vision. She eventually became famous for her spectacular, larger-than-life paintings of natural objects, including flowers, animal skulls, and shells. She loved nature, especially the desert of New Mexico, where she spent the last half of her life. O'Keeffe was married to the famous American photographer Alfred Stieglitz and appears in many of his photographs.

Study

▶ In *Free Fall*, students might point to the leaves, swans, boy, water, and fish.

▶ In *Autumn Leaves—Lake George*, students will point to various leaves in the painting.

■ For more examples of art from North America, see the ***Art Around the World Collection.***

Art Journal: Concept

Have students draw a picture in their Art Journals of what they think are free-form shapes.

Aesthetic Perception

Seeing Like an Artist Encourage students to find free-form shapes in the classroom decor or classroom materials, such as crayons or glue bottles. Have them name what they see and trace the shape of the object with their fingers.

Developing Visual Literacy Ask students to describe how the picture makes them feel. What is it about the picture that makes them feel that way?

Web Connection

Visit **www.okeeffemuseum.org/** to find out more about Georgia O'Keeffe and her exhibitions.
NSAE 5.a; 5.c

LESSON 3 • Free-Form Shapes   75

Teach

Time: About 30 minutes

"Let's look at some free-form shapes in nature." *"Vamos a observer algunas figuras abstractas en la naturaleza".*

- Have students bring in objects found in nature. Discuss how these free-form shapes look different from geometric shapes.

Practice

Materials: various, large free-form shapes to hold up for the class to see

- Hold up each object one at a time for the class to see.

- Have students trace the free-form shapes in the air as directed on page 76.

Creative Expression

Materials: collection of leaves, 12" × 18" white paper, water soluble printing ink, brayer, inking plate, newspapers to cover inking area of table

Alternate Materials: crayons and watercolors (Make crayon rubbings of leaves and fill shapes with watercolors.)

- Direct one student through the steps while the others watch.

- Ink the brayer. Roll ink over the side of the leaf with raised veins.

- Place the inked leaf, ink side down, on your white paper.

- Press the leaf to the paper with the heel of your hand. Remove the leaf immediately so it won't stick to the paper.

- Repeat until the page is full of leaf prints.

- Distribute the materials and have the students follow the directions on page 77.

- See page 226 in Technique Tips for information and tips about printmaking.

- See the Activity Tips on page 236 for visual examples of this lesson's activity.

NSAE 1.c

 Art Journal: Brainstorming

Ask students to draw in their Art Journals their favorite leaf shapes and choose a few they want to print.

Using Free-Form Shapes

Artists use **free-form shapes** to show people, animals, and other things.

Practice

1. Look at the objects your teacher shows you.

2. Trace the shape of each object in the air.

Differentiated Instruction

Reteach

Find free-form shapes in picture books and trace them with your finger.

Special Needs

Some students with physical difficulties may benefit from having their paper taped down as they are printing. Also, an inking tray or container with raised edges may help students with poor motor control as they roll paint onto the brayer.

ELL Tips

Display on individual cards a few outlines of shapes, such as a leaf, a fried egg, and a fish. Say the name of each shape and explain that these shapes are called free-form shapes. Have students repeat the term and trace the outline of each free-form shape.

▲ **Steven Roth.** Age 6.

Think about how the student used free-form shapes in this artwork.

 Creative Expression

Where do you see free-form shapes in nature? Print some free-form shapes using leaves.

1. Roll ink onto leaves.

2. Press the leaves on your paper.

 **Art Criticism**

Decide Which leaf shape do you think is most interesting? Why?

Art Across the Curriculum

Use these simple ideas to reinforce art concepts across the curriculum.

★ **Narrative Writing** Show students the entire *Free Fall* story by David Wiesner. Discuss how the story was told without words. Have students draw a picture using free-form shapes to make up their own story.

★ **Math** Give students a copy of a calendar for the month of November. Discuss how leaves like those seen in *Free Fall* fall off the trees in November. Have students trace the numbers on the calendar.

★ **Science** Discuss plant parts. Have students draw a plant using free-form shapes.

★ **Social Studies** Have students draw pictures to illustrate relative locations such as near, far, up, and down. Discuss how these words apply to *Free Fall*. For example, *down* tells the direction the boy is falling in *Free Fall*.

★ **Technology** Use the freehand tool in a paint program to draw a picture with free-form shapes. Visit **SRAonline.com** to print detailed instructions for this activity.

Reflect

Time: About 5 minutes

Review and Assess

"What kinds of things are free-form shapes?"
"¿Qué tipos de cosas son figuras abstractas?"

Think

Discuss the student art question. Students should point out various leaves in picture.

■ Identify free-form shapes in *Large Prints 3 Le Gourmet* and *4 Fruit Displayed on a Stand*.

Informal Assessment

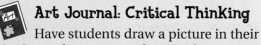 **Art Journal: Critical Thinking**
Have students draw a picture in their Art Journals to answer the Decide question.

 **Art Criticism**

Have students ask themselves the following questions.

Describe ▶ What shapes are your leaves? Are they curved? Slanted? Pointed?

Analyze ▶ Are all the shapes different? Are the shapes different sizes?

Interpret ▶ Do your leaf prints remind you of a tree full of leaves or a pile of raked leaves?

Decide ▶ Which leaf shape do you think is most interesting? Why?

■ For standardized-format test practice using this lesson's art content, see pages 22–23 in **Reading and Writing Test Preparation.**

Lesson 3 Wrap-Up

Free-Form Shapes

Focus

Use *Transparency 9* and *Large Prints 3 Le Gourmet* and *4 Fruit Displayed on a Stand.* Discuss how the artists used free-form shapes. Count the number of free-form shapes in the pictures.

Teach

Have the students tear paper to form free-form shapes to arrange in a collage.

Reflect

Have students use the four steps of art criticism to evaluate their work. Did they effectively use free-form shapes to create a collage?

Alternate Activity

Materials:
- 9″ × 12″ construction paper
- construction paper in various colors
- glue

1. Show students examples of shapes cut with scissors and shapes torn from paper. Ask them to describe the differences in these shapes. Help students see that the lines in torn paper shapes are not perfectly straight just like the lines in nature are not perfectly straight.

2. Demonstrate how to hold the paper and tear large and small shapes.

3. Have students tear shapes and arrange them to create an animal or place in nature.

4. Then have students glue their arrangements on the 9″ × 12″ paper.

NSAE 1.c

Research in Art Education

"The child's artistic responses in the early primary grades, reflecting the nuances of their world, are usually wonderfully fresh and disarmingly naive" (Kent, Robert, and Mark Luca, *Art Education: Strategies of Teaching.* New Jersey: Prentice Hall, 1968).

Assessment

Use the following rubric to evaluate the artwork students make in the Create activity and to assess students' understanding of free-form shapes.

Have students complete page 25 or 26 in their *Assessment* books.

	Art History and Culture	Aesthetic Perception	Creative Expression	Art Criticism
3 POINTS	The student recognizes that illustrators are artists.	The student accurately locates free-form shapes in artwork and in the environment.	The student's leaf prints clearly illustrate free-form shapes.	The student thoughtfully and honestly evaluates his or her own work using the four steps of art criticism.
2 POINTS	The student's recognition that illustrators are artists is weak or incomplete.	The student shows emerging awareness of free-form shapes.	The student's leaf prints show some awareness of free-form shapes.	The student attempts to evaluate his or her own work, but shows an incomplete understanding of evaluation criteria.
1 POINT	The student does not recognize that illustrators are artists.	The student does not locate free-form shapes in artwork or in the environment.	The student's leaf prints show no understanding of free-form shapes.	The student makes no attempt to evaluate his or her own artwork.

Assessment, p. 25

Name _____ Date _____

Free-Form Shapes

Lesson **3** UNIT 2

For the teacher: Use the following prompts for this activity.
1. Use a crayon or a pencil to draw an imaginary free-form shape in box 1.
2. Draw something you know and can see that is a free-form shape in box 2.

Level K — Unit 2 • An Introduction to Shape — 25

Lesson 4 Overview

More About Shapes

Lesson 4 provides additional instruction about geometric and free-form shapes. Students distinguish between these shapes and use them to create a drawing of their neighborhood.

Objectives

 Art History and Culture

To recognize that artists use geometric and free-form shapes in their works of art

 Creative Expression

To create a drawing of their house using geometric and free-form shapes

Aesthetic Perception

To locate geometric and free-form shapes in artwork and in the environment

Art Criticism

To evaluate one's own work using the four steps of art criticism

Vocabulary Reading

Review the following vocabulary words with students before beginning the lesson.

Geometric shape figura geométrica—a mathematical shape, such as a circle, square, rectangle, or triangle

free-form shape figura abstracta—an irregular and uneven shape, whose outline is curved, angular, or both.

See page 89B for additional vocabulary and Spanish vocabulary resources.

 Art Journal: Vocabulary

Have students add these words to the Vocabulary section of their Art Journals.

Lesson Materials

- write-over markers
- 12" × 18" paper (light-colored)
- large outline drawings of obvious shapes found in a classroom, such as a pencil, glue bottle, chair, table, book, and computer or television

Alternate Materials
- any drawing media

Program Resources

- *Reading and Writing Test Prep.*, pp. 24–25
- *Transparency 10*
- *Flash Cards 7–11*
- *Artist Profiles*, pp. 7, 42
- *Assessment*, pp. 27–28
- *Large Prints 3* Le Gourmet and *4 Fruit Displayed on a Stand*
- *The National Museum of Women in the Arts Collection*

Concept Trace
Geometric and Free-form Shapes
Introduced: Level K, Unit 2, Lessons 2 and 3

Reinforced: Level K, Unit 2, Lessons 4, 5, and 6
Level 1, Unit 2, Lessons 2 and 3

Lesson 4 Arts Integration

Theatre

Complete Unit 2, Lesson 4 on pages 42–43 of *Theatre Arts Connections.*

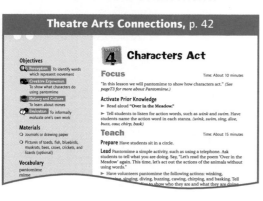

Music

 A piece of music suggests different ways to move. Separate the class into two groups. Have one group move to the song *Summertime* from *Porgy and Bess.* Freeze after 30 seconds. The other group can look for shapes in the students' bodies. Change groups. Use the song *I am the Very Model for a Modern Major General.* Were the shapes the same? Why or why not?

Movement & Dance

Give students specific verbal directions in guiding them to create geometric and free-form shapes. For example: four counts to create a circle on the floor, four counts to transition, four counts to create a twisted shape standing. Now reverse, using the twisted shape on the floor and the circle while standing.

Activate Prior Knowledge

"What do you like best about school?" "¿Qué es lo que más les gusta de la escuela?"

- Lead a discussion about the many things students see, do, and learn at school.

Using Literature ★ Reading

- Read *Billy and the Big New School* by Catherine and Lawrence Anholt. Encourage students to find geometric and free-form shapes in the illustrations.

Thematic Connection
Comparing and Contrasting ★ Reading

- **School:** Ask students to study the buildings in the pictures and describe how the schools are similar or different to their own school. Search for geometric and free-form shapes in your school.

Introduce the Art

Look

"Where are the children going in Allan Crite's painting? The title gives us a clue." "¿Adónde van los niños en la pintura de Allan Crite? El título nos da una pista".

Classify and Categorize ★ Reading

- The people in the paintings are free-form, organic shapes. What other things in the pictures are free-form shapes?

- The school building is a *rectangle*. Have students identify other geometric shapes in the paintings.

- Study how both artists used geometric and free-form shapes.

NSAE 4.a

 Art History and Culture

Share information from the Art History and Culture sections with students. Artists often describe their experiences through their art. Ask students to think about why these artists might have painted these pictures. Possible answers: The artists live near these schools. The artists were remembering when they went to school when they were little.

NSAE 4.a

 Web Connection

Visit **www.nmaa.si.edu/** for more information about the Smithsonian American Art Museum in Washington, D.C.

78 UNIT 2 • Shape

▲ **Allan Rohan Crite.** (American). *School's Out.* 1936.
••••••••••••••••••••••
Oil on canvas. $30\frac{1}{4} \times 36\frac{1}{8}$ inches (76.84 × 91.75 cm.). Smithsonian American Art Museum, Washington, D.C.

Look how you can find **geometric shapes** and **free-form shapes** outside.

 **Art History and Culture**

Sometimes artists create art to tell us about people and places they have seen.

78 Unit 2 • Lesson 4

 Art History and Culture

Allan Rohan Crite

Allan Rohan Crite (a´lən rō´ ən krīt)(1910–) is known for his paintings that document the lives of urban African Americans during the 1930s and 1940s in Boston, Massachusetts. He made a series of neighborhood paintings that showed African Americans in ordinary light, enjoying the usual pleasures of life.

See pages 16–21 and 24–25 for more about subject matter and art history.

Artist Profiles, p. 7

◄ Artist Profile ►
Allan Rohan Crite
b. 1910

Allan Rohan Crite (al´ ən rō´ ən krīt) was born in Plainfield, New Jersey. He moved to Boston the year he was born and has lived there ever since. He studied art at several Boston schools and earned degrees from the School of the Museum of Fine Arts, Boston, and Harvard University. During the Depression the government hired Crite and other African American artists to create paintings. This was the beginning of a long, successful career for Crite. He once said, "The business of art is communication, and the middle of that word is community. It is one story and one inheritance that we all share."

▲ **Ben Shahn.** (American).
World's Greatest Comics.
1946.
....
Tempera on panel. 35 × 48 inches
(88.9 × 121.92 cm.). Amon Carter
Museum, Fort Worth, Texas.

Study the pictures.

▶ Find different shapes in the paintings and name them.

Aesthetic Perception

Seeing Like an Artist Name a free-form shape you see. Trace the shape with your finger.

Study

▶ The windows, doorways, and buildings are rectangular.

▶ There are circular rings hanging from the swing set (in *World's Greatest Comics*).

▶ The young girl in the green dress near the middle of the street (in *School's Out*) is holding a circular-shaped object.

▶ The body parts of the people are made of many different free-form shapes.

▶ The trees and clouds are free-form shapes.

■ For more examples of genre art, see *The National Museum of Women in the Arts Collection.*

Art Journal: Concept

Have students draw in their Art Journals one geometric shape and one free-form shape.

Aesthetic Perception

Seeing Like an Artist Ask students to name things they use in school and identify the shapes as geometric or free-form.

Developing Visual Literacy Take students outside to study the school building and to observe the activity around the building. Ask them if their school is more like *School's Out* or *World's Greatest Comics*.
NSAE 3.a; 3.b

Art History and Culture

Ben Shahn

Ben Shahn (ben shän) (1899–1969) was born in Lithuania and moved to the United States with his family at age 8. In his teens he left school to work as an apprentice for a lithographer. His interest in letters and calligraphy was evident in his art throughout his career. A social realist, Shahn's paintings and prints often reflected his personal feelings about social and political issues. In his later years, Shahn focused on photography and painting murals.

See pages 16–21 and 24–25 for more about subject matter and art history.

Artist Profiles, p. 42

◆ Artist Profile ◆
Ben Shahn
1898-1969

Ben Shahn (ben shän) was born in Kovno, Lithuania, and immigrated with his parents to New York City when he was eight years old. His early education consisted primarily of studying passages from the Torah and copying its texts, which inspired his lifelong interest in lettering and the visual character of words. He furthered this interest through an apprenticeship with a lithographer and often used his artwork as an expression of his commitment to social justice. Shahn's political views and activism were also a primary element in his work, and his creations became some of the most widely collected works in America.

Web Connection

Browse the *Teachers and Family Guides* at **www.artmuseums.harvard.edu/Shahn/** to learn more about Ben Shahn's artwork.

 **Teach**

 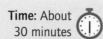

"Let's play a shapes game." "*Vamos a jugar un juego de figuras*".

Practice

Materials: large outline drawings of obvious shapes found in a classroom, such as a pencil, scissors, glue bottle, chair, table, book, and computer or television.

- Display visuals of the outlines of obvious shapes found in a classroom.

- Have students identify an object in the classroom that matches that shape as directed on page 80.

 **Creative Expression**

Materials: write-over markers, 12" × 18" drawing paper (light-colored)

Alternate Materials: any drawing tools

- Distribute the materials and have students follow the directions on page 81.

- Direct students to use geometric shapes to draw a real or imaginary house.

- Encourage them to fill the background space with free-form shapes from nature.

- Have students use write-over markers to color and decorate the drawing.

- Have students color the geometric and free-form shapes a solid color. Then add lines, patterns, and textures to the shapes.

- See the Activity Tips on page 236 for visual examples of this lesson's activity.

- Have students exhibit their art and express ideas about each other's work.

NSAE 1.a; 1.c

Art Journal: Brainstorming

Ask students to think about the shapes around them. Show students how to divide their journal page into two sections. Have students draw geometric shapes that they see around them on one half of the page and free-form shapes on the other half.

Using Geometric and Free-Form Shapes

You can find different shapes everywhere you look.

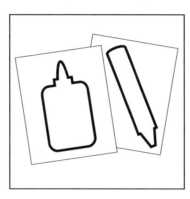

Practice

1. Look at the outlines of the objects.
2. Name the objects.

80 Unit 2 • Lesson 4

Differentiated Instruction

Reteach
Create cutout pairs of geometric and free-form shapes to use in a matching game. Have students identify the names of the shapes as they play.

Special Needs
Help students increase shape recognition by using pre-cut shapes with the name of the shape written on them during instruction.

ELL Tips
Write the terms *geometric shape* and *free-form shape* on the board. Have students say the terms and use them to identify paper cutouts or flash cards of geometric forms and pictures of free-form shapes.

▲ **Barbara Kipreos.**
Age 5.

Think about the different geometric and free-form shapes the student used.

How many geometric shapes and free-form shapes can you find?

1. Draw a picture of your house. Use geometric shapes.

2. Draw the background with free-form shapes from nature.

Analyze What geometric and free-form shapes did you use?

Art Across the Curriculum

Use these simple ideas to reinforce art concepts across the curriculum.

★ **Expository Writing** Have students draw pictures to explain what students, such as those in the pictures, learn at school.

★ **Math** Count the windows in pictures.

★ **Science** Draw a picture of how *School's Out* might look if it were a winter day.

★ **Social Studies** Have a discussion to identify the people who help students stay safe and healthy throughout the school day.

★ **Technology** Use a paint program to draw a picture with free-form and geometric shapes. Visit **SRAonline.com** to print detailed instructions for this activity.

Reflect

Time: About 5 minutes

Review and Assess

"In what way is a free-form shape different from a geometric shape?" "¿En qué se diferencia una figura abstracta de una geométrica?"

Think

■ Discuss the student art question. Possible answers: She used a triangle for the roof and girl's body and a square for the house and windows. The girl's face is a circle. The door is a rectangle. The animal on the tree, the tree top, and the design on the roof are free-form shapes.

■ Use **Large Prints 3** *Le Gourmet* and **4** *Fruit Displayed on a Stand* for more examples of geometric and free-form shapes.

Informal Assessment

Art Journal: Critical Thinking
Have students draw a picture in their Art Journals to answer the Analyze question.

Have students ask themselves the following questions.

Describe ► What parts of your house did you show in your picture?

Analyze ► What geometric and free-form shapes did you use?

Interpret ► What does your picture tell others about your house?

Decide ► Can the objects in your picture be identified by their shape?

NSAE 2.b; 5.a; 5.c

■ For standardized-format test practice using this lesson's art content, see pages 24–25 in **Reading and Writing Test Preparation.**

More About Shapes

 Extra! **For the Art Specialist**

Focus

Study **Large Prints 3** *Le Gourmet* and **4** *Fruit Displayed on a Stand* and look for free-form and geometric shapes. Direct the students to name all the objects that are made with free-form shapes and all the objects made with geometric shapes.

Teach

Ask the students to name a variety of pets. List their ideas on the board. Then ask students to think of the types of houses where these pets would live. For example, a dog might live in a dog house, a hamster in a cage, and a fish in a glass bowl or tank. Have students draw a pet and the house the pet lives in using free-form and geometric shapes.

Reflect

Have students use the four steps of art criticism to evaluate their work. Did they effectively use free-form and geometric shapes to draw a pet and its house?

Alternate Activity

Materials
- 9" × 12" white drawing paper or watercolor paper
- black permanent markers
- water container
- watercolor brushes
- tissue paper, cut or torn into squares

1. Ask the students to choose a pet and identify the shapes they would use to draw this animal and its house. Which shapes are free-form shapes? Which shapes are geometric shapes?

2. Have students use permanent markers to draw a pet in its home.

3. Next have students wet the paper and lay tissue squares on the paper. As the ink bleeds out of the tissue, it will color the paper.

4. Then students pick up the tissue square and move it to another place on the drawing. Continue this process until the paper is covered with color.

NSAE 1.a; 1.c

Research
in Art Education

One study demonstrated that students involved with the arts were "less likely to drop out of school, watched fewer hours of television, were less likely to report boredom in school, had a more positive self-concept, and were more involved in community service." These social and practical outcomes show the need to give all students a chance at arts involvement ("Involvement in the Arts and Success in Secondary School" in *Critical Links*, p. 68). As students think about their house and the shapes around it, encourage them to discuss how they could help make their community a better place to live.

Assessment

Use the following rubric to evaluate the artwork students make in the Create Expression activity and to assess students' understanding of geometric and free-form shapes.

Have students complete page 27 or 28 in their *Assessment* books.

	Art History and Culture	Aesthetic Perception	Creative Expression	Art Criticism
3 POINTS	The student recognizes that artists use geometric and free-form shapes to create works of art and can identify these shapes in fine art.	The student accurately locates geometric and free-form shapes in artwork and in his or her environment.	The student's drawing clearly illustrates geometric and free-form shapes.	The student thoughtfully and honestly evaluates his or her own work using the four steps of art criticism.
2 POINTS	The student shows emerging awareness that artists use geometric and free-form shapes to create works of art and can identify some shapes in fine art.	The student shows emerging awareness of geometric and free-form shapes.	The student's drawing shows some awareness of geometric and free-form shapes.	The student attempts to evaluate his or her own work, but shows an incomplete understanding of evaluation criteria.
1 POINT	The student cannot recognize that artists use geometric and free-form shapes to create works of art and cannot identify these shapes in fine art.	The student cannot locate geometric and free-form shapes in artwork or in his or her environment.	The student's drawing shows no understanding of geometric or free-form shapes.	The student does not attempt to evaluate his or her own artwork.

Assessment, p. 27

Name _____ Date _____

Lesson 4 UNIT 2

More About Shapes

For the teacher: Use the following prompts for this activity.
1. Use a crayon or a pencil to draw a free-form shape in box 1.
2. Draw a geometric shape in box 2.

Level K   Unit 2 • An Introduction to Shape   **27**

Lesson 5 · Overview

Body Shapes

Lesson 5 teaches students how to create a self-portrait using body parts.

Objectives

 Art History and Culture

To recognize that artists help us learn about different people and places

Creative Expression

To create a self-portrait using body shapes

 Aesthetic Perception

To recognize major body parts and note differences in sizes among parts

Art Criticism

To evaluate one's own work using the four steps of art criticism

Vocabulary Reading

Review the following vocabulary word with students before beginning the lesson.

free-form shape **figura abstracta**—an irregular and uneven shape whose outline is curved, angular, or both.

See page 89B for additional vocabulary and Spanish vocabulary resources.

Art Journal: Vocabulary

Have students add this word to the Vocabulary section of their Art Journals.

Lesson Materials
- colored markers
- 12″ × 18″ paper
- large mirror

Alternate Materials
- crayons

Program Resources
- *Reading and Writing Test Prep.*, pp. 26–27
- *Transparency 11*
- *Flash Cards 8* and *18*
- *Artist Profiles*, pp. 22, 23
- *Assessment*, pp. 29–30
- *Large Print 3* Le Gourmet
- *The National Museum of Women in the Arts Collection*

Concept Trace
Body Shapes
Introduced: Level K, Unit 2, Lesson 5

Reinforced: Level K, Unit 2, Lesson 6
Level 1, Unit 2, Lessons 4 and 5

Lesson 5 Arts Integration

Theatre

Complete Unit 2, Lesson 5 on pages 44–45 of *Theatre Arts Connections.*

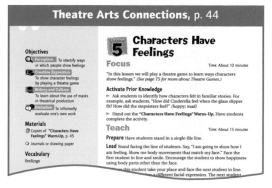

Music

 Sing and dance the *Hokey Pokey.* As you put a body part in, study it for the shapes it contains.

Movement & Dance

Create a movement sequence focused on body part isolations. Students make a large group circle, all standing with feet slightly apart. Instruct them to take eight counts to move each body part. Explore different movements. For example, heads can roll smoothly, shoulders can lift and lower sharply, arms can swing forward and back or side-to-side, and feet can stomp.

Focus

Activate Prior Knowledge

"A picture of you is called a portrait." "Un dibujo de ustedes se llama un retrato".

- Explain that a portrait is often an image of only the face and upper body, and a self-portrait is your own portrayal of yourself.

Using Literature 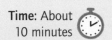 Reading

Read *My Friends* by Taro Gomi. Ask students to identify body parts in the illustrations.

Thematic Connection

Feelings: Ask students to describe how the people are feeling in the fine art pictures. How do the students know the people are feeling that way?

Introduce the Art

Look

"This is a portrait by William H. Johnson called *Li'l Sis.*" "Éste es un retrato hecho por William Johnson titulado *Li'l Sis*".

Main Idea and Details Reading

- Ask students to describe what is happening in the painting.

Comparing and Contrasting Reading

- Compare the shape of the baby's body to the girl's body. Did the artist use some of the same shapes in the baby's body as in the little girl's?

Bodies Have Parts Science

- Ask students to point to body parts on the girl and the baby, and name them.

NSAE 4.a

Art History and Culture

Share information from the Art History and Culture sections with students. Discuss who and where the people in the paintings could be. Possible answers: The girl in Johnson's painting appears to be the big sister of the baby in the carriage. She might be taking her little sister for a walk in her neighborhood. The people in the Lawrence painting might be friends or siblings. They look like they are outside in a big field.

NSAE 4.a

Web Connection

Visit **www.nmaa.si.edu/** to find more works of art by William H. Johnson.

Body Shapes

Look at both works of art. The artists used shapes to show body parts. Body parts have many different shapes.

◄ **William H. Johnson.** (American). *Li'l Sis.* 1944.

Oil on paperboard. 26 × 21¼ inches (66.04 × 53.98 cm.). Smithsonian American Art Museum, Washington, D.C.

Art History and Culture

The art of both artists helps us learn about the history of African Americans.

Art History and Culture

William H. Johnson

William H. Johnson (wil´ yəm h jän´ sən) (1901–1970) was an African American painter. He was born in South Carolina, but he later moved to New York and Paris to study art. Johnson began his art career as a realist but later practiced expressionism in Europe. After returning to the United States he developed a primitive, simple style.

See pages 16–21 and 24–25 for more about subject matter and art history.

Artist Profiles, p. 22

Artist Profile

William H. Johnson
1901–1970

William Johnson (wil´ yəm jän[t]´ sən) was born in Florence, South Carolina. When he was young, a teacher saw him drawing in the dirt with a stick. She gave him pencils and encouraged him to draw more pictures. At age 17, Johnson went to New York to study art. While there he won many prizes. A teacher collected money so that Johnson could go to Paris, France, in 1926 to study art.

In the late 1930s, Johnson and his wife returned to the United States. For a time he worked as a teacher, and in the early 1940s, he worked for the Works Progress Administration (WPA). The WPA was a

▲ **Jacob Lawrence.**
(American) *Harriet Tubman Series #4.*
1939-1940.
....
Casein tempera on gessoed
hardboard, Hampton
University Art Museum,
Hampton, Virginia.

Study the pictures.

▶ Name the body parts you see
in the pictures.

Aesthetic Perception

Seeing Like an Artist Is your hand a free-form
shape or a geometric shape?

Art History and Culture

Jacob Lawrence

Jacob Lawrence (jā´ kəb lär´ ənz) (1917–2000) was raised in Harlem
in New York City. He attended the Harlem Art Workshop and won a
scholarship to the American Artists School. Lawrence's paintings
are known not only for contributing to the art world, but also for
adding to our knowledge of African American history. His paintings
often depict the struggle for freedom and justice for African-
Americans in the United States. Lawrence was the first African
American artist to receive sustained mainstream recognition in the
United States.

See pages 16–21 and 24–25
for more about subject
matter and art history.

Artist Profiles, p. 23

◄ Artist Profile ►
Jacob Lawrence
1917-2000
Jacob Lawrence (jā´ kəb lär´ ənz) had
parents who met on their migration to
the North. His father was born in South
Carolina, and his mother in Virginia.
Lawrence was born in Atlantic City, New
Jersey, in 1917. The family finally settled
in Harlem in 1929 at the end of the Harlem
Renaissance. Because his mother worked
all day, she enrolled Lawrence in the Harlem
Art Workshop after school to keep him out
of trouble. He had many excellent teachers
there, including Charles Alston. Lawrence
won a scholarship to the American Artists
School. He taught at New York's Pratt
Institute from 1958 to 1965. From 1970, he
taught at the University of Washington in
Seattle, where he also served as head of the

Study

▶ Possible answers include arms, shoulders,
elbows, hands, fingers, legs, knees, feet,
toes, back, stomach, chest, neck, head,
eyes, ears, nose, and mouth.

■ For more examples of portraits, see *The
National Museum of Women in the Arts
Collection.*

Art Journal: Concept
Have students draw pictures of free-
form body shapes, such as legs or hands.

Aesthetic Perception

Seeing Like an Artist Have students study
their hands and determine if they are free-
form or geometric shapes. Students can trace
their hands as a way to check their answers.

Developing Visual Literacy Ask students to
describe the mood of each picture. "What did
each artist do to create this mood?"

Web Connection
Visit **www.jacoblawrence.org/** or
www.whitney.org/jacoblawrence/ to find out
more about Jacob Lawrence and his exhibitions.
NSAE 5.a; 5.c

**each** Time: About 30 minutes

"Let's talk about the shapes of our bodies."
"Hablemos de las figuras de nuestros cuerpos".

Practice

■ Have students trace with their fingers the shape of their heads, and then trace the outside edge of their shoes or feet as directed on page 84.

■ Discuss the variety of free-form, organic shapes that can be used to show different parts of the body.

Creative Expression

Materials: 12" × 18" paper, colored markers, large mirror

Alternate Materials: crayons

■ See page 215 in Technique Tips for information about drawing with markers.

■ Distribute the materials and have students follow the directions on page 85.

■ Allow students to view themselves in a mirror. Encourage them to observe the shapes of their body parts and the relationship of body parts to each other.

■ Guide students to fill the page with their self-portraits.

■ Encourage students to draw and color the clothes they are wearing and to add details such as hair and glasses.

■ Students might add a favorite toy or other small thing to their self-portraits to indicate something personal about themselves.

■ See the Activity Tips on page 237 for visual examples of this lesson's activity.

NSAE 1.a; 1.c

Art Journal: Brainstorming

Encourage students to think about how they would pose if someone were painting their portrait. Discuss different poses and possible ways to position arms and legs for a portrait. Have students sketch possible poses in their Art Journal.

Using Free-Form Shapes

All body parts are **free-form shapes.**

Practice

1. Use your finger to trace around your head.

2. Trace around your foot. How is its shape different from your head?

84   Unit 2 • Lesson 5

Differentiated Instruction

Reteach
Play "Simon Says" with the students. "Simon says touch your arm. Simon says touch your leg."

Special Needs
Help to foster students' body awareness by having a long mirror in the classroom for the introduction to this lesson. One at a time, have students come to the mirror and trace with their hands the free-form shapes they see.

ELL Tips
Display a simple outline picture of a person standing. Identify with students the body parts (head, arm, leg, and so on), and then label them. Also have students decide if a particular body part is a geometric or free-form shape.

Think about the kinds of free-form shapes this student used in her drawing.

◀ **Stephanie Gowdy.** Age 6.

 Creative Expression

How many free-form shapes does your body have?

1. Draw a big picture of yourself. Fill the entire sheet of paper.
2. Show how you look today. Draw the clothes you are wearing.

 **Art Criticism**

Describe What shapes did you use to create your self-portrait?

Art Across the Curriculum

Use these simple ideas to reinforce art concepts across the curriculum.

★ **Persuasive Writing** Draw a picture of how you would look if you were trying to persuade your teacher to take you outside for recess.

★ **Math** Identify examples of the relationship of objects in the paintings. For example, in *Li'l Sis* the girl is **in front of** the doll buggy. In *Harriet Tubman Series Number 4,* the person wearing red is **next to** the person wearing light blue. Also use words such as *on, behind, under,* and *above.*

★ **Science** Name the major body parts and identify the function of each part.

★ **Social Studies** Discuss how the girl in *Li'l Sis* is taking care of the child. Ask students to tell you about something they take care of (pet, baby sibling, toys, plants, and so on). Have students draw a picture that shows them taking care of something.

★ **Technology** Have students use a paint program to draw a self-portrait. Visit **SRAonline.com** to print detailed instructions for this activity.

Reflect

Review and Assess

"Are most body parts geometric shapes or free-form shapes?" "¿Tienen figura geométrica o abstracta la mayoría de las partes del cuerpo?"

Think

■ Discuss the student art question. Students might mention the head and neck, the hair, the upper body and arms, the legs, the hands, and the facial features.

■ Identify geometric and free-form shapes in *Large Print 3 Le Gourmet.*

Informal Assessment

Art Journal: Critical Thinking
Have students draw a picture in their Art Journals to answer the Describe question.

 Art Criticism

Have students ask themselves the following questions.

Describe ▶ What shapes did you use to create your self-portrait?

Analyze ▶ Are the shapes all the same size? Are the clothing shapes the same as the body shapes?

Interpret ▶ Does your self-portrait look like you? What does your picture tell about you?

Decide ▶ Did you use more geometric or free-form shapes?

NSAE 2.b; 5.a; 5.c

■ For standardized-format test practice using this lesson's art content, see pages 26–27 in *Reading and Writing Test Preparation.*

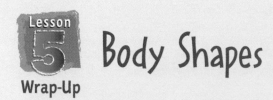

Lesson 5 Wrap-Up

Body Shapes

Extra! For the Art Specialist

Time: About 30 minutes

Focus

Use *Transparency 11* and *Large Print 3 Le Gourmet*. Ask students to look for body shapes. How are body shapes and free-form shapes the same? How are these shapes different?

Teach

Ask students to describe the free-form shapes that make up the body. Trace the students' bodies onto large paper and have the students add details.

Reflect

Have students use the four steps of art criticism to evaluate their work. Did they effectively use free-form shapes to draw their self-portraits?

Alternate Activity

Materials
- roll paper 36" wide
- pencils
- tempera paint
- paint brushes
- water containers
- paper towels

1. Ask students to look at their hands, arms, feet, and legs. Discuss how people wear clothes to protect and cover most of their body.

2. Ask the students to think of their favorite clothing. Is it a special outfit, or uniform, or a costume?

3. Direct the students to lie on a long sheet of roll paper. Trace around their body shape.

4. Invite the students to add their favorite clothes to the drawing. Include eyes, nose, mouth, and hair to complete the drawing.

5. Have students paint their drawing with tempera paint.

NSAE 1.a; 1.c

Research in Art Education

"Talk about art, or art criticism, is probably one of the ways we share the contents of our inner lives without embarrassment. Art criticism is very much like teaching: it is the sharing of discoveries about art, or in some cases about life, where art has its ultimate source" (Hurwitz, Al, and Stanley Madeja. *The Joyous Vision.* New Jersey: Prentice Hall, 1997).

Assessment

Use the following rubric to evaluate the artwork students make in the Creative Expression activity and to assess students' understanding of body shapes.

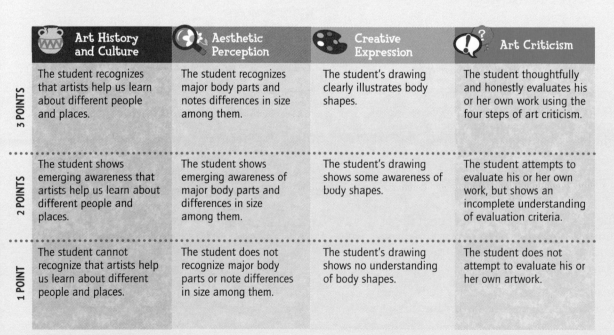

	Art History and Culture	Aesthetic Perception	Creative Expression	Art Criticism
3 POINTS	The student recognizes that artists help us learn about different people and places.	The student recognizes major body parts and notes differences in size among them.	The student's drawing clearly illustrates body shapes.	The student thoughtfully and honestly evaluates his or her own work using the four steps of art criticism.
2 POINTS	The student shows emerging awareness that artists help us learn about different people and places.	The student shows emerging awareness of major body parts and differences in size among them.	The student's drawing shows some awareness of body shapes.	The student attempts to evaluate his or her own work, but shows an incomplete understanding of evaluation criteria.
1 POINT	The student cannot recognize that artists help us learn about different people and places.	The student does not recognize major body parts or note differences in size among them.	The student's drawing shows no understanding of body shapes.	The student does not attempt to evaluate his or her own artwork.

Have students complete page 29 or 30 in their *Assessment* books.

Assessment, p. 29

Name _____ Date _____

Lesson 5 UNIT 2

Body Shapes

For the teacher: Use the following prompts for this activity.
1. Use a crayon or a pencil to trace your hand with your fingers together in box 1.
2. Draw the shape of your hand without tracing it in box 2. The shapes should be similar.

Level K   Unit 2 • An Introduction to Shape   **29**

 Lesson
6
Overview

The Shape of People

Lesson 6 teaches how to show different-sized body parts to create different-sized people.

Objectives

 Art History and Culture

To recognize that artists from the same period use different materials and styles to tell stories about families

 Creative Expression

To create a family portrait using different-sized body shapes

 Aesthetic Perception

To compare sizes of body shapes in relation to sizes of people

Art Criticism

To evaluate one's own work using the four steps of art criticism

Vocabulary 🌟 Reading

Review the following vocabulary word with students before beginning the lesson.

shape figura—a two-dimensional area that is defined in some way. While a form has depth, a shape has only height and width.

See page 89B for additional vocabulary and Spanish vocabulary resources.

 Art Journal: Vocabulary

Have students add this word to the Vocabulary section of their Art Journals.

Lesson Materials

- 12″ × 18″ drawing paper
- markers (multicultural colors)
- patterned papers or wall paper samples
- glue sticks
- an assortment of objects ranging in size from small to large (such as a golf ball, a baseball, and a basketball)

Alternate Materials
- any drawing media

Program Resources
- *Reading and Writing Test Prep.,* pp. 28–29
- *Transparency 12*
- *Flash Cards 8* and *18*
- *Artist Profiles,* pp. 3, 38
- *Assessment,* pp. 31–32
- *Large Print 3 Le Gourmet*
- *The National Museum of Women in the Arts Collection*

Concept Trace
Body Shapes
Introduced: Level K, Unit 2, Lesson 5

Reinforced: Level K, Unit 2, Lesson 6
Level 1, Unit 2, Lessons 4 and 5

Lesson 6 Arts Integration

Theatre

Complete Unit 2, Lesson 6 on pages 46–51 of *Theatre Arts Connections.*

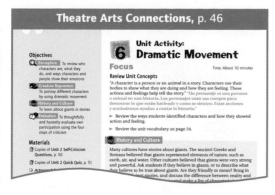

Music

 We can use our voice and suggest the three sizes of bears in the story *The Three Bears.* Choose one classroom instrument to accompany the three characters. Tell the story using the largest instrument with each syllable of Papa Bear, the middle-sized instrument with Mama Bear, and a tiny-sized instrument for Baby Bear.

Movement & Dance

Identify the three levels of low, middle, and high. Look around the classroom and identify objects at these different levels. Students then create specific geometric shapes with their bodies choosing one for each level. Now create a free form shape using their bodies, at each level. Use words to assist in creating free form shapes for example, twist, bend, and reach.

 **ocus**

 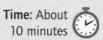

Activate Prior Knowledge

"Has anyone taken a photograph of your family?" "¿Alguien ha fotografiado a su familia?"

- Encourage students to share a picture-taking experience. Was everyone smiling?

Using Literature ⭐ Reading

Read *JoJo's Flying Side Kick,* written and illustrated by Brian Pinkney. Have students find people of different sizes in the illustrations.

Thematic Connection

Family Customs and Traditions ⭐ Social Studies

Families: Encourage students to discuss their family customs and traditions.

Introduce the Art

Look

"Let's look at the paintings of the families."
"Miremos las pinturas de las familias".

Drawing Conclusions ⭐ Reading

- Who is the youngest in each picture? Who is the oldest? How can you tell?

- How do the sizes of the heads change as people get older? How do the shapes on their faces change as they get older?

Main Idea and Details ⭐ Reading

- What kind of details did the artists use?

NSAE 4.a

🏺 Art History and Culture

Share information from the Art History and Culture sections with students. Ask students to describe what the people are doing in each picture and how the artists created the people differently. Possible answers: *Father and Daughter* has busy, colorful designs on the clothing, walls, and floor. *Family* has mostly solid colors with bold, thick lines. The people in *Father and Daughter* look like they are dancing. The people in *Family* are calm and still.

NSAE 4.a

💻 **Web Connection**

Explore collage at The National Gallery of Art's site for children by visiting **www.nga.gov/kids/kids.htm**.

The Shape of People

Look at these works of art. The people are all different sizes. Some people are big. Some people are small.

◀ **Miriam Schapiro.** (Canadian American). *Father and Daughter.* 1997.
Acrylic and fabric on canvas. 72 × 60 inches (182.88 × 152.4 cm.). Private collection.

🏺 Art History and Culture

Artists have different ways of showing people in their works of art. What are the people doing in these works of art?

🏺 Art History and Culture

Miriam Schapiro

Miriam Schapiro [mir´ ē əm shə pir´ ō] (1923–   ) created abstract expressionist art in the beginning of her career. In the 1950s she began to include feminist themes in her work. Schapiro was very involved in the feminist art movement of the early 1970s. Schapiro created her own style called *femmage,* in which she combined commonplace hand-sewn work by women, such as quilting needlework, with canvas and acrylic paint to create multi-layered compositions.

See pages 16–21 and 24–25 for more about subject matter and art history.

Artist Profiles, p. 38

Artist Profile
Miriam Schapiro
b. 1923
Miriam Schapiro (mir´ē am sha pir´ō) is an American artist who was born in Toronto, Canada. She grew up in the Flatbush section of Brooklyn, New York. Her parents encouraged her pursuit of a career in art and sent her to art classes at the Museum of Modern Art. She met her husband, artist Paul Brach, while attending college. They married in 1946 and have a son who is a writer. Schapiro organizes her home life so that art is woven into it. She can move from baking in the kitchen to painting in her studio and back to the kitchen without feeling interrupted. Her husband says that she has learned to live a "seamless life."

◀ **Romare Bearden.**
(American). *Family.* 1988.
· ·
Collage on wood. 28 × 20 inches
(71.12 × 50.8 cm.). Smithsonian
American Art Museum,
Washington, D.C.

Study the pictures.

▶ Point to the smallest person in each picture.

▶ Point to the biggest person in each picture.

Aesthetic Perception

Seeing Like an Artist Who is the tallest person in the room?

Study

▶ Students should identify the daughter in *Father and Daughter* as the smallest person in the picture, and the father as the biggest.

▶ The baby being held in *Family* is the smallest in the picture, and the man or woman sitting down is the biggest.

■ For more examples of genre art, see *The National Museum of Women in the Arts Collection.*

Art Journal: Concept
Have students draw rectangles of different sizes in their Art Journals to represent each member of their families.

Aesthetic Perception

Seeing Like An Artist Ask students to stand and look around the room to determine who the tallest person is.

Developing Visual Literacy Encourage students to discuss the main idea of each picture. What was the artist trying to show us?

Art History and Culture

Romare Bearden

Romare Bearden (rō mâr´ bēr´ dən) (1911–1988) focused on his career as an artist much later than many of his contemporaries. Not until after studying math at New York University did he focus his attention on studying art. Much of Bearden's work was influenced by African American life and his distinguished artist, intellectual, and musician friends. Bearden was well known for his collages that combined painting and photographs.

See pages 16–21 and 24–25 for more about subject matter and art history.

Artist Profiles, p. 3

┌ Artist Profile ▶ ─
Romare Bearden
1911–1988
· · · · · · · · · · · · · · · · · · ·
Romare Bearden (rō mar´ bēr dən) was born in North Carolina. His family moved to Harlem in New York City when he was three years old. His family's home became a meeting place for artists, writers, and musicians during the Harlem Renaissance. Bearden studied math, not the arts, in college, but he worked as a cartoonist and illustrator to pay for it. When he was 21, he decided to become a professional artist. Over the years, Bearden studied art in New York City and Paris, France. He also worked as a social worker, served in the army, and wrote several songs and books. Bearden was known as a warmhearted, friendly man.

Web Connection
Visit **www.beardenfoundation.org/** to find out more about Romare Bearden.

Teach

Time: About 30 minutes

"Let's sort objects according to size, and then let's draw the different-sized shapes of those objects." "Vamos a clasificar los objetos de acuerdo con su tamaño y luego vamos a dibujar las figuras de diferentes tamaños de esos objetos".

■ Have students classify objects according to size.

Practice

Materials: an assortment of objects ranging in size from small to large

■ Have students classify the items according to size as directed on page 88.

■ Explain that students can draw different-sized shapes to show different-sized objects.

Creative Expression

Materials: 12" × 18" drawing paper, markers (multicultural colors), patterned papers or wallpaper samples, glue sticks

Alternate Materials: any drawing media

■ Direct the students to close their eyes and imagine the people in their family. Who is the tallest? Who is the smallest? What is each person wearing?

■ Using patterned paper or wallpaper samples, students cut shapes to be the people's clothing.

■ Have students arrange and glue the shapes on a sheet of drawing paper.

■ Then have students use markers to add heads, arms, and legs to the paper shapes.

■ Distribute the materials and have the students follow the directions on page 89.

■ See the Activity Tips on page 237 for visual examples of this lesson's activity.

NSAE 1.a; 1.c

Art Journal: Brainstorming

Have students draw a quick sketch of their family showing how the people in their family are different sizes.

Using Shapes to Create People

The **shapes** used to draw people are different sizes.

Practice

1. Sort the objects by size.

2. Draw shapes that are the same sizes as the objects.

Differentiated Instruction

Reteach
Divide students into groups of five. Have each group arrange themselves from the tallest to the shortest. Let the other groups decide whether each order is correct.

Special Needs
Have students bring in a picture of their family as a visual reference for this activity.

ELL Tips
Display pictures showing the full body of three people of different height. Have students point to the smallest, largest, and in-between sizes of arms, legs, and heads shown. Say the names of the body parts with students.

Think about who each person in the
picture might be.

How many different people sizes
do you have in your family?

1. Think about the size of people
   in your family.
2. Cut out different size shapes to
   show the people in your
   family.
3. Arrange the shapes on your
   paper.

Decide Do you think
your family members will
recognize themselves in
your portrait? Why?

Unit 2 • Lesson 6   **89**

Art Across the Curriculum

Use these simple ideas to reinforce art concepts across the curriculum.

★ **Narrative Writing** Have students draw a picture that illustrates
one of their family traditions. Then have students tell the class
about what is happening in their pictures.

★ **Math** Have students select an individual shape from the fine art
and draw it in graduated sizes.

★ **Science** Show the students pictures of baby and adult animals.
Discuss how they have similar body shapes in different sizes, just as
adult people and children do.

★ **Social Studies** Discuss how life for the people in the fine art
pictures might be the same and different from what the students
experience.

★ **Technology** Use a paint program to draw a family portrait. Visit
SRAonline.com to print detailed instructions for this activity.

Reflect   Time: About 5 minutes

Review and Assess
"What kinds of shapes did you use to show
your family?" "¿Qué tipos de figuras usaron
para mostrar a sus familias?"

Think

Discuss the student art question. Possible
answers: The tall man is the father, the tall
woman is the mother, one child is the artist
and the other child is her sister or brother.

■ Identify body shapes in **Large Print 3**
Le Gourmet.

Informal Assessment

Art Journal: Critical Thinking
Have students answer the Decide
question by writing *Yes* or *No* in their Art
Journals. Discuss why they answered the
way they did.

Have students ask themselves the following
questions.

Describe ▶ How many people did you
draw in your portrait? What
are they wearing?

Analyze ▶ Where are the free-form
shapes in your family
portrait? Who has the
smallest shape? The
largest? Where are you in
the family portrait?

Interpret ▶ Why did you use the
different-sized shapes and
colors for each member?

Decide ▶ Do you think family
members will recognize
themselves in your
portrait? Why?

NSAE 2.b; 5.a; 5.c

■ For standardized-format test practice
using this lesson's art content, see pages
28–29 in **Reading and Writing Test**
Preparation.

Lesson 6 Wrap-Up
The Shape of People

Extra! For the Art Specialist

Time: About 30 minutes

Focus

Use **Transparency 12** and **Large Print 3** *Le Gourmet*. Ask students to look for body shapes. How did the artist use size and place to tell us about this person?

Teach

Discuss activities that happen on a playground. Have students use chalk and oil pastels to make a drawing of a playground.

Reflect

Have students use the four steps of art criticism to evaluate their work. Did they effectively show various body shapes and sizes in their drawings?

Alternate Activity

Materials
- 12" x 18" light blue construction paper
- chalk
- oil pastels

1. Ask students to think of being on the playground at your school. What are the students doing? Are they playing jump rope, running, laughing, or sitting together? Are all the students the same age? Are they the same size?

2. Have students use chalk to make a drawing of the playground by using their imaginations. If possible, take the students outside to sketch each other on the playground.

3. Then have students use oil pastels to color their chalk drawings.

NSAE 1.a; 1.c

Research in Art Education

"The making of art is an essential activity for elementary children. They need and want hands-on experiences in this 'other language.' Art lessons must include cycles of experiences with basic media and techniques, allowing students to acquire and then build upon skills fundamental to creative expression" (Kay Alexander, "Art Curricula by and for Art Educators," in *Art Education: Elementary* ed. Andra Johnson [1992]).

Assessment

Use the following rubric to evaluate the artwork students make in the Creative Expression activity and to assess students' understanding of different-sized body shapes.

Have students complete page 31 or 32 in their **Assessment** books.

	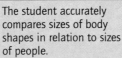 Art History and Culture	Aesthetic Perception	Creative Expression	Art Criticism
3 POINTS	The student recognizes that artists from the same period use different materials and styles to tell stories about families.	The student accurately compares sizes of body shapes in relation to sizes of people.	The student's family portrait clearly illustrates various sizes of body shapes.	The student thoughtfully and honestly evaluates his or her own work using the four steps of art criticism.
2 POINTS	The student shows emerging awareness that artists from the same period use different materials and styles to tell stories about families.	The student shows emerging awareness of sizes of body shapes in relation to sizes of people.	The student's family portrait shows some awareness of various sizes of body shapes.	The student attempts to evaluate his or her own work, but shows an incomplete understanding of evaluation criteria.
1 POINT	The student does not recognize that artists from the same period use different materials and styles to tell stories about families.	The student does not accurately compare sizes of body shapes in relation to sizes of people.	The student's family portrait shows no understanding of various sizes of body shapes.	The student does not attempt to evaluate his or her own artwork.

Assessment, p. 31

Name _____ Date _____

The Shape of People

Lesson **6** UNIT 2

For the teacher: Use the following prompt for this activity.
Use a crayon to draw a series of five different geometric shapes from small to large in the box.

Level K

Unit 2 • An Introduction to Shape   **31**

Vocabulary Review

circle círculo—

free-form shape—an irregular and uneven shape whose outline is curved, angular, or both **figura abstracta**—una figura irregular y desigual en que su contorno es curvado, angular o ambos

geometric shape—a mathematical shape, such as a circle, square, rectangle, or triangle **figura geométrica**—una figura matemática, como un círculo, cuadrado rectángulo o triángulo

outline—a line that shows or creates the outer edges of a shape **contorno**—una línea que muestra o crea los bordes exteriores de una figura

rectangle rectángulo—

shape—a two-dimensional area that is defined in some way. While a form has depth, a shape has only height and width. **figura**—un área bidimensional que se define en alguna manera. Mientras una forma tiene profundidad, una figura tiene solamente altura y ancho

square cuadrado—

triangle triángulo—

Vocabulary Practice

 Display *Transparency 38* to review unit vocabulary words.

Context Clues Vocabulary
Have students complete sentences using the vocabulary words from this unit. For example: A square is a geometric _____.

Word Games Vocabulary
Play "I Spy" using the vocabulary words and items in the classroom. For example: "I spy a circle" or "I spy a free-form shape."

Examples Vocabulary
Show students pictures and objects to illustrate the meanings of the vocabulary words, such as examples of free-form shapes and geometric shapes.

Art Criticism

Critical Thinking Art Criticism is an organized system for looking at and talking about art. You can criticize art without being an expert. The purpose of art criticism is to get the viewer involved in a perception process that delays judgment until all aspects of the artwork have been studied.

■ See pages 28–29 for more about art criticism.

Describe

▶ Ask students to describe what the people are doing. Possible answers: The man is playing a guitar while sitting in a chair. His right foot is wrapped around the chair leg. A woman is resting her feet on the arm of a sofa. The two young people are standing, facing each other in a doorway.

▶ Ask the students how many people they see in *Big Blues Man II*. Possible answers: There are four people. We see a man's back, a woman's feet and skirt, and two young people.

▶ Discuss what is in the background. Possible answers: Part of the background is dark. The other part, the open doorway, is blue with small light circles and dots.

Analyze

▶ Ask students to find some geometric shapes. Possible answers: The guitar neck is represented by a thin and thick rectangle joined together. The chair back has two thin rectangles. The background seems to be divided into two rectangles.

▶ Discuss where they see free-form shapes. Possible answers: The man's body and the woman's feet are free-form shapes. Her skirt is a free-form shape. The people in the background, the man's hat, and the sofa arm are also free-form shapes.

▶ Where do students see lines that outline shapes? Possible answers: The shapes of the young people are outlined. The woman's skirt and feet and the guitar are outlined in white.

90 UNIT 2 • Shape

▲ **Leo Twiggs.** (American). *Big Blues Man II.* 1993.
• •
Batik painting on cotton. 24 × 19 inches (60.96 × 48.26 cm.). Private collection.

90   Unit 2

Art History and Culture

Leo Twiggs

Leo Twiggs (lē´ ō twigs) (1934–   ) was born and raised in the low country of South Carolina. He has enjoyed blues music all his life and began watching blues performers from the time he was young. These masterful storytellers were his inspiration for *Big Blues Man II*.

Twiggs studied art at numerous schools, including New York University, where he studied under African American artist Hale Woodruff. Twiggs credits Woodruff with teaching him about color and composition that have become the foundation of his work.

See pages 16–21 and 24–25 for more about subject matter and art history.

Artist Profiles, p. 51

Artist Profile ●

Leo Twiggs
b. 1934

Leo Twiggs (lē´ ō twigs) often draws from his experiences as a youth in South Carolina to produce his artwork. He has a doctorate of art from the University of Georgia and has won numerous awards and recognitions from organizations around the United States. Twiggs's accomplishments in teaching art to disadvantaged African American students earned him the title "Outstanding Young Man of America" in 1970. He is also the first visual artist to receive the Governor's Trophy for outstanding contribution to the arts in South Carolina.

 **Art Criticism** Critical Thinking

Describe

► What are the people doing?

Analyze

► What geometric shapes do you see in the painting? What free-form shapes do you see?

Interpret

► Who do you think are the other people with the Blues Man in the painting?

Decide

► Did this painting tell you a story?

Interpret

► Ask students to explain what is happening in this picture and who they think these people are. Possible answers: Some might say this is after supper and the man is the father playing music for the family. Some might say a friend is visiting.

► Discuss where the people in this painting are. Possible answer: Because the bare feet on the sofa indicate the woman is lying down or at least reclining comfortably, students may guess that the people are in a home.

► Encourage students to think about what these people did before this scene and what will happen next. Possible answers: Students may invent a variety of stories about the people in this scene. This would be a good time to have the students act out their stories about this painting.

Decide

► Ask students if this painting tells them a story. Possible answer: Some students might make up a story that comes to mind when looking at this painting.

NSAE 5.a; 5.c

Art Journal: Writing
Have students draw a picture in their Art Journals to answer the Interpret question. Discuss the other questions aloud.

 Aesthetic Perception

Critical Thinking Show students a guitar or other instrument.

Describe ► Point to and name the kinds of lines you see on the instrument.

Analyze ► Are any of these lines the same as the lines you saw in *Big Blues Man II*?

Interpret ► How does music make you feel?
► Does all music make you feel the same way?

Decide ► Do you like this kind of instrument?
► Why or why not?

"Artists use different kinds of lines in their artworks." "Los artistas usan diferentes tipos de líneas en sus obras de arte".

T Review unit vocabulary with students using *Transparency 38.*

► Review the different types of geometric and free-form shapes.

► Have students name geometric and free-form shapes they see in the classroom.

► Ask students to identify shapes that they see every day and what the shapes mean. (Examples: a stop sign, a traffic light, a clock.) Is the shape geometric or free-form?

Art Journal: Writing
Read the questions on page 92 to students. Have students write their answers in their Art Journals or on a separate sheet of paper. 1. A, 2. A, 3. B.

T For further assessment, have students complete the unit test on *Transparency 44.*

CAREERS IN ART
Illustration

► Shows students examples of illustrations from children's books, catalogs, and various food products.

► Discuss how illustrating is an occupation just like others with which they may be familiar.

► Have students make a drawing to illustrate their favorite story or poem. Then have students create a drawing as an advertisement for a product.

"Art is an extension of language--an expression of sensations too subtle for words."
            —Robert Henri

Show What You Know

Answer these questions on a separate sheet of paper.

❶ Which of these is a geometric shape?

A.   B.

❷ Which of these is a free-form shape?

A.   B.

❸ What kind of shapes are body parts?
A. geometric
B. free-form

92   Unit 2

Unit Assessment Options

Aesthetic Perception

Practice Show students classroom objects and have them identify the shapes as geometric or free-form. If geometric, ask students to name the shape.

Creative Expression

Student Portfolio Have students review all the artwork they have created during this unit and select the pieces they wish to put into their portfolios. Have students share their portfolios with classmates and comment constructively about the art.
NSAE 5.a; 5.c

Art Criticism

Activity Have students select their favorite work of art from the unit. Guide students through study of their selected work using the four steps of art criticism. (See pages 28–29 for more about Art Criticism.)

CAREERS IN ART
Illustrator

Some artists create pictures to help us understand what we are reading.

Children's book illustrators draw pictures to help us understand what is happening in stories.

Advertising illustrators draw pictures of items that are for sale. They draw pictures for things like catalogs and food packages.

▲ **Book Illustrator**

Shape in Dance

Jerry Duke creates dances. His dancers make lots of circles. His dancers sometimes work with puppets.

What to Do Create circle shapes and forms.

1. Draw five circles of different sizes.
2. Make circles with your body.
3. Make circles with a partner.
4. Make a circle with a group.
5. Do a circle dance.

▲ AMAN International Folk Ensemble: "Suite of Appalachian Music and Dance."

 Art Criticism

 **Analyze** How did you create circular shapes with a partner?

 ## Art History and Culture

Appalachian Folk Music and Dance

AMAN International Folk Ensemble was founded in 1964 to research, preserve, and present the traditional dance, music, and folklore of ethnic groups residing in America. *The Suite of Appalachian Music and Dance* is a collage of different dance forms that are found in a wide geographical area of the Appalachians. Big circle dancing is a style that was brought to the Appalachian Mountain region of the Eastern United States by settlers from the British Isles (England, Wales, Ireland, Scotland).

 ## Shape in Dance

Objective: To create a variety of sizes and types of circle shapes through body design and motion

Materials: *Suite of Appalachian Music and Dance* performed by the AMAN International Folk Ensemble. Running Time: 7:24

Focus

Time: About 10 minutes

■ Read and discuss the information on page 93.

Art History and Culture

■ Encourage students to think about why the circle shape is often used in dances.

Teach

Time: About 20 minutes

Aesthetic Perception

■ Discuss how students can use their bodies to create circular shapes.

Creative Expression

■ Have students find their own space. Ask them to make three different circle shapes with their bodies. Repeat with a partner. Encourage them to vary levels and size.

■ Form groups of 6–8 for a circle dance: walk right 8 counts; walk left 8 counts; walk into the center 4 counts; walk out 4 counts; jump together in place 8 counts.

■ **Informal Assessment** Did students create circle shapes alone, with partners, and with groups?

Reflect

Time: About 5 minutes

Art Criticism

■ Have students draw in their Art Journals to answer the Analyze question on page 93.

Describe ▶ Describe the ways you formed circles alone.

Interpret ▶ How did it feel to create a group circle dance?

Decide ▶ Were you successful in creating different types of circular shapes?

Unit 3 Planning Guide

	Lesson Title	Suggested Pacing	Creative Expression Activity
Lesson 1	A Garden of Colors	45 minutes	Create a flower garden.
Lesson 2	Recognizing Objects by Color	55 minutes	Create a fruit collage.
Lesson 3	Looking at Colors	55 minutes	Create a collage, using one color.
Lesson 4	Primary Colors	45 minutes	Create a drawing of an object using primary color markers.
Lesson 5	Colors Show Feelings	55 minutes	Create a self-portrait that uses color to show an emotion.
Lesson 6	Light and Dark Colors	60 minutes	Create a sea picture.
ART SOURCE ARTSOURCE	Color in Storytelling and Music	40 minutes	Make sound patterns for different animals and create appropriate movements.

Materials	Program Resources	Fine Art Resources	Literature Resources
jumbo crayons, 12" × 18" white paper	*Reading and Writing Test Preparation*, pp. 30–31 *Flash Cards*, 1–6 *Assessment*, pp. 33–34 *Home and After-School Connections*, pp. 15–18	*Transparency*, 13 *Artist Profiles*, pp. 52, 57 *Large Prints*, 5 and 6 *The National Museum of Women in the Arts Collection*	*George and Martha One Fine Day* by James Marshall
Eating the Alphabet by Lois Elhert, 12" × 18" colored paper, 6" × 6" construction paper squares, construction paper scraps, glue, scissors, pieces of fruit (real or plastic)	*Reading and Writing Test Preparation*, pp. 32–33 *Flash Cards*, 7, 9, 10, and 11 *Assessment*, pp. 35–36	*Transparency*, 14 *Artist Profiles*, pp. 12, 23 *Large Prints*, 5 and 6 *The National Museum of Women in the Arts Collection*	*Stone Soup* by Heather Forest
old magazines, scissors, glue, 9" × 12" paper (spectral colors)	*Reading and Writing Test Preparation*, pp. 34–35 *Flash Cards*, 1–6 *Assessment*, pp. 37–38	*Transparency*, 15 *Artist Profiles*, pp. 6, 47 *Animals Through History Time Line* *Large Prints*, 5 and 6 *Women in the Arts Collection*	*You'll Soon Grow into Them, Titch* by Pat Hutchins
9" × 12" white drawing paper; red, yellow, and blue markers	*Reading and Writing Test Preparation*, pp. 36–37 *Flash Card*, 7 *Assessment*, pp. 39–40	*Transparency*, 16 *Artist Profiles*, pp. 27, 72 *Large Prints*, 5 and 6 *The National Museum of Women in the Arts Collection*	*Sun Up, Sun Down* by Gail Gibbons
12" × 18" construction paper (blue and violet, yellow and orange), oil pastels (separate into bright and dull colors, skin tones, and black and white)	*Reading and Writing Test Preparation*, pp. 38–39 *Assessment*, pp. 41–42	*Transparency*, 17 *Artist Profiles*, pp. 11, 34 *Large Prints*, 5 and 6 *The National Museum of Women in the Arts Collection*	*The 100th Day of School* by Angela Shelf Medearis
12" × 18" white paper, liquid tempera paint (blue, black, white), small sponges, water dishes, large and medium brushes, mixing trays, paper towels, oil pastels	*Reading and Writing Test Preparation*, pp. 40–41 *Flash Cards*, 9 and 10 *Assessment*, pp. 43–44	*Transparency*, 18 *Artist Profiles*, pp. 18, 50 *Large Prints*, 5 and 6 *Art Around the World*	*In the Ocean* by Claire Henley and *Oceans* by Kristin Ward
"The Girl on the Rock" retold by Paul Tracey from Hugh Tracey's book, The Lion on the Path			

3 Color

Lesson 1: Color names are taught in this lesson.

Lesson 2: Color recognition explores the recognition of objects by color.

Lesson 3: Color is observed in fine art and in the environment.

Lesson 4: Primary colors are red, yellow, and blue.

Lesson 5: Colors and feelings are discussed in this lesson. Artists use colors to show emotions.

Lesson 6: Color value is the darkness or lightness of a color.

Introduce Unit Concepts

"Let's discover some things about colors."
"Vamos a descubrir algunas cosas sobre los colores".

Color
- Play "I Spy" using colors to describe the answer.
- Name various emotions (happy, sad, excited, bored) and have students select a color that expresses each emotion.

Color

◄ **Henri Matisse.** (French). *Woman in a Purple Coat.* 1937.
....
Oil on canvas. 31⅞ × 25¹¹⁄₁₆ inches (80.9 × 65.2 cm). Museum of Fine Arts, Houston, Houston, Texas.

Colors are everywhere.

Look around you to find colors.

94 Unit 3

Fine Art Prints

Display **Large Prints 5** *Capriccio Musicale* and **6** *Point of Tranquility*. Refer to the prints throughout the unit as students learn about color.

Large Print 5

Large Print 6

ILLUSTRATOR PROFILE

David Diaz
(1958–)

As a first-grader in Fort Lauderdale, Florida, David Diaz already knew that he would become an artist. The realization came one day as he drew a face around the simple outline of a nose on his phonics worksheet. Drawing was fun!

Diaz continued to enjoy art and made it the emphasis of his studies in high school and college. With a degree from Fort Lauderdale Art Institute, Diaz headed to California and started his own design and illustration business in 1979. Diaz's client list included such well-known companies and publications as Pepsi®, American Express®, *The Atlantic Monthly*, and *The Washington Post*. Eventually Diaz began to turn down design projects in favor of illustration assignments, which he found more gratifying.

Diaz began his career as a children's book illustrator with Gary Soto's *Neighborhood Odes*. His second effort in this field, illustrating Eve Bunting's *Smoky Night*, earned Diaz the prestigious Caldecott Medal in 1995. Diaz has since created the images for many more children's books, and he treats his young audience with the same respect granted his corporate clients. Diaz does not alter or simplify his style when drawing for children, but tries to make powerful images that are appropriate to the story.

While studying Unit 3, share David Diaz's illustrations with the class and discuss the use of color in his works of art. Ask students to name colors they know. Do they see any light colors or dark colors?

Music

Color is used in music to refer to the distinctive tone quality, or timbre, of each instrument and voice. Tone colors of classroom instruments can be classified as woods, metals, drums, and rattles/shakers. To help students become aware of tone color, have them listen with eyes closed to a few classroom instruments. Have them classify the instruments as wood, metal, drum, or rattle/shaker color.

Literature

Watch the video or DVD *The Great Kapok Tree* by Lynne Cherry at any time throughout the unit to practice the unit concepts and to discover the vivid colors shown in the illustrations.

Literature and Art

Performing Arts

 Listen to *The Girl on the Rock* by Paul Tracey. Notice the different kinds of sounds Tracey makes for each animal.

Artsource®

Artists use many different **colors** in their art. What colors in the painting can you name?

Henri Matisse

(1869–1954)

▶ was a great French artist.

▶ loved to paint with bright colors.

Unit 3   **95**

Art History and Culture

Henri Matisse

Henri Matisse (än rē´ mä tēs) (1869–1954) grew up in a small town in northern France. As a child he showed little interest in art. When he finished high school he studied law in Paris. He became ill at age twenty-one and had to stay in bed for a long time. His mother gave him paints to keep him from being bored, and he discovered both a talent and an interest in art.

See pages 16–21 and 24–25 for more about subject matter and art history.

Artist Profiles, p. 27

Artist Profile

Henri Matisse
1869–1954

Henri Matisse (än´ rē ma tēs´) was the son of a middle-class couple in the north of France. He was not interested in art while he was in school. After high school his father sent him to law school in Paris. When he was 21 an appendicitis attack changed his life. Because he had to spend a long time in the hospital, his mother brought him a paint box to help him pass the time. Matisse eventually convinced his father to let him drop out of law school and study art. Matisse married and started a family soon after. His paintings were not selling, so he worked for a decorator and his wife opened a hat shop. During the last years of his life he suffered from arthritis. Unable to hold a brush in his hands, he devoted his efforts to

Examine the Artwork

"Let's see how the artist used colors in this painting." "Vamos a observar cómo el artista usó los colores en esta pintura".

■ Have students observe the painting on page 94 and describe what they see.

■ Have students answer the question pertaining to color on page 95.

Acceptable answers include red, orange, pink, gray, black, white, green, or yellow.

Unit Pretest

T Display *Transparency 45* as a pretest. Answers: 1. B; 2. A; 3. B

A Garden of Colors

Lesson 1 introduces color names. Red, blue, yellow, orange, violet, green, brown, black, and white are covered in this lesson.

Objectives

 Art History and Culture

To recognize that artists use different colors to create landscapes

 Aesthetic Perception

To locate colors in the artwork and in the environment

Creative Expression

To create a drawing with a variety of colors

Art Criticism

To evaluate one's own work using the four steps of art criticism

Vocabulary  Reading

Review the following vocabulary words with students before beginning the lesson. Definitions for these words appear as art on **Student Edition** page 98 and in the glossary.

red (rojo), **orange** (anaranjado)

yellow (amarillo), **green** (verde)

blue (azul), **violet** (violeta)

brown (marrón), **black** (negro)

white (blanco)

See page 119B for additional vocabulary and Spanish vocabulary resources.

 Art Journal: Vocabulary

Have students add these words to the Vocabulary section of their Art Journals.

Lesson Materials

- colored paper (1 sheet each of red, orange, yellow, green, blue, violet, brown, black, and white)
- jumbo crayons
- 12" × 18" white paper

Alternate Materials

- solid-colored fabric in the colors mentioned above
- markers

Program Resources

- *Reading and Writing Test Prep.,* pp. 30–31
- *Transparency 13*
- *Flash Cards 1–6*
- *Artist Profiles,* pp. 52, 57
- *Assessment,* pp. 33–34
- *Large Prints 5* Capriccio Musicale and *6 Point of Tranquility*
- *The National Museum of Women in the Arts Collection*

Concept Trace

Color Names

Introduced: Level K, Unit 3, Lesson 1

Reinforced: Level K, Unit 3, Lessons 2–6

Lesson 1 Arts Integration

Theatre

Complete Unit 3, Lesson 1 on pages 54–55 of the **Theatre Arts Connections** book.

Music

Learning to identify the sounds of musical instruments takes experience with both hearing and seeing the instrument. Some pieces are titled with the names of the instruments that it is written for. Listen to "Trumpet and Drum" from *Jeux d'enfants* by Georges Bizet. Have students raise their hands when they hear the trumpet.

Movement & Dance

Have students call out different colors then identify each color and where it can be seen in the classroom. How do those colors make us feel? Teach the song *I Can Sing a Rainbow.* Create actions or movements to accompany each of the colors in the song: "I can sing a rainbow, red, yellow, pink and green, purple and orange and blue."

ocus

Time: About 10 minutes

Activate Prior Knowledge

"What colors can you name?" "¿Qué colores pueden nombrar?"

- Encourage students to look around the classroom and name colors they see.

Using Literature 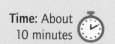 Reading

- Read *George and Martha One Fine Day* by James Marshall. Ask students to identify the colors they see in the illustrations.

Thematic Connection ⭐ Science

- **Observing Plants:** Have students plant seeds and record observations about parts of plants including leaves, roots, stems, and flowers. Identify plant parts in the fine art pictures.

Introduce the Art

"Let's look at the colors in these garden scenes." "Vamos a mirar los colores en estas escenas de jardines".

Discussing the Selection ⭐ Reading

- Describe each garden.
- Which color stands out the most in each picture? Why?
- Have students point to the flowers and name their colors.

Adjectives and Adverbs ⭐ Language Arts

- List on a chart the adjectives and adverbs students use to describe the fine art.
NSAE 4.a

Art History and Culture

Share information from the Art History and Culture sections with students. Discuss the different colors that artists use to make objects look real. Possible answers: Students could mention any color. Encourage students to tell how the colors are used, such as an artist might use green to paint grass.

 Web Connection

Visit **www.zalucha.com/studio/index1.html** to find out more about Peggy Flora Zalucha. Visit the gallery to study a portfolio of her work.
NSAE 5.a; 5.c

Lesson 1 A Garden of Colors

▲ **Peggy Flora Zalucha.** (American). *Sprinkler Garden.* 1994.
Transparent watercolor on paper. 36 × 52 inches (91.44 × 132.08 cm.). Courtesy of Peggy Flora Zalucha.

Look at the flower gardens. They are full of **colors.**

Art History and Culture

The flowers in this painting look real. Artists sometimes paint in a realistic style.

Art History and Culture

Peggy Flora Zalucha

Peggy Flora Zalucha (peg´ ē flor´ a zə lōō´ kə) (1948–) was born in Peoria, Illinois. She is an artist who deems herself a product of the 1960s. She was raised to appreciate photography, and she was encouraged to take pictures of the world around her. When Zalucha was in college, women were not advised to obtain studio degrees. Seeing this ideology as a potential obstacle in her path, Zalucha sought a degree in teaching instead.

Her first official job was as an art teacher in rural Nebraska. Zalucha has been making and teaching art for more than twenty years.

See pages 16–21 and 24–25 for more about subject matter and art history.

Artist Profiles, p. 57

Artist Profile
Peggy Flora Zalucha
b. 1948
Peggy Flora Zalucha (peg´ ē flor´ a za lōō´ kə) was born in Peoria, Illinois. She was raised to appreciate photography and encouraged to take pictures of the world around her. When Zalucha was in college, women were not advised to get studio degrees, so Zalucha got her degree in teaching instead. Her first official job was as an art teacher in a rural Nebraska school. Zalucha has been making and teaching art for more than 20 years.

Study the pictures.

▶ Does the second picture have any colors that you did not see in the first picture?

◀ **Edouard Vuillard.**
(French). *Morning in the Garden at Vaucresson.* 1937.
••••••••••••••••••••••
Tempera on canvas.
59½ × 43⅝ inches
(151.13 × 110.80 cm.).
The Metropolitan Museum of Art, New York, New York.

 Aesthetic Perception

Seeing Like an Artist Look around you. What colors do you see?

Art History and Culture

Edouard Vuillard

Edouard Vuillard (ed wärd´ vwē yär´) (1868–1940) grew up in Paris with his mother and siblings in an apartment that also served as his mother's lingerie and dressmaking business. This environment seemed to be the inspiration of Vuillard's many paintings of women in domestic interiors. Later Vuillard's interest turned to larger scale artwork such as wall paintings, folding screens, and portraits of wealthy French families. Edouard Vuillard was a part of *Nabis,* a group of young artists who rejected academic art and impressionism and wanted to restore feeling and imagination to the arts.

See pages 16–21 and 24–25 for more about subject matter and art history.

Artist Profiles, p. 52

Artist Profile
Edouard Vuillard
1868-1940
Edouard Vuillard (ed wärd´ vwē yär´) was born in a small French town on the border of Switzerland, and then moved to Paris with his family when he was nine years old. His father died a few years after the move, and his mother supported their family on the small income from her dressmaking business. Vuillard grew up in a strong domestic environment and was always encouraged by his mother. Vuillard's decision to pursue a career in art set him apart as the first person in his family to have a career outside the military. He chose to paint in a style independent from the conservative Parisian schools of his time.

Study

▶ Possible answers may include orange, gray, brown, light blue, light green, or violet.

■ For more examples of landscapes, see *The National Museum of Women in the Arts Collection.*

📖 **Art Journal: Concept**
Name a color and ask students to draw a circle of that color in their Art Journals.

🔍 **Aesthetic Perception**

Seeing Like an Artist Encourage students to identify colors they see in the classroom and around the school.

Developing Visual Literacy Encourage students to observe the plants and flowers outside the school and their homes. Ask them to identify the colors they see.
NSAE 3.a; 3.b

💻 **Web Connection**
Learn more about Edouard Vuillard and Nabis at
www.encyclopedia.com/html/N/Nabis.asp.

 **each**

Time: About 30 minutes

"Let's play a color name game." *"Vamos a jugar un juego de nombrar colores".*

■ Display a piece of colored paper. Have children identify the color name and hold up the same color crayon.

Practice

Materials: colored paper (1 sheet each of red, orange, yellow, green, blue, violet, brown, black, and white)

Alternate Materials: solid-colored fabric in the previously mentioned colors

■ Have the students identify colors as directed on page 98.

■ Ask students to find something in the classroom that matches the color of the crayon they are holding.

■ Repeat this procedure with other pieces of colored paper and crayons.

Creative Expression

Materials: jumbo crayons, 12" × 18" white paper

Alternate Materials: markers

■ Display pictures of different kinds of flowers. Provide names as necessary. Let students name the colors.

■ Ask students to decide which flowers they would like to have in a garden of their own.

■ Distribute the materials and have students follow the directions on page 99.

■ See the Activity Tips on page 238 for visual examples of this lesson's activity.

■ Review the Technique Tips on page 214 for information on using crayons.
NSAE 1.a; 1.c

Art Journal: Brainstorming

Have students brainstorm ideas for different kinds of flowers and draw these flowers in their Art Journals.

Using Color

Colors have names.

red   orange   yellow   green   blue

violet   brown   black   white

Practice

1. Look at the paper your teacher shows the class.

2. Show a crayon that matches the paper color.

Differentiated Instruction

Reteach
Play a game of "I Spy" using colored paper squares labeled with color names. Have students find something in a particular color. Let students take turns being the "spy."

Special Needs
To reinforce skills of color recognition, have real flowers for students to observe as they begin the lesson activity.

ELL Tips
Display a bouquet of real, plastic, or silk flowers. Say the names of the color(s) of each flower and have students repeat them. Then create a color chart. Call on students to point to different colors that you name.

▲ **Lauren Knutti.**
Age 5.

Think about the colors you see in this student's work.

Creative Expression

What colors would you put in your garden?

1. Think about the types of flowers you like best.
2. Draw your own flower garden.

 **Art Criticism**

Decide Would your garden look real if you used only one color? Why?

● **Art Across the Curriculum** ●

Use these simple ideas to reinforce art concepts across the curriculum.

★ **Expository Writing** Have students draw a series of pictures to show the steps of plant growth such as seed, small plant receiving water and sun, adult plant.

★ **Math** Have students observe the growth of classroom plants, and then compare and order them according to size.

★ **Science** Observe plant growth and draw a picture to predict what will happen next.

★ **Social Studies** Distinguish between things that are needed and things that are wanted, first identifying these things in the works of art.

★ **Technology** Explore the color palette in a paint program while drawing a colorful garden. Visit **SRAonline.com** to print detailed instructions for this activity.

Reflect

Time: About 5 minutes

Review and Assess

"What are the names of the nine colors you learned?" "¿Cuáles son los nombres de los nueve colores que aprendieron?"

Think

■ Discuss the student art question. Answers may include blue, yellow, violet, red, green, pink, and black.

■ Identify colors in *Large Prints 5 Capriccio Musicale* and *6 Point of Tranquility*.

Informal Assessment

Art Journal: Critical Thinking
Have students answer the Decide question in their Art Journals by drawing a picture of their garden using only one color. Discuss the second Decide question aloud.

 **Art Criticism**

Have students ask themselves the following questions.

Describe ► What is growing in your garden picture?

Analyze ► What color did you use?

Interpret ► What time of year is it in your garden? Spring, summer, or fall?

Decide ► Would your garden look real if you used only one color? Why?

NSAE 2.b; 5.a; 5.c

■ For standardized-format test practice using this lesson's art content, see pages 30–31 in *Reading and Writing Test Preparation*.

A Garden of Colors

 For the Art Specialist

Time: About 30 minutes

Focus

Study **Large Prints 5** *Capriccio Musicale* and **6** *Point of Tranquility* and discuss how the artists used color. Name the colors you see in these works of art. Point to your favorite colors in the pictures.

Teach

Tell students to imagine that they are butterflies flying from flower to flower in a garden. Ask students to describe the colors they see and how the flowers are arranged. Are they in a straight line or are they bunched together? Have students use watercolors to paint a garden scene.

Reflect

Have students use the four steps of art criticism to evaluate their work. Did they effectively use color to paint a garden scene?

Alternate Activity

Materials
- 9" × 12" white drawing paper or watercolor paper
- watercolor sets
- brushes
- sponges
- water containers
- markers

1. Demonstrate for the students how to wet the paper with a sponge.

2. Have students select two or three colors for their flowers.

3. Then students apply drops of watercolor paint onto the wet paper. Tell students to leave a space between each color because the paint will spread.

4. Allow time so the papers can dry. Then have students use markers to draw stems and leaves and add details such as butterflies, bees, and other insects.

NSAE 1.a; 1.c

Research in Art Education

"Enriched and stimulated in art classes by a teacher's varied and challenging motivations, children learn to see more, sense more, and recall more . . . Some people, however, think that anything a child draws, paints, or constructs is art . . . It may indeed be a child's visual statement, but it is not necessarily a quality work of art. To have quality, it must, as much as possible, be expressed in the language, structure, and form of art" (Wachowiak, Frank, and Robert Clements, *Emphasis Art: A Qualitative Art Program for Elementary and Middle Schools* (7th ed.). New York: Longman, 2001).

Assessment
Use the following rubric to evaluate the artwork students make in the Creative Expression activity and to assess students' understanding of colors.

Have students complete page 33 or 34 in their *Assessment* books.

	Art History and Culture	Aesthetic Perception	Creative Expression	Art Criticism
3 POINTS	The student recognizes that artists use different colors to create landscapes.	The student accurately locates colors in works of art and in the environment.	The student's drawing clearly shows a variety of colors.	The student thoughtfully and honestly evaluates his or her own work using the four steps of art criticism.
2 POINTS	The student shows emerging awareness that artists use different colors to create landscapes.	The student shows emerging awareness of colors in works of art and in the environment.	The student's drawing shows some use of different colors.	The student attempts to evaluate his or her own work, but shows an incomplete understanding of evaluation criteria.
1 POINT	The student does not recognize that artists use different colors to create landscapes.	The student does not locate colors in works of art or in the environment.	The student's drawing does not show a variety of colors.	The student makes no attempt to evaluate his or her own artwork.

Assessment, p. 33

Name _____ Date _____ **Lesson 1** UNIT 3

A Garden of Colors

For the teacher: Use the following prompts for this activity.
1. Using a crayon, color a different color in each box.
2. Say the name of each color out loud.

Level K

Unit 3 • Color **33**

Lesson 2 Overview

Recognizing Objects by Color

Lesson 2 explores color recognition—the recognition of objects in our environment by color.

Objectives

 Art History and Culture

To recognize that artists with different styles get inspiration for their artwork from everyday objects

 Creative Expression

To create a fruit collage using appropriate colors to make the fruit recognizable

 Aesthetic Perception

To locate colors in the environment and identify objects that are recognizable by their color

 Art Criticism

To evaluate one's own work using the four steps of art criticism

Vocabulary Reading

Review the following vocabulary word with students before beginning the lesson.

collage collage—artwork consisting of pieces of paper and fabric glued onto a background

See page 119B for additional vocabulary and Spanish vocabulary resources.

 Art Journal: Vocabulary

Have students add this word to the Vocabulary section of their Art Journals.

Lesson Materials

- *Eating the Alphabet* by Lois Elhert
- 12" × 18" colored paper (any color)
- 6" × 6" construction paper squares (red, yellow, orange, green, blue, violet)
- construction paper scraps (various colors)
- glue and scissors
- various pieces of fruit (real or plastic)

Alternate Materials
- crayons or oil pastels

Program Resources
- *Reading and Writing Test Prep.*, pp. 32-33
- *Transparency 14*
- *Artist Profiles*, pp. 12, 23
- *Assessment*, pp. 35-36
- *Large Prints 5 Capriccio Musicale* and *6 Point of Tranquility*
- *The National Museum of Women in the Arts Collection*

Concept Trace
Color Identification
Introduced: Level K, Unit 3, Lesson 2

Reinforced: Level 1, Unit 3, Lesson 1

Lesson 2 Arts Integration

Theatre

Complete Unit 3, Lesson 2 on pages 56–57 of the *Theatre Arts Connections* book.

Theatre Arts Connections, p. 56

Music

 Borrow from the music teacher one rhythm instrument from each category of wood, metal, drum, or rattle/shaker. Play the instruments behind a screen and have the students identify one at a time. Explain that it is the tone color that can be recognized.

Movement & Dance

Identify certain foods that have bold colors. How do those colors help us recognize how the food might taste? Then find words that describe the color and food, for example, pepper—red, hot, sizzle; banana—yellow, soft, peel; popcorn—white, light, pop. Explore movements using these different descriptions.

Activate Prior Knowledge

"What is your favorite fruit?" "¿Cuál es su fruta favorita?"

- Ask students to also mention the color(s) of their favorite fruits.

Using Literature

- Read *Stone Soup* by Heather Forest, illustrated by Susan Gaber. Have students identify items used in the soup and name the colors of these items.

Thematic Connection
Healthy Foods ⭐ Health

- **Fruit:** Identify healthy foods that help the body grow. List types of fruit and their colors.

Introduce the Art

"Let's look at the pictures of fruit." "Vamos a mirar las pinturas de frutas".

- Ask students to describe what they see in each painting.

Main Idea ⭐ Reading

- How were you able to identify the kinds of fruit in the pictures?

- Have students point to the fruits and name their colors.

- Share and discuss information from *Artist Profiles* pages 12 and 23 with students.

Adjectives and Adverbs ⭐ Language Arts

- List on a chart the adjectives and adverbs students use to describe the fine art.

NSAE 4.a

 Art History and Culture

Share information from the Art History and Culture sections with students. Ask students to name some everyday objects that these artists were inspired to portray in these works of art. Possible answers: fruit, watercolor paints, flowers, and plants.

💻 **Web Connection**
Find out more about photorealism and Audrey Flack by visiting www.artcyclopedia.com/history/photorealism.html.

◀ **Audrey Flack.** (American). *Energy Apples.* 1980.
Acrylic and oil on canvas. 47¾ × 48¼ inches (121.29 × 122.56 cm.). Private Collection.

Look at both pictures. What kinds of food do you see in these works of art?

 Art History and Culture

Sometimes artists get ideas for their art from objects they see every day. What everyday objects are in these works of art?

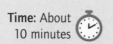 **Art History and Culture**

Audrey Flack

Audrey Flack (ô´ drē flak) (1931–) is one of America's best known artists. Flack is most often recognized for her photo-realist paintings. Photo-realists work from photographs and paint with such tremendous detail that the painting looks almost like a photograph. Flack also enjoys sculpture and has created numerous sculptures that depict female strength.

See pages 16–21 and 24–25 for more about subject matter and art history.

Artist Profiles, p. 12

▶ Artist Profile ◀
Audrey Flack
b. 1931
Audrey Flack (ô´ drē flak) grew up in New York City and lives there still. She earned a fine arts degree from Yale. She also studied anatomy, the structure of the human body. This helps her make her paintings more realistic. Flack is married to a musician. Early in her career she painted while raising two daughters. She has also taught at Pratt Institute and New York University.

Study the pictures.

▶ Would it be harder to name each food if they were not colored?

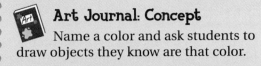
▲ **Jacob Lawrence.** (American).
Still Life with Grapes and Roses.
1954.
••
Egg tempera on hardboard. 17¾ × 23⅞ inches
(45.09 × 58.42 cm.). Private collection.

🔍 Aesthetic Perception

Seeing Like an Artist Look around. What objects do you see that are the color red?

🏺 Art History and Culture

Jacob Lawrence

Jacob Lawrence (jā´ kəp lô´ rens) (1917–2000) was born in Atlantic City, New Jersey, and raised in Harlem. He attended the Harlem Art Workshop and won a scholarship to the American Artists School. Lawrence's paintings are known not only for contributing to the art world, but also for adding to our knowledge of African American history. His paintings often depicted the struggle for freedom and justice in post-Civil War America. Lawrence was the first African American artist to receive sustained mainstream recognition in the United States.

See pages 16–21 and 24–25 for more about subject matter and art history.

Artist Profiles, p. 23

◀ Artist Profile ▶
Jacob Lawrence
1917–2000

Jacob Lawrence (jā´ kəb lãr´ əns) had parents who met on their migration to the North. His father was born in South Carolina, and his mother in Virginia. Lawrence was born in Atlantic City, New Jersey, in 1917. The family finally settled in Harlem in 1929 at the end of the Harlem Renaissance. Because his mother worked all day, she enrolled Lawrence in the Harlem Art Workshop after school to keep him out of trouble. He had many excellent teachers there, including Charles Alston. Lawrence won a scholarship to the American Artists School. He taught at New York's Pratt Institute from 1958 to 1965. From 1970, he taught at the University of Washington in Seattle, where he also served as head of the

---

Study

▶ It would be hard to recognize objects that have similar shapes like apples, peaches, and plums or lemons and limes.

■ For more examples of still lifes, see *The National Museum of Women in the Arts Collection.*

📓 Art Journal: Concept

Name a color and ask students to draw objects they know are that color.

🔍 Aesthetic Perception

Seeing Like an Artist Encourage students to identify red objects they see in the classroom.
NSAE 3.a; 3.b
Developing Visual Literacy
Comparing and Contrasting 🌟 Reading
Show students pieces of real fruit. Compare the colors in the paintings to the colors of the real fruit.

💻 Web Connection

Visit **www.whitney.org/jacoblawrence/** to find out more about Jacob Lawrence.

Teach

Time: About 40 minutes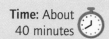

"Let's sort colors and identify different foods that we know by these colors." "Vamos a clasificar colores e identificar diferentes comidas que reconocemos por estos colores".

Practice

- Choose four colors and list them on the board. Have students name foods that can be identified by each color as directed on page 102.

 Creative Expression

Materials: *Eating the Alphabet* by Lois Elhert, 12" × 18" colored paper (any color), 6" × 6" construction paper squares (red, yellow, orange, green, blue, violet), construction paper scraps (various colors), glue, scissors, various pieces of fruit (real or plastic)

Alternate Materials: crayons or oil pastels

- Read aloud *Eating the Alphabet* by Lois Elhert. Ask students to name the shapes and colors of the fruit depicted in the book.

- Show students a variety of fruit (real or plastic). Allow students to handle the fruit and match the real or plastic fruit to the fruit they see in the fine art still lifes.

- Distribute the materials and have students follow the directions on page 103.

- See the Activity Tips on page 238 for visual examples of this lesson's activity.

- Ask students to look at the 6" × 6" squares of paper and find colors that match the fruit.

- Have students cut fruit shapes from the paper squares and then arrange and glue them to their 12" × 18" paper.

- Encourage students to use the paper scraps to add details to their fruit collages.

NSAE 1.a; 1.c

Art Journal: Brainstorming
Have students brainstorm ideas for different kinds of fruit and draw these in their Art Journals.

102 UNIT 3 • Color

Using Color To Recognize Objects

Colors help us identify things.

Practice

1. Think about the color your teacher says.
2. Name food that is that color.

102 Unit 3 • Lesson 2

Differentiated Instruction

Reteach
Show students a picture cookbook. Ask them to identify the colors and food they see.

Special Needs
To help students with the skill of color naming, create a poster showing the different colors and their names.

ELL Tips
Identify the food and the colors in the art with students. Display pictures of food and other familiar objects and say the names and colors with students. (Suggested objects: those that are consistently the same color and are easily recognizable because of their color, such as a stop sign, school bus, fire truck, and grass).

Think about the kinds of fruit you see in the student's artwork.

▲ **Michael Lazzario.** Age 6.

 **Creative Expression**

What kinds of fruit do you see?

1. Choose paper that matches the fruit colors.
2. Cut shapes and make a collage.

 **Art Criticism**

Describe What colors did you use for your collage?

 **Reflect** Time: About 5 minutes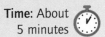

Review and Assess

"What are two things we can identify by color?" "¿Cuáles son dos cosas que podemos identificar por sus colores?"

Think

■ Discuss the student art question. Possible answers: oranges and apples or strawberries.

■ Identify colors in **Large Prints 5** *Capriccio Musicale* and **6** *Point of Tranquility*.

Informal Assessment

Art Journal: Critical Thinking

Have students answer the Describe question in their Art Journals by writing the color words or drawing with the appropriate colors.

 **Art Criticism**

Have students ask themselves the following questions.

Describe ► What colors did you use for your collage?

Analyze ► How can the fruit in your collage be identified?

Interpret ► What food does each color represent?

Decide ► Do you think your fruit looks like fruit you have eaten in real life? Explain.

NSAE 2.b; 5.a; 5.c

■ For standardized-format test practice using this lesson's art content, see pages 32–33 in **Reading and Writing Test Preparation.**

Art Across the Curriculum

Use these simple ideas to reinforce art concepts across the curriculum.

★ **Descriptive Writing** Have students draw pictures to create a grocery list of the fruit they would like their parent to buy. Encourage them to choose their colors carefully so there will be no doubt as to what kind of fruit they want.

★ **Math** Observe and recognize parts that are less than a whole by dividing fruit and other food into halves.

★ **Science** Discuss animal coloring and generate a list of animals that are identified more easily because of their color(s).

★ **Social Studies** Identify the state and national flag. Discuss how flags are recognized because of their colors and patterns.

★ **Technology** Encourage students to use the fill tool in a paint program to paint pictures of fruit. Visit **SRAonline.com** to print detailed instructions for this activity.

Recognizing Objects by Color

Extra! For the Art Specialist

Time: About 40 minutes

Focus

Study **Large Prints 5** *Capriccio Musicale* and **6** *Point of Tranquility* and discuss how the artists used color. Have students use color wheels to help them find colors in the works of art. Could they find every color on the color wheel? Were there any colors that were missing?

Teach

Have students draw a farm scene using a variety of colors.

Reflect

Have students use the four steps of art criticism to evaluate their work. Did they effectively use variety of colors to draw a farm scene?

Alternate Activity

Materials
- 12" × 18" white or light-colored drawing paper
- markers

1. Read the story *The Little Red Hen*. Ask students to help you make a list of all the animals in the story and the color of each animal.

2. Encourage students to think of their favorite scene from the story. Have students use the markers to make a colorful illustration of the scene, including the sky, barn, plants, and other animals.

NSAE 1.a; 1.c

Research in Art Education

Arts involvement increases student self-image. Students involved in the arts are "far more likely than their low-arts counterparts to think of themselves as competent in academics" ("Learning in and Through the Arts: Curriculum Implications" in *Champions of Change*, p. 40). Observe students' confidence levels as they participate in the Art Across the Curriculum activities.

Assessment

Use the following rubric to evaluate the artwork students make in the Creative Expression activity and to assess students' understanding of color recognition.

Have students complete page 35 or 36 in their *Assessment* books.

	Art History and Culture	Aesthetic Perception	Creative Expression	Art Criticism
3 POINTS	The student recognizes that artists with different styles get inspiration for their artwork from everyday objects.	The student accurately locates colors in the environment and identifies objects that are recognizable by color.	The student's collage clearly demonstrates using color to help make objects recognizable.	The student thoughtfully and honestly evaluates own work using the four steps of art criticism.
2 POINTS	The student is sometimes able to recognize that artists with different styles get inspiration for their artwork from everyday objects.	The student shows emerging awareness of colors in the environment and can sometimes identify objects that are recognizable by color.	The student's collage shows some use of color to help make objects recognizable.	The student attempts to evaluate own work, but shows an incomplete understanding of evaluation criteria.
1 POINT	The student does not recognize that artists with different styles get inspiration for their artwork from everyday objects.	The student does not locate colors in the environment or identify objects that are recognizable by color.	The student's collage does not demonstrate using color to help make objects recognizable.	The student makes no attempt to evaluate own artwork.

Assessment, p. 35

Name _____ Date _____

Lesson 2 UNIT 3

Recognizing Objects by Color

1	2

For the teacher: Use the following prompt for this activity.
Using a crayon, draw an object in each box that is identified by its color.

Level K   Unit 3 • Color **35**

Lesson 3 Overview

Looking at Colors

Lesson 3 continues the observation and study of color. Students will identify colors around them and look at the colors artists use.

Objectives

 Art History and Culture

To recognize that artists use many colors in their paintings

 Creative Expression

To create a color shape collage using one color

 Aesthetic Perception

To identify colors in fine art and in the environment

 Art Criticism

To evaluate one's own work using the four steps of art criticism

Vocabulary Reading

Review the following vocabulary word with students before beginning the lesson.

painting pintura—a picture or design created with paint

See page 119B for additional vocabulary and Spanish vocabulary resources.

 Art Journal: Vocabulary

Have students add this word to the Vocabulary section of their Art Journals.

Lesson Materials
- old magazines
- scissors
- glue
- 9″ × 12″ paper (spectral colors)

Alternate Materials
- construction paper in a variety of colors

Program Resources
- *Reading and Writing Test Prep.,* pp. 34–35
- *Transparency 15*
- *Flash Cards 1–6*
- *Artist Profiles,* pp. 6, 47
- *Animals Through History Time Line*
- *Assessment,* pp. 37–38
- *Large Prints 5 Capriccio Musicale* and *6 Point of Tranquility*
- *The National Museum of Women in the Arts Collection*

Concept Trace
Looking at Color
Introduced: Level K, Unit 3, Lesson 1
Reinforced: Level K, Unit 3, Lesson 3

Lesson 3 Arts Integration

Theatre
Complete Unit 3, Lesson 3 on pages 58–59 of the *Theatre Arts Connections* book.

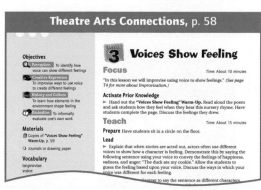

Music
 A composer can choose certain instruments to depict certain aspects of nature. What instrument could depict a bird call? What in nature fits a cymbal crash? Camille Saint-Saen chose the string bass to portray an elephant dancing in "The Elephant" from *The Carnival of the Animals.*

Movement & Dance
Brainstorm descriptive or action words that help identify specific colors and how they make us feel, for example: gold–sparkle; green–dash; blue–float. Divide the class into small groups. Each group is given a color and word that they will demonstrate through movement. Give each group 12 counts to perform their ideas.

Focus

Activate Prior Knowledge

"What color is your favorite candy?" "¿De qué color es su caramelo favorito?"

- Discuss different colors used in candy. Talk about the jawbreaker machines in the picture.

Using Literature

- Read *You'll Soon Grow into Them, Titch* by Pat Hutchins. Ask students to identify colors they see in the illustrations.

Thematic Connection

- **Colors:** Ask students to name their favorite colors and explain why they like them.

Introduce the Art

"Let's look at this painting of jawbreaker machines by the artist Wayne Thiebaud." "Vamos a mirar esta pintura de las máquinas de hacer caramelos duros del artista Wayne Thiebaud".

Main Idea and Details ⭐ Reading

- Ask students to describe the machines they see in the painting. Where have they seen machines like that?

- Have students point to and name the colors of the jawbreakers.

- Share and discuss information from *Artist Profiles* pages 6 and 47 with students.

Adjectives and Adverbs ⭐ Language Arts

- List on a chart the adjectives and adverbs students use to describe the fine art.
NSAE 4.a

🏺 Art History and Culture

Share information from the Art History and Culture sections with students. Discuss how Chagall's art has decorated buildings in many different communities. Encourage students to think about why we decorate buildings with art. Possible answers: People like to look at art because it is beautiful. People like to talk about what they see in the art. Art reminds people of events that have happened.
NSAE 4.a

💻 Web Connection

Find out more about Wayne Thiebaud at www.artnet.com.

Looking at Colors

▲ **Wayne Thiebaud.** (American). *Three Machines.* 1963.
••••••••••••••••
Oil on canvas. 30 × 36½ inches (76.2 × 92.71 cm.). Fine Arts Museum of San Francisco, San Francisco, California.

Look at these works of art. Sometimes artists use many colors.

🏺 Art History and Culture

Chagall has made murals, stained-glass windows, and mosaics that help decorate buildings in different communities.

🏺 Art History and Culture

Wayne Thiebaud

Wayne Thiebaud (wān tē′ bō) (1920–) became interested in art during high school while doodling and drawing cartoons when recuperating from a sports injury. He started his art career as a commercial artist and sign painter. Later, after working as a food preparer, he became fascinated with cafeteria and convenience food displays and began painting pictures of food.

See pages 16–21 and 24–25 for more about subject matter and art history.

Artist Profiles, p. 47

Artist Profile
Wayne Thiebaud
b. 1920
Wayne Thiebaud (wān tē′ bō), one of California's most famous contemporary painters, has earned as many awards for excellence in teaching as he has for his painting and printmaking. He became interested in drawing in high school and later worked as a freelance cartoonist and illustrator. He continued his artwork during his military service in the U.S. Air Force during World War II. He drew cartoons for the military base newspaper. In 1949 Thiebaud decided to become a painter. His first one-person show in New York City was praised by the critics. At that time his subjects were mass-produced consumer goods, particularly junk food, and he was mistakenly classified with the pop artists

◄ **Marc Chagall.**
(Russian). *I and the Village.* 1911.
Oil on canvas. 75⅝ × 59⅝ inches (192.1 × 151.4 cm.). Museum of Modern Art, New York, New York.

Study the pictures.

▶ How do you think the artists decided which colors to use?

Aesthetic Perception

Seeing Like an Artist What colors would you use to paint a picture of your favorite toy?

Art History and Culture

Marc Chagall

Marc Chagall (mark sha gäl´) (1887–1985) was born in Russia but spent many years studying art and painting in Paris. Chagall was not known to follow one particular artistic movement, but instead explored many different techniques. His paintings and prints, stained-glass windows, and large murals are remembered for their bright colors and dreamlike quality.

See pages 16–21 and 24–25 for more about subject matter and art history.

Artist Profiles, p. 6

• Artist Profile •
Marc Chagall
1887-1985

Marc Chagall (mark sha gäl´) was born in a small town in Russia, Vitebsk, which is now part of Belarus. He studied art in Saint Petersburg and then in Paris, France. After the Russian revolution he served as the director of the art academy in his hometown. From 1919 to 1922, Chagall was the art director of the Moscow Jewish State Theater. He painted murals in the theater lobby and created sets for the shows. In 1923, he moved to France. He spent most of the rest of his life there, except for a brief period of residence in the United States from 1941 to 1948.

Study

▶ Possible answers: The artists painted objects realistically. The artists painted the objects as they imagined they might look. Or, the artists painted the objects with their favorite colors. Artists may have chosen colors to depict a particular mood or feeling.

■ For more examples of abstract art, see *The National Museum of Women in the Arts Collection.*

Art Journal: Concept

Ask students to draw and color a balloon. Then have students name the color they used and explain why they chose it.

Aesthetic Perception

Seeing Like an Artist Lead a discussion about favorite toys. Ask students what colors they would use to paint a picture of their favorite toy.

Developing Visual Literacy Ask students where they have seen candy machines. How does the candy painting make them feel? How do they feel when they see a real candy machine?

Web Connection
Learn more about Marc Chagall by visiting www.artchive.com/artchive/C/chagall.html.

Teach

Time: About 40 minutes

"Let's go on a color search." "Vamos a buscar colores".

Practice

Materials: 9" × 12" paper (spectral colors)

- Separate students into groups. Assign each group a different color by giving them a piece of colored construction paper. Have group members search for objects in the classroom with that color.

- Allow groups to show their findings to the other groups.

 ## Creative Expression

Materials: old magazines, scissors, glue, 9" × 12" paper (spectral colors)

Alternate Materials: construction paper in a variety of colors

- Have students follow the directions on page 107.

- See the Activity Tips on page 239 for visual examples of this lesson's activity.

- Encourage students to think about different objects they see every day.

- Have students decide on a shape they would like to show.

- Give each child at a table a different colored sheet of the 9" × 12" paper for the background. This is his or her assigned color.

- Encourage students to be aware that the magazine pictures they find of the same color as their background paper do not have to match exactly. The pieces may be lighter or darker (value), or brighter or duller (intensity).

- Remind students that each cut piece should touch the piece next to it.

- Have students guess each other's shapes.

NSAE 1.c

Art Journal: Brainstorming

Have students brainstorm ideas for different kinds of shapes and draw these in their Art Journals.

Using Colors

Artists use colors to make their artwork look interesting.

Practice

1. Find objects in the room that are the same color as your piece of paper.

2. Tell the class what you found.

Differentiated Instruction

Reteach
Encourage students to match all six colors on a color wheel with something they see in their lives (for example, blue = police uniform, sky, water, and so on).

Special Needs
Students who have difficulty cutting may benefit from the use of adaptive scissors for this lesson's activity.

ELL Tips
Show students colored paper squares and name the colors with them. Then display a toy and talk about it with students. "This is a toy. What color is the toy? What color would you paint this toy?"

▲ **Susan Morris.**
Age 5.

Think about what shape the student created in her collage.

 **Creative Expression**

Where can you find colors?

1. Create a collage using the color your teacher gives you.

2. Find that color in magazine pictures. Cut out pieces of that color to make your collage.

 **Art Criticism**

Describe Name the color that you collected. What shape did you create?

Art Across the Curriculum

Use these simple ideas to reinforce art concepts across the curriculum.

★ **Descriptive Writing** Have students draw pictures of something else that could be a part of the village in *I and the Village*.

★ **Math** Count jawbreakers or other candies and practice writing the numbers to represent the candies counted.

★ **Science** Recognize that the jawbreaker dispenser is a machine and name other kinds of machines.

★ **Social Studies** Discuss the types of jobs being shown in *I and the Village*. What kinds of machines might help these people?

★ **Technology** Use a paint program to create jawbreakers of many colors. Visit **SRAonline.com** to print detailed instructions for this activity.

 **Time:** About 5 minutes

Review and Assess

"Where do artists get their ideas for colors?"
"¿Dónde obtienen los artistas sus ideas para los colores?"

Think

■ Discuss the student art question. Possible answers include a dog, cat, or other animal.

■ Identify colors in *Large Prints 5 Capriccio Musicale* and *6 Point of Tranquility*.

Informal Assessment

Art Journal: Critical Thinking
Have students answer the Describe question in their Art Journals by naming the color word and drawing the shape with the appropriate color.

? Art Criticism

Have students ask themselves the following questions.

Describe ▶ Name the color that you collected. What shape did you create?

Analyze ▶ How do your color pieces look different from the color of your background paper? In what way does the color look the same?

Interpret ▶ How does your collage make you feel? Give your collage a title.

Decide ▶ What do you like about using one color for an artwork? What don't you like?

NSAE 2.b; 5.a; 5.c

■ For standardized-format test practice using this lesson's art content, see pages 34–35 in *Reading and Writing Test Preparation*.

Looking at Colors

Extra! For the Art Specialist

Time: About 40 minutes

Focus

Study **Large Prints 5** *Capriccio Musicale* and **6** *Point of Tranquility* and discuss how the artists used color. Ask students to find a color in these works of art that they like best. Then have students name two other things that are also this color.

Teach

Ask the students to name their favorite color. Have them think of objects that are this color. Have students create a paper weaving using this color.

Reflect

Have students use the four steps of art criticism to evaluate their work. Did they effectively create a paper weaving of just one color?

Alternate Activity

Materials
- 9" × 12" paper (Draw lines on one paper and make copies for the students so they can use the lines as guides when cutting. See Technique Tips page 225.)
- 1" × 9" paper strips (approximately 8 per student)
- ruler
- scissors
- pencils

1. Show an example of a paper weaving that is one color.

2. Demonstrate how to fold the paper and cut on the lines.

3. Have the students select one color for weaving and show them how to weave the strips in and out of their paper loom.
NSAE 1.a; 1.c

Research in Art Education

"The purposes of Art Education are to build awareness of the aesthetic components in human experience: the feeling of kinship between the young 'artist-analyst' and the traditions of artistic creation and comprehension of the language of visual form as embodied and as experienced through the visual impact of everyday objects" (*Report of the Commission on Art Education,* 1965, NAEA).

Assessment

Use the following rubric to evaluate the artwork students make in the Creative Expression activity and to assess students' understanding of color.

Have students complete page 37 or 38 in their *Assessment* books.

	Art History and Culture	Aesthetic Perception	Creative Expression	Art Criticism
3 POINTS	The student recognizes that artists use many colors in their paintings.	The student identifies colors in fine art and in the environment.	The student's collage clearly demonstrates his or her recognition of the assigned color.	The student thoughtfully and honestly evaluates his or her own work using the four steps of art criticism.
2 POINTS	The student shows emerging awareness that artists use many colors in their paintings.	With teacher help the student identifies colors in fine art and in the environment.	The student's collage shows some recognition of the assigned color.	The student attempts to evaluate his or her own work, but shows an incomplete understanding of evaluation criteria.
1 POINT	The student does not recognize that artists use many colors in their paintings.	The student does not identify colors in fine art or in the environment.	The student's collage does not demonstrate recognition of the assigned color.	The student makes no attempt to evaluate his or her own artwork.

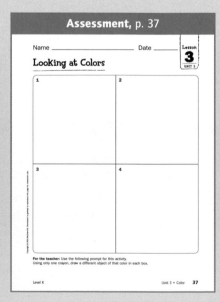

Lesson 4 Overview

Primary Colors

Lesson 4 teaches the primary colors—red, yellow, and blue. The primary colors are pure colors and cannot be made by mixing other colors.

Objectives

 Art History and Culture

To compare how different artists use primary colors in their art

 Creative Expression

To create a drawing of an object using primary color markers

Aesthetic Perception

To identify primary colors in art and in the environment

Art Criticism

To evaluate one's own work using the four steps of art criticism

Vocabulary Reading

Review the following vocabulary words with students before beginning the lesson.

primary colors colores primarios—the colors red, yellow, and blue

See page 119B for additional vocabulary and Spanish vocabulary resources.

 Art Journal: Vocabulary

Have students add these words to the Vocabulary section of their Art Journals.

Lesson Materials

- 9" × 12" white drawing paper
- red, yellow, and blue markers
- multi-colored fabric scraps (each scrap should have at least one primary color on it)

Alternate Materials
- crayons

Program Resources
- *Reading and Writing Test Prep.,* pp. 36–37
- *Transparency 16*
- *Flash Card 7*
- *Artist Profiles,* pp. 27, 72
- *Assessment,* pp. 39–40
- *Large Prints 5 Capriccio Musicale* and *6 Point of Tranquility*
- *The National Museum of Women in the Arts Collection*

Concept Trace
Primary Colors
Introduced: Level K, Unit 3, Lesson 4

Reinforced: Level 1, Unit 3, Lesson 2

Lesson 4 Arts Integration

Theatre

Complete Unit 3, Lesson 4 on pages 60–61 of the *Theatre Arts Connections* book.

Theatre Arts Connections, p. 60

Music

 SPOTLIGHT on MUSIC

There are some musical sounds that cannot be duplicated with instruments or by electronic means. It is primary to every student; he or she carries it around with him or her every day. It is the voice. Impress upon students that their voice is an instrument and it needs to be cared for. Harsh talking and shouting causes damage and hurts our ability to sing and speak with flexibility.

Movement & Dance

Identify the primary colors and use them as signals in a movement experience. For example: red will stop quickly; green will move fast or run; yellow will move in a slow motion. Call out each color in different sequences once the connection between the action and the color is clear.

Focus

Activate Prior Knowledge

"What is something you have seen that is red? That is yellow? That is blue?" "¿Pueden nombrar algo que hayan visto que sea rojo? ¿Que sea amarillo? ¿Que sea azul?"

Using Literature

- Read *Sun Up, Sun Down* by Gail Gibbons. Have students identify primary colors in the illustrations.

Thematic Connection
Creative Expression ★ Music

- **Music:** Encourage students to play classroom instruments independently or in a group.

Introduce the Art

"Let's look at both works of art." "Vamos a mirar ambas obras de arte".

Comparing and Contrasting ★ Reading

- Discuss how the works of art are similar and different.

- Have students name the colors they see in each work of art and identify the objects or areas that are red, yellow, and blue in each artwork.

- Ask students to identify the color they see the most in each artwork.

- Share and discuss information from *Artist Profiles* pages 27 and 72 with students.

Adjectives and Adverbs ★ Language Arts

- List on a chart the adjectives and adverbs students use to describe the fine art.

🏺 Art History and Culture

Share information from the Art History and Culture sections with students. Discuss how art helps us learn about different places and times. Ask students who they think might have used the *Octopus Bag*. Answers will vary. Students might say Native Americans because of the way the bag is decorated. Some students might suggest that a woman used the bag because it resembles a purse.

💻 **Web Connection**

Learn more about Henri Matisse and fauvism at www.nga.gov/feature/artnation/fauve/.

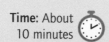 **Primary Colors**

◀ **Henri Matisse.** (French). *La Musique (Music)*. 1939.
....
Oil on canvas. 45¼ × 45⅜ inches (114.93 × 115.25 cm). Albright-Knox Art Gallery, Buffalo, New York.

Look at these works of art. They have some of the same colors.

🏺 Art History and Culture

Art like the *Octopus Bag* helps us learn what it is like to live in different places and times.

🏺 Art History and Culture

Henri Matisse

Henri Matisse (än rē´ mä tēs) (1869–1954) a French painter and sculptor, was one of the most influential artists of the late nineteenth and early twentieth centuries. Matisse was a leader of the fauves—a group of artists dedicated to showing strong emotionalism, wild colors, and distortion of shape in their paintings.

See pages 16–21 and 24–25 for more about subject matter and art history.

Artist Profiles, p. 27

◆ Artist Profile ◆
Henri Matisse
1869-1954

Henri Matisse (än´ rē´ ma tēs´) was the son of a middle-class couple in the north of France. He was not interested in art while he was in school. After high school his father sent him to law school in Paris. When he was 21 an appendicitis attack changed his life. Because he had to spend a long time in the hospital, his mother brought him a paint box to help him pass the time. Matisse eventually convinced his father to let him drop out of law school and study art. Matisse married and started a family soon after. His paintings were not selling, so he worked for a decorator and his wife opened a hat shop. During the last years of his life he suffered from arthritis. Unable to hold a brush in his hands, he devoted his efforts to

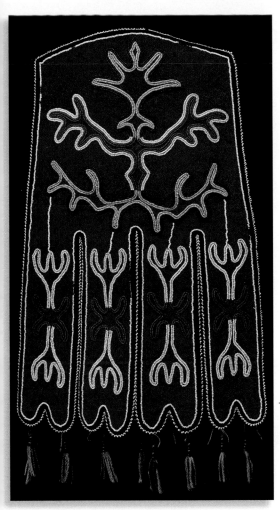

Study the pictures.

▶ Where do you see the colors red, yellow, and blue?

◀ **Artist Unknown.**
Tlingit. (Canadian.)
Octopus Bag.
c. 1890.
• • • • • • • • • • • • • • • • • • • •
Wool cloth, wool tape, glass beads, yarn, cotton cloth lining. 21½ × 12 inches (54.61 × 30.48 cm.). Seattle Museum of Art, Seattle, Washington.

Aesthetic Perception

Seeing Like an Artist Look around your classroom. Do you see any objects that are red, yellow, or blue?

 Art History and Culture

Tlingit, Angoon (Northwest Coastal Native Americans)

The Tlingit are a group of Native Americans who live predominantly in the heavily forested and damp coastal islands of southeastern Alaska, but also in Washington state and British Columbia, Canada. Octopus bags like the one shown in this lesson are worn by the Tlingit during ceremonies. The bags got their name from the four long pieces of fabric resembling octopus tentacles that dangle at the bottom of the bag. Octopus bags are worn on the body overlapping the other clothing.

See pages 16–21 and 24–25 for more about subject matter and art history.

Artist Profiles, p. 72

Artist Profile

Octopus Bag

This octopus bag was made by an unidentified Tlingit artist from the Alaskan coastal region of Angoon. Tlingit peoples living in this region have supported themselves through hunting, fishing, and fur trading for generations. The area has become home to several American whaling and fish processing businesses, and many Tlingit have taken to working at these facilities to support their families.

◀ Artist unknown (Tlingit). (Canadian.)
Octopus Bag. c. 1890.
Wool cloth, wool tape, glass beads, yarn, cotton cloth lining

Study

▶ *Music:* Red: the apple, floor, the blanket/wall behind the woman in blue and red bricks or wall behind the lady in yellow. Yellow: the lines on the floor, the yellow triangles on the blue dress, the guitar, the yellow dress and the lines in the wall behind the woman in yellow. Blue: the woman's dress.

▶ *Octopus Bag:* Red: the main color of the bag. It fills the entire area behind the design. Yellow: the outline of the top and bottom of the large shape at the top of the bag. Blue: the outline of the center of the shape at the top of the bag and the four shapes in the center of the four "legs" or sections hanging at the bottom of the bag.

■ For more examples of utilitarian art, see ***The National Museum of Women in the Arts Collection.***

Art Journal: Concept

Ask students to draw three free-form shapes and color one red, another yellow, and the third blue.

 Aesthetic Perception

Seeing Like an Artist Ask students to point out objects in the room that are red, yellow, or blue.   NSAE 3.a

Developing Visual Literacy Ask students if they have ever played or seen a musical instrument before. Do they own a bag, such as a book bag, backpack, or purse? What colors are these objects?
NSAE 3.a

Web Connection

Visit **www.carnegiemuseums.org/cmnh/exhibits/ north-south-east-west/tlingit/** to find out more about the Tlingit.

Teach

Time: About 30 minutes

"Let's look at the primary colors." "Vamos a mirar los colores primarios".

Practice

Materials: multi-colored fabric scraps (each scrap should have at least one primary color on it)

- Display a piece of red paper in one corner of the room, yellow paper in another corner, and blue paper in another corner.

- Give each student a scrap of fabric to hold behind their backs. Ask them not to look at the fabric until you tell them to.

- Ask students to look at their fabric and decide which primary colors they see the most on their fabric.

- Ask students to walk to the corner of the room that is displaying that primary color.

Creative Expression

Materials: 9" × 12" white drawing paper; red, yellow, and blue markers

Alternate Materials: crayons

- Distribute the materials and have students follow the directions on page 111.

- See the Activity Tips on page 239 for visual examples of this lesson's activity.

- Review the Technique Tips on page 215 for information about using markers.

- Have students exhibit their art and express ideas about each other's work.

NSAE 1.a; 1.c; 5.a; 5.c

Art Journal: Brainstorming

Have students look around them and think about an object they would like to draw. Ask students to sketch this object in their Art Journals.

Using Primary Colors

The **primary colors** are red, yellow, and blue. They are very special because no other colors can be mixed to make them. They are the first colors.

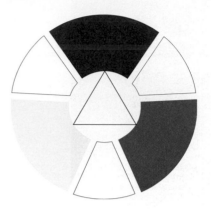

Practice

1. Look at the fabric your teacher gave you.

2. Decide which primary color you see the most on your fabric. Go to the corner of the room that shows that color.

Differentiated Instruction

Reteach
Have students create a paper chain by alternating red, yellow, and blue strips of paper.

Special Needs
Some students may have trouble locating objects in the room to draw. Have an assortment of objects from which students will choose.

ELL Tips
Have three volunteers stand next to one another. Ask students to name the colors of the volunteers' shirts and identify primary colors on the shirts.

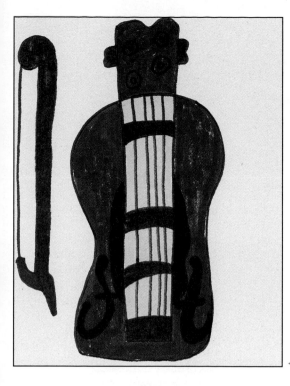

Think about the colors you see in the student's drawing.

◀ **Jed Woodward.** Age 6.

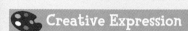 **Creative Expression**

What object will you draw?

1. Find an object you like.
2. Use red, yellow, and blue markers only. Draw and color a picture of your object.

 **Art Criticism**

Analyze What colors did you use? What are these colors called?

Art Across the Curriculum

Use these simple ideas to reinforce art concepts across the curriculum.

★ **Personal Writing** Show students pictures of various instruments. Have students draw a picture to show what kind of instrument they might like to learn to play.

★ **Math** Listen to a song. Clap the rhythm and count the beats out loud in each measure. (For example, "One, two, three, four. One, two, three, four.")

★ **Science** Record observations about parts of animals, including wings, feet, heads, and tails. Note which animals have one or more primary color.

★ **Social Studies** Look at portraits of historical figures in American or state history, such as George Washington. Identify primary colors in the portraits.

★ **Technology** Direct students to use a paint program for this assignment. Have students draw a picture using the primary colors. Visit **SRAonline.com** to print detailed instructions for this activity.

Reflect

Time: About 5 minutes

Review and Assess

"What colors did you use?" "¿Qué colores usaron?"

Think

■ Discuss the student art question. The student used red, yellow, and blue.

■ Identify primary colors in *Large Prints 5 Capriccio Musicale* and *6 Point of Tranquility*.

Informal Assessment

Art Journal: Critical Thinking
Have students answer the Analyze question in their Art Journals.

 Art Criticism

Have students ask themselves the following questions.

Describe ▶ What object did you draw?

Analyze ▶ What colors did you use? What are these colors called?

Interpret ▶ Give your drawing a title. Use a color name in the title, such as *Mountain of Red Blocks*.

Decide ▶ What other details might you add to your drawing?

NSAE 2.b; 5.a; 5.c

■ For standardized-format test practice using this lesson's art content, see pages 36–37 in *Reading and Writing Test Preparation*.

Primary Colors

Extra! For the Art Specialist

Focus

Study **Large Prints 5** *Capriccio Musicale* and **6** *Point of Tranquility* and discuss how the artists used color. Ask students to describe where they see red, yellow, and blue in these works of art. Have students point to these colors.

Teach

Using a color wheel, have the students find red, yellow, and blue. Explain to the students that the primary colors are the colors that are mixed to make other colors. Have students create a tissue paper collage using primary colors.

Reflect

Have students use the four steps of art criticism to evaluate their work. Did they create a collage using only primary colors?

Alternate Activity

Materials
- 9″ × 12″ white construction paper
- colored tissue paper (red, yellow, blue) torn or cut into squares
- liquid starch
- brushes

1. Study the colors that are next to the primary colors on the color wheel. Explain how two primary colors are mixed to make those colors.

2. Demonstrate how to use liquid starch to wet the 9″ × 12″ white construction paper.

3. Have students place a sheet of primary colored tissue in the wet starch. Then students place a different colored piece of tissue next to the first piece so the colors overlap on one side.

4. Tell students to continue wetting the paper and overlapping the tissue until the paper is filled.
NSAE 1.a; 1.c

Research in Art Education

Case studies have indicated that students perceive "that the arts facilitate their personal and social development." It also appeared that to gain the full benefit of arts education, students should be exposed to all of the arts, including fine arts, dance, theater, and music ("Arts Education in Secondary School: Effects and Effectiveness" in *Critical Links*, p. 76). The study of music is featured in this lesson.

Assessment
Use the following rubric to evaluate the artwork students make in the Creative Expression activity and to assess students' understanding of primary colors.

Have students complete page 39 or 40 in their *Assessment* books.

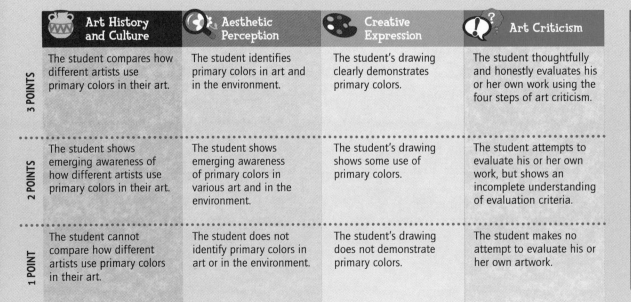

	Art History and Culture	Aesthetic Perception	Creative Expression	Art Criticism
3 POINTS	The student compares how different artists use primary colors in their art.	The student identifies primary colors in art and in the environment.	The student's drawing clearly demonstrates primary colors.	The student thoughtfully and honestly evaluates his or her own work using the four steps of art criticism.
2 POINTS	The student shows emerging awareness of how different artists use primary colors in their art.	The student shows emerging awareness of primary colors in various art and in the environment.	The student's drawing shows some use of primary colors.	The student attempts to evaluate his or her own work, but shows an incomplete understanding of evaluation criteria.
1 POINT	The student cannot compare how different artists use primary colors in their art.	The student does not identify primary colors in art or in the environment.	The student's drawing does not demonstrate primary colors.	The student makes no attempt to evaluate his or her own artwork.

Assessment, p. 39

Name _____ Date _____

Lesson 4 UNIT 3

Primary Colors

For the teacher: Use the following prompt for this activity. Using crayons, draw a picture using only the primary colors.

Level K

Unit 3 • Color 39

Lesson 5 Overview

Colors Show Feelings

Lesson 5 discusses the effects of color. Artists use colors to show emotions.

Objectives

 Art History and Culture

To recognize that artists use bright and dull colors to express feelings in their works of art

 Creative Expression

To create a self-portrait that uses color to show an emotion

 Aesthetic Perception

To learn how bright and dull colors are used in works of art

Art Criticism

To evaluate one's own work using the four steps of art criticism

Vocabulary ⭐ Reading

Review the following vocabulary words with students before beginning the lesson.

bright color color brillante—a pure spectral color

dull color color opaco—a low-intensity color that has been subdued by the addition of its complement; brown, gray, dull red, and so on.

See page 119B for additional vocabulary and Spanish vocabulary resources.

 Art Journal: Vocabulary

Have students add these words to the Vocabulary section of their Art Journals.

Lesson Materials

- 12″ × 18″ construction paper (blue and violet, yellow and orange)
- oil pastels (separate into bright and dull colors, skin tones, and black and white)
- 9″ × 12″ paper in a variety of bright and dull colors

Alternate Materials

- crayons or markers
- large swatches of bright and dull-colored fabric

Program Resources

- *Reading and Writing Test Prep.*, pp. 38–39
- *Transparency 17*
- *Artist Profiles*, pp. 11, 34
- *Assessment*, pp. 41–42
- *Large Prints 5* Capriccio Musicale and *6* Point of Tranquility
- *The National Museum of Women in the Arts Collection*

Concept Trace
Colors Show Feelings
Introduced: Level K, Unit 3, Lesson 5

Reinforced: Level 2, Unit 2, Lesson 6

Lesson 5 Arts Integration

Theatre

Complete Unit 3, Lesson 5 on pages 62–63 of the *Theatre Arts Connections* book.

Theatre Arts Connections, p. 62

Music

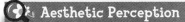

Listen to "Run, Run!" from *Memories of Childhood,* by Octavio Pinto. The sound of musical instruments can show feelings. From the title, we know that running is taking place. Is the running done for fun or to escape from something?

Movement & Dance

Identify parts of nature that make us feel a particular way. Students create words to describe their feelings. For example: lake, blue, calm; lightning, white, excited; daisy field, yellow, playful. Explore each of these ideas in movement by using different qualities of force or energy.

Focus

Time: About 10 minutes

Activate Prior Knowledge

"How does the color red make you feel? The color green?" "¿Cómo se sienten cuando ven el color rojo? ¿El color verde?"

■ Show students color swatches of red, green, and so on. Encourage them to associate the colors with objects or ideas to help them explore their reactions to colors. Prompt students with questions such as, "What does the color red remind you of? What does the color green remind you of?"

Using Literature

■ Read *The 100th Day of School* by Angela Shelf Medearis, illustrated by Joan Holub. Ask students to identify bright and dull colors in the illustrations. Discuss how the colors make them feel. Then have students create their own artwork to be an illustration for the story.

Thematic Connection

■ **Feelings:** Brainstorm and list different types of feelings. Discuss events that can lead up to each feeling.

Introduce the Art

"Let's look at the colors in these works of art."
"Vamos a mirar los colores en estas obras de arte".

Main Idea and Details Reading

■ Ask students to describe what they see in each painting.

Making Inferences Reading

■ How are the people feeling in each painting?

Cause and Effect Reading

■ What might have caused the people to feel this way?

NSAE 4.a

Art History and Culture

Share information from the Art History and Culture sections with students. Tell students that artists use colors to show feelings. Ask students why they think Picasso chose blue for many of his paintings. Possible answers: Picasso chose blue to make the paintings look calm or sad. Blue fit the mood of what he was painting.

 Web Connection

Visit www.artnet.com and search for Janet Fish to view more of her art.

Colors Show Feelings

▲ **Janet Fish.** (American). *Feeding Caitlin.* 1988.
Oil on canvas. 54¼ × 70 inches (137.80 × 177.8 cm.). Butler Institute of American Art, Youngstown, Ohio.

Look at these paintings. Notice how the colors are different.

Art History and Culture

Artists use colors to help show feelings. During one period Picasso painted many blue paintings. Why do you think he chose blue?

Art History and Culture

Janet Fish (jan´ ət fish)(1938–   ) is known as a contemporary realist painter. Contemporary realism is a realistic style of painting in which people, places, and other objects are represented in a natural manner. Working out of her home in New York City, Fish often paints brightly colored, large still lifes of everyday objects.

See pages 16–21 and 24–25 for more about subject matter and art history.

Artist Profiles, p. 11

▸ Artist Profile ◂
Janet Fish
b. 1938

Janet Fish (jan´ ət fish) earned two degrees in fine arts from Yale University but struggled to find work. For a while, she supported herself by painting bars of soap for a department store. Since then her large, lively still lifes have become much admired. Fish has taught at art schools across the nation. She now spends half her time in New York and half in Vermont.

◀ **Pablo Picasso.** (Spanish).
The Tragedy. 1903.
....
Oil paint on wood. 41½ × 27 inches
(105.4 × 69 cm.). National Gallery of
Art, Washington, D.C.

Study the pictures.

▶ How does each painting make you feel?

Aesthetic Perception

Seeing Like an Artist Name a creature you have seen in a cartoon. What color is it?

Unit 3 • Lesson 5   **113**

Study

▶ Answers will vary. *Feeding Caitlin* might make you feel happy or excited because of its bright colors and the expressions on the people's faces. You might think *The Tragedy* looks sad because of the dull colors, the expressions and body language, and the title.

■ For more examples of narrative art, see **The National Museum of Women in the Arts Collection.**

Art Journal: Concept
Ask students to draw shapes with colors that make them feel happy on the top half of the page. Below that have the students draw shapes in colors that make them feel sad.

Aesthetic Perception

Seeing Like an Artist Encourage students to think about cartoon characters and their colors. Ask students why they think the artists chose those colors. Discuss how the colors can help show how a character is feeling.

Developing Visual Literacy Ask students to describe how each picture makes them feel. What makes them feel that way?

Art History and Culture

Pablo Picasso

Pablo Picasso (päb´ lō pi kä´ sō) (1881–1973) was recognized for his artistic talent at an early age. At the age of 15 he attended advanced classes at the Royal Academy of Art in Barcelona. Picasso's work is usually referred to in terms of "periods." Work done during his early twenties (1901–1904) is referred to as the Blue Period. These predominately blue paintings often depicted the poor and were very melancholy. The mood of this period was likely influenced by the suicidal death of Picasso's friend.

See pages 16–21 and 24–25 for more about subject matter and art history.

Artist Profiles, p. 34

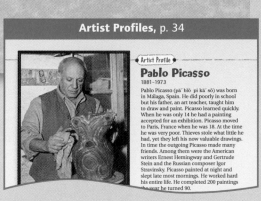

◆ Artist Profile ◆
Pablo Picasso
1881–1973
Pablo Picasso (pä´ blō pi kä´ sō) was born in Málaga, Spain. He did poorly in school but his father, an art teacher, taught him to draw and paint. Picasso learned quickly. When he was only 14 he had a painting accepted for an exhibition. Picasso moved to Paris, France when he was 18. At the time he was very poor. Thieves stole what little he had, yet they left his now valuable drawings. In time the outgoing Picasso made many friends. Among them were the American writers Ernest Hemingway and Gertrude Stein and the Russian composer Igor Stravinsky. Picasso painted at night and slept late most mornings. He worked hard his entire life. He completed 200 paintings the year he turned 90.

Web Connection
Click **www.tamu.edu/mocl/picasso/** to find out more about Pablo Picasso.

LESSON 5 • Colors Show Feelings **113**

Teach

Time: About 40 minutes

"Show on your face how a color makes you feel." *"Muestren en su cara cómo los hace sentir un color".*

Practice

Materials: 9" × 12" paper in a variety of bright and dull colors

Alternate Materials: large swatches of bright and dull-colored fabric

- Display a piece of colored paper and demonstrate a facial expression that shows your reaction to the color.

- Ask students to use facial expressions to show how a color makes them feel as directed on page 114.

Creative Expression

Materials: 12" × 18" construction paper (blue and violet, yellow and orange), oil pastels (separate into bright and dull colors, skin tones, and black and white)

Alternate Materials: crayons or markers

- Ask students which colors they think of as happy colors and which colors they think of as sad colors.

- Distribute the materials and have students follow the directions on page 115.

- Allow students to choose either bright or dull colors for their self-portraits. Provide the students with a piece of paper in the same color family as their oil pastel choices.

- Instruct the students to begin their drawing by using a circle or oval to create a face shape and then draw a body.

- Have students use the oil pastels to color in the face completely and then add facial features such as eyes, nose, and mouth. Then have students complete their self-portaits.

- See the Activity Tips on page 240 for visual examples of this lesson's activity.

NSAE 1.c

Art Journal: Brainstorming
Direct the students to imagine themselves as happy or sad. Have students draw a quick sketch of how they look in this mood in their journals.

Using Color To Show Feelings

Artists use **bright colors** to make us feel happy.

Dull colors can make us feel sad or scared.

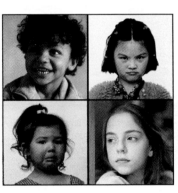

Practice

1. Look at the color your teacher shows you.

2. Show with your face how the color makes you feel.

Differentiated Instruction

Reteach
You may wish to read the book *Hailstones and Halibut Bones,* which is about color. Discuss the feelings about each color expressed by the writer. Ask students whether they agree with those feelings.

Special Needs
To assist students in making connections among colors and feelings, ask them to draw an event where they felt happy or sad, including some of the colors they observed.

ELL Tips
Arrange colors on a chart from bright and happy to dark and scary. Review colors with students by saying the color name and showing a facial expression to convey a reaction to the color. Have students do the same. Use words such as *happy, scary, peaceful,* and *sad* to help students tell how a color makes them feel.

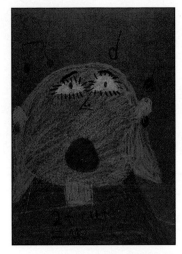

 Michael Olson. Age 6.

Emily Wyatt. Age 6.

Think about how these students' artwork makes you feel.

 Creative Expression

How do different colors make you feel?

1. Choose bright or dull colors for your portrait.
2. Draw your face and body. Then add details.

 Art Criticism

Interpret How do the colors in your picture make you feel? Give your picture a title.

Art Across the Curriculum

Use these simple ideas to reinforce art concepts across the curriculum.

★ **Narrative Writing** Have students draw pictures to tell a story. Use colors that demonstrate the feeling of the story.

★ **Math** Use language such as before and after to describe relative position in a sequence of events relating to the fine art. For example: "After the girl feeds Caitlin she is going to go swimming."

★ **Science** Discuss ways the Earth can provide resources for life, such as water. Identify other uses of water, including ways it might be used by the people in the fine art paintings.

★ **Social Studies** Identify physical characteristics of bodies of water. How are the bodies of water different in the two paintings? What other bodies of water have they seen?

★ **Technology** Have students use bright or dull colors in a paint program to draw a happy or sad picture. Visit **SRAonline.com** to print detailed instructions for this activity.

Reflect
Time: About 5 minutes

Review and Assess

"What are the different ways that colors can make us feel?" "¿Qué diferentes sentimientos nos hacen experimentar los colores?"

Think

- Discuss the student art question. Possible answers: The bright portrait makes me feel happy and excited. The dull blue portrait makes me feel calm or sad.

- Identify the feelings the colors evoke in **Large Prints 5** *Capriccio Musicale* and **6** *Point of Tranquility*.

Informal Assessment

Art Journal: Critical Thinking
Have students answer the Interpret question by drawing a picture in their Art Journals.

 **Art Criticism**

Have students ask themselves the following questions.

Describe ▶ How do you look in your self portrait?

Analyze ▶ What colors make the shapes seem larger? Smaller? What colors are the brightest? The darkest?

Interpret ▶ How do the colors in your picture make you feel? Give your picture a title.

Decide ▶ What other details could you add to your self-portrait?

NSAE 2.b; 5.a; 5.c

- For standardized-format test practice using this lesson's art content, see pages 38–39 in **Reading and Writing Test Preparation**.

Lesson 5 Wrap-Up

Colors Show Feelings

  For the Art Specialist

Time: About 40 minutes

Focus

Study *Large Prints 5* *Capriccio Musicale* and *6* *Point of Tranquility* and discuss how the artists used color. Ask students to describe how these works of art make them feel when they look at them. Discuss how colors show feelings.

Teach

Discuss how artists choose colors to express feelings in their art work. Show the students several squares of construction paper and ask them how each color makes them feel. Ask the students to select a favorite color and create a finger painting that shows different facial expressions.

Reflect

Have students use the four steps of art criticism to evaluate their work. Did they use their favorite color to create a finger painting that effectively shows different facial expressions?

Alternate Activity

Materials
- finger paint paper or white drawing paper
- finger paints (red, yellow, blue, orange, green, violet)
- paper towels

1. Direct the students to select one color of finger paint.

2. Have students paint one vertical and one horizontal line through the middle of the paper to divide it into four rectangles.

3. Ask students to think about how their color makes them feel. Have students paint in each rectangle a different facial expression that shows how this color might make them feel.

NSAE 1.a; 1.c

Research in Art Education

One case study showed that students who were "learning disabled and who were 'reluctant' readers" were better able to engage in reading when the creation and analysis of visual art was incorporated in their discussions of stories. This suggests that combining visual art with reading may help certain readers ("Reading *Is* Seeing: Using Visual Response to Improve the Literary Reading of Reluctant Readers" in *Critical Links,* p. 144). In the Using Literature section, students create art to illustrate the story the teacher reads.

Assessment
Use the following rubric to evaluate the artwork students make in the Creative Expression activity and to assess students' understanding of bright and dull colors.

Have students complete page 41 or 42 in their *Assessment* books.

	Art History and Culture	Aesthetic Perception	Creative Expression	Art Criticism
3 POINTS	The student recognizes that artists use bright and dull colors to express feelings in their works of art.	The student understands how bright and dull colors are used to express feelings.	The student's self-portrait clearly demonstrates the use of color to show a feeling.	The student thoughtfully and honestly evaluates own work using the four steps of art criticism.
2 POINTS	The student shows emerging awareness that artists use bright and dull colors to express feelings in their works of art.	The student shows emerging awareness of how bright and dull colors are used to express feelings.	The student's self-portrait shows some use of color to show a feeling.	The student attempts to evaluate own work, but shows an incomplete understanding of evaluation criteria.
1 POINT	The student cannot recognize that artists use bright and dull colors to express feelings in their works of art.	The student does not understand how bright and dull colors are used to express feelings.	The student's self-portrait does not demonstrate using color to show a feeling.	The student makes no attempt to evaluate own artwork.

Assessment, p. 41

Name _____ Date _____

Colors Show Feelings

Lesson **5** UNIT 3

For the teacher: Use the following prompts for this activity.
1. Using a crayon, draw a line using a color that represents a happy feeling in box 1.
2. Draw a line using a color that represents a sad feeling in box 2.
3. Draw a line using a color that represents an angry feeling in box 3.
4. Draw a line using a color that represents a silly feeling in box 4.

Level K

Unit 3 • Color **41**

Light and Dark Colors

Lesson 6 explores color value—the darkness or lightness of a color. Mixing black with a color makes it darker. Adding white to a color makes it lighter.

Objectives

 Art History and Culture

To recognize that artists have different styles for depicting water in art.

 Creative Expression

To create a painting with light and dark values of one color

 Aesthetic Perception

To locate light and dark values in the fine art

Art Criticism

To evaluate one's own work using the four steps of art criticism

Lesson Materials

- white paper (any size)
- liquid tempera paint (blue, black, white)
- 12" × 18" white paper
- small sponges
- water dishes
- large and medium brushes
- mixing trays
- paper towels
- oil pastels

Alternate Materials

- crayons
- light or white paper

Program Resources

- *Reading and Writing Test Prep.*, pp. 40–41
- *Transparency 18*
- *Flash Cards 9–10*
- *Artist Profiles*, pp. 18, 50
- *Assessment*, pp. 43–44
- *Large Prints 5* Capriccio Musicale and *6* Point of Tranquility
- *Art Around the World Collection*

Concept Trace

Color Value

Introduced: Level K, Unit 3, Lesson 6

Reinforced: Level 2, Unit 2, Lessons 5–6

Vocabulary  Reading

Review the following vocabulary words with students before beginning the lesson. The following words appear as art on student page 118 and in the glossary.

darker más oscuro

lighter más claro

See page 119B for additional vocabulary and Spanish vocabulary resources.

Art Journal: Vocabulary

Have students add these words to the Vocabulary section of their Art Journals.

Lesson 6 Arts Integration

Theatre

Complete Unit 3, Lesson 6 on pages 64–69 of the *Theatre Arts Connections* book.

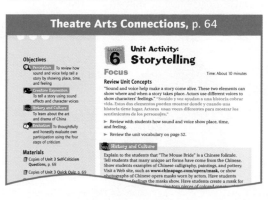

Theatre Arts Connections, p. 64

Music

 Listen to "Cuckoo in the Woods" from *Carnival of the Animals* by Camille Saint-Saen. The sound of the bird is brighter than the background instruments. How would music feel if there were only bright colors? Would you get tired of it?

Movement & Dance

Pick two colors with contrasting qualities, such as red and blue and create a word web for each color. Some examples are: red—explosive, bold, piercing; blue—cool, soothing, expansive. Ask students to try a red color idea and then a blue color idea, exploring all of the qualities using movement. Then identify the contrasts between them.

Focus

Activate Prior Knowledge

"Have you ever seen a waterfall?" "¿Alguna vez han visto una catarata?"

Using Literature

■ Read *In the Ocean* by Claire Henley and *Oceans* by Kristin Ward. Ask students to identify light and dark colors in the illustrations.

Thematic Connection Science

■ **Caring for the Environment:** Discuss ways we can help take care of the environment.

Introduce the Art

"Let's look at the waterfall paintings." "Vamos a mirar las pinturas de cataratas".

Comparing and Contrasting ⭐ Reading

■ Ask students to describe what they see in each painting. How are these paintings alike and different?

■ Ask students to name the colors they see in the paintings. Have them point to the lighter and darker colors.

■ Share and discuss information from *Artist Profiles* pages 18 and 50 with students.

Adjectives and Adverbs ⭐ Language Arts

■ List on a chart the adjectives and adverbs students use to describe the fine art.

NSAE 4.a

🏺 Art History and Culture

Share information from Art History and Culture sections with students. Discuss how Japanese prints were usually made by a team of four artists, but Hokusai created many by himself. Ask students why people might work as a team to create an artwork. Possible answers: It might take a long time to create the art and having more people speeds up the process. Some people might be better at some steps of the process than others.

💻 **Web Connection**

Visit **www.johnhtwachtman.com/index.htm** to learn more about John Henry Twachtman.

Light and Dark Colors

▲ **John Henry Twachtman.** (American). *Waterfall Blue Brook.* c. 1895–1900.

Oil on canvas. 25⅛ × 30⅛ inches (63.81 × 77.72 cm.). Cincinnati Art Museum, Cincinnati, Ohio.

Look at the pictures of water. They have light and dark colors.

🏺 Art History and Culture

Long ago Japanese prints were made by a team of four artists. Each person did one step to help make the print.

🏺 Art History and Culture

John Henry Twachtman

John Henry Twachtman (jän hen´ rē twäkt´ mən) (1853–1902) was born in Cincinnati, Ohio. After studying art in Cincinnati, he continued his studies in Munich and Paris. French Impressionist artists had a great influence on Twachtman's painting, but Twachtman differed in that he was more likely to paint a landscape depicting fall or winter rather than the more traditional spring or summer. In 1888 he returned to the United States and settled in Connecticut, where the countryside landscapes served as his inspiration.

See pages 16–21 and 24–25 for more about subject matter and art history.

Artist Profiles, p. 50

◆ Artist Profile ◆

John Henry Twachtman
1853–1902

Born in Cincinnati, Ohio, John Henry Twachtman (jän hen´ rē twäkt´ mən) began studying art when he was 18. As his artistic style evolved, he moved from harsh, radical impressionist compositions to a calmer style. Near the end of his career, when he was painting some of his most famous works on his country farm, he came to believe that a person is most true and content in the solitude of nature.

◄ **Katsushika Hokusai.**
(Japanese). *Kirifuri Waterfall on Mount Kurokami in Shimotsuke Province.* *c. 1833-1834*
••••••••••••••••••••••••••
Color woodblock print. 15⁵⁄₁₆ × 10⅝ inches (38.9 × 26.3 cm.). Honolulu Academy of Arts, Honolulu, Hawaii.

Study the works of art.

▶ Point to a dark blue part in the pictures. Now point to a light blue part.

Study

▶ A possible answer is the dark blue around the rocks in *Waterfall Blue Brook* or the dark blue vertical lines on the *Kirifuri Waterfall.* Light blue is found in the splashing water at the base of each falls.

■ For more examples of art from Asia, see the **Art Around the World Collection.**

Art Journal: Concept
Ask students to demonstrate light and dark values by coloring a light red shape and a dark red shape.

Aesthetic Perception

Seeing Like an Artist Show students a book illustration. Ask students to point out examples of light and dark green in the picture.

Developing Visual Literacy Discuss the frequent use of blue in the fine art. Encourage students to look around and find as many examples of light and dark blue as possible.
NSAE 3.a

Aesthetic Perception

Seeing Like an Artist Look in a book. Find a picture that has light green and dark green.

Art History and Culture

Katsushika Hokusai

Katsushika Hokusai (kät sū shē kä hō kū sī) (1760–1849) produced nearly 30,000 pieces of art in his lifetime including paintings, wood engravings, and prints. He was most famous for his colored prints on woodblocks. Hokusai used a separate block of wood to print each color. During the 1830s he produced several series of prints. *Kirifuri Waterfall* is from his Waterfall Series, a set of eight prints.

See pages 16–21 and 24–25 for more about subject matter and art history.

Artist Profiles, p. 18

◄ Artist Profile ►
Katsushika Hokusai
1760–1849
Katsushika Hokusai (kät sōō´ shē kä hō´ kōō sī) was born in the city that is now Tokyo. He changed his name more than 30 times. No one knows why. When his home became dirty, he moved. Hokusai lived in 93 different places! Hokusai supported himself by illustrating comic books, greeting cards, and novels. During his lifetime he had two wives and seven children.

Hokusai was not interested in money. To pay his bills he would hand over an envelope of money he had received for a painting. Sometimes it was enough, and sometimes it wasn't. When he was broke, he bought art supplies after dark, hoping to avoid people he owed. Hokusai painted

Web Connection
Learn more about Hokusai by visiting the Web site for the Hokusai Museum. Go to www.book-navi.com/hokusai/hokusai-e.html.

LESSON 6 • Light and Dark Colors 117

Teach

Time: About 45 minutes

"Let's create light and dark colors of the same main color." "Vamos a crear colores claros y oscuros del mismo color principal".

Practice

Materials: white paper (any size), liquid tempera paint (blue, black, white)

- Have students follow directions on page 118.

- On a sheet of paper, mix one drop of black paint with blue. Discuss what happens each time more black paint is added. Use a similar procedure in mixing blue paint with white paint.

- "What color was added to create the lightest color? What color was added to create the darkest color?"

Creative Expression

Materials: liquid tempera paint (blue, black, white), 12" × 18" white paper, small sponges, water dishes, large and medium brushes, mixing trays, paper towels, oil pastels

Alternate Materials: crayons, light or white paper

- Have students create a seascape by sponge painting light and dark colors of blue.

- Distribute the materials and have the students follow the directions on page 119.

- See the Activity Tips on page 240 for visual examples of this lesson's activity.

- Encourage students to mix the black paint into the blue to create a darker color for the bottom of their seascape.

- Have students make their colors lighter as they move to the top of the page so their paintings resemble a real seascape.

- Encourage students to add details like fish, waves, and plants, with oil pastels.

NSAE 1.a; 1.c

Art Journal: Brainstorming

Ask students to think about different ocean creatures. Have students draw several of these creatures in their Art Journals.

Using Light and Dark Colors

Mixing colors with black makes them **darker.**

Mixing colors with white makes them **lighter.**

Practice

1. Mix one drop of black paint with blue.

2. Mix one drop of blue paint with white.

Differentiated Instruction

Reteach

Show a picture with light and dark values of a color, for example, red. Have students point to the light and dark areas.

Special Needs

Check students' understanding of light and dark colors by having them choose a second color with which to complete the practice exercise.

ELL Tips

Display light and dark values of colored pencils. Have students draw lines of light and dark colors. Then have students pick out light blue, dark blue, light green, dark green, and so on. Each time a color is named, have students repeat the name with you.

▲ Yung Kipreos.
Age 6.

Think about where you see light colors in the student's work. Where do you see dark colors?

 Creative Expression

What things in the sea have light and dark colors?

1. Create a sea picture with light and dark colors.

2. Add details like fish, waves, and plants.

Art Criticism

Decide Do you like the light and dark colors in your painting? Which part do you like best?

Art Across the Curriculum

Use these simple ideas to reinforce art concepts across the curriculum.

★ **Poetry Writing** Help students generate a list of words that rhyme with *sea*. Have students draw a picture for each rhyming word.

★ **Math** Compare and order two or three concrete objects according to height. Study the waterfalls in the fine art and determine which is taller.

★ **Science** Discuss animal habitats and name animals that live in the water.

★ **Social Studies** Show students pictures of various waterfalls. Identify common physical characteristics, such as rocks, water, and hills.

★ **Technology** Ask students to study the color palette in a paint program. Find light and dark shades of the same hue. Create a picture using the lighter and darker shades of one color. Visit **SRAonline.com** to print detailed instructions for this activity.

 **eflect**   **Time:** About 5 minutes

Review and Assess

"How can you make a color darker? How can you make a color lighter?" "¿Cómo pueden oscurecer un color? ¿Cómo pueden aclarar un color?"

Think

■ Discuss the student art question. Dark colors are near the bottom and on the fish. Light colors are in the top area.

■ Identify light and dark colors in *Large Prints 5 Capriccio Musicale* and *6 Point of Tranquility*.

Informal Assessment

Art Journal: Critical Thinking
Have students answer the Decide question by writing *yes* or *no* in their Art Journals. Then ask students to draw their favorite part from their painting.

Art Criticism

Have students ask themselves the following questions.

Describe ▶ What is happening in your seascape?

Analyze ▶ How did you make the light blue part in your picture? How did you make the dark blue part?

Interpret ▶ Is your ocean calm or rough? How can you tell?

Decide ▶ Do you like the light and dark colors in your painting? Which part do you like best?

NSAE 2.b; 5.a; 5.c

■ For standardized-format test practice using this lesson's art content, see pages 40–41 in *Reading and Writing Test Preparation*.

Lesson 6 Wrap-Up
Light and Dark Colors

Extra! For the Art Specialist
Time: About 45 minutes

Focus
Study **Large Prints 5** *Capriccio Musicale* and **6** *Point of Tranquility* and discuss how the artists used color. Ask students to describe how the use of light and dark colors affects the mood of the works of art. Discuss how each picture makes them feel.

Teach
Ask the students to draw a nighttime scene using colored chalk and white tempera paint.

Reflect
Have students use the four steps of art criticism to evaluate their work. Did they effectively use light and dark colors to draw a nighttime scene?

Alternate Activity

Materials
- 9" × 12" black paper
- colored chalk or oil pastels
- white tempera paint
- shallow bowls or plates for the tempera paint
- paper towels

1. Ask students to imagine a nighttime scene and describe what they see. Are there stars and a moon? What animals like to come out when it is dark?

2. Have students use colored chalk or oil pastels to draw the nighttime scene from their imaginations. Demonstrate for the students how to dip chalk in white tempera paint and draw with it on the black paper. Point out how the colors become light when mixed with white paint.

NSAE 1.a; 1.c

Research in Art Education

". . . [T]he kind of deliberately designed tasks students are offered in school help define the kind of thinking they will learn to do. The kind of thinking students learn to do will influence what they come to know and the kind of cognitive skills they acquire" (Eisner, Elliot W. *The Arts and the Creation of Mind.* New Haven: Yale Univ. Press, 2002).

Assessment
Use the following rubric to evaluate the artwork students make in the Creative Expression activity and to assess students' understanding of light and dark colors.

Have students complete page 43 or 44 in their *Assessment* books.

	Art History and Culture	Aesthetic Perception	Creative Expression	Art Criticism
3 POINTS	The student recognizes that artists have different styles for depicting water in art.	The student accurately locates light and dark values in the fine art.	The student's painting clearly demonstrates light and dark values.	The student thoughtfully and honestly evaluates own work using the four steps of art criticism.
2 POINTS	The student shows emerging awareness that artists have different styles for depicting water in art.	The student shows emerging awareness of light and dark values and can identify some in the fine art.	The student's painting shows some use of light and dark values.	The student attempts to evaluate own work, but shows an incomplete understanding of evaluation criteria.
1 POINT	The student does not recognize that artists have different styles for depicting water in art.	The student does not locate light and dark values in the fine art.	The student's painting does not demonstrate light and dark values.	The student makes no attempt to evaluate own artwork.

Assessment, p. 43

Name _____ Date _____ Lesson **6** UNIT 3

Light and Dark Colors

For the teacher: Use the following prompts for this activity.
1. Find four different pictures of the same color in a magazine.
2. Sort the pictures according to value and glue them in the box in order from lightest to darkest.

Level K   Unit 3 • Color   **43**

Unit 3 Vocabulary Review

black negro

blue azul

bright color—a pure spectral color **color brillante**—un color puro del espectro

brown marrón

collage—artwork consisting of pieces of paper and fabric glued onto a background **collage**—una obra de arte que contiene pedazos de papel y tela pegados en el fondo.

darker más oscuro

dull color—a low-intensity color that has been subdued by the addition of its complement; such as brown, gray, or dull red **color opaco**—un color de baja intensidad que ha sido sojuzgado por la adición de un color que lo completa; como marrón, gris o rojo opaco.

green verde

lighter más claro

orange anaranjado

painting—a picture or design created with paint **pintura**—un retrato o diseño creado con pintura.

primary colors—the colors red, yellow, and blue **colores primarios**—los colores rojo, amarillo y azul

red rojo

violet morado

white blanco

yellow amarillo

Vocabulary Practice

T Display **Transparency 39** to review unit vocabulary words.

Word Games ⭐ Vocabulary
Practice color words by playing "I Spy." One student leads the game by thinking of an item in the classroom and saying, "I spy something green (or whatever color the object is that the student sees)." The other students try to guess what the object is. The person who guesses correctly becomes the leader. Write the color words on the board as students say them.

Word Meanings ⭐ Vocabulary
List the vocabulary words. Tell students a definition of a word from the vocabulary list and ask them to identify the word that matches the meaning. Or, show a piece of colored paper and ask students to identify the word that matches the color.

Picture Clues ⭐ Vocabulary
Show pictures to help students understand the meanings of vocabulary words, such as pictures containing dull, light, or dark colors.

Art Criticism

Critical Thinking Art Criticism is an organized system for looking at and talking about art. You can criticize art without being an expert. The purpose of art criticism is to get the viewer involved in a perception process that delays judgment until all aspects of the artwork have been studied.

■ See pages 28–29 for more about art criticism.

Describe

▶ Ask students to describe this work of art. Possible answers include the following: It is a painted and decorated wooden chair. There are 5 casters under each side of the chair. The seat and back are a red padded material that is held down with upholstery nails. Behind the head area of the seat is the face of a storybook character. This is Milo who has exciting adventures in *The Phantom Tollbooth* that was published by Random House in 1961. There is a switch and electric outlets on the arms of the chair. There are lights on two triangular forms that stick out from the back of the chair.

Analyze

▶ Discuss the colors seen on the chair. Possible answers: The padded seat and back are red. The boy's face, the triangle shapes, and the painted wiggly stripes are orange. Yellow is painted on the top of the chair, the trim on the arms, and the front. Green is painted on the castle rooftops. Two masks on the front of the chair are green. There are green lines in the yellow circle with the boy's head. Blue is painted on the back, both the inside and the outside of the arms, and on the front of the chair. The front of the arms have violet stars and stripes on a black background. The boy's shirt is violet. There are some brown areas on the castles. The front of the arms are black, the casters are black, and the armrest areas look black.

120 UNIT 3 • Color

▲ **Rodney Alan Greenblat.** (American). *Control Chair.* 1986.

Painted wood, leather, lights, electrical outlets, and casters. 39 × 26¾ × 27½ inches (99.06 × 67.95 × 69.85 cm.). Birmingham Museum of Art, Birmingham, Alabama.

120   Unit 3

Art History and Culture

Rodney Alan Greenblat

Rodney Alan Greenblat (räd´ nē al´ ən grēn´ blat) (1960–   ) attended the New York School of Visual Arts. After graduating in 1982 he moved to New York City's East Village area, where he began promoting and exhibiting his work with the help of gallery owner Gracie Mansion. Much of Greenblat's work is inspired by cartoons, children's stories and his own imagination. Some of his creations show the influence of pop artists such as Roy Lichtenstein and Richard Hamilton.

See pages 16–21 and 24–25 for more about subject matter and art history.

Artist Profiles, p. 14

Artist Profile
Rodney Alan Greenblat
b. 1960

Rodney Alan Greenblat was born in Daly City, California, in 1960. Greenblat attended the New York School of Visual Arts. After graduating in 1982, he moved to New York City's East Village area, where he began promoting and exhibiting his work with the help of gallery owner Gracie Mansion. Rodney Alan Greenblat has participated in many successful art exhibitions all over the world.

 **Art Criticism** **Critical Thinking**

Describe

▶ What is this work of art?

Analyze

▶ What colors do you see on this chair?

Interpret

▶ What do you think it would feel like to sit in this chair?

Decide

▶ Do you think this chair is a work of art? Why or why not?

 Aesthetic Perception

Critical Thinking Show students an interesting piece of furniture in the school, perhaps a cozy chair from a classroom or library.

Describe ▶ What kind of furniture is this?

Analyze ▶ Are the colors like the colors on *Control Chair?* Why or why not?

Interpret ▶ How would you use this piece of furniture?

Decide ▶ Do you think this piece of furniture is a work of art?
▶ Why or why not?

Interpret

▶ Encourage students to explain the feeling the colors give to the chair. How do the colors make the chair look? Exciting? Scary? Relaxing? Possible answers: Answers will vary. Some might say that the bright colors make it look exciting.

▶ Ask students to tell how they think it would feel to sit in this chair. Possible answers: Some may say the chair is comfortable because of the padded seat. Some may think about the emotional quality of the piece and say exciting.

▶ Discuss what would happen if the switch was pulled. Possible answers: Some might say the lights would blink and the wheels would roll. The more adventurous will imagine flights of fancy to another place or time. Some may think about the castles on the sides and imagine going to them. Some may think about fantasy adventures. Encourage storytelling about the adventures that are possible in this chair.

Decide

▶ Ask students if they think the chair is a work of art. Why or why not? Possible answers: Some might say no because it is a chair, but remind them that chairs are works of art. Some might say yes because it looks exciting, or because it is full of bright colors. Encourage a discussion as to whether or not this is art, but always make the student defend his or her decision with a reason. If they ask you, you might say that a museum thinks enough of it to put it in its collection.

NSAE 5.a; 5.c

 Art Journal: Writing
Have students draw a picture in their Art Journals to answer the Interpret Aesthetic Perception question. Discuss the other questions aloud.

"Artists use different colors in their art." "Los artistas usan diferentes colores en sus obras de arte".

T Review unit vocabulary with students using *Transparency 39.*

■ Review the different colors and properties of colors in the student lessons.

Art Journal: Writing
Read the questions on page 122 to students. Have students write their answers in their Art Journals or on a separate sheet of paper. 1. B., 2. A., 3. A.

T For further assessment, have students complete the unit test on *Transparency 45.*

LEARN ABOUT MUSEUMS
► The Yale University Art Gallery has collections from a variety of countries and cultures all over the world, as well as impressionist, modernist, and contemporary paintings and sculpture. The gallery also holds a collection of American paintings and decorative arts that is considered to be one of the finest collections of its kind in the world.

► Discuss with students the different kinds of artwork in a museum.

► Discuss proper museum etiquette.

► For information about preparing for and experiencing a visit to a museum, including appropriate behavior, see the Museum Guide from the *National Museum of Women in the Arts Collection.*

"There is a logic of colors, and it is with this alone, and not with the logic of the brain, that the painter should conform."

—Paul Cézanne

Show What You Know
Answer these questions on a sheet of paper.

❶ Which of these is blue?

A.   B.

❷ Which of these is a dull color?

A.   B.

❸ Which of these would you add to make a color lighter?

A.   B.

The Yale University Gallery

This museum has art from all over the world. It is best known for its collection of paintings and works of art by American artists.

Unit Assessment Options

🔍 Aesthetic Perception
Practice Ask students to identify colors they see around them. Are any of them primary colors? Light or dark colors? Bright or dull colors?

🎨 Creative Expression
Student Portfolio Have students review all the artwork they have created during this unit and select the pieces they wish to put into their portfolios. Have students share their portfolios with classmates and comment constructively about the art.
NSAE 5.a; 5.c

❓ Art Criticism
Activity Have students select their favorite work of art from the unit. Guide students through study of their selected work using the four steps of art criticism. (See pages 28–29 for more about Art Criticism.)

Color in Storytelling and Music

Paul Tracey is a storyteller. He tells stories about Africa. His stories teach people about right and wrong. In this story, each animal makes its own interesting sound.

What to Do Make the sounds and movements of some animals.

1. Make the African sounds for each animal.

2. Find a way to move like each animal as you say their sounds.

3. Make up your own sounds and movements for Eagle and Hyena.

4. Perform them for others.

▲ **Paul Tracey.**
"The Girl on the Rock"

 **Art Criticism**

Decide Were you successful in expressing different kinds of moods and feelings?

 Art History and Culture

African Storytelling and Music

In the stories of the Shona-speaking people of Zimbabwe, Elephant and Lion are the undisputed chiefs. Baboon is their assistant; Antelope is their obedient subject. Hyena and Jackal are portrayed as servants; Tortoise is the creature of unhurried wisdom. Rabbit is quick-witted and playful; Python is the healer; and Crocodile can take on the traits of a husband or father. Birds are messengers and also serve as a nagging conscience.

 Color in Storytelling and Music

Objective: To make sound patterns for different animals and create appropriate movements.

Materials: *The Girl on the Rock* retold by Paul Tracey. Running time: 9:48

ocus   Time: About 10 minutes

- Read and discuss page 123.

- Have students make animal sounds.

Art History and Culture

- Have students predict the characteristics of animals in the story.

Teach   Time: About 20 minutes

Aesthetic Perception

- Ask students to identify the movements of the animals they know.

Creative Expression

- Listen to *The Girl on the Rock*.

- Have students practice the sound pattern for each animal.

- Chant the animal sound patterns and explore ways that each animal might move.

- **Informal Assessment** Comment positively on their interpretations.

eflect   Time: About 10 minutes

Art Criticism

- Have students draw a picture in their Art Journals to answer the Decide question.

Describe ► What movements did you make for each animal?

Analyze ► How did the sounds match the characteristics of each animal?

Interpret ► How did the animal sounds make you feel?

Unit 4 Planning Guide

	Lesson Title	Suggested Pacing	Creative Expression Activity
Lesson 1	Space in Art	45 minutes	Create a landscape drawing with a horizontal line.
Lesson 2	Form	45 minutes	Create a clay form of themselves.
Lesson 3	Space and Form	45 minutes	Create a puppet.
Lesson 4	Building Forms	45 minutes	Create a sculpture of a house.
Lesson 5	Animal Forms	45 minutes	Create a four-legged animal sculpture using clay.
Lesson 6	Forms Can Be Used	45 minutes	Create a pinch pot with clay.
▲ RT S ● U RC ◼ ARTSOURCE	Space and Form in Music and Dance	35 minutes	Create a dance that uses different movements and include sounds of clapping and stomping.

Materials	Program Resources	Fine Art Resources	Literature Resources
12" × 18" construction paper (light and dark blue), oil pastels	*Reading and Writing Test Preparation,* pp. 42–43 *Flash Card,* 20 *Assessment,* pp. 45–46 *Home and After School Connections,* pp. 19–22	*Transparency,* 19 *Artist Profiles,* pp. 10, 20 *Large Prints,* 7 and 8 *The National Museum of Women in the Arts Collection*	*Commotion in the Ocean* by Giles Andreae
assorted colors of oil-based modeling clay, clay mats (muslin), wood or cardboard (for a base), full-length mirror	*Reading and Writing Test Preparation,* pp. 44–45 *Assessment,* pp. 47–48	*Transparency,* 20 *Artist Profiles,* pp. 49, 63 *Large Prints,* 7 and 8 *Art Around the World*	*The Pledge of Allegiance* by Scholastic Editors
short paper-towel tubes, markers, scissors, glue, 2" × 3" construction paper strips, 1" × 3" felt strips, craft items such as buttons, feathers, or yarn	*Reading and Writing Test Preparation,* pp. 46–47 *Flash Card,* 20 *Assessment,* pp. 49–50	*Transparency,* 21 *Artist Profiles,* pp. 15, 30 *Large Prints,* 7 and 8 *Art Around the World*	*Fish Faces* by Norbert Wu
glue, markers, scissors, colored paper lunch bags, 6" × 6" construction paper squares, construction paper scraps, newspaper, craft items such as yarn and beads	*Reading and Writing Test Preparation,* pp. 48–49 *Assessment,* pp. 51–52	*Transparency,* 22 *Artist Profiles,* pp. 55, 76 *Large Prints,* 7 and 8 *The National Museum of Women in the Arts Collection*	*The Village of Round and Square Houses* by Ann Grifalconi
earthen clay, clay mats (muslin), pencils, wood or cardboard (for a base)	*Reading and Writing Test Preparation,* pp. 50–51 *Assessment,* pp. 53–54	*Transparency,* 23 *Artist Profiles,* pp. 58, 60 *Large Prints,* 7 and 8 *Art Around the World* *Animals Time Line*	*May I Bring a Friend?* by Beatrice Schenk de Regniers
clay, wood or cardboard (for a base), clay mats (muslin), clay tools (plastic forks and knives, paper clips, craft sticks, pencils)	*Reading and Writing Test Preparation,* pp. 52–53 *Flash Card,* 20 *Assessment,* pp. 55–56	*Transparency,* 24 *Artist Profiles,* pp. 61, 73 *Large Prints,* 7 and 8 *Art Around the World*	*Mouse Views: What the Class Pet Saw* by Bruce McMillan
"Dhon Dholak Cholam" performed by the Ranganiketan Manipuri Cultural Arts Troupe			

Unit Overview

Space and Form

Lesson 1: **Space** is the emptiness between shapes.

Lesson 2: **Form** refers to objects having three dimensions.

Lesson 3: **Space and Form** focuses on space around three-dimensional objects.

Lesson 4: **Building forms** are part of a category of art known as architecture.

Lesson 5: **Animal forms** can also be three-dimensional. A four-legged animal sculpture can be a solid form.

Lesson 6: **Uses for forms** refers to pottery that is both pretty and useful.

Introduce Unit Concepts

"Look for space and forms in your world."
"Busquen espacios y formas en su ambiente".

Shape, Space, and Form

- Draw various shapes on the board. Have students differentiate between shape and space.

- Arrange several objects on a table. Have students identify the space that surrounds the objects.

- Arrange several objects on a table. Have students draw one of the objects. Hold their drawings next to the actual three-dimensional object and discuss the differences between a flat shape and the three-dimensional form.

Cross-Curricular Projects

- See the *Language Arts and Reading, Mathematics, Science,* and *Social Studies Art Connections* books for activities that further develop space and form.

Space and Form

A form is a solid object that takes up space.

◄ **Allan Houser.** (American). *Earth Song.* 1978.
••••••••••••••••••••••••••••••
Alabama marble. 48 × 24 × 24 inches (121.92 × 60.96 × 60.96 cm.). The Herald Museum, Phoenix, Arizona.

124 Unit 4

Fine Art Prints

Display *Large Prints 7 Bear and Seal* and *8 Armoured Carousel Horse.* Refer to the prints throughout the unit as students learn about space and form.

Large Print 7

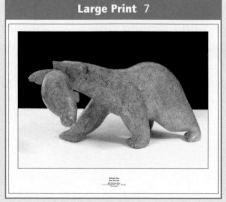

Large Print 8

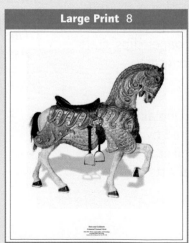

You can see all around a form. There is space around the form.

► Point to a form in the picture.
► Point to space in the picture.

In This Unit you will:
► learn about space and form.
► practice using them in your artwork.

Allan Houser
(1914–1994)

► was a Native American artist.
► was an art teacher.
► painted before he became a sculptor.

Unit 4   **125**

Examine the Artwork

"Let's find space and form in Allan Houser's *Earth Song*." "Vamos a buscar espacio y forma en Allan Houser's Earth Song".

■ Have students follow the directions on page 125 for identifying forms and space in the pictures.

► The Native American, his drum, and the tool he is using to beat the drum all stand and invade space.

► The Native American is surrounded by space on all sides and can therefore be seen from all sides.

► The drum and tool are held close to him and can be seen from most sides.

Unit Pretest

Display *Transparency 46* as a pretest. Answers: 1. B, 2. A, 3. A

Home Connection

■ See *Home and After-School Connections* for family newsletters and activities for this unit.

 Art History and Culture

Allan Houser

The artwork of Allan Houser (a´ lən hou´ zər) (1914–1994) often paid tribute to Houser's Native American roots. Houser was born Allan C. Haozous to Sam and Blossom Haozous. His parents were members of the Chirichua Apache tribe in New Mexico. Houser's paintings and sculptures frequently depicted the daily life and traditional roles of Native Americans, such as women gathering food and water, or men hunting.

See pages 16–21 and 24–25 for more about subject matter and art history.

Artist Profiles, p. 21

◆ Artist Profile ◆

Allan Houser
1915–1994

Born in Oklahoma, Allan Houser (a´ lan hou´ zar) was the great-nephew of the Apache chief Geronimo. In 1929, he left high school to help out on his family's farm, but he was also able to study his passion—art. In 1936, his paintings were shown at the World's Fair in New York. After he painted several large murals for government buildings in Washington, D.C. in 1939 and 1940, he began to explore sculpture. Houser made small wood carvings while he taught art and worked as a pipe fitter's assistant.

ILLUSTRATOR PROFILE

Mitsumasa Anno
(1926–   )

Born in Japan in 1926, Mitsumasa Anno wanted to become an artist from an early age. Prior to realizing this dream, however, Anno pursued another path that contributed to his work in the field of children's publishing. After receiving his degree from the Yamaguchi Teacher Training College, Anno spent ten years as an elementary school teacher.

As a teacher, and then as an author and illustrator, Anno has sought to broaden children's thinking. In the postscript of his first picture book, *Topsy Turvies,* Anno wrote, "I have purposely added no words to these . . . pictures of mine, so you can make them mean whatever you want them to mean." Anno continued to stretch young imaginations in his subsequent books, many of which were based on his travels or his interests in mathematics.

The more time a reader spends with one of Anno's inventive books, the more he or she is rewarded with the discovery of hidden surprises in his watercolor and ink illustrations. When Anno employs the technique of tromp l'oeil, as in *Upside-Downers,* the eye is not only tricked, but also treated.

While studying Unit 4, share Anno's illustrations with the class. What kinds of building and animal forms do students see in the illustrations? Where is there space in and around objects?

Music

Spaces in music are called rests. Have the students find "spaces" in a song they sing. *Form* in music relates to the way sections of a musical composition are organized.

Literature

Watch the video or DVD *Henry and Mudge Under the Yellow Moon* by Cynthia Rylant to explore how the artist used space and form.

Literature and Art

Performing Arts

 Show *Dhon Dholak Cholam.* Discuss how the dance incorporates space and form.

Artsource®

Lesson 1 Overview

Space in Art

Lesson 1 introduces space. **Space** is the emptiness between shapes. This lesson looks at space in paintings, collages, drawings, and prints. If you lay one shape next to another, there will likely be a gap, or empty area between the shapes. This empty area is space. There will also be space above, below, and on each side of the shape. The shapes will look different if the space around them changes.

Objectives

 Art History and Culture

To recognize a few facts about the art and life of Raoul Dufy and Edward Hopper

Creative Expression

To create a landscape drawing with a horizon line

Aesthetic Perception

To locate space in the artwork and in their environment

Art Criticism

To evaluate one's own work using the four steps of art criticism

Vocabulary  Reading

Review the following vocabulary words with students before beginning the lesson.

space *espacio*—the element of art that refers to the area between, around, above, below, and within objects

See page 149B for additional vocabulary and Spanish vocabulary resources.

 Art Journal: Vocabulary

Have students add this word to the Vocabulary section of their Art Journals.

Lesson Materials
- oil pastels
- 12″ × 18″ construction paper (light and dark blue)

Alternate Materials:
- crayons

Program Resources
- *Reading and Writing Test Prep.*, pp. 42–43
- *Transparency 19*
- *Flash Card 20*
- *Artist Profiles*, pp. 10, 20
- *Assessment*, pp. 45–46
- *Large Prints 7* Bear and Seal and *8* Armoured Carousel Horse
- *The National Museum of Women in the Arts Collection*

Concept Trace
Space in Art
Introduced: Level K, Unit 4, Lesson 1

Reinforced: Level K, Unit 4, Lesson 3

Lesson 1 Arts Integration

Theatre

Complete Unit 4, Lesson 1 on pages 72–73 of the ***Theatre Arts Connections*** book.

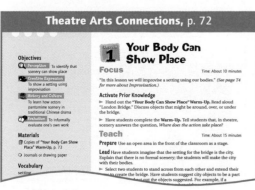

Music

 Many composers, like painters, describe nature in their work. Paul Winter has taken his soprano saxophone outdoors and imitated nature for many years. Listen to *Antarctica* by Paul Winter. What sounds does he use to describe animals and the freezing cold?

Movement & Dance

Have students sit in a small huddle in the center of the room. Then have students stand and spread out, finding their own space (home base) in which to stand. Have them circle their arms slowly to make sure they are not touching anyone else. Direct students to return to the huddle and then back to their "home base." Repeat this several times, asking them to identify the difference between group space and personal space.

Focus

Activate Prior Knowledge

"What are some things that you see outdoors in the country? In the city?" "¿Cuáles son algunas de las cosas que observan en el campo? ¿En la ciudad?"

■ Show students a country scene and a city scene. Discuss the shapes and the space between shapes in each picture.

Using Literature

■ Read *Commotion in the Ocean* by Giles Andreae, illustrated by David Wojtowycz. Encourage students to identify space in the illustrations.

Thematic Connection

■ **Journeys:** Encourage students to describe the places where they have traveled. Do the places in the fine art look like places they have visited?

Introduce the Art

"Let's see how artists used shapes and space to create these paintings." "Vamos a observar cómo los artistas usan las figuras y el espacio para crear estas pinturas".

■ Have students trace different shapes and the space around those shapes in the paintings. Ask students to identify the shapes they are tracing, such as "building" or "light."

Visualizing [★] Reading

■ Ask students what they think it would be like to live in the places shown in each painting. What kinds of things could they do if they lived there?

Adjectives and Adverbs [★] Language Arts

■ List on a chart the adjectives and adverbs students use to describe the fine art.
National Standards for Arts Education in Visual Arts 4.a

 Art History and Culture

Share and discuss information from the Art History and Culture sections with students. Edward Hopper was an American realist. Realism was an art movement in the mid-nineteenth century. Realists painted everyday scenes and events as they actually looked.

 Web Connection
Visit **www.albrightknox.org** to learn more about Raoul Dufy and the Albright-Knox Art Gallery in Buffalo, New York.

 Lesson **1**   Space in Art

▲ **Raoul Dufy.** (French). *Le Pantheon et Saint-Etienne-du-Mont.* c. 1903–1906.
Oil on canvas. 25½ × 31¼ inches (64.77 × 79.38 cm.). Albright-Knox Art Gallery, Buffalo, New York.

Look at the many shapes artists use in their art. **Space** is the empty area between shapes.

 Art History and Culture

Hopper liked to paint pictures of objects and places that are familiar to people, such as towns, trains, and stores.

 Art History and Culture

Raoul Dufy

In 1900 Raoul Dufy (rä ool´ dū´ fē) (1877–1953) was awarded a scholarship to study art in Paris at École des Beaux-Arts. He was influenced by impressionism, which was popular at the time. In 1905 Dufy discovered Matisse's work and was inspired to paint with the intense colors common to fauvism. Although generally associated with the fauves and painting, Raoul Dufy also created woodcuts, fabric designs, lithographs, and ceramics, and he worked as an illustrator and stage designer.

See pages 16–21 and 24–25 for more about subject matter and art history.

 **Artist Profiles, p. 10**

▶ Artist Profile ◀
Raoul Dufy
1877–1953
Raoul Dufy (rä ool´ dū´ fä) was born in Le Havre, France, to an impoverished but happy family. He had an early interest in art and a passion for drawing. At the age of 15, he enrolled at the Le Havre School of Fine Arts, where he met Georges Braque, who was a pioneer of cubism, along with Picasso. Braque became a lifelong friend and major artistic influence. In 1900, Dufy received a grant to attend the École des Beaux-Arts in Paris. His interest in impressionism was directed toward fauvism under the influence of Matisse in 1905. He also worked as an illustrator, fabric designer, and decorator. *Time* magazine awarded him the moniker "Grandaddy of Modern Chic."

▲ **Edward Hopper.**
(American).
***The Lighthouse at
Two Lights.*** 1929.
....
Oil on canvas. 29½ × 43¼
inches (74.93 × 109.86 cm.).
The Metropolitan Museum of
Art, New York, New York.

Study the pictures.

▶ Point to empty areas around the
shapes in the works of art.

🔍 Aesthetic Perception

Seeing Like an Artist Do you see space around
the clouds when you look in the sky?

🏺 Art History and Culture

Edward Hopper

Edward Hopper (ed´ wərd häp´ ər) (1882–1967) established himself
as one of the premier American realist painters of the twentieth
century. His subject matter was usually objects and places that are
familiar to the public, such as towns, stores, trains, and restaurants.
Hopper's art was often thought to convey a mood of loneliness. He
sometimes painted people who were alone or people who were not
interacting with each other in introspective scenes.

See pages 16–21 and 24–25 for more about subject matter and art
history.

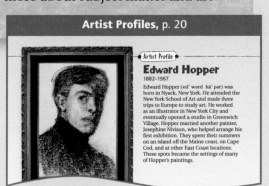

Artist Profiles, p. 20

◆ Artist Profile ◆
Edward Hopper
1882-1967
Edward Hopper (ed´ ward hä´ pər) was
born in Nyack, New York. He attended the
New York School of Art and made three
trips to Europe to study art. He worked
as an illustrator in New York City and
eventually opened a studio in Greenwich
Village. Hopper married another painter,
Josephine Nivison, who helped arrange his
first exhibition. They spent their summers
on an island off the Maine coast, on Cape
Cod, and at other East Coast locations.
These spots became the settings of many
of Hopper's paintings.

Study

▶ Possible answers: the sky in either
painting or the black spaces between the
pillars in the building in the top right
corner of the Dufy painting.

■ For more examples of landscapes, see ***The
National Museum of Women in the Arts
Collection.***

📓 Art Journal: Concept
Have students draw a picture that
shows a space between objects. Ask them
to point to the space.

🔍 Aesthetic Perception

Seeing Like an Artist Ask students if there are
spaces around the clouds in the sky. Then
allow them to look out the window or go
outside to look at the clouds to check their
answer.

Developing Visual Literacy Ask students to
share their personal experiences about visits
they have taken to places like the city and
lighthouse shown in the paintings. What else
might they see at these places?
NSAE 3.a; 3.b; 4.a

💻 Web Connection
Learn more about Edward Hopper at **http://nmaa-
ryder.si.edu/collections/exhibits/hopper/**.
NOTE: This site is for teacher use only.

 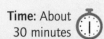**each**

"Let's find space that surrounds shapes."
"Vamos a buscar el espacio que rodea las figuras".

Practice

- Have two students stand in front of the group. Tell them to hold hands and stand as far apart as they can. Have another student point out the empty space between them.

- Have the same two students stand back to back as close as they can. Discuss what happened to the space between them.

 ## Creative Expression

Materials: oil pastels, 12" × 18" construction paper (light and dark blue)

Alternate Materials: crayons

- Direct students to envision their outdoor scene. Is it daytime or nighttime? Do they see trees, buildings, or the sky?

- Distribute the materials and have the students follow the directions on page 129.

- Allow the students to select from dark or light blue construction paper to create a day or night scene.

- Instruct the students to divide their paper using a horizon line. Ask students to think about the amount of sky and land they want in their drawings.

- Direct students to draw the horizon line with oil pastels. Is it straight or curved?

- On the horizon line and on the area below it, ask students to make shapes in their landscape of objects such as trees, buildings, and animals.

- Have students color the shapes and ground area with oil pastels and then add shapes in the sky for clouds, sun, or moon.

- See the Activity Tips on page 241 for visual examples of this lesson's activity.

NSAE 1.a; 1.c

Art Journal: Brainstorming
Have students imagine an outdoor scene. Ask them to draw in their Art Journals some things they might see outdoors.

Using Space in Art

The empty places around and between shapes are called **space.**

Practice

1. Hold hands with your partner. Notice the space between you.

2. Stand back to back with your partner. What happened to the space?

Differentiated Instruction

Reteach
Line up students in a circle and ask them to join hands. Have them walk toward the center and then back out again. Discuss with them how the space changes.

Special Needs
To further reinforce the concept of space in landscape, create a silhouette landscape, cutting away all negative space.

ELL Tips
Display a set of colored rings and ask students to tell you what is in the center of each ring. Put your hand through the center of one ring and say, "Nothing is in the center. The center is empty." An empty place is called *space.*

▲ **Zoe Lequeux.** Age 5.

Think about where you see space in this student's art.

 Creative Expression

How could you show space on paper?

1. Draw a landscape with trees or houses.
2. Color the sky.

 **Art Criticism**

Interpret Is it daytime or nighttime in your picture? How can you tell?

Art Across the Curriculum

Use these simple ideas to reinforce art concepts across the curriculum.

★ **Personal Writing** Have students draw a landscape of a place they have visited. Encourage students to share their pictures and tell the class about their visit.

★ **Math** Have students identify geometric shapes in the fine art that are used to make the buildings around them.

★ **Science** Observe and identify the pattern of day and night. Ask students to identify the time of day in the fine art and predict what time of day would occur next. How would the painting look different at a different time of day?

★ **Social Studies** Study different kinds of landforms, first looking at how the artists created different landforms in the fine art.

★ **Technology** Use a paint program to draw a landscape. Visit **SRAonline.com** to print detailed instructions for this activity.

 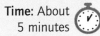 **R**eflect   Time: About 5 minutes

Review and Assess

"What is space?" "¿Qué es el espacio?"

Think

■ Use *Large Print 7* Bear and Seal to compare its use of space to that of the art in this lesson. Have students describe the difference they see.

■ Discuss the student art question. Possible answers: There is space around the clouds and birds and between each sun ray. There is space between the mountain peaks.

Informal Assessment

Art Journal: Critical Thinking
Have students answer the Interpret question by drawing a picture in their Art Journals.

 **Art Criticism**

Have students ask themselves the following questions.

Describe ▶ Can you point to the shapes in your landscape? Point to the space that surrounds the shapes.

Analyze ▶ What happened to the empty space in the sky when you drew pictures in it?

Interpret ▶ Is it day or nighttime in your picture? How can you tell?

Decide ▶ What do you like best about your drawing?

NSAE 2.b; 5.a; 5.c

■ For standardized-format test practice using this lesson's art content, see pages 42–43 in *Reading and Writing Test Preparation.*

Space in Art

Extra! For the Art Specialist

Time: About 30 minutes

Focus

Use *Transparency 19* and discuss how the artists used space. Where is the horizon line in each work of art? What objects are closest to the horizon? What objects are farthest away?

Teach

Have students create a seascape by tearing sheets of paper into small shapes.

Reflect

Have students use the four steps of art criticism to evaluate their work. Did they effectively use space in their seascapes?

Alternate Activity

Materials:
- light blue 9" × 12" paper
- scraps of dark blue construction paper and other assorted colors
- glue

1. Have students look outside and identify the horizon line. Where is the horizon line on the ocean?

2. Direct students to create a seascape by tearing pieces of dark blue paper into small shapes.

3. Before gluing the shapes, have students use glue to draw a horizon line on their light blue paper.

4. Then have students place their torn paper shapes on the glue line. Continue gluing torn shapes in the space from the horizon line to the bottom of the paper. Tear more shapes for details such as boats, clouds, or fish.

NSAE 1.c

Research in Art Education

"The arts help students develop their abilities to appreciate and interpret art of other cultures and to learn about people of the past through exposure to reproductions, to art works in museums and galleries, or through discussions about contemporary artists and art works" (Andra Nyman, "Cultural Content, Identity, and Program Development: Approaches to Art Education for Elementary Educators," in *Contemporary Issues in Art Education*, edited by Y. Gaudelius and P. Speirs, 61–69. New Jersey: Prentice Hall, 2002).

Assessment
Use the following rubric to evaluate the artwork students make in the Creative Expression activity and to assess students' understanding of space in art.

Have students complete page 45 or 46 in their *Assessment* books.

	Art History and Culture	Aesthetic Perception	Creative Expression	Art Criticism
3 POINTS	The student recognizes a few facts about the art and life of Raoul Dufy and Edward Hopper.	The student accurately locates spaces in the artwork and in their environment.	The student's drawing clearly illustrates space.	The student thoughtfully and honestly evaluates his or her own work using the four steps of art criticism.
2 POINTS	The student shows some knowledge of the art and life of Raoul Dufy and Edward Hopper.	The student shows emerging ability to locate spaces in the artwork and in their environment.	The student's drawing shows some awareness of space.	The student attempts to evaluate his or her own work, but shows an incomplete understanding of evaluation criteria.
1 POINT	The student shows no knowledge of the art and life of Raoul Dufy and Edward Hopper.	The student does not locate spaces in the artwork and in their environment.	The student's drawing shows no understanding of space.	The student makes no attempt to evaluate his or her own artwork.

Assessment, p. 45

Name _____ Date _____

Space in Art

Lesson **1** UNIT 4

For the teacher: Use the following prompts for this activity.
1. Using a blue crayon, draw a shape in the center of the box.
2. Color the space around the shape with a red crayon.

Level K   Unit 4 • Space and Form   **45**

Lesson 2 Form

Form refers to objects having three dimensions. Like a shape, a form has height and width, but it also has depth. Unlike shapes which are flat, forms are solid shapes and take up space. They stand, move, hang from above, or project from a wall. You can see all around a form. Sculpture as a form is covered in Lesson 2.

Objectives

 Art History and Culture

To recognize a few facts about the art and life of Felipa Trujillo

Creative Expression

To create a clay form of themselves

 Aesthetic Perception

To locate forms in their environment

Art Criticism

To evaluate one's own work using the four steps of art criticism

Vocabulary ⭐ Reading

Review the following vocabulary words with students before beginning the lesson.

form forma—any object that can be measured in three ways: height, width, and depth

sculpture escultura—a three-dimensional work of art

See page 149B for additional vocabulary and Spanish vocabulary resources.

 Art Journal: Vocabulary

Have students add these words to the Vocabulary section of their Art Journals.

Lesson Materials

- assorted colors of oil-based modeling clay
- pencils, crayons, paper
- clay mats (muslin)
- wood or cardboard (for a base)
- full-length mirror

Alternate Materials:
- pencils
- paper
- scissors
- earthen clay

Program Resources

- *Reading and Writing Test Prep.*, pp. 44–45
- *Transparency 20*
- *Artist Profiles*, pp. 49, 63
- *Assessment*, pp. 47–48
- *Large Prints 7* Bear and Seal and *8* Armoured Carousel Horse
- *Art Around the World Collection*

Concept Trace

Form

Introduced: Level K, Unit 4, Lesson 2

Reinforced: Level K, Unit 4, Lessons 3–6

Lesson 2 Arts Integration

Theatre

Complete Unit 4, Lesson 2 on pages 74–75 of the *Theatre Arts Connections* book.

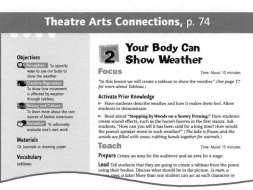

Theatre Arts Connections, p. 74

Music

 Form in music describes the way sections are put together. If a song has a verse and refrain it is AB, (unless the tune of the refrain is the same as the verse, as in *This Land is My Land,* which is AA). Sing *The Happy Wanderer* by Friedrich W. Moller. Pat the pulse on the refrain, the B section.

Movement & Dance

Have students spread out, each person in his or her own space (home base). Assign each student either number 1 or 2. All the "1s" create a shape by sitting or standing in their space. The "2s" take 16 counts to travel (perhaps by skipping or galloping) around the space, moving through the shapes made by the "1s." At the end of the 16 counts, the "2s" return to their home bases. Alternate groups and repeat.

Focus

Time: About 10 minutes

Activate Prior Knowledge

"Can you point to the front, back, top, bottom, and sides of your body?" "¿Pueden señalar el frente, la parte posterior, la parte superior, la parte inferior y los lados de su cuerpo?"

- Discuss the idea of a person being a form and being able to see a person from all sides.

Using Literature

- Read *The Pledge of Allegiance* by Scholastic Editors. Have students identify forms in the photographs.

Thematic Connection

- **Body:** Name a major body part such as arm or leg. Direct students to identify each part on themselves as you name the parts. Then have students identify these parts on the fine art sculptures.

Introduce the Art

"These sculptures are forms. They can be seen from all sides." "Estas esculturas son formas. Se pueden ver por todos los lados".

- Have students describe the forms in the pictures.

Making Inferences | Reading

- Ask students what they think the sculptures in the pictures would look like from the other side.
- Direct students to point out the space in and around the sculptures.

Adjectives and Adverbs | Language Arts

- On a chart list the adjectives and adverbs students use to describe the fine art.

Art History and Culture

Share information from the Art History and Culture sections with students. Encourage students to discuss what they have learned from people in their families. Is there something that a family member can do that they would like to learn? Discuss how artists sometimes learn their art skills from family members.

NSAE 4.a

Web Connection

Learn more about folk art at **www.moifa.org/**, the Web site for the Museum of International Folk Art.

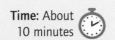

2 Form

Look at this form. It is a **sculpture.** It has a front, back, top, bottom, and sides.

◀ **Felipa Trujillo.** (American). *Man.* Early 1900s.
....
Museum of International Folk Art, a unit of the Museum of New Mexico, Santa Fe, New Mexico.

Art History and Culture

This artist was taught how to make pottery by people in her family. What has someone in your family taught you?

Art History and Culture

Felipa Trujillo

Felipa Trujillo (fä lē´ pä trū hē´ yō) (1908–1986) was a Native American potter from the Cochiti Pueblo in New Mexico. She came from a long line of potters. Her mother, Estepanita Herrera, taught Felipa about pottery. They worked together making pitchers, bowls, and figurines until her mother's death in 1960. Felipa Trujillo was one of the most well-known artists of "storyteller" figurines, a unique art form invented by her niece, the master potter Helen Cordero.

See pages 16–21 and 24–25 for more about subject matter and art history.

Artist Profiles, p. 49

◆ Artist Profile ◆

Felipa Trujillo
1908–1986
Felipa Trujillo (fä lē´ pä trū hē´ yō) was a Native American potter from the Cochiti Pueblo in New Mexico. She was one of the first potters to make clay figures called *storytellers*. She came from a long line of potters. Her mother, Estepanita Herrera, taught Trujillo about pottery. They worked together making pitchers, bowls, and figurines until her mother's death in 1960. It was then that Trujillo began to make storyteller figurines.

◀ **Felipa Trujillo.** (American). *Man.*
Museum of International Folk Art, a unit of the Museum of New Mexico

Study both sculptures.

▶ Describe what you think each one would look like from all sides.

◀ **Artist Unknown.** (Italy). *Camillus.*
A.D. 41–54.
....
Bronze. 46⅞ inches high (119.08 cm.). The
Metropolitan Museum of Art, New York, New York.

🔍 Aesthetic Perception

Seeing Like an Artist What are the different sides of a form you see in your classroom?

🏺 Art History and Culture

Camillus

This work is a statue portrait of the Roman dictator Marcus Furius Camillus, who was made chief executive by the Roman people in the year 396 B.C. Under the leadership of Camillus, the Romans finally conquered the Etruscan peoples and destroyed their cities. Later Camillus organized and led an army of 40,000 Romans to counter an attack by the Gauls. After his army drove the Gauls out of Roman lands, Camillus was honored with the title Second Founder of the City. These victories in battle, along with his later work maintaining peace and justice in the Roman Empire, earned Camillus the respect of his people and a permanent place in Roman history.

See pages 16–21 and 24–25 for more about subject matter and art history.

Artist Profiles, p. 63

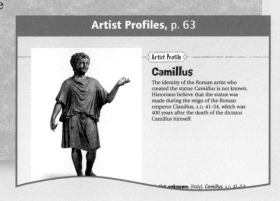

⟨ Artist Profile ⟩
Camillus
The identity of the Roman artist who created the statue *Camillus* is not known. Historians believe that the statue was made during the reign of the Roman emperor Claudius, A.D. 41–54, which was 400 years after the death of the dictator Camillus himself.

Artist unknown. (Italy). *Camillus.* A.D. 41–54.

Study

▶ Possible answers: the hair on the back of the sculptures' heads or body parts that would now be visible, such as the back, the heels, and the elbows. Additional clothing might be visible from different angles.

■ For more examples of art from Europe, see the ***Art Around the World Collection.***

Art Journal: Concept
Have students draw a picture in their Art Journals that shows a space between objects. Ask them to point to the space.

🔍 Aesthetic Perception

Seeing Like an Artist Ask students to name the different sides of a form they see in the classroom. For example, students might identify the front, back, sides, top, and bottom of a bottle of glue.

Developing Visual Literacy Encourage students to speculate on why the artists created these sculptures. Who are the people in the sculptures?
NSAE 3.a; 3.b; 5.a; 5.c

💻 **Web Connection**
Visit **www.metmuseum.org/** to search for other examples of statues of famous leaders.

Teach

Time: About 30 minutes

"Let's discover the difference between a shape and a form." "Vamos a descubrir la diferencia entre una figura y una forma".

Practice

Materials: crayons or pencils, paper

- Have students follow the directions on student page 132.

- Compare the flat, two-dimensional shape of the drawing to the three-dimensional form of the object. How does the object take up more space than the drawing the student created?

Creative Expression

Materials: assorted colors of oil-based modeling clay, pencils, clay mats (muslin), wood or cardboard (for a base), full-length mirror

Alternate Materials: pencils, paper, scissors, earthen clay

"In what pose would you like to show yourself in clay?" "¿Cómo les gustaría posar en arcilla?"

- Provide a full-length mirror so students can stand in front of it and make poses.

- Distribute the materials and have the students follow the directions on page 133.

- See the Activity Tips on page 241 for visual examples of this lesson's activity.

- Remind students that they will be showing all sides of their body in clay. Encourage them to shape the head first, followed by the arms and legs.

- See pages 230–231 for additional information about using clay.

- Students can add facial and clothing details by using a pencil or adding small pieces of clay.

- You may wish to place the figures on wood or cardboard bases.

NSAE 1.a; 1.c

Art Journal: Brainstorming

Have students sketch in their Art Journals different poses that they could use to make their clay forms.

Using Forms

A **form** is a solid. You can look all around a form.

Practice

1. Draw your favorite thing in the classroom.

2. Look at your drawing next to the real object.

Differentiated Instruction

Reteach

Play "Simon Says" to get students to identify the forms of their bodies.

Special Needs

Some students may have difficulty combining the clay slab and the posterboard base. Students can still gain an understanding of additive sculpture if the base is omitted.

ELL Tips

Display a toy car or bus, or another small toy. Have students walk around the object, stop at different points, and describe what they see from that view. Explain that the toy is a form. Ask, "Can you walk around it? Can it be seen on all sides?"

◀ **Aaron Ragans.**
Age 6.

Think about what you might see if you looked at this artwork from the side.

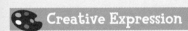

Creative Expression

What do you look like from different sides?

1. Make a clay form of yourself.
2. Use a pencil to add a face and clothing.

Art Criticism

Analyze Does your sculpture have a front, back, top, bottom, and sides?

Art Across the Curriculum

Use these simple ideas to reinforce art concepts across the curriculum.

★ **Poetry Writing** Ask students to draw pictures for things that rhyme with *ran*.

★ **Math** Have students stand and model addition and subtraction problems, for example, 2 girls plus 1 girl equals 3 girls.

★ **Science** Identify animal parts, noting how the parts of the body work together to move and eat.

★ **Social Studies** Discuss similarities and differences among people, including physical attributes and cultural differences.

★ **Technology** Use a paint program to draw a landscape. Visit **SRAonline.com** to print detailed instructions for this activity.

Reflect

Time: About 5 minutes

Review and Assess

"How is a form different from a shape?" "¿En qué se diferencia una forma de un figura?"

Think

- Use *Large Prints 7* Bear and Seal and *8* Armoured Carousel Horse to compare the shapes in them to those of the art in this lesson.

- Discuss the student art question. Answers might include the back of the head and body, details to represent hair or clothing, and a profile view of the face.

Informal Assessment

Art Journal: Critical Thinking
Have students answer the Analyze Art Criticism question by drawing a picture in their Art Journals.

Art Criticism

Have students ask themselves the following questions.

Describe ▶ In what ways does your clay form—your statue—look like you?

Analyze ▶ Does your sculpture have a front, back, top, bottom, and sides?

Interpret ▶ What is your statue doing?

Decide ▶ How does your statue take up space?

NSAE 2.b; 5.a; 5.c

- For standardized-format test practice using this lesson's art content, see pages 44–45 in *Reading and Writing Test Preparation.*

Lesson 2 Form

Extra! For the Art Specialist

Time: About 30 minutes

Focus

Use *Transparency 20* and *Large Prints 7 Bear and Seal* and *8 Armoured Carousel Horse* to discuss how the artists used form. How is a person or animal a form? Explain.

Teach

Study forms by having students create an animal sculpture from clay.

Reflect

Have students use the four steps of art criticism to evaluate their work. Did they effectively create a form using clay?

Alternate Activity

Materials:
- clay (one baseball-sized ball of clay per student)
- pencils
- craft sticks

1. Discuss how people and animals are forms because they occupy space.

2. Demonstrate modeling techniques with a piece of clay. Show the students how to pinch, squeeze and pull the clay to make a head, legs, or a tail.

3. Brainstorm a list of animals they could create from a ball of clay.

4. Have students make animal sculptures and then use pencils and craft sticks to add eyes, mouths, and textures to them.

NSAE 1.a; 1.c

Research in Art Education

"At a time when the development of thinking skills is particularly important . . . the presence of a program that fosters flexibility, promotes a tolerance for ambiguity, encourages risk taking and depends upon the exercise of judgment outside the sphere of rules is an especially valuable resource" (Eisner, Elliot W. *The Arts and the Creation of Mind.* New Haven: Yale Univ. Press, 2002).

Assessment
Use the following rubric to evaluate the artwork students make in the Creative Expression activity and to assess students' understanding of form in art.

Have students complete page 47 or 48 in their *Assessment* books.

	Art History and Culture	Aesthetic Perception	Creative Expression	Art Criticism
3 POINTS	The student recognizes a few facts about the art and life of Felipa Trujillo.	The student accurately locates forms in his or her environment.	The student's clay form demonstrates a strong understanding of form.	The student thoughtfully and honestly evaluates his or her own work using the four steps of art criticism.
2 POINTS	The student shows emerging awareness of facts about the art and life of Felipa Trujillo.	The student shows emerging ability to locate forms in his or her environment.	The student's clay form demonstrates emerging awareness of form.	The student attempts to evaluate his or her own work, but shows an incomplete understanding of evaluation criteria.
1 POINT	The student does not recognize facts about the art and life of Felipa Trujillo.	The student does not locate forms in his or her environment.	The student's clay form demonstrates no understanding of form.	The student makes no attempt to evaluate his or her own artwork.

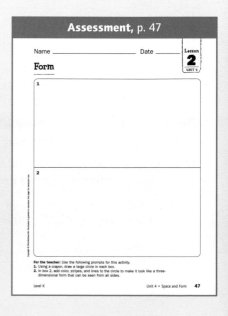

Assessment, p. 47

Name _____ Date _____ Lesson **2** UNIT 4

Form

1

2

For the teacher: Use the following prompts for this activity.
1. Using a crayon, draw a large circle in each box.
2. In box 2, add color, stripes, and lines to the circle to make it look like a three-dimensional form that can be seen from all sides.

Level K   Unit 4 • Space and Form   **47**

Space and Form

Lesson 3 discusses space and form. Space is all around forms. It can be above, below, around, and even through forms.

Objectives

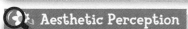
Art History and Culture

To recognize that artists have different styles for creating sculpture

Creative Expression

To create a puppet

Aesthetic Perception

To recognize that sculptures are forms

Art Criticism

To evaluate one's own work using the four steps of art criticism

Vocabulary Reading

Review the following vocabulary word with students before beginning the lesson.

space *espacio*—the element of art that refers to the area between, around, above, below, and within objects

See page 149B for additional vocabulary and Spanish vocabulary resources.

Art Journal: Vocabulary

Have students add this word to the Vocabulary section of their Art Journals.

Lesson Materials

- short paper-towel tubes (cut whole tubes in half or use toilet paper rolls)
- markers, scissors, glue
- 2" × 3" construction paper strips (various colors)
- 1" × 3" felt strips
- craft items such as buttons, feathers, yarn, or beads
- stuffed animals (bring several or ask students to bring one from home)

Alternate Materials:
- roll and staple 10" square pieces of posterboard

Program Resources

- *Reading and Writing Test Prep*, pp. 46–47
- *Transparency 21*
- *Flash Card 20*
- *Artist Profiles*, pp. 15, 30
- *Assessment*, pp. 49–50
- *Large Prints 7 Bear and Seal* and *8 Armoured Carousel Horse*
- *Art Around the World Collection*

Concept Trace
Space and Form
Introduced: Level K, Unit 4, Lesson 3

Reinforced: Level 1, Unit 4, Lesson 2

Lesson 3 Arts Integration

Theatre

Complete Unit 4, Lesson 3 on pages 76–77 of the *Theatre Arts Connections* book.

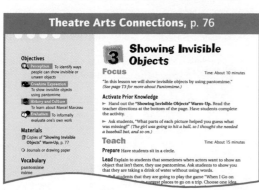

Music

 Listen to "March" from *The Nutcracker*. Determine that it is in ABA form. Another way to illustrate form without using letters is with geometric shapes. "March" would be triangle-circle-triangle. Have students march in place during the triangle music and scurry like mice during the B music.

Movement & Dance

Have each student create a shape that reaches out into a space, but is at a different level from those around him or her. Divide the class in half. The first half spreads out and creates their shapes. The second half walks around and through the space, viewing each shape created from the front, side, and back. Discuss how the shapes are different when viewed from various angles.

Look at how space is used in all the forms in these works of art. Space is above, below, and through the forms.

▲ **Henry Moore.**
(British). *Reclining Figure.* 1939.
. . . .
Elm. 37 inches high (93.98 cm.).
Detroit Institute of The Arts,
Detroit, Michigan.

Art History and Culture

Different artists like to make sculptures in different ways. Some sculptures look like real people.

ocus

Time: About 10 minutes

Activate Prior Knowledge

Show students an empty container, like a bucket. "What is in this bucket?" Demuestre a los estudiantes un recipiente vacío, como un cubo. "¿Qué se encuentra en este cubo?"

- Discuss that the bucket is full of air, or empty space.

- Point out the space around the bucket and through the handle of the bucket.

Using Literature ⭐ Reading

- Read *Fish Faces* by Norbert Wu. Ask students to identify space and forms in the pictures.

Thematic Connection

- **Look Again:** Discuss students' reactions when they first looked at the fine art. Encourage students to tell you about times when they have taken a second look at something or studied it from different angles to see it better.

Introduce the Art

"These sculptures are forms. They can be seen from all sides. They have space all around them." "Estas esculturas son formas. Se pueden ver por todos los lados. Tienen espacio en todo su alrededor".

- Make sure students realize that *Old Couple on a Bench* is a three-dimensional sculpture and not a photograph of real people.

- Ask students to describe the sculptures.

Comparing and Contrasting ⭐ Reading

- Discuss the similarities and differences in the sculptures, noting that artists use different media to create sculptures and have different styles.

Finding Details ⭐ Reading

- Ask students to describe details that make Hanson's sculpture look real. Why doesn't Moore's sculpture look real?

Art History and Culture

Share information from the Art History and Culture sections with students. Duane Hanson created life-size sculptures and tried to make them as realistic as possible.
NSAE 4.a

 Web Connection
Browse Henry Moore exhibitions online at **www.henry-moore-fdn.co.uk/**.
NSAE 5.a; 5.c

Art History and Culture

Henry Moore

Henry Moore (hen´ rē môr) (1898–1986) was influenced by Mexican, Egyptian, and African sculptures he saw while studying at the Royal Academy of Art in London. In his early years as an artist, Moore's work was often criticized for being too abstract and simplified. In 1948, however, Henry Moore was awarded the International Prize for sculpture.

Henry Moore created numerous sculptures of reclining figures, including *Reclining Figure, 1956–1958,* that he was commissioned to create for the UNESCO Building in Paris.

See pages 16–21 and 24–25 for more about subject matter and art history.

Artist Profiles, p. 30

Artist Profile

Henry Moore
1898-1986

Henry Moore (hen´ rē mor) was born in Castleford, England. When he was ten, he told his father he wanted to become a sculptor. At 18, he left home to join the army during World War I. He began studying art after the war. By age 23, he was a serious sculptor.

Study the pictures.

▶ Where do you see forms in the pictures?

▶ Where do you see space?

▲ **Duane Hanson.** (American).
Old Couple on a Bench. 1994–1995.
....
Bronze, polychromed, mixed media with
accessories. Palm Springs Desert Museum,
Palm Springs, California.

Aesthetic Perception

Seeing Like an Artist Point to the space around a form in your classroom.

Art History and Culture

Duane Hanson

Duane Hanson (dwān han´ sən) (1925–1996) is renowned for his hyperrealist, life-size sculptures of ordinary people in everyday poses. Hanson created his sculptures from live models, using partial body molds cast in polyester resin and fiberglass. He painted the skin with great detail and added jewelry, hair, clothing, and accessories.

See pages 16–21 and 24–25 for more about subject matter and art history.

Artist Profiles, p. 15

• Artist Profile •
Duane Hanson
1925-1996

Duane Hanson (dwān han´san) carved little figures out of logs using kitchen knives as a boy in his native Minnesota. Later he attended art school and taught art in Atlanta, Georgia and Miami, Florida. The same art dealer who discovered Andy Warhol arranged for Hanson's first solo exhibition. His life-size sculptures of ordinary people were an immediate success with the public. People could identify with his work. Hanson married and had five children. He continued to plan and create sculpture until the end of his life.

Study

▶ The reclining figure is a form, and so are the man and woman, her purse, the bench, and the paper the man is holding.

■ For more examples of art from Europe, see the *Art Around the World Collection.*

Art Journal: Concept

Have students draw a picture in their Art Journals that shows a space between objects. Ask them to point to the space.

Aesthetic Perception

Seeing Like an Artist Ask students to choose a form they see in the room and point out the space that is around the form.

Developing Visual Literacy Ask students how the sculptures make them feel. What did the artists do to their sculptures to help create that feeling?
NSAE 3.a; 3.b; 5.a; 5.c

Web Connection

Learn more about Duane Hanson and see examples of his work at **www.artmolds.com/ali/halloffame/ duane_hanson.htm**.

Teach

Time: About 30 minutes

"Let's explore the space around a form."
"Vamos a explorar el espacio alrededor de una forma".

Practice

Materials: stuffed animals (bring several or ask students to bring one from home)

- Provide several stuffed animals for students.

- While one student holds a stuffed animal, have another student point to the space above, below, around and (if possible) through the animal.

Creative Expression

Materials: short paper-towel tubes, markers, scissors, glue, 2" × 3" construction paper strips (various colors), 1" × 3" felt strips, craft items

Alternate Materials: roll and staple 10" square pieces of posterboard

"What kinds of puppets have you seen?"
"¿Qué tipos de títere han visto?"

- Encourage students to describe the puppets they have seen.

- Distribute the materials and have the students follow the directions on page 137.

- See the Activity Tips on page 242 for visual examples of this lesson's activity.

- Have students select 2–3 pieces of the 2" × 3" strips of construction paper and glue them around the tube.

- Then have students draw a head and body on the puppet.

- Students can glue felt strips to the sides and bottom of the tube to be the arms and legs of the puppet.

- Encourage students to add craft items like buttons and beads to decorate the puppet.

NSAE 1.a; 1.c

Art Journal: Brainstorming

Ask students to draw a sketch in their Art Journals of a puppet they would like to make.

Using Space and Form

The empty areas around and through a form are **space.**

Practice

1. Look at a stuffed animal.
2. Point to the space around the animal.

Differentiated Instruction

Reteach

Show students various forms, like a vase, desk, and computer. Point to the space above, below, around, and inside the forms.

Special Needs

To reinforce the concept of form and space, have a student pose in a three quarter position in front of an overhead screen. The shadow they cast will include their form and the space around their form. Have their classmates identify the spaces and form.

ELL Tips

Explore the following words through role-play: *above, below, over, under, around,* and *through.* For example, have students hold an object above the table and below the table. Have students walk around a blanket or sit under a blanket.

◀ **Sarah Stewart.**
Age 6.

Think about where you see space around the student's puppet.

 **Creative Expression**

Where is the space around your puppet?

1. Practice holding and moving your paper-towel tube.

2. Use the tube to make a puppet.

 **Art Criticism**

Analyze Is your puppet more like the sculpture of the man and woman, or is it more like the wood sculpture? Why?

Art Across the Curriculum

Use these simple ideas to reinforce art concepts across the curriculum.

★ **Narrative Writing** Discuss *Old Couple on a Bench*. Where are these people? Ask students to draw a picture that shows where the people are and what they might do next.

★ **Math** Model the length of *Reclining Figure* with a piece of masking tape on the floor. Have students find concrete objects that are about the same as, less than, and greater in length than the sculpture.

★ **Science** Record observations about plant parts, including leaves, roots, stems, and flowers. Identify which part of the plant Henry Moore used to create his sculpture.

★ **Social Studies** Discuss basic human needs such as food, clothing, and shelter. Are any of these needs identifiable in Hanson's sculpture?

★ **Technology** Have students use a paint program to draw a person. Then ask students to use one color to paint the space around the person. Visit **SRAonline.com** to print detailed instructions for this activity.

Reflect
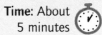
Time: About 5 minutes

Review and Assess

"Can you find space and forms?" "¿Pueden encontrar espacios y formas?"

■ Have students identify the forms in *Large Prints 7 Bear and Seal* and *8 Armoured Carousel Horse* and then point to the space around the forms.

■ Discuss the student art question. There is space around the puppet and between some of the strands of yarn.

Informal Assessment

Art Journal: Critical Thinking
Have students answer the *Analyze* question in their Art Journals by drawing a picture.

 **Art Criticism**

Have students ask themselves the following questions.

Describe ▶ Is your puppet an animal, person, or something else? Describe it.

Analyze ▶ Is your puppet more like the sculpture of the man and woman or the wood sculpture? Why?

Interpret ▶ If your puppet was in a puppet show, what would the story be about?

Decide ▶ Does the space around your puppet change when you move it? How?

NSAE 2.b; 5.a; 5.c

■ For standardized-format test practice using this lesson's art content, see pages 46–47 in *Reading and Writing Test Preparation*.

Space and Form

Extra! For the Art Specialist

Time: About 30 minutes

Focus

Use *Transparency 21* and *Large Prints 7 Bear and Seal* and *8 Armoured Carousel Horse* discuss how the artists used space and form. Point to the forms in each work of art. How do these forms occupy space? Explain.

Teach

The students will learn about space and form by creating a small pillow.

Reflect

Have students use the four steps of art criticism to evaluate their work. Did they learn about form by creating a pillow? How did they incorporate space in their design?

Alternate Activity

Materials:
- 4" × 6" paper
- fabric crayons
- 5" × 7" white cotton muslin
- iron
- polyester fill
- thread

1. Explain how artists make objects that are meant to be held and touched. Show examples of handmade objects such as puppets, pillows, or quilts.

2. Ask the students to think of a favorite person or animal and draw a picture of the person or animal using fabric crayons.

3. Transfer the students' drawings to fabric using an iron.

4. Attach the printed fabric to a backing and have the students stuff the pillow with polyester fill. Stitch the pillow closed.

NSAE 3.a; 3.b

Research in Art Education

Research suggests that when arts are integrated in schools, students tend to perform better on standardized reading and math tests. This seems to be especially true for low socio-economic status students at the elementary school level ("Chicago Arts Partnerships in Education (CAPE): Evaluation Summary" in *Critical Links,* p. 72).

Assessment

Use the following rubric to evaluate the artwork students make in the Creative Expression activity and to assess students' understanding of space and form.

Have students complete page 49 or 50 in their *Assessment* books.

	Art History and Culture	Aesthetic Perception	Creative Expression	Art Criticism
3 POINTS	The student recognizes that artists have different styles for creating sculpture and can identify some of these differences in the fine art.	The student recognizes that sculptures are forms.	The student's puppet demonstrates a strong understanding of space and form.	The student thoughtfully and honestly evaluates his or her own work using the four steps of art criticism.
2 POINTS	The student shows emerging awareness of artists using different styles to create sculpture and can identify some of these differences in the fine art with help.	The student shows emerging ability to recognize that sculptures are forms.	The student's puppet demonstrates emerging awareness of space and form.	The student attempts to evaluate his or her own work, but shows an incomplete understanding of evaluation criteria.
1 POINT	The student does not recognize that artists have different styles for creating sculpture and cannot identify these differences in the fine art.	The student does not recognize that sculptures are forms.	The student's puppet demonstrates no understanding of space and form.	The student makes no attempt to evaluate his or her own artwork.

Assessment, p. 49

Name _____ Date _____

Lesson 3 UNIT 4

Space and Form

For the teacher: Use the following prompts for this activity.
1. Using a crayon, draw a large circle.
2. Add color, stripes, and lines to the circle to make it look like a three-dimensional form that can be seen from all sides.
3. Color the space around the circle with a green crayon.

Level K   Unit 4 • Space and Form   **49**

Lesson 4 Overview

Building Forms

Lesson 4 explores buildings as forms. Buildings are forms that have many parts. An artist who designs buildings is called an architect.

Objectives

 Art History and Culture

To recognize that architecture is the art of designing and creating buildings

 Creative Expression

To create a sculpture of a house

 Aesthetic Perception

To locate and identify building forms in their environment

 Art Criticism

To evaluate one's own work using the four steps of art criticism

Vocabulary Reading

Review the following vocabulary words with students before beginning the lesson.

form forma—any object that can be measured in three ways: height, width, and depth

See page 149B for additional vocabulary and Spanish vocabulary resources.

 Art Journal: Vocabulary

Have students add this word to the Vocabulary section of their Art Journals.

Lesson Materials

- crayons or pencils
- light-colored paper
- glue, markers, scissors
- colored paper lunch bags (1 per student)
- 6" × 6" construction paper squares (any color, 1 per student)
- construction paper scraps (various colors)
- newspaper (2 sheets per student)
- craft items such as buttons, feathers, yarn, and beads

Alternate Materials:
- clean, empty milk cartons from the cafeteria

Program Resources
- *Reading and Writing Test Prep.*, pp. 48–49
- *Transparency 22*
- *Artist Profiles*, pp. 55, 76
- *Assessment*, pp. 51–52
- *Large Prints 7 Bear and Seal* and *8 Armoured Carousel Horse*
- *The National Museum of Women in the Arts Collection*

Concept Trace
Building Forms
Introduced: Level K, Unit 4, Lesson 4

Reinforced: Level 1, Unit 4, Lesson 5

Lesson 4 Arts Integration

Theatre
Complete Unit 4, Lesson 4 on pages 78–79 of the *Theatre Arts Connections* book.

Theatre Arts Connections, p. 78

Objectives
To recognize that costumes help create characters
To create a spider costume
To learn more about the holiday costumes of Mexico
To informally evaluate one's own work

Choosing Costumes

Focus   Time: About 10 minutes
"In this lesson we will create a spider costume." *(See page T18 for more about Costumes.)*

Activate Prior Knowledge
▶ Provide examples of familiar stories and rhymes. Have students describe the costumes that actors might wear as characters.
▶ Read aloud or sing **"The Itsy, Bitsy Spider."** Have students make the hand gestures as they listen to the poem. Ask students to describe a spider. *(eight legs, round body, fuzzy, and so on)* Tell students that a costume for a spider should look at least a little like a real spider. Discuss how a spider costume might look.

Teach   Time: About 15 minutes
Prepare Have students sit at their desks.
Lead Provide each student with a brown paper bag, streamers (for legs), crayons or markers, and glue.
Have students to roll up the edges of the paper bag to make a hat around the brim of the hat to create spider legs.

Materials
Black streamers, brown paper bags, various art supplies, such as streamers, felt, fabric, and so on
Crayons or nontoxic markers
Nontoxic glue/glue sticks
Journals or drawing paper

Music
 The form of a song can be built. Listen to *Colors* by M.L. Reilly and L.F. Olson. This song starts with AAB form. Each time a color line is added, another A is added before the B. Sing the song and create more A sections.

Movement & Dance
Have students work with a partner to explore ways to create different structures. Standing with feet together and toes touching, students clasp each others' wrists or elbows and lean away from each other, maintaining balance. How stable is this structure? Now have each student stand with one foot forward and the other back, as in a lunge. Then they reach upward and toward each other, pressing both hands together to form an arch. How stable is this structure?

Focus

Time: About 10 minutes

Activate Prior Knowledge

"Have you ever seen a building being built?"
"¿Alguna vez han visto un edificio en construcción?"

■ Show pictures of different kinds of buildings. Focus on different parts of buildings, their shapes, and their purposes.

Using Literature ⭐ Reading

■ Read *The Village of Round and Square Houses* by Ann Grifalconi. Study the buildings and identify the different parts, their shapes, and their purposes.

Thematic Connection

■ **Buildings:** Name physical characteristics that help make buildings useful. For example, a barn might have a large open space for housing animals.
NSAE 4.a

Introduce the Art

"These buildings have many different parts that are put together." "Estos edificios tienen muchas diversas partes que se ponen juntas".

■ Ask students to point to different parts of the buildings.

Making Inferences ⭐ Reading Skill

■ Ask students how they think the parts of the buildings are put together.

■ Explain that buildings are a kind of art form known as *architecture.* An artist who designs buildings is called an *architect.*

■ Have students point to and trace shapes, patterns, and forms on this building.

Adjectives and Adverbs ⭐ Language Arts

■ On a chart list the adjectives and adverbs students use to describe the fine art.

Art History and Culture

Share information from the Art History and Culture sections with students. Answers will vary. Possible answers include school, store, library, and church.

🖥 **Web Connection**
Learn more about Frank Lloyd Wright and the Guggenheim Museum in New York City by visiting www.guggenheim.org/the_building.html.

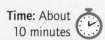 Lesson 4

A Building Is a Form

▲ **Frank Lloyd Wright.** (American). *Stockman House.* 1908.
Mason City, Iowa.

Look at these pictures of buildings. Buildings are forms with many different parts.

🏺 Art History and Culture

Artists who design buildings are called **architects.** What kinds of buildings have you visited?

🏺 Art History and Culture

Frank Lloyd Wright

Frank Lloyd Wright (frangk loid rīt) (1867–1959) is known internationally for his innovative building designs that were influenced by and built to be a part of nature. He completed 532 of his 1141 designs, including the Guggenheim Museum in New York City and *Fallingwater,* a house in Pennsylvania that was built around a waterfall. Wright might be best known for the houses he designed, but his work included a variety of building types, bridges, furniture, fabrics, glass, and more.

See pages 16–21 and 24–25 for more about subject matter and art history.

Artist Profiles, p. 55

● Artist Profile ●
Frank Lloyd Wright
1867-1959
Frank Lloyd Wright (frangk loid rīt) was born in Richland Center, Wisconsin. As a young boy, he and his mother arranged blocks, paper, and other simple materials into shapes of buildings and furniture. Wright studied engineering at the University of Wisconsin for less than two years before moving to Chicago. He eventually found a job at the architectural firm of Adler and Sullivan, where he worked with the important modern architect Louis Henri Sullivan for five years. In 1893, Wright began his own business. He traveled in Europe and then lived in Japan between 1915 and 1922, during the construction of the Imperial Hotel in Tokyo that he designed. In 1928, he declared personal and professional

▲ **Artist Unknown.**
(India). *Taj Mahal.*
1638–1648.

Marble. 240 feet tall
(73.15 meters). Agra, India.

Study the pictures.

▶ Name some of the different parts of these buildings.

🔍 Aesthetic Perception

Seeing Like an Artist What parts of your school building do you see when you are outside?

🏺 Art History and Culture

Taj Mahal

Taj Mahal is an Islamic tomb in Agra, India. This masterpiece of architecture and its surrounding buildings and gardens were built in the 1600s over a period of 22 years. The Taj Mahal was designed by Iranian master architect Ustad Isa, as well as numerous chief architects and craftsmen, and construction involved more than 20,000 workers. Muslim Emperor Shah Jahan ordered the building of Taj Mahal to honor his wife, Mumtaz Mahal, after her death.

See pages 16–21 and 24–25 for more about subject matter and art history.

Artist Profiles, p. 76

◇ Artist Profile ◇

Taj Majal

Shah Jehan, one of the great Mughal rulers of India, ordered the construction of the Taj Mahal. To at least some degree, Ustad Ahmad Lahori was responsible for designing the Taj Mahal. He is also said to have been a highly regarded mathematician and astronomer. The great calligrapher 'Abd ul-Haq Amanat Khan, already famous before Shah Jehan's reign, played an important role in the creation of the Taj Mahal. He is credited with having selected the Koranic verses (words taken from the Koran, the sacred book of Islam) used on the Taj Mahal.

Study

▶ Possible answers: roof, windows, pillars, arches, domes, towers, chimney, window box, front, sides, and back.

■ For more examples of utilitarian art, see *The National Museum of Women in the Arts Collection.*

📓 Art Journal: Concept
Have students draw a picture in their Art Journals that shows a building with various parts.

🔍 Aesthetic Perception

Seeing Like an Artist Take students outside to look at the school building, or ask them to think about how the school looks on the outside. Ask students to name some of the different parts of the school building.

Developing Visual Literacy Ask students what they think of the Taj Mahal and Stockman House. Encourage students to speculate on why the architects designed these buildings. How might these buildings be used?
NSAE 3.a; 3.b; 5.a; 5.c

💻 Web Connection
Learn more about the Taj Mahal at http://www.taj-mahal.net/.

Teach

Time: About 30 minutes

"Let's draw the parts of buildings you saw on your way to school today." *"Vamos a dibujar las partes de los edificios que observaron hoy camino a la escuela".*

Practice

Materials: crayons or pencils, light-colored paper

Alternate Materials: any drawing media

- Ask students to think about the buildings they saw on their way to school today. Help students name the different parts of a building.

- Discuss how students can use different shapes and forms to show the parts of a building.

Creative Expression

Materials: glue, markers, scissors, colored paper lunch bags 6" × 6" construction paper squares (any color, 1 per student), construction paper scraps, newspaper (2 sheets per student), craft items

Alternate Materials: clean, empty school milk cartons

- Distribute the materials and have the students follow the directions on page 141.

- See the Activity Tips on page 242 for visual examples of this lesson's activity.

- Ask students to look at the flat paper bag and identify how many sides it has. Then have students open the paper bag and stuff it with newspaper. How many sides does it have now?

- Help students gather the top of the paper bag and staple a folded 6" × 6" piece of paper to the top.

- Encourage students to decorate their house with doors and windows they cut from construction paper. They can also add craft items to make their house unique.

NSAE 1.a; 1.c

Art Journal: Brainstorming

Have students sketch their house from different views. How does it look from the side? From the top?

Using Building Forms

A building is a **form.** You can walk around and inside a building and see all the parts.

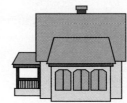

Practice

1. Think about the buildings you saw on your way to school.

2. Draw one of the buildings you saw.

Differentiated Instruction

Reteach
Display a picture of a house or building from a magazine. Lead students in a discussion about how the sides that are not visible look.

Special Needs
Students with limited upper body strength may have difficulty drawing on the sculpture. Pre-cut various doors and windows that the students can choose and place onto their sculptures.

ELL Tips
Take students on a walk around the outside of your school. Name the different parts of the school building with students, or display pictures of a building that show all its sides. Name the parts of the building with students.

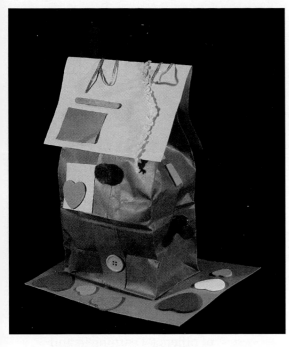

Think about the different parts you see in this house.

◄ **Anwesha Nandi.**
Age 5.

 **Creative Expression**

What kinds of houses have you seen? Design your own house.

1. Fill the paper bag with newspaper. Staple a folded piece of paper to the top so it looks like a roof.

2. Decorate your house with doors and windows.

 **Art Criticism**

Decide What parts might you add to make your house more interesting?

Art Across the Curriculum

Use these simple ideas to reinforce art concepts across the curriculum.

★ **Narrative Writing** Ask students to imagine that they are architects. Have them draw a building and explain what kind of building it is, how it is used, and by whom.

★ **Math** Have students count the windows in the classroom or the school building.

★ **Science** Study how parts make up buildings as well as machines, and identify some common parts used in machines.

★ **Social Studies** Learn about taking care of buildings in the community, like churches, schools, and homes.

★ **Technology** Have students use a paint program to draw their school. Visit **SRAonline.com** to print detailed instructions for this activity.

 # Reflect
Time: About 5 minutes

Review and Assess

"Is a building a form or shape? Why?" "¿Un edificio es una forma o una figura? ¿Por qué?"

■ Discuss the student art question. The house has a roof, walls, door, and window.

Informal Assessment

 Art Journal: Critical Thinking
Have students answer the *Decide* question by drawing a picture in their Art Journals.

Art Criticism

Have students ask themselves the following questions.

Describe ► Can you name the parts of your house?

Analyze ► Where are the big parts? The little parts?

Interpret ► What might others say about your house when they see it?

Decide ► What parts might you add to make your house more interesting?

NSAE 2.b; 5.a; 5.c

■ For standardized-format test practice using this lesson's art content, see pages 48–49 in *Reading and Writing Test Preparation.*

Building Forms

Extra! For the Art Specialist

Time: About 30 minutes

Focus

Use **Transparency 22** and **Large Prints 7** *Bear and Seal* and **8** *Armoured Carousel Horse* to discuss how the artists used forms. How many different forms do you go in and out of each day? List them.

Teach

Have students use clay to create a relief sculpture of a house.

Reflect

Have students use the four steps of art criticism to evaluate their work. Did they effectively use clay to create a form of a house?

Alternate Activity

Materials:
- clay (9" × 12" slabs rolled $\frac{3}{4}$" thick)
- tools for texture
- craft sticks

1. Discuss the different materials people use to make houses. Encourage students to describe how wood, stone, brick or rock would feel. Have students think of different ways to show these textures in clay.

2. Give each student a slab of clay approximately 9" × 12". Have students use craft sticks to press lines for the door and window shapes. Use other objects to create textures for the walls and roof.

3. Using a craft stick or other flat tool, students cut a point at the top of the rectangle to be the roof.

4. Fire the clay and then have students paint their work.

NSAE 1.a; 1.c

Research in Art Education

Collaboration is an important benefit of the arts. In the visual arts students may engage in "enterprises such as painting murals and scenery, producing books, and organizing exhibitions." They also often have the opportunity to learn to appropriately critique the work of others ("Learning in and Through the Arts: Curriculum Implications" in *Champions of Change*, p. 40). Discuss how students need to work together and take turns as they create their art projects and share supplies.

Assessment

Use the following rubric to evaluate the artwork students make in the Creative Expression activity and to assess students' understanding of building forms.

Have students complete page 51 or 52 in their *Assessment* books.

	Art History and Culture	Aesthetic Perception	Creative Expression	Art Criticism
3 POINTS	The student recognizes that architecture is the art of designing and creating buildings.	The student accurately locates and identifies building forms in his or her environment.	The student's sculpture demonstrates an understanding that buildings are forms.	The student thoughtfully and honestly evaluates his or her own work using the four steps of art criticism.
2 POINTS	The student shows emerging awareness of architecture being the art of designing and creating buildings.	The student shows emerging ability to locate and identify building forms in his or her environment.	The student's sculpture demonstrates emerging awareness that buildings are forms.	The student attempts to evaluate his or her own work, but shows an incomplete understanding of evaluation criteria.
1 POINT	The student does not recognize that architecture is the art of designing and creating buildings.	The student does not locate or identify building forms in his or her environment.	The student's sculpture demonstrates no understanding that buildings are forms.	The student makes no attempt to evaluate his or her own artwork.

Assessment, p. 51

Name _____ Date _____

A Building Is a Form

Lesson **4** UNIT 4

For the teacher: Use the following prompts for this activity.
Using geometric shapes, draw the parts of a building. First, draw the bottom.
Then, add shapes onto the sides. Next, add shapes to make a roof.

Level K

Unit 4 • Space and Form **51**

Lesson 5 Animal Forms

 Overview

Lesson 5 introduces animal forms. Animal forms can be three-dimensional. A four-legged animal sculpture can be a solid form. In this lesson you will create animal sculptures from clay.

Objectives

 Art History and Culture

To recognize that *William* is a sculpture from ancient Egypt

 Creative Expression

To create a four-legged animal sculpture using clay

 Aesthetic Perception

To identify four-legged animals that could be used as the subjects of a sculpture

Art Criticism

To evaluate one's own work using the four steps of art criticism

Vocabulary ⭐ Reading

Review the following vocabulary words with students before beginning the lesson.

sculpture *escultura*—a three-dimensional work of art

solid form *forma sólida*—a three-dimensional object, having height, width, and depth

See page 149B for additional vocabulary and Spanish vocabulary resources.

Art Journal: Vocabulary

Have students add these words to the Vocabulary section of their Art Journals.

Lesson Materials

- crayons
- paper
- earthen clay
- clay mats (muslin)
- pencils
- wood or cardboard (for a base)

Alternate Materials:
- modeling clay

Program Resources

- *Reading and Writing Test Prep.,* pp. 50–51
- *Transparency 23*
- *Artist Profiles,* pp. 58, 60
- *Animals Through History Time Line*
- *Assessment,* pp. 53–54
- *Large Print 7 Bear and Seal* and *8 Armoured Carousel Horse*
- *Art Around the World Collection*

Concept Trace

Animal Forms

Introduced: Level K, Unit 4, Lesson 5

Reinforced: Level 1, Unit 4, Lesson 3

Lesson 5 Arts Integration

Theatre

Complete Unit 4, Lesson 5 on pages 80–81 of the *Theatre Arts Connections* book.

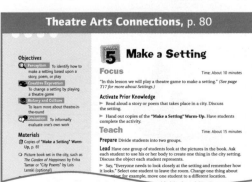

Theatre Arts Connections, p. 80

Music

 Listen to the silly animal song by Bill Harley, *Sittin' Down to Eat.* Point out how the music of the A section is always the same, even in the different verses and that the animals change. Therefore the form is AB.

Movement & Dance

Select three animals with three contrasting qualities. Ask students to identify how their speed, size, and motion vary. Have students spread out and explore moving as each animal. Use words to help students access the movement. Examples: snake—long, light, slithering; eagle—fast, expansive, gliding; elephant—slow, heavy, trudging.

Focus

Time: About 10 minutes

Activate Prior Knowledge

"Do you have a special stuffed animal toy that has four legs?" "¿Tienen un muñeco de peluche que tenga cuatro patas?"

- Discuss the stuffed animal as having a head, body, legs, and a tail.

Using Literature

- Read *May I Bring a Friend?* by Beatrice Schenk de Regniers, illustrated by Beni Montresor. Ask students to identify animal forms they see in the illustrations.

Thematic Connection Science

- **Animals:** Discuss the basic needs of animals, and compare them with the needs of humans.

Introduce the Art

"Let's look at these sculptures of four-legged animals." "Vamos a observar estas esculturas de animales con cuatro patas".

- Ask students to identify the animals in the pictures and name the body parts they see. Then have students count the animals' legs.

Identifying Details ☆ Reading

- Discuss the designs on the hippopotamus. The designs on the hippo's body are lotus flowers. Lotus flowers grow in a hippo's environment. What is on the camel's back? The camel has a saddle on its back so a person can ride on the camel.

- Share with students that both sculptures are very old. The *Bactrian Camel* sculpture is from China. *William* is from ancient Egypt and is a symbol of great strength.

Drawing Conclusions ☆ Reading

- Ask students why a hippopotamus might have been chosen to represent strength.

🏺 Art History and Culture

Share information from the Art History and Culture sections with students. Answers will vary. Students might suggest that these works of art are valuable or have special meaning.
NSAE 4.a

💻 Web Connection

Visit www.pbs.org/kratts/world/africa/hippo/ to find out more about hippopotamuses.

An Animal Is a Form

Look at these animals. Sometimes artists make forms of animals. We can look at every side of animal forms.

◀ **Artist Unknown.** (China.) *Bactrian Camel with Packsaddle.* C. A.D. 700–750.
Earthenware with three-colored glaze. 36⅛ inches high (91.75 cm.). Nelson Atkins Museum, Kansas City, Missouri.

🏺 Art History and Culture

These animals are very old works of art. Why do you think they have been kept for so many years?

🏺 Art History and Culture

Bactrian Camel

During the Tang Dynasty, camels carried people and goods between China and the Middle East through Bactria. The camel became a symbol of wealth because of the trade goods they carried on their backs. Earthenware figures of these camels were often made as burial figures for tombs. The figures were made of clay and then painted and glazed. Lead glazing became popular at this time because it melted completely, resulting in a bright clear glaze that allowed the paint colors to remain brilliant.

See pages 16–21 and 24–25 for more about subject matter and art history.

Artist Profiles, p. 58

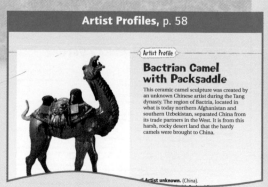

⌐ Artist Profile ¬
Bactrian Camel with Packsaddle
This ceramic camel sculpture was created by an unknown Chinese artist during the Tang dynasty. The region of Bactria, located in what is today northern Afghanistan and southern Uzbekistan, separated China from its trade partners in the West. It is from this harsh, rocky desert land that the hardy camels were brought to China.

◀ Artist unknown. (China.)

Study the pictures.

▶ What kinds of animal forms do you see in the pictures?

▲ **Artist Unknown.**
(Egypt). *Ancient Egyptian Hippo "William".*
1991–1786 B.C.
....
$4\frac{3}{8} \times 7\frac{7}{8}$ inches (11.13 × 20.02 cm.). The Metropolitan Museum of Art, New York, New York.

 Aesthetic Perception

Seeing Like an Artist What other animals with four legs could be made as a sculpture?

Study

▶ Hippopotamus and camel.

■ For more examples of art from the Middle East, see the *Art Around the World Collection.*

 Art Journal: Concept
Have students draw a picture in their Art Journals of a four-legged animal.

 Aesthetic Perception

Seeing Like an Artist Ask students to think of animals with four legs that could be made as a sculpture. Look at pictures of animals for more ideas.

Developing Visual Literacy Ask students if they have seen a real camel or hippopotamus. Where did they see them? How were they similar or different to the sculptures in the lesson?
NSAE 4.a

Art History and Culture

Ancient Egyptian Hippo "William"

This animal sculpture is part of the Egyptian Collection of the Metropolitan Museum of Art in New York City. Nicknamed "William," it now serves as the official museum mascot. The animal figure is a charm, or amulet, that was buried in the tomb of a great leader to act as a protector of that tomb from thieves and evil spirits. *William* stands only 4 inches high, yet is a symbol of great strength.

See pages 16–21 and 24–25 for more about subject matter and art history.

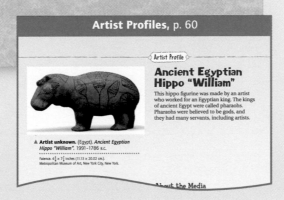

Artist Profiles, p. 60

Artist Profile

Ancient Egyptian Hippo "William"

This hippo figurine was made by an artist who worked for an Egyptian king. The kings of ancient Egypt were called pharaohs. Pharaohs were believed to be gods, and they had many servants, including artists.

▲ **Artist unknown.** (Egypt). *Ancient Egyptian Hippo "William".* 1991–1786 B.C.
Faience. $4\frac{3}{8} \times 7\frac{7}{8}$ inches (11.13 × 20.02 cm.). Metropolitan Museum of Art, New York, New York.

Web Connection
Learn more about Bactrian camels at www.lpzoo.com/tour/factsheets/mammals/bactrian_camel.html.

Teach

Time: About 30 minutes

"Let's draw an animal with four legs." "Vamos a dibujar un animal con cuatro patas".

Practice

Materials: crayons, paper

Alternate Materials: any drawing media

- Have students use crayon to draw a picture of an animal with four legs as directed on page 144.

- Ask students to point to and count the animal's legs.

Creative Expression

Materials: earthen clay, clay mats (muslin), pencils, wood or cardboard (for a base)

Alternate Materials: modeling clay

"Let's create an animal form in clay." "Vamos a crear en arcilla la forma de un animal".

- Distribute the materials and have the students follow the directions on page 145.

- See the Activity Tips on page 243 for visual examples of this lesson's activity.

- Have students roll a ball of clay about the size of a small apple into the shape of a potato. Then, have them squeeze the clay to make a head and body.

- For legs, have students add four additional pieces of clay by thoroughly rubbing the spot where they connect. This will blend the pieces and make them stick.

- Remind students that they will need to place each leg at a corner of the body so that their animal will stand up.

- Have students use a pencil to add eyes and other details to all sides of their forms.

- See the Technique Tips on pages 230–231 for additional information about using clay.

NSAE 1.a; 1.c

Art Journal: Brainstorming

Have students think about different four-legged animals and then draw their favorite.

The *Animals Through History Time Line* provides many examples of animals that would be helpful for this activity.

Using Animal Forms

An animal **sculpture** is a **form.** You can walk around this animal form and see all four legs.

Practice

1. Draw an animal with four legs.
2. Count the legs.

Differentiated Instruction

Reteach

Have students role-play different animal movements by walking on hands and knees. Ask them to identify their animal forms (for example, paws, trunk, and so on) as they go.

Special Needs

If using Pleistocene clay, ensure that it has been heated so that it is not difficult for students with limited upper body strength to manipulate.

ELL Tips

Display a stuffed animal. Invite students to walk around it to view it from all sides. Ask them if this animal is a form, and why. Then ask students to name animals with four legs and list them on a chart.

◄ **Davis Hays.**
Age 6.

Think about the kind of animal form this student made.

What do your favorite animals look like? Design an animal form.

1. Make an animal with four legs out of clay.
2. Use a pencil to add eyes and other details.

Interpret What is your animal doing? What sound would it make if it could speak?

Unit 4 • Lesson 5 **145**

● Art Across the Curriculum ●

Use these simple ideas to reinforce art concepts across the curriculum.

★ **Expository Writing** Ask students to draw three pictures to illustrate how the clay changed when they created their animal form, beginning with a picture of a ball of clay. Then have students explain the steps.

★ **Math** Have students count the number of arms, legs, or eyes on an animal sculpture.

★ **Science** Learn more about the needs of living things, like the hippo depicted in the Egyptian sculpture.

★ **Social Studies** Ask students to draw some of the things they do to have fun, just as some people look at art for fun.

★ **Technology** Have students use a paint program to draw a four-legged animal. Visit **SRAonline.com** to print detailed instructions for this activity.

Reflect Time: About 5 minutes

Review and Assess

"Is a clay animal a solid form or a flat shape?"
"¿Un animal de arcilla es una forma sólida o una figura plana?"

■ Use *Large Prints 7 Bear and Seal* and *8 Armoured Carousel Horse* to compare animal sculptures. Remind students that you can see all sides of solid forms.

■ Discuss the student art question. This animal could be a horse, donkey, or perhaps unicorn.

Informal Assessment

Art Journal: Critical Thinking
Have students answer the first Interpret question by drawing a picture in their Art Journals. Allow them to answer the second question aloud.

Have students ask themselves the following questions.

Describe ► What kind of animal did you create?

Analyze ► How does your clay animal form look different from a human form? How does the animal form look similar?

Interpret ► What is your animal doing? What sound would it make if it could speak?

Decide ► How did you make sure that your animal form would stand on its four legs?

NSAE 2.b; 5.a; 5.c

■ For standardized-format test practice using this lesson's art content, see pages 50–51 in *Reading and Writing Test Preparation*.

LESSON 5 • Animal Forms **145**

Lesson 5 — Animal Forms
Wrap-Up

 For the Art Specialist

Time: About 30 minutes

Focus

Use *Transparency 23* and *Large Prints 7 Bear and Seal* and *8 Armoured Carousel Horse* to discuss how the artists used form. Have students think of animal forms that they can hug with both arms. List them.

Teach

Have students create a four-legged animal sculpture using found objects.

Reflect

Have students use the four steps of art criticism to evaluate their work. Did they effectively create a four-legged animal sculpture using found objects?

Alternate Activity

Materials:

- empty toilet paper tube (one per student)
- variety of found objects such as yarn, buttons, tag board, foam shapes, and colored tissue
- scissors
- craft glue
- craft sticks
- low-melt hot glue (for the teacher)

1. Discuss how animals are forms. Some animals are small enough to hold in your hands. Some animals can be hugged with two arms, and others are so big you have to walk around them.

2. Make a list of small, medium, and large animals.

3. Direct students to choose their favorite animals and construct sculptures with found objects.

4. Assist students by gluing craft sticks for the legs of the animals. Have students use craft glue to attach other objects for the face, hair, or tails of the animals.

NSAE 1.a; 1.c

Research in Art Education

Research has shown that assessing knowledge through a combination of drawing and writing can lead to higher scores for content knowledge. This applied to native English speakers and limited English speakers alike. This suggests "that drawing may be one way to reveal what students know but cannot put into words" ("The Arts, Language, and Knowing: An Experimental Study of the Potential of the Visual Arts for Assessing Academic Learning by Language Minority Students" in *Critical Links*, p. 141). Observe students' illustrations in their Art Journals as they draw pictures to explain how they made their animal forms.

Assessment

Use the following rubric to evaluate the artwork students make in the Creative Expression activity and to assess students' understanding of animal forms.

Have students complete page 53 or 54 in their *Assessment* books.

	Art History and Culture	Aesthetic Perception	Creative Expression	Art Criticism
3 POINTS	The student recognizes that *William* is a sculpture from ancient Egypt.	The student accurately identifies four-legged animals that could be used as the subjects of a sculpture.	The student's animal sculpture demonstrates a strong understanding of form.	The student thoughtfully and honestly evaluates his or her own work using the four steps of art criticism.
2 POINTS	The student shows emerging awareness that *William* is a sculpture from ancient Egypt.	The student shows emerging ability to identify four-legged animals that could be used as the subjects of a sculpture.	The student's animal sculpture demonstrates emerging awareness of form.	The student attempts to evaluate his or her own work, but shows an incomplete understanding of evaluation criteria.
1 POINT	The student does not recognize that *William* is a sculpture from ancient Egypt.	The student does not identify four-legged animals that could be used as the subjects of a sculpture.	The student's animal sculpture demonstrates no understanding of form.	The student makes no attempt to evaluate his or her own artwork.

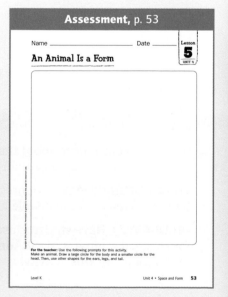

Assessment, p. 53

Name _____ Date _____
Lesson **5** UNIT 4

An Animal Is a Form

For the teacher: Use the following prompts for this activity. Make an animal. Draw a large circle for the body and a smaller circle for the head. Then, use other shapes for the ears, legs, and tail.

Level K   Unit 4 • Space and Form   **53**

Lesson 6 Overview

Forms Can Be Used

Lesson 6 is about uses for forms. Students will study pottery that is both pretty and useful and learn to recognize jars and bowls as art forms.

Objectives

Art History and Culture
To recognize that some art forms have a practical, useful purpose

Aesthetic Perception
To identify artwork that has everyday uses

Creative Expression
To create a pinch pot with clay

Art Criticism
To evaluate one's own work using the four steps of art criticism

Vocabulary ★ Reading
Review the following vocabulary word with students before beginning the lesson.

art form forma artística—a type of art

See page 149B for additional vocabulary and Spanish vocabulary resources.

Art Journal: Vocabulary
Have students add this word to the Vocabulary section of their Art Journals.

Lesson Materials
- clay, wood or cardboard (for a base)
- clay mats (muslin)
- clay tools: plastic forks/knives, paper clips, craft sticks, and pencils

Alternate Materials:
- cornstarch dough

Program Resources
- *Reading and Writing Test Prep.*, pp. 52–53
- *Transparency 24*
- *Flash Card 20*
- *Artist Profiles*, pp. 61, 73
- *Assessment*, pp. 55–56
- *Large Print 7 Bear and Seal* and *8 Armoured Carousel Horse*
- *Art Around the World Collection*

Concept Trace
Forms Can Be Used
Introduced: Level K, Unit 4, Lesson 6

Reinforced: Level 2, Unit 2, Lesson 4

Lesson 6 Arts Integration

Theatre
Complete Unit 4, Lesson 6 on pages 82–87 of the *Theatre Arts Connections* book.

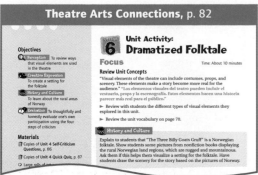

Music
 Sometimes songs can be used to do a job. A lullaby puts a child to sleep. A sea chant is sung to keep the beat so that the workmen are synchronized in their movements. Listen to *Chairs to Mend*. Songs like this advertise the job someone does, or things they sell.

Movement & Dance
Some dances are created to show physical skill and to look beautiful; others are created to show the customs of a particular community. Some dances tell stories or express emotions. Ask students to identify dances they have seen that fit into these categories. Examples: ballet, folk dance, modern dance, and tap dance.

Focus

Time: About 10 minutes

Activate Prior Knowledge

"Name something that holds water." "Vamos a nombrar algo que retiene agua".

- Discuss the various containers and their uses: glass jar, pitcher, bowl, pan, and pot.

Using Literature

- Read *Mouse Views: What the Class Pet Saw* by Bruce McMillan. Are any of the forms in the photographs both pretty and useful?

Thematic Connection ★ Social Studies

- **Cultural Diversity:** Discuss differences among people who live in different places, such as the Chinese and Native Americans who created the fine art examples.

Introduce the Art

"People have been making clay jars for thousands of years. This jar might have been used for holding water a long time ago." "Las personas han elaborado jarras de arcilla por miles de años. Esta jarra se pudo haber utilizada para retener agua hace mucho tiempo".

- Have students describe the jar. Is it large or small? What is unusual about the handles?

Making Inferences ★ Reading

- Ask students what other things might have been put in this jar.

- Explain to students that some works of art have practical purposes.

- The height of the *Painted Storage Jar* suggests that it was used for long-term storage of grains or perhaps beans. The handles appear to be quite small for the size of the vessel and look as though they might be held with a rope.

Adjectives and Adverbs ★ Language Arts

- On a chart list the adjectives and adverbs students use to describe the fine art.

🏺 Art History and Culture

Share information from the Art History and Culture sections with students. Answers will vary. Possible answers: vase, pitcher, bowl, dish, and flower pot.

💻 Web Connection

Visit the Web site for the Kimbell Art Museum in Fort Worth, Texas, at **www.kimbellart.org/** to learn more about *Painted Storage Jar.*

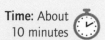 **Lesson 6**

Forms Can Be Used

◀ **Artist Unknown.** (China.) *Painted Storage Jar.* c. 2500–1700 B.C.

Clay, iron oxide, and magnesium pigments. 15 inches high × 16 inches in diameter (38.1 × 40.64 cm.). Kimbell Art Museum, Fort Worth, Texas.

Look at these works of art. Artwork can be pretty and useful.

🏺 Art History and Culture

Sometimes artists make forms that can be used to do a job. What forms do you have at home that can be used to do a job?

146 Unit 4 • Lesson 6

🏺 Art History and Culture

Yangshou Culture

This jar was made during the Neolithic era—the final stage of the Stone Age—and comes from the Yangshou culture, where it was excavated from a Chinese tomb. This civilization was named after a site in the Hunan Province, located on the Central Plain of northern China. The Yangshou made pottery for general, daily use and pottery to be used as funerary jars.

See pages 16–21 and 24–25 for more about subject matter and art history.

Artist Profiles, p. 73

Painted Storage Jar

The artist who made this painted storage jar is not known. However, this artist was a specially trained craftsperson who more than likely belonged to a family of potters.

◀ **Artist unknown.** (China.) *Painted Storage Jar.* c. 2500–1700 B.C.

Clay, iron oxide, and magnesium pigments. 15 inches high × 16 inches in diameter (38.1 × 40.64 cm.). Kimbell Art Museum, Fort Worth, Texas.

Study the pictures.

▶ How would you use the forms in the pictures?

▲ **Artist Unknown.** (Native American, Cherokee or Iroquois.) *Bowl.* c. 1800.

Wood and brass. 13⅝ inches high (34.60 cm.). Detroit Institute of the Arts, Detroit, Michigan.

Aesthetic Perception

Seeing Like an Artist Where do you see forms that are pretty and useful?

Art History and Culture

Cherokee or Iroquois *Bowl*

This Cherokee or Iroquois *Bowl* might have been used for serving food at meals during religious rituals. Each end of the bowl has a carved image, one male and the other female, possibly recognizing the importance of each gender in community life.

See pages 16–21 and 24–25 for more about subject matter and art history.

Artist Profiles, p. 61

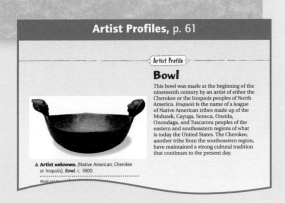

⌐ Artist Profile ⌐
Bowl

This bowl was made at the beginning of the nineteenth century by an artist of either the Cherokee or the Iroquois peoples of North America. *Iroquois* is the name of a league of Native American tribes made up of the Mohawk, Cayuga, Seneca, Oneida, Onondaga, and Tuscarora peoples of the eastern and southeastern regions of what is today the United States. The Cherokee, another tribe from the southeastern region, have maintained a strong cultural tradition that continues to the present day.

▲ **Artist unknown.** (Native American, Cherokee or Iroquois). *Bowl.* c. 1800.

Study

▶ Possible answers: *Painted Storage Jar* could be used as a vase or for storing dry foods like spaghetti or rice. The *Bowl* could be used for serving food or for storing small items like crayons or paper clips.

■ For more examples of art from Asia, see the *Art Around the World Collection.*

Art Journal: Concept
Have students draw a picture that shows a building with various parts.

Aesthetic Perception

Seeing Like an Artist Ask students to look around and identify forms that are both pretty and useful.

Developing Visual Literacy Ask students if they have any forms at home that are both pretty and useful like the *Painted Storage Jar* and *Bowl.* What do they look like? How are they used?
NSAE 3.a; 3.b; 4.a

💻 **Web Connection**
Visit **www.dia.org/collections/aonwc/ nativeamericanart/nativeamericanart.html** to learn more about Native American art at the Detroit Institute of Arts.

 **Teach** **Time:** About 30 minutes

"Let's practice forming clay." "*Vamos a moldear arcilla*".

 Practice

Materials: small chunk of clay

Alternate Materials: cornstarch dough

- Give each student a tangerine-size ball of clay to work with. As directed on page 148, have the students pinch it with their thumb and fingers to flatten it.

- Ask students if it is easier to flatten the clay using both hands or just one.

Creative Expression

Materials: clay, wood or cardboard (for a base), clay mats (muslin), clay tools: plastic forks/knives, paper clips, craft sticks, pencils

Alternate Materials: cornstarch dough

- Lead a discussion that gets students thinking of different containers they could use in their homes and the containers' purposes—to hold water, food, flowers, pencils, and so on.

- Distribute the materials and have the students follow the directions on page 149.

- See the Activity Tips on page 243 for visual examples of this lesson's activity.

- Explain that one way of creating a pot is by pinching the clay to create a bowl form.

- Have students roll their clay into a ball.

- Keeping their fingers outside the clay ball, the students should push their thumb into it to make an impression.

- Encourage the students to use their fingers now to pinch around the clay ball to shape the pot.

- Have the students decorate their pots with designs using the tip of a pencil or pen.

- See the Technique Tips on pages 230–231 for more information about using clay.

NSAE 1.a; 1.c

Art Journal: Brainstorming
Have students sketch pictures in their Art Journals of different kinds of containers.

Using Forms

Jars and bowls are **forms** that people look at and use.

Practice

1. Flatten the clay your teacher gives you.

2. Did you use both hands or just one?

Differentiated Instruction

Reteach
Show students pictures from magazines that have useful objects in them and discuss their design as created by an artist.

Special Needs
Encourage student creativity by showing students examples of pinch pots that are shaped in non-traditional ways and decorated to give the viewer clues about their purpose.

ELL Tips
Display a jar of jam, a flower vase, a cookie jar, and a soup can. Have students say with you the name of each container. Then have students walk around the containers so they can see them from all sides. Ask, "Are these forms? How are they used?"

Think about how you could use this student's pot.

 Creative Expression

How could you design a piece of art to use at home? Create a pinch pot.

1. Pinch your clay ball to form a pot.
2. Use a pencil to make a design on your pot.

 Art Criticism

Interpret What will you keep inside your pinch pot?

Art Across the Curriculum

Use these simple ideas to reinforce art concepts across the curriculum.

★ **Descriptive Writing** Remind students that *Painted Storage Jar* was from China. Help students practice writing words that name things from China, such as *kite, panda,* and *rice.*

★ **Math** Have students study the patterns on *Painted Storage Jar,* and then create their own patterns with geometric shapes.

★ **Science** Discover how putting things in a jar will add weight to the jar. Determine which of several jars is heaviest and which is lightest.

★ **Social Studies** Discuss tasks and chores that the students do every day. Ask how *Painted Storage Jar* and *Bowl* might have been used to help with daily activities.

★ **Technology** Have students use a paint program to draw a storage jar or bowl. Use various tools to add a design. Visit **SRAonline.com** to print detailed instructions for this activity.

Reflect

Time: About 5 minutes

Review and Assess

"What kinds of art forms also have everyday uses?" "¿Qué clases de formas artísticas también tienen utilidad actualmente?"

Think

■ Discuss the student art question. Answers may include using the pot as a flower pot or for storing school supplies or small toys.

Informal Assessment

Art Journal: Critical Thinking
Have students answer the Interpret question in their Art Journals by drawing a picture.

 Art Criticism

Have students ask themselves the following questions.

Describe ▶ Is your pinch pot deep, wide, short, or tall?

Analyze ▶ Describe the textures you added to your pot. Why did you choose these textures?

Interpret ▶ What will you keep inside your pinch pot?

Decide ▶ How does your pinch pot resemble the bowls or jars you use at home? How is it different?

NSAE 2.b; 5.a; 5.c

■ For standardized-format test practice using this lesson's art content, see pages 52–53 in *Reading and Writing Test Preparation.*

Forms Can Be Used

 Extra! For the Art Specialist

Focus

Use *Transparency 24* and *Large Prints 7 Bear and Seal* and *8 Armoured Carousel Horse* to discuss how the artists used form. Encourage students to think of forms that they can hold in their hands. Ask students to describe the forms.

Teach

Help students learn about uses for forms by having them decorate a cardboard container with collage.

Reflect

Have students use the four steps of art criticism to evaluate their work. Did they create a form that is both decorative and useful?

Alternate Activity

Materials:
- empty cardboard juice containers
- magazine scraps
- white glue
- 1" brushes
- easel

1. Forms can be very big or very small. Some forms are small enough to hold in your hand. They can be beautiful objects like jewelry or they can be useful objects like a bowl. Show the students how a bowl has an empty space inside that can be used to hold many things.

2. Direct the students to collect 2–3 pages from a magazine. Have them tear the pages into smaller shapes.

3. Then have students cover the cardboard juice containers with white glue that has been slightly thinned. Students place the magazine pieces on the wet glue.

4. Then students apply more glue over the paper. Continue these steps until the container is completely covered.

NSAE 1.a; 1.c

Research in Art Education

An ideal arts curriculum would be "one that offers in-depth, carefully sequenced teaching in several art forms for the entire span of young peoples' schooling." It is also beneficial to have extended times of learning in which students may visit museums and concert halls ("Learning in and Through the Arts: Curriculum Implications" in *Champions of Change*, p. 44). These visits are an excellent way of learning more about the art of other cultures, like the Native American and Chinese cultures that are presented in this lesson.

Assessment

Use the following rubric to evaluate the artwork students make in the Creative Expression activity and to assess students' understanding of forms that can be used.

Have students complete page 55 or 56 in their *Assessment* books.

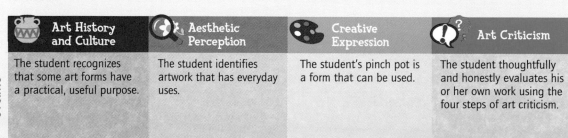

	Art History and Culture	Aesthetic Perception	Creative Expression	Art Criticism
3 POINTS	The student recognizes that some art forms have a practical, useful purpose.	The student identifies artwork that has everyday uses.	The student's pinch pot is a form that can be used.	The student thoughtfully and honestly evaluates his or her own work using the four steps of art criticism.
2 POINTS	The student shows emerging awareness that some art forms have a practical, useful purpose.	The student shows emerging ability to identify artwork that has everyday uses.	The student demonstrates emerging ability to create a form that can be used.	The student attempts to evaluate his or her own work, but shows an incomplete understanding of evaluation criteria.
1 POINT	The student does not recognize that some art forms have a practical, useful purpose.	The student does not identify artwork that has everyday uses.	The student's pinch pot is not a form that can be used.	The student makes no attempt to evaluate his or her own artwork.

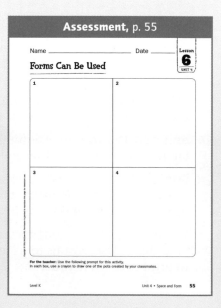

Assessment, p. 55

Name _____ Date _____ Lesson **6** UNIT 4

Forms Can Be Used

1	2
3	4

For the teacher: Use the following prompt for this activity.
In each box, use a crayon to draw one of the pots created by your classmates.

Level K   Unit 4 • Space and Form   **55**

space—the element of art that refers to the area between, around, above, below, and within objects **espacio**—el elemento artístico que se refiere al área entre, alrededor, arriba, debajo y adentro de los objetos.

form—any object that can be measured in three ways: height, width, and depth **forma**—cualquier objeto que se puede medir en tres maneras: la altura, el ancho y la profundidad

sculpture—a three-dimensional work of art **escultura**—tridimensional una obra de arte

solid form—a three-dimensional object, having height, width, and depth **forma sólida**—un objeto tridimensional, teniendo altura, anchura y profundidad

art form—a type of art **forma artística**—un tipo de arte

Vocabulary Practice

T Display *Transparency 40* to review unit vocabulary words.

Words in Context ⭐ Vocabulary
Have students use vocabulary words to complete sentences.

Visualization Strategies ⭐ Vocabulary
Create a word wall and include the vocabulary words from this unit.

Words and Sounds ⭐ Vocabulary
Help students create tongue twisters with the vocabulary words, such as *Sculptures are solid forms that are surrounded by space.*

Wrapping Up Unit 4
Space and Form

Art Criticism

Critical Thinking Art Criticism is an organized system for looking at and talking about art. You can criticize art without being an expert. The purpose of art criticism is to get the viewer involved in a perception process that delays judgment until all aspects of the artwork have been studied.

- See pages 28–29 for more about art criticism.

Describe

▶ Ask students how many people they see in the sculpture and to describe what they are doing. There is a man and a woman. The man sits on a stool at a counter, and the woman stands in front of a coffee maker, holding a cup and saucer.

▶ Ask students to identify the objects they see. Part of a restaurant counter, one stool, an overhead light, fountain equipment that includes tall faucets, syrup dispensers, a drain for water, and a big coffee maker. On the counter, there is a plate, cup and saucer, a napkin holder and a sugar jar. There are three metal cup holders. A large red rectangle hangs on the wall behind the woman and there is a brown mat on the floor.

Analyze

▶ Ask students where they see empty spaces. There is space between the man and the counter, and under his stool. There is space between the woman and the coffee maker, and between the man and the woman. There is space above and around the whole work.

▶ Can you walk around this form? If it were not in the corner we could walk around it.

▶ What is unusual about the people forms? They are white and bumpy.

▶ What is unusual about the objects? They look like real restaurant objects.

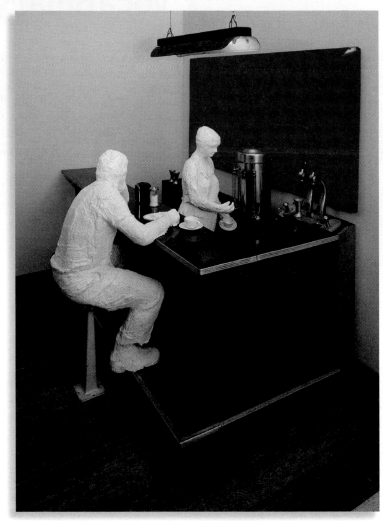

▲ **George Segal.** (American). *The Diner.*
1964–1966.
....
Plaster, wood, chrome, laminated plastic, masonite, and fluorescent lamp. 98$\frac{3}{4}$ × 144$\frac{1}{4}$ × 96 inches (250.83 × 366.40 × 243.84 cm.). The Walker Art Center, Minneapolis, Minnesota.

150   Unit 4

Art History and Culture

George Segal

George Segal (jôrj sē´ gǝl) (1924–2000) was born in the Bronx. After college he started a chicken farm and taught high school. In 1958 he sold his chickens and used the chicken houses as his studio. He created plaster figures on wood and chicken-wire frames. He used gauze to create his sculptures.

In 1961 Segal hit upon the idea of making a plaster cast of his own body, and placing the hollow figure in a real-life setting. Soon he was at the center of the pop art movement. After that Segal was asked to create his special sculptures around the world.

See pages 16–21 and 24–25 for more about subject matter and art history.

Artist Profiles, p. 40

Artist Profile ♦
George Segal
1924–2000
Not long before George Segal (jôrj sē´ gǝl) was born, his parents emigrated from eastern Europe to the Bronx in New York. They did not consider art to be a legitimate profession, but Segal insisted on studying art in college. After graduating in 1947, he started a chicken farm in New Jersey and taught at a high school to support his wife and two children. In 1958, he sold his chickens and used the buildings the chickens were housed in as his studio. For the next two years he created plaster figures on wood and chicken wire frames. All the art teachers in that area received surplus gauze embedded with plaster from a nearby Johnson & Johnson plant to give to Segal. He used this gauze to create his sculptures.

 **Art Criticism** **Critical Thinking**

Describe

▶ How many people do you see in the sculpture?

Analyze

▶ Where do you see space around the people?

Interpret

▶ What do you think the people are saying to each other?

Decide

▶ Does this look like a place you would like to go to get something to eat?

Interpret

▶ What do you think the people are saying to each other? Answers will vary. Students might say the man is ordering his meal, or that they are discussing the weather. Some might say the people are friends and sharing information about their families; some might say they are not talking at all.

▶ If you could stand next to the man in the sculpture, what sounds would you hear? Answers will vary. Students may list the sound of the coffee maker, cups and saucers rattling, or music playing.

▶ What would you smell? Answers will vary. Students may mention the smells of coffee or fried foods.

▶ Why do you think the diner has only one stool? Answers will vary. Students may say the artist wanted to make it look lonely, or that he was showing only one part of the diner.

▶ Why do you think the people are all white and everything else looks real? Answers will vary. Encourage students to see these as real people in a real setting.

Decide

▶ Ask students if this looks like a place where they would like to go to get something to eat. Answers will vary.

NSAE 5.a; 5.c

Art Journal: Writing

Have students draw a picture in their Art Journals to answer the Analyze Aesthetic Perception question. Discuss the other questions out loud.

Aesthetic Perception

Critical Thinking Ask students if they have ever eaten in a restaurant.

Describe ▶ What did it look like inside the restaurant?

Analyze ▶ What kinds of forms did you see in the restaurant? Was there space between the forms?

Interpret ▶ What do you think it would be like to work in this restaurant?

Decide ▶ Did you like eating at this restaurant? Why or why not?

"Where do we see space and form every day?" "¿Dónde observamos espacio y forma diariamente?"

T Review unit vocabulary with students using **Transparency 40.**

► Review the concepts of space and form.

► Have students name different forms around the room (such as desks, chairs, books, and people) and identify the space that the forms use.

Art Journal: Writing
Read the questions on page 152 to students. Have students write their answers in their Art Journals or on a separate sheet of paper. 1. A, 2. A, 3. A.

T For further assessment, have students complete the unit test on **Transparency 46.**

CAREERS IN ART
Motion Pictures

► Ask students about movies they have seen. Did any actors wear make-up? How would the movie have been different if the actor(s) did not have on make-up?

► Discuss how animators make still pictures appear to move. Encourage students to think about the advantages of moving animation over still pictures. What are the disadvantages?

"Each form is a world."
—Kasimir Malevich

Show What You Know

Answer these questions on a sheet of paper.

❶ Which of these works of art is a form?

A.   B.

❷ Which of these is **not** a form?

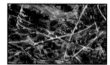

A.   B.

❸ A form can be seen

  A. from all sides.
  B. from only the front.

Unit Assessment Options

🔍 Aesthetic Perception

Practice Ask students to identify forms they see around them. Where is there space around the forms?

🎨 Creative Expression   NSAE 5.a; 5.c

Student Portfolio Have students review all the artwork they have created during this unit and select the pieces they wish to put into their portfolios. Have students share their portfolios with classmates and comment constructively about the art.

💬 Art Criticism

Activity Have students select their favorite work of art from the unit. Guide students through study of their selected work using the four steps of art criticism. (See pages 28–29 for more about Art Criticism.)

CAREERS IN ART
Motion Pictures

Do you like to watch movies? Artists help create movies.

Animators draw still pictures and make them look like they are moving, like you see in a cartoon.

Make-up artists put make-up on actors to change how they look.

▲ Animator

Space and Form in Music and Dance

▲ Ranganiketan Manipuri Cultural Arts Troupe. *Dhon Dholak Cholam.*

These drummers dance as they play music. They leap around a circle.

What to Do Create a dance that includes clapping and stomping.

1. Make clapping patterns that have long (ta) and short (ti-ti) sounds.

2. Try walking on just the *ta* sounds. Try walking on just the *ti-ti* sounds.

3. Make up your own sound patterns with *ta* and *ti-ti*. Walk in the same rhythm that you are saying with your voice.

4. Watch and listen to your teacher. Repeat what your teacher did.

 Art Criticism

Describe What movements did you do to match the sounds you made?

Unit 4 **153**

 Art History and Culture

Body Percussion

Dhon Dholak Cholam is a piece showing the traditional music and costumes of Manipur, India. The performers dance barefoot, turning leaps around a circle as they play their drums. The beautiful drums have a long, oval form with animal skin stretched over the ends.

Musicians and dancers use body percussion. Clapping the hands and other body parts are ways to make rhythm patterns. Also, stamping, walking and tapping the feet give other possibilities. Rhythm patterns are a group of beats that can be echoed or repeated. The drummers from Manipur learned their rhythm patterns by repeating combinations of vocal sounds which they played.

Space and Form in Music and Dance

Objective: To create a dance that uses different movements and includes sounds of clapping and stamping

Materials: *Dhon Dholak Cholam* performed by Ranganiketan Manipuri Cultural Arts Troupe. Running Time: 2:26

Focus
Time: About 10 minutes

■ Read the information on page 153.

■ Have students brainstorm the types of forms they might see in a dance. How will space be used?

 Art History and Culture

■ Encourage students to create percussion sounds with their bodies.

Teach
Time: About 20 minutes

Aesthetic Perception

■ Ask students to describe what they see in *Dhon Dholak Cholam.*

Creative Expression

■ Follow the steps on student page 153.

■ Have students experiment by clapping patterns of beats that have long *(ta)* and short *(ti-ti)* sounds.

■ If you wish, you can also add the sound pattern of *tik-a-ti.* Try this combination alone and then combine it with *ta* and *ti.*

■ **Informal Assessment** Comment positively as students move to the patterns you create.

Reflect
Time: About 5 minutes

 **Art Criticism**

■ Have students draw in their Art Journals to answer the Describe question.

Analyze How were the rhythms of *ta* and *ti-ti* different?

Interpret What did you feel as you moved and spoke the rhythm patterns?

Decide Were you successful in making the different sound patterns with movement?

Unit 5 Planning Guide

	Lesson Title	Suggested Pacing	Creative Expression Activity
Lesson 1	Texture You Can Touch	45 minutes	Create a collage with textured materials.
Lesson 2	Texture You Can See	45 minutes	Create a texture rubbing using crayon.
Lesson 3	Designing with Texture	45 minutes	Create a puppet by gluing materials onto a paper bag.
Lesson 4	Fiber Textures	45 minutes	Create a basket by weaving yarn, ribbon, or raffia into a prepared cup base.
Lesson 5	Real Texture on Forms	45 minutes	Create textures on a sculptural form by drawing lines and pressing textures into clay.
Lesson 6	Texture on Shapes	45 minutes	Sew yarn on burlap to create a stitched artwork.
ART SOURCE ARTSOURCE	Texture in Music and Dance	35 minutes	Create a dance using paper fans as props.

Materials	Program Resources	Fine Art Resources	Literature Resources
scrap paper, tissue paper, construction paper, recycled paper, 12" × 18" paper for background, scissors, glue	*Reading and Writing Test Preparation*, pp. 54–55 *Assessment*, pp. 57–58 *Home and After-School Connections*, pp. 23–26	*Transparency*, 25 *Artist Profiles*, pp. 19, 33 *Animals Through History Time Line* *Large Prints*, 9 and 10 *Women in the Arts Collection*	*Animal Orchestra* by Scott Gustafson
textured surfaces, jumbo unwrapped crayons or crayon pieces, 9" × 12" white paper	*Reading and Writing Test Preparation*, pp. 56–57 *Assessment*, pp. 59–60	*Transparency*, 26 *Artist Profiles*, pp. 24, 31 *Large Prints*, 9 and 10 *The National Museum of Women in the Arts Collection*	*Yo! Yes?* by Chris Raschka
small paper lunch bags, scissors, glue, paper scraps, different types of fabrics, yarn, buttons	*Reading and Writing Test Preparation*, pp. 58–59 *Assessment*, pp. 61–62	*Transparency*, 27 *Artist Profiles*, pp. 65, 70 *Large Prints*, 9 and 10 *The National Museum of Women in the Arts Collection*	*Olivia . . . and the Missing Toy* by Ian Falconer
plastic cups (precut with five cuts from the lip to base), precut yarn, ribbon, or raffia	*Reading and Writing Test Preparation*, pp. 60–61 *Assessment*, pp. 63–64	*Transparency*, 28 *Artist Profiles*, pp. 59, 69 *Large Prints*, 9 and 10 *Art Around the World*	*Little Red Riding Hood* by Trina Schart Hyman
clay, plastic utensils, pressing objects, such as buttons and thread spools, clay mats (muslin), paper clips	*Reading and Writing Test Preparation*, pp. 62–63 *Assessment*, pp. 65–66	*Transparency*, 29 *Artist Profiles*, pp. 67, 75 *Animals Through History Time Line* *Large Prints*, 9 and 10 *Art Around the World*	*The Seashore Book* by Charlotte Zolotow
12" × 12" pieces of burlap (taped around the edges), large, plastic sewing needles, various precut yarns, jumbo crayons	*Reading and Writing Test Preparation*, pp. 64–65 *Assessment*, pp. 67–68	*Transparency*, 30 *Artist Profiles*, pp. 35, 66 *Animals Through History Time Line* *Large Prints*, 9 and 10 *Art Around the World*	*The Keeping Quilt* by Patricia Polacco
"Korean Classical Music & Dance" video and "Toraji Taryong" audio			

5 Texture

Lesson 1: **Real texture** is texture you can touch.

Lesson 2: **Visual texture** is texture you see with your eyes but cannot feel.

Lesson 3: **Designing with texture** is done with different kinds of fibers, or cloth, such as velvet, lace, wool, and yarn.

Lesson 4: **Natural fibers** come directly from nature, such as straw, leaves, and grass.

Lesson 5: **Textures on Forms** focuses on understanding how texture can be created on clay.

Lesson 6: **Texture on Shapes** focuses on creating real texture by sewing with yarn.

Introduce Unit Concepts

"Search for real and visual textures in your world." "Busquen texturas reales y visuales en su ambiente".

Real Texture
- Have a variety of objects with different surfaces available for students to touch and describe.

Visual Texture
- Have various wallpapers, patterns, or fabrics available for students to describe the visual textures they portray.

Cross-Curricular Projects
- See the ***Language Arts and Reading, Mathematics, Science,*** and ***Social Studies Art Connections*** books for activities that further develop texture concepts.

Texture

Texture is the way something feels.

▲ **Beau Dick.** (Kwakwaka'wakw Tribe, Canadian). *Urban Raven/Urban Indian Transformation Mask.* 2002.
Hand-carved and painted red cedar. 10 × 12 × 23 inches when closed (25.4 × 30.48 × 58.42 cm.). Douglas Reynolds Gallery, Vancouver, British Columbia.

154 Unit 5

Fine Art Prints
Display **Large Prints 9** *Cat* and **10** *Child with Puzzle*. Refer to the prints throughout the unit as students learn about texture.

Large Print 9

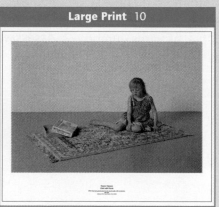

Large Print 10

Artists use different materials to create texture. Some texture is real. You can feel it. Some texture can be seen but not felt.

► How do you think this mask feels to the touch?

In This Unit you will:

► learn about texture.

► see how artists use texture on their works of art.

► use texture on your artwork.

Beau Dick

(1955–   )

Beau Dick

► is a member of the Tsawataineuk First Nation.

► carves masks, poles, rattles, and talking sticks.

► learned to carve from his father and grandfather.

Examine the Artwork

"There are two types of textures in this mask. Let's look at those textures." "Hay dos tipos de texturas en esta máscara. Veamos esas texturas".

■ Have students study the mask and describe what they see.

■ Read the definitions of real and visual texture, and then have students answer the question pertaining to texture on page 155.

► Possible answers: The straw hair feels rough and dry. The beak feels smooth on the side, but the edges might feel a little sharp. On the open mask the raised eyebrows and hands might feel bumpy and a little rough.

Unit Pretest

T Display **Transparency 41** as a pretest. Answers: 1. A, 2. A, 3. B

Home Connection

■ See **Home and After-School Connections** for family newsletters and activities for this unit.

Art History and Culture

Beau Dick

Beau Dick (bō dik) (1955–   ) lives in Kingcome Inlet, British Columbia, where he was born and raised. His father and grandfather taught him how to carve when he was a teenager, and he has since received wide acclaim for his carvings that are on display locally and around the world. Dick's carvings often reflect his Kwakwaka'wakw culture, as well as other tribal traditions. The raven is considered a symbol of creation for the Kwakwaka'wakw people and often appears as the subject matter of artwork, as it does in Dick's *Urban Raven/Urban Indian Transformation Mask.*

See pages 16–21 and 24–25 for more about subject matter and art history.

Artist Profiles, p. 9

◄ Artist Profile ►
Beau Dick
b. 1955
Beau Dick (bō dik) was born in 1955 in the isolated village of Kingcome in British Columbia, Canada. He is a Northwest Coast Native American of the Kwakwaka'wakw tribe. Dick started his artistic career painting native North American ceremonial scenes and legends. He later studied carving with master carvers Doug Cranmer and Henry Hunt. He has become known for his carved masks in the styles of different tribes. Dick currently lives in Vancouver, British Columbia, Canada. Kwakiutl traditions are the foundation for his art.

Unit 5 Arts Integration

ILLUSTRATOR PROFILE

Molly Bang
(1943–   )

Molly Bang was born in Princeton, New Jersey, in 1943, but this was only the first of many places she would call home. After graduating from college, Bang lived in Japan, India, Bangladesh, and Mali. In her extensive travels and experiences with various cultures, Bang collected folktales that became her first books. Bang wrote the translations and created original illustrations.

While Bang's works are characterized by a sense of whimsy, many of her books spring from personal convictions. For example, her retelling of multicultural tales reflects Bang's belief in the importance of a global heritage, just as many of her own stories present her ideas about protecting the environment.

Bang uses a variety of techniques, including watercolor, gouache, collage, and three-dimensional dioramas, to produce her award-winning illustrations. The subjects of her three Caldecott Honor books are equally diverse. *The Grey Lady and the Strawberry Snatcher* is a wordless, fantastical picture book; *Ten, Nine, Eight* is a bedtime story that originated as a poem for Bang's young daughter; and *When Sophie Gets Angry—Really, Really Angry* is about how a disgruntled little girl finds solace in the woods.

While studying Unit 5, share Bang's illustrations with the class and discuss the use of texture in her works of art. Ask students to identify real and visual texture. Encourage students to describe how they think Molly Bang might have created some of the textures on her works of art.

Music

Texture in music refers to the way that melody and harmony, or rhythm patterns, are combined to create layers of sound. Students can become aware of texture by simply noticing whether they are hearing melody alone or with an accompaniment.

Literature

Watch the video or DVD *The Pig's Picnic* by Keiko Kasza to observe different forms of texture.

Literature and Art

Performing Arts

 Show the video *Korean Classical Music & Dance* and ask students to identify the colors and textures they see.

Artsource®

Texture You Can Touch

Lesson 1 introduces real texture. Real texture is texture you can touch. It is created with materials such as wood, cloth, paper, and aluminum. We use words like *rough, smooth, fuzzy, prickly,* and *bumpy* to describe how textures feel.

Objectives

Art History and Culture

To recognize that artists use a variety of materials to create texture

Creative Expression

To create a collage with textured materials

Aesthetic Perception

To locate and verbally describe textures in their environment

Art Criticism

To evaluate one's own work using the four steps of art criticism

Vocabulary ⭐ Reading

Review the following vocabulary words with students before beginning the lesson.

real texture textura real—texture you can feel

collage collage—bits and pieces of things glued onto paper

See page 179B for additional vocabulary and Spanish vocabulary resources.

Art Journal: Vocabulary

Have students add this word to the Vocabulary section of their Art Journals.

Lesson Materials

- a variety of textured materials (foil, tree bark, burlap, leaves, grasses, sandpaper, and pieces of fabric such as velvet and satin)
- scrap paper, tissue paper, construction paper, recycled paper
- 12" × 18" paper for background
- scissors, glue

Alternate Materials
- crayons
- paper towels

Program Resources
- *Reading and Writing Test Prep.,* pp. 54–55
- *Transparency 25*
- *Artist Profiles,* pp. 19, 33
- *Assessment,* pp. 57–58
- *Large Prints 9* Cat and *10* Child with Puzzle
- *Animals Through History Time Line*
- *The National Museum of Women in the Arts Collection*

Concept Trace
Texture You Can Touch
Introduced: Level K, Unit 5, Lesson 1

Reinforced: Level 1, Unit 5, Lesson 1

Lesson 1 Arts Integration

Theatre

Complete Unit 5, Lesson 1 on pages 90–91 of the *Theatre Arts Connections* book.

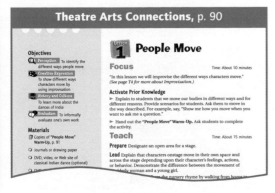

Music

Sing *Shoo, Fly.* Change the texture on the B section by adding a pat–clap pattern or sing it *a cappella* and then add piano accompaniment. As you add layers of sound you create thicker texture.

Movement & Dance

Organize students into pairs, and assign each pair a number. Have students make a circle with partners standing on opposite sides. As a number is called, each pair skips to the center of the circle, and without touching they move in a circle around each other, changing places. Then call each number again, but this time students link elbows as they turn. Discuss how it feels to be physically connected while dancing.

Focus

Time: About 10 minutes

Activate Prior Knowledge

"Have you ever seen a frog? What do frogs look like? Sound like? Feel like?" "¿Han visto alguna vez una rana? ¿Cómo son las ranas? ¿Cómo suenan? ¿ Cómo se sienten?"

■ Encourage students to role-play a frog and make its sound and movements.

Using Literature ⭐ Reading

■ Read *Animal Orchestra* by Scott Gustafson. Ask students to identify examples of texture in the story. Is it texture they can touch? No.

Thematic Connection ⭐ Reading

■ **Living Things:** Discuss the difference between living and nonliving objects. Have students identify and group objects as living or nonliving, including the animals shown in the fine art.

Introduce the Art

Look

"This sculpture of a frog is made of wood. A sculpture is a form that you can see on all sides." "Esta escultura de una rana está hecha de madera. Una escultura es una forma que pueden ver desde todos los lados".

■ Describe the frog and its various parts.

Drawing Conclusions ⭐ Reading

■ Why do you think the artist used wood to make the frog? Possible answer: The artist may have used wood to represent the skin texture of a real frog.

■ Have students tell what they think parts of the frog sculpture would feel like.

Adjectives and Adverbs ⭐ Language Arts

■ List on a chart the adjectives and adverbs students use to describe the fine art.

Art History and Culture

Share information from the Art History and Culture sections with students. Art dealers are knowledgable about many artists and types of art. They play an important role in bringing new or low-profile artists to the attention of art collectors, museum professionals, and the community.

Web Connection

Visit The National Museum of Women in the Arts at www.nmwa.org/.

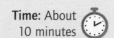
Lesson 1 Texture You Can Touch

Look at the works of art. They are made of wood.

◀ **Betty Parsons.** (American). *Winged Frog.* 1978.
Mixed-media wood construction. 27 × 20 inches (68.58 × 50.8 cm.). The National Museum of Women in the Arts, Washington, D.C.

Art History and Culture

Betty Parsons was an artist and an art dealer. She had a gallery where she showed other artists' works of art.

Art History and Culture

Betty Parsons

Betty Parsons (bet´ tē pär´ sənz) (1900–1982) was an art dealer, collector, painter, and sculptor. She started her own contemporary art gallery called the Betty Parsons Gallery. She helped attract attention for many new artists by exhibiting their work. Parsons also collected more than 300 works of art, many of which were given to her by other artists.

Betty Parson's early paintings were realistic, but her style changed to abstract in the 1940s. Her sculptures often contained pieces of wood and other materials that she found on the beach by her home.

See pages 16–21 and 24–25 for more about subject matter and art history.

Artist Profiles, p. 33

Artist Profile
Betty Parsons
1900–1982
Strong-willed and rebellious, Betty Parsons (bet´ tē pär´ sənz) defied her family to become both an artist and a pioneering art dealer. As a young woman she was forbidden by her wealthy parents to attend college, but she persuaded them to let her study art. In 1922 she left New York for Europe. She studied sculpture and drawing in Paris, France. She returned to the United States, where her watercolors and painted constructions of weathered wood were shown in both group and solo exhibitions. She was an early supporter of abstract expressionism and opened her first art gallery on 57th Street in 1946. Mark Rothko, Jackson Pollock, Hedda Sterne, and Barnett Newman were among the artists who

Study both works of art.

▶ Which parts look rough?

▶ Which parts look smooth?

◀ **John Hoover.** (Native American, Aleut). *Eagle and Salmon.* 1987.
······································
Cedar. 48 × 24 inches (121.92 × 60.96 cm.).
Private Collection.

 Aesthetic Perception

Seeing Like an Artist Describe how textures in your classroom feel.

Art History and Culture

John Hoover

John Hoover (jän hōō´ vər) (1919–) grew up in Cordova, Alaska, where for many years he earned his living as a commercial fisherman. During the off-season Hoover pursued his interest in art, focusing first on painting and later on sculpture. John Hoover is now well-known for his wood carvings that are inspired by numerous native cultures as well as myths he creates himself.

See pages 16–21 and 24–25 for more about subject matter and art history.

Artist Profiles, p. 19

Artist Profile
John Hoover
b. 1919
John Hoover (jän hōō´ vər) was born in Cordova, Alaska, to an Aleut-Russian mother and a German father. Growing up, he spent a lot of time fishing and making art, and his early involvement in boat building inspired his interest in sculpture. Hoover has always been fascinated with traditional Northwest Coast Native American carvings, and continues to reference them in his work today. As one of the most respected contemporary Native American sculptors, Hoover has exhibited around the country and continues to make art at his home in Washington.

Study

▶ On *Winged Frog*, the area of peeled paint below the mouth looks rough. The jagged wood across the lower front of the frog also looks rough. *Eagle and Salmon* looks rough where the wood has been carved on the eagle heads, salmon bodies, and the face in the middle of the sculpture.

▶ *Winged Frog* looks smooth around the eyes. *Eagle and Salmon* looks smooth around the edges.

■ For more examples of abstract/ nonobjective art, see *The National Museum of Women in the Arts Collection.*

Art Journal: Concept
Have students draw a picture of an object that has real texture, such as a tree trunk or sweater.

 **Aesthetic Perception**

Seeing Like an Artist Encourage students to touch objects in the classroom. Ask students to describe how various objects feel.

Developing Visual Literacy Identify the animals in the sculptures. Why do you think the artists chose these animals to show in their sculptures?
National Standards for Arts Education in Visual Arts 3.a; 3.b; 5.a; 5.c

Web Connection
Learn more about John Hoover's Aleutian heritage by visiting http://arcticcircle.uconn.edu/ HistoryCulture/Aleut/aleutindex.html.

Teach

Time: About 30 minutes

"Let's describe how different textures feel to the touch." "Vamos a describir cómo se sienten al tacto las diferentes texturas".

Practice

Materials: a variety of textured materials (foil, tree bark, burlap, leaves, grasses, sandpaper, and pieces of fabric such as velvet and satin)

- Display a variety of materials with different textures.

- Have the students touch each texture and offer one word to tell how each item feels.

 Creative Expression

Materials: scrap paper, tissue paper, construction paper, recycled paper, 12" × 18" paper for background, scissors, glue

Alternate Materials: crayons, paper towels

- Review the Technique Tips on pages 221–223 for additional information on making a collage.

- Distribute the materials and have the students follow the directions on page 159.

- Ask students to choose a shape from the shapes they drew in their Art Journals.

- Display your texture collection so that students can select some textured materials.

- Heavier materials may need to be precut into small swatches for the students. Avoid materials that are too difficult to cut.

- Show students how to apply drops of glue onto the textures they are gluing onto their background paper.

- Encourage students to view their collage each time they finish a part of it to help them decide what else they would like to add to it.

Art Journal: Brainstorming
Encourage students to think about different shapes they have seen or made in artwork, shapes around them in the classroom, shapes outdoors, animals, toys, and so on. Ask students to draw these shapes in their Art Journals.

Using Real Texture

Something you can feel with your fingers is called **real texture.**

Practice

1. Feel each object your teacher shows you.

2. Use one word to tell how each object feels.

158   Unit 5 • Lesson 1

Differentiated Instruction

Reteach
Have students play a compare-and-contrast game with textures. Let them hold two items of different textures and describe the way one texture feels compared to the other.

Special Needs
Increase students' skills of word recognition by writing the textures they describe on a class chart. The actual objects whose texture matches each word can also be added to the chart.

ELL Tips
Display samples of materials with a variety of textures to illustrate textures that are rough, smooth, and fuzzy. Introduce the word *texture,* and have students use it in a descriptive sentence such as, "This cloth is rough."

▲ **Grayson Gunn.** Age 5.

Think about the kinds of texture you see in the student's artwork. How would these textures feel?

 Creative Expression

How many different textures can you put in a **collage**?

1. Think about the shapes you see in a landscape.
2. Cut out the shapes.
3. Use these shapes to make a landscape with textures.

 Art Criticism

Analyze How many different real textures are there in your collage? Describe how the different textures in your collage feel to the touch.

Art Across the Curriculum

Use these simple ideas to reinforce art concepts across the curriculum.

★ **Narrative Writing** Have students draw a picture to illustrate a story they make up about the eagle and salmon.

★ **Math** Divide objects into equal parts, understanding that parts make up a whole. Use the creation of the collage as an example.

★ **Science** Study the textures of different things you find in nature, such as the animals represented in the fine art.

★ **Social Studies** Learn about parts of the United States flag.

★ **Technology** Use the tools in a paint program to explore texture. Visit **SRAonline.com** to print detailed instructions for this activity.

 **Reflect** Time: About 5 minutes

Review and Assess

"What is real texture?" "¿Qué es la textura real?"

Think

Discuss the student art question. The clouds are fluffy. The tree trunk is rough and bumpy. The roof is smooth.

■ Identify texture in *Large Prints 9 Cat* and *10 Child with Puzzle*.

Informal Assessment

Art Journal: Critical Thinking
Have students answer the first Analyze question by writing the number in their Art Journals. Discuss the second Analyze question out loud.

 **Art Criticism**

Have students ask themselves the following questions.

Describe ▶ What shape is your collage? What kinds of real textures did you use in your collage?

Analyze ▶ How many different real textures are there in your collage? Describe how the different textures in your collage feel to the touch.

Interpret ▶ How does your collage make you feel? Give your collage a name.

Decide ▶ Do you have enough different textures, or would you like to add more? What would you add?

NSAE 2.b; 5.a; 5.c

■ For standardized-format test practice using this lesson's art content, see pages 54–55 in *Reading and Writing Test Preparation.*

Texture You Can Touch

Extra! **For the Art Specialist**

Time: About 30 minutes

Focus

Use *Transparency 25* and *Large Prints 9 Cat* and *10 Child with Puzzle* to discuss how the artists used texture. Describe all the textures you would feel if you could touch the objects in these works of art.

Teach

Ask students to imagine taking a walk in the woods. What do they see? How does it feel when they touch the bark of a tree or leaves? Help students learn about texture by creating a collage with materials from nature.

Reflect

Have students use the four steps of art criticism to evaluate their work. Did they effectively create a textured collage with materials from nature?

Alternate Activity

Materials:
- objects from nature (twigs, rocks, leaves)
- glue
- 9" × 12" poster or mat board
- markers

1. Have students use materials from nature to make a person, animal, or nature scene.

2. First students arrange the materials how they want them. Then students glue the objects to their cardboard.

3. Have students use markers to add lines and colors to their scenes.

NSAE 1.a; 1.c; 3.a

Research in Art Education

Research has shown that incorporating the arts in education can lead to positive school change. Pilot projects demonstrate that "the arts do contribute to the general school curriculum, to learning for all students, to school and professional culture, to educational and instructional practices, and to the schools' neighborhoods and communities" ("The Arts and Education Reform: Lessons from a Four-Year Evaluation of the A+ Schools Program, 1995–1999" in *Critical Links*, p. 84).

Assessment
Use the following rubric to evaluate the artwork students make in the Creative Expression activity and to assess students' understanding of texture.

Have students complete page 57 or 58 in their *Assessment* books.

	Art History and Culture	Aesthetic Perception	Creative Expression	Art Criticism
3 POINTS	The student recognizes that artists use a variety of materials to create texture.	The student locates and verbally describes textures in his or her environment.	The student's collage clearly illustrates use of textured materials.	The student thoughtfully and honestly evaluates his or her own work using the four steps of art criticism.
2 POINTS	The student shows emerging awareness that artists use a variety of materials to create texture.	The student can sometimes locate and verbally describe textures in his or her environment.	The student's collage shows some use of textured materials.	The student attempts to evaluate his or her own work, but shows an incomplete understanding of evaluation criteria.
1 POINT	The student does not recognize that artists use a variety of materials to create texture.	The student cannot locate or verbally describe textures in his or her environment	The student's collage shows no use of textured materials.	The student makes no attempt to evaluate his or her own artwork.

Assessment, p. 57

Name _____ Date _____

Lesson **1** UNIT 5

Texture You Can Touch

1

2

For the teacher: Use the following prompts for this activity.
1. In box 1, use crayons to draw a picture of something that feels smooth.
2. In box 2, draw a picture of something that feels rough.

Level K

Unit 5 • Texture **57**

Lesson 2
Overview

Texture You Can See

Lesson 2 introduces visual texture. **Visual texture** is texture you see with your eyes but cannot feel. Artists copy textures from real life by painting and drawing with lines, shapes, and colors.

Objectives

 Art History and Culture

To identify facts about the life and art of Gabriele Münter and Jean Étienne Liotard

 Creative Expression

To create a texture rubbing using crayon

 Aesthetic Perception

To locate textures in the environment and describe how they would visually recreate the texture in a work of art

 Art Criticism

To evaluate one's own work using the four steps of art criticism

Vocabulary Reading

Review the following vocabulary word with students before beginning the lesson.

visual texture textura visual—the way something looks like it might feel if you could touch it

See page 179B for additional vocabulary and Spanish vocabulary resources.

 Art Journal: Vocabulary

Have students add these words to the Vocabulary section of their Art Journals.

Lesson Materials

- textured surfaces
- jumbo unwrapped crayons or crayon pieces
- 9" × 12" white paper

Alternate Materials
- crayons or markers on white or light-colored paper

Program Resources
- *Reading and Writing Test Prep.*, pp. 56–57
- *Transparency 26*
- *Artist Profiles*, pp. 24, 31
- *Assessment*, pp. 59–60
- *Large Prints 9* Cat and *10* Child with Puzzle
- *The National Museum of Women in the Arts Collection*

Concept Trace
Visual Texture
Introduced: Level K, Unit 5, Lesson 2

Reinforced: Level 1, Unit 5, Lesson 2

Lesson 2 Arts Integration

Theatre

Complete Unit 5, Lesson 2 on pages 92–93 of the *Theatre Arts Connections* book.

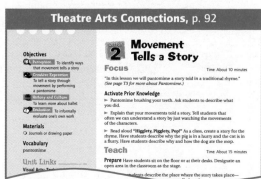

Theatre Arts Connections, p. 92

Music

In ensemble music the texture can be very thick when all the instruments are playing or thin when only a few are playing. Listen to *Fascinating Rhythm* by George Gershwin. Every arrangement of this song can be different. The melody can be passed around from a singer to one individual player to another, or they can all play and sing at the same time.

Movement & Dance

Ask students how we express feelings and emotions through our bodies. Have students look at a series of photographs of people expressing specific emotions. (Example: A football player after scoring.) What do we see in body language that helps us identify the feelings or emotions of that person at the time the picture was taken? Have students try each of the postures in the photographs.

Focus

Activate Prior Knowledge

"Feel your hair. What kinds of lines would you use to draw the texture of your hair?" "Toquen su cabello. ¿Qué tipos de líneas usarían para trazar la textura de sus cabellos?"

- Have students use as many adjectives as they can when describing how their hair feels.

Using Literature Reading

- Read *Yo! Yes?* by Chris Raschka. Ask students to identify visual texture in the illustrations.

Thematic Connection

- **Friends:** Discuss *Yo! Yes?* By Chris Raschka. Ask students how they make friends.

Introduce the Art

Look

"Artists copy the real textures we touch by using lines, shapes, and colors." "Los artistas copian las texturas reales que tocamos usando líneas, figuras y colores".

- Ask students to describe what they see in the works of art.

Making Inferences Reading

- Have students describe how they think various objects in the portraits would feel, such as the hats, coats, pillow, and ball.

- Have students trace with their fingers the lines used to create these objects.

Adjectives and Adverbs Language Arts

- List on a chart the adjectives and adverbs students use to describe the fine art.

Art History and Culture

Share information from the Art History and Culture sections with students. Ask students if they think the people in the pictures are from now or long ago and why. Possible answers: The people are from long ago. The dates of the portraits give us a clue as well as the clothes the people are wearing.

Web Connection

Visit **www.nmwa.org/collection/profile.asp?LinkID=620** to learn more about Gabriele Münter and other female artists.

Texture You Can See

Look at the paintings. Can you see texture?

◀ **Gabriele Münter.** (German). *Child with Ball.* c. 1916.
••••••••••••••••••••••••
Oil on canvas. 20 ½ × 17 inches (52.07 × 43.18 cm.). The National Museum of Women in the Arts, Washington, D.C.

Art History and Culture

Do you think the people in the paintings are from now or long ago? Why?

Art History and Culture

Gabriele Münter

Gabriele Münter (gä´ brē ā lā mūn´ tər) (1877–1962) was an artist of the German Expressionist and Blaue Reiter movements in art history. Her work is characterized by broad areas of color and expressive color contrasts. Münter's work as an artist was constricted by social and political situations during her lifetime. She studied art at the Ladies' Art School in Dusseldorf, Germany, because women students were not then admitted to the established art schools. Later, she had to work in secrecy because German modern art was declared "degenerate" by the Nazis.

See pages 16–21 and 24–25 for more about subject matter and art history.

Artist Profiles, p. 31

Artist Profile

Gabriele Münter
1877–1962

Gabriele Münter (gä brä´ lā mūn´ tər) was one of the founders of modern German expressionism. She studied in Düsseldorf, Germany before traveling to the United States for two years. She resumed her studies in Munich, Germany, where she met many artists who were developing new styles of painting. She traveled throughout Europe, spending two years near Paris, France, where she learned about innovations in French art. In 1911, she joined with other radical artists in Munich to form the Blue Rider group. She painted in secret when German expressionist art was outlawed. After World War II she continued to paint and promoted the history of the Blue Rider group.

◄ **Jean Etienne Liotard.** (Swiss).
Portrait of Marthe Marie Tronchin.
c. 1758–1761.

Pastel and stumping on vellum. 24$\frac{9}{16}$ × 18$\frac{5}{8}$ inches (62.38 × 47.30 cm.). The Art Institute of Chicago, Chicago, Illinois.

Study both pictures.

► How do you think the child's hat would feel?

► How do you think the woman's coat would feel?

 Aesthetic Perception

Seeing Like an Artist How could you draw the texture of something you see?

Study

► The child's hat would probably feel fuzzy. The artist has used curved lines to show the fuzzy curves of the hat. The woman's coat would probably feel smooth. The artist used smooth lines to create the coat.

■ For more examples of portraits, see *The National Museum of Women in the Arts Collection.*

Art Journal: Concept
Have students draw a picture of something that looks soft.

Aesthetic Perception

Seeing Like an Artist Ask students how they could draw the texture of something they see. Possible answers: Different lines, shapes, and colors help create different textures. For example, zigzag lines could make something look sharp.

Developing Visual Literacy Take students outside to look for textures in the environment. Ask students to explain how they could draw these textures in a work of art.

Art History and Culture

Jean Étienne Liotard

Jean Étienne Liotard (zhän´ ā tyen´ lē ō tär´) (1702–1789) was born in Geneva, Switzerland and studied art in Paris, France. Early in his career he had the opportunity to paint portraits of Pope Clement XII and several other religious figures in Naples. After these paintings were viewed, he gained a reputation as one of the best portrait painters in Europe. He was invited to Austria, England, and the Netherlands to paint portraits of emperors, generals, and queens. He was nicknamed "the Turkish painter" because he wore eccentric Asian costumes. Besides creating art, Liotard wrote a book called *Treatise on the Art of Painting.* He was also an art collector.

See pages 16–21 and 24–25 for more about subject matter and art history.

Artist Profiles, p. 24

◄ Artist Profile ►
Jean-Étienne Liotard
1702–1789

Jean-Étienne Liotard (zhän´ ā tyen´ lē ō tär´) was born in Geneva, Switzerland. He and his twin brother were expected to grow up and become tradesmen, but at a young age, each of them showed such artistic talent that they were encouraged to become artists. Liotard studied art in Paris, France. Early in his career he had the opportunity to paint portraits of Pope Clement XII and several other religious people in Naples. After these paintings were viewed, he gained a reputation as one of the best portrait painters in Europe. He was invited to Austria, England, and the Netherlands to paint portraits of emperors, generals, and queens. He was nicknamed

Web Connection
Visit the Art Institute of Chicago online at **www.artic.edu/aic/.**

 **each**

Time: About 30 minutes

"Let's look at some different textures and name the lines you could use to draw them."

"Vamos a observar algunas de las diferentes texturas y nombren las líneas que usarían para trazarlas".

Practice

- Have students feel the bottom of their shoes and provide a word to describe the texture.

- Repeat with other items. List on the board the kinds of lines that could create each texture on paper.

 Creative Expression

Materials: textured surfaces, jumbo unwrapped crayons or crayon pieces, 9" × 12" white paper

Alternate Materials: crayons or markers on white or light-colored paper

- Distribute the materials and have the students follow the directions on page 163.

- See the Activity Tips on page 244 for visual examples of this lesson's activity.

- Have students draw their favorite hat on a piece of paper. Encourage them to draw it large.

- Guide students through the process of making crayon rubbings on different textured surfaces. Have students place parts of their white paper over different textured objects and rub their crayon over their paper.

- Review the Technique Tips on page 215 for information on crayon rubbings.

NSAE 1.a; 1.c

Art Journal: Brainstorming

Have students brainstorm different kinds of hats. If necessary, suggest they think about hats for sports; for cold, snowy weather; for hot, sunny weather; and for different kinds of jobs. You might also display some pictures of different kinds of hats. Have students draw a hat in their Art Journals.

Using Visual Texture

Texture you can see but cannot touch is **visual texture.**

Practice

1. Feel the bottom of your shoe.

2. What kinds of lines would you use to draw the bottom of your shoe?

Differentiated Instruction

Reteach

Show students numerous pictures and have them describe the textures they see.

Special Needs

Students with motor impairments may benefit from having their textured paper taped down as they create the crayon rubbings.

ELL Tips

List on the board the words *rough, smooth, fuzzy,* and *fluffy.* Draw different items with each of these textures. Use different kinds of lines to create each texture.

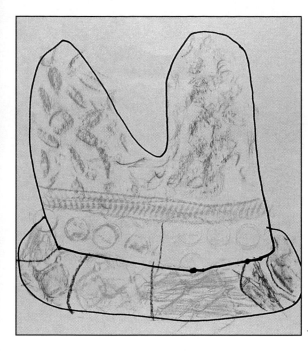

Think about the kinds of lines the student used to show texture.

◀ **Catherine Burton.** Age 5.

How can you show how different things feel?

1. Design a hat that has different textures.

2. Make crayon rubbings to create different textures.

 **Art Criticism**

Interpret Who might wear the hat you made?

Art Across the Curriculum

Use these simple ideas to reinforce art concepts across the curriculum.

★ **Poetry Writing** Have students draw pictures of objects that rhyme with *hat.* Help students write the rhyming words below their pictures.

★ **Math** Describe one object in relation to another using informal language. For example, in *Child with Ball,* the girl is *on* a chair. The pillow is *behind* the girl's head.

★ **Science** Observe objects with real texture and discuss which senses are used for observation. Repeat with pictures of objects that have visual texture.

★ **Social Studies** Identify basic needs such as clothing, noting how the girl and woman are dressed for cold weather.

★ **Technology** Use the tools in a paint program to draw a portrait that has visual texture. Visit **SRAonline.com** to print detailed instructions for this activity.

Reflect Time: About 5 minutes

Review and Assess

"What is visual texture?" "¿Qué es la textura visual?"

Think

Discuss the student art question. The student used curvy, straight, and diagonal lines that are rough. There are two horizontal, smooth lines through the middle of the hat.

Informal Assessment

Art Journal: Critical Thinking
Have students answer the Interpret question by drawing a picture in their Art Journals.

 **Art Criticism**

Have students ask themselves the following questions.

Describe ▶ Tell about different textures you used for your hat. How did you decide what texture rubbing to use for each part of your hat?

Analyze ▶ In what way do the visual textures look different from real textures? In what way do the visual textures look different from each other?

Interpret ▶ Who might wear the hat you made?

Decide ▶ Do you like the visual textures that you used for your hat? Tell why or why not.

NSAE 2.b; 5.a; 5.c

■ For standardized-format test practice using this lesson's art content, see pages 56–57 in *Reading and Writing Test Preparation.*

Texture You Can See

Extra! For the Art Specialist

Time: About 30 minutes

Focus

Use *Transparency 25* and *Large Prints 9 Cat* and *10 Child with Puzzle* to discuss how the artists used texture. Ask students to count the different textures they see.

Teach

Talk about the textures of animals. Ask students to think of words to describe these textures. Have students create a wet-into-wet painting of animal textures.

Reflect

Have students use the four steps of art criticism to evaluate their work. Did they effectively create textures on their paintings?

Alternate Activity

Materials:
- 12" × 18" watercolor or drawing paper
- sponges
- watercolor paint
- brushes
- oil pastels

1. Show students how to wet their paper with a sponge. Direct students to paint several circles with watercolor paint. Tell students to notice the soft, fuzzy edges that develop as the paint mixes with the water on the paper.

2. After the paper dries, have students use oil pastels to draw the eyes, nose, mouth, legs, tail, and other details.

3. Ask students to think about where their animals would live and draw a background to complete the scene.

NSAE 1.c

Research in Art Education

"Since the matter of aesthetic criticism is the perception of aesthetic objects, natural and artistic criticism is always determined by the quality of firsthand perception; obtuseness in perception can never be made good by any amount of learning, however extensive, nor any command of abstract theory however correct" (John Dewey, *Art As Experience* [1934]).

Assessment

Use the following rubric to evaluate the artwork students make in the Creative Expression activity and to assess students' understanding of visual texture.

Have students complete page 59 or 60 in their *Assessment* books.

	Art History and Culture	Aesthetic Perception	Creative Expression	Art Criticism
3 POINTS	The student identifies facts about the life and art of Gabriele Münter and Jean Étienne Liotard.	The student locates textures in the environment and describes how they would visually recreate the texture in a work of art.	The student's crayon rubbing effectively demonstrates visual texture.	The student thoughtfully and honestly evaluates his or her own work using the four steps of art criticism.
2 POINTS	The student shows emerging awareness of the life and art of Gabriele Münter and Jean Étienne Liotard.	The student can sometimes locate textures in the environment and describe how they would visually recreate the texture in a work of art.	The student's crayon rubbing shows some visual texture.	The student attempts to evaluate his or her own work, but shows an incomplete understanding of evaluation criteria.
1 POINT	The student cannot identify facts about the life and art of Gabriele Münter and Jean Étienne Liotard.	The student cannot locate textures in the environment or describe how they would visually recreate the texture in a work of art.	The student's crayon rubbing does not demonstrate visual texture.	The student makes no attempt to evaluate his or her own artwork.

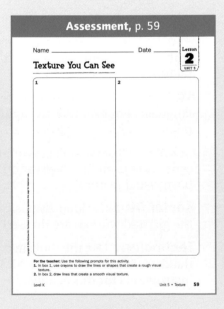

Assessment, p. 59

Name _____ Date _____ Lesson **2** UNIT 5

Texture You Can See

1.   2.

For the teacher: Use the following prompts for this activity.
1. In box 1, use crayons to draw the lines or shapes that create a rough visual texture.
2. In box 2, draw lines that create a smooth visual texture.

Level K   Unit 5 • Texture **59**

Designing with Texture

Lesson 3 introduces designing with texture. This is done with different kinds of fibers, or cloth, such as velvet, lace, wool, and yarn. Using fibers to create different textures for a puppet is developed in this lesson.

Objectives

 Art History and Culture

To recognize that puppetry and toy making are arts that have been around for a long time

 Creative Expression

To create a puppet by gluing materials onto a paper bag

Aesthetic Perception

To describe textures of puppets and toys that students have seen in art, in real life, or in the mass media

Art Criticism

To evaluate one's own work using the four steps of art criticism

Vocabulary  Reading

Review the following vocabulary word with students before beginning the lesson.

texture *textura* —the element of art that refers to how things feel, or look as if they might feel if touched

See page 179B for additional vocabulary and Spanish vocabulary resources.

 Art Journal: Vocabulary

Have students add this word to the Vocabulary section of their Art Journals.

Lesson Materials
- small paper lunch bags
- scissors
- glue
- paper scraps
- yarn and buttons
- different types of fabric

Alternate Materials
- paper towels
- aluminum foil

Program Resources
- *Reading and Writing Test Prep,* pp. 58–59
- *Transparency 27*
- *Artist Profiles,* pp. 65, 70
- *Assessment,* pp. 61–62
- *Large Prints 9* Cats and *10* Child with Puzzle
- *The National Museum of Women in the Arts Collection*

Concept Trace
Designing with Texture
Introduced: Level K, Unit 5, Lesson 3

Reinforced: Level 1, Unit 5, Lesson 1

Lesson 3 Arts Integration

Theatre

Complete Unit 5, Lesson 3 on pages 94–95 of the *Theatre Arts Connections* book.

Music

You can create an interesting performance with one song by changing the texture on every repeat. Start with these ideas and then create your own.

- All sing, no accompaniment
- All sing, add piano
- One child sings alone with piano
- No piano, all sing with a pat-clap accompaniment
- All sing, pat-clap, and add piano

Movement & Dance

A marionette puppet's movement is isolated and controlled by strings. Ask students to imagine that there are strings attached to their head, wrists, elbows, and knees. Explore how the body parts move when an imaginary string is pulled.

A wind up toy moves all parts at the same time. Ask students to move as if they were a wind up toy. How are the movements of the puppet and the robot different?

Time: About 10 minutes

Activate Prior Knowledge

"Have you ever made or worked with a puppet? What did the puppet look like?"

"Alguna vez han elaborado o manejado un títere? ¿Cómo era el títere?"

■ Encourage students to describe their puppets in detail, using words that describe their texture. If they cannot think of their own puppets, have them describe a few of the Muppets™.

Using Literature ★ Reading

■ Read *Olivia . . . and the Missing Toy* by Ian Falconer. Ask students to identify texture in the illustrations.

Thematic Connection

■ **Toys:** Discuss *Olivia . . . and the Missing Toy* by Ian Falconer. Ask students if they have ever lost a favorite toy.

Introduce the Art

Look

"Puppets and wooden toys are an art form."

"Los títeres y los juguetes de maderas son una forma de arte".

Identifying Details ★ Reading

■ Ask students to describe the different materials used to make the puppets and pull toys.

■ Share and discuss information from *Artist Profiles* pages 65 and 70.

Adjectives and Adverbs ★ Language Arts

■ List on a chart the adjectives and adverbs students use to describe the fine art.

 Art History and Culture

Share information from the Art History and Culture sections with students. Puppets have been used for many years to act out the action and dialogue in stories or to teach lessons to children. Puppets help make a story more entertaining and easier to understand.

Web Connection

Go to **www.moifa.org/** to visit the Museum of International Folk Art online.

◀ **Artist Unknown.** (Western Europe). *Hand Puppets.* Late nineteenth century.
....
Painted wood. 16 inches high on average (40.64 cm.). Museum of International Folk Art, Santa Fe, New Mexico.

Look at the art on both pages. The artists used texture on these toys.

 Art History and Culture

Artists have made puppets and toys for a long time. Puppets are often used for telling stories.

Art History and Culture

Hand Puppets

The artist who made these puppets was probably a master puppet maker. This person was also most likely a master puppeteer, or person who tells great stories with puppets. It takes a lot of practice to learn how to control the strings of the puppets so they appear to walk, talk, and wave.

See pages 16–21 and 24–25 for more about subject matter and art history.

Artist Profiles, p. 70

Artist Profile

Hand Puppets

The artist who made these puppets was probably a master puppet maker. This person was also most likely a master puppeteer, or person who tells great stories with puppets. It takes a lot of practice to learn how to control the strings of the puppets so they appear to walk, talk, and wave.

◀ **Artist unknown.** (Western Europe). *Hand Puppets.* Late nineteenth century.
Painted wood. 16 inches (40.64 cm.) average height. Museum of International Folk Art, Santa Fe, New Mexico.

Study the puppets and toys.

▶ Name the kinds of textures you see on the heads and bodies of the puppets and toys.

▲ **Artist Unknown.** (Mexico). *Conchero Pull Toys.* 1930s.

Wood, painted earthenware, feathers, cloth, cardboard, bottle caps, paper, and fur. Maximum height 20 inches (50.8 cm.). San Antonio Museum of Art, San Antonio, Texas.

Aesthetic Perception

Seeing Like an Artist Tell about the textures of a puppet or toy you have seen.

Art History and Culture

Conchero Pull Toys

These *Conchero Pull Toys* were made by an unknown artist from the geographic area in or around the Mexican state of Guanajuato. It is estimated that these toys were made in the 1930s or 1940s, although they may have been made more recently. Many Mexican artisans create pull toys similar to the ones featured here. Pull toys are typically made to be sold in street markets and fairs, often during the celebrations of special saints' days.

See pages 16–21 and 24–25 for more about subject matter and art history.

Artist Profiles, p. 65

Artist Profile

Conchero Pull Toys

These toys were made by an unknown artist from the geographic area in or around the Mexican state of Guanajuato. It is estimated that these toys were made in the 1930s. Many Mexican artisans create pull toys similar to the ones featured here. Pull toys are typically made to be sold in street markets and fairs, often during the celebrations of special saints' days.

▲ **Artist unknown.** (Mexican). *Conchero Pull Toys.* 1930s.

Wood, painted earthenware, feathers, cloth, cardboard, bottle caps,

Study

Encourage students to point to and describe as many of the textures on the puppets and pull toys as they can. Possible answers:

▶ Some lace on the puppets would probably feel bumpy. The checked material on the puppet on the right looks like it would feel smooth.

▶ The feathers on the pull toys' heads look fuzzy. The bottle cap-like pieces on the pull toys' arms look hard and somewhat sharp on the edges.

■ For more examples of utilitarian art, see *The National Museum of Women in the Arts Collection.*

Art Journal: Concept

Have students draw a picture of a puppet that is wearing textured fabric.

Aesthetic Perception

Seeing Like an Artist Ask students to describe the textures of a puppet or toy they have seen. Answers will vary. Encourage students to name the materials used and to describe how the textures feel.

Developing Visual Literacy Ask students to think about why the artists chose these textures for the puppets and pull toys. Discuss how they think the puppets and toys were used. How would they look different if they were made with different materials?

Web Connection

Visit the San Antonio Museum of Art online at **www.samuseum.org/**.

Teach

Time: About 30 minutes

"Let's discover the textures of the fibers in your clothing." *"Vamos a descubrir las texturas de las fibras en su ropa".*

Practice

■ Have students feel different parts of their clothing and suggest words to describe the different textures. You may want to suggest the words *smooth, rough, bumpy, fuzzy,* and *scratchy,* and have students use them.

Creative Expression

Materials: small paper lunch bags, scissors, glue, paper scraps, different types of fabrics, yarn and buttons

Alternate Materials: paper towels, aluminum foil

■ Distribute the materials and have the students follow the directions on page 167.

■ See the Activity Tips on page 245 for visual examples of this lesson's activity.

■ Have students select different textured materials to use in making their puppet.

■ Have students glue the materials onto their paper bag. Encourage students to try to have their puppets show whether they're feeling happy, sad, scared, or silly.

■ When students finish their puppets, model how to put a hand inside the bag and move the puppet's mouth.

■ Invite students to make up a story that their puppet can tell the class.

■ Review the Technique Tips on page 222 for information on using glue.

NSAE 1.c

Art Journal: Brainstorming

Have students brainstorm ideas for puppet characters. Have students draw a picture in their Art Journals of how their puppet will look.

Using Texture

Cloth and yarn have different **textures.**

Practice

1. Feel your sleeve.
2. How does it feel?

Differentiated Instruction

Reteach
Play "I Spy" with students. Choose an object in the room and provide clues about its color and texture. Have students guess what you are looking at.

Special Needs
Develop students' awareness of their sense of touch and their textural preferences by asking them to choose textures that they think feel the best for use in this activity.

ELL Tips
Show students pieces of fabric that have a variety of textures. Write the words *smooth, rough, bumpy, fuzzy,* and *scratchy* on individual cards. Have pairs of students select fabrics to place with each label. As they place the materials, have students repeat the word labels.

Think about the different textures you see in the artwork.

◀ **Rose Valentine.** Age 5.

 Creative Expression

Where would you place different textures on a puppet?

1. Think about a puppet you would like to make.

2. Choose textured materials for your puppet.

3. Glue the materials on your paper bag.

Art Criticism

Interpret Is your puppet feeling happy? Scared? Sad? Silly? Give your puppet a name.

Unit 5 • Lesson 3   **167**

Art Across the Curriculum

Use these simple ideas to reinforce art concepts across the curriculum.

★ **Narrative Writing** Write a play for the puppets you made. Then perform the play as a puppet show.

★ **Math** Count the puppets the class made, noting that the number is the same as the number of students. Sort the puppets according to characteristics, such as all animal puppets or boy puppets.

★ **Science** Identify things that are living and nonliving, noting how we pretend puppets are living things in plays.

★ **Social Studies** Create puppets of historical figures and perform a play to explore their contributions to the community, state, or nation.

★ **Technology** Use the tools in a paint program to design a toy that has visual texture. Visit **SRAonline.com** to print detailed instructions for this activity.

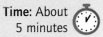 **Reflect** Time: About 5 minutes

Review and Assess

"Why do artists use different fibers, or materials, to make puppets and toys?"
"¿Por qué los artistas usan diferentes fibras o materiales para hacer títeres y juguetes?"

Think

Discuss the student art question. The student used a fuzzy-looking fiber for the hair and a smooth-looking fabric for the clothing. The buttons look bumpy.

Informal Assessment

Art Journal: Critical Thinking
Have students answer the Interpret question by drawing a picture in their Art Journals.

 Art Criticism

Have students ask themselves the following questions.

Describe ▶ Describe your puppet. What is it?

Analyze ▶ What different types of materials and textures did you use to create your puppet?

Interpret ▶ Is your puppet feeling happy? Scared? Sad? Silly? Give your puppet a name.

Decide ▶ Do the textured materials help tell more about your puppet? Do the textures make your puppet seem more real? Are there any other textures that you would like to add?

NSAE 2.b; 5.a; 5.c

■ For standardized-format test practice using this lesson's art content, see pages 58–59 in *Reading and Writing Test Preparation.*

Designing with Texture

Extra! For the Art Specialist

Time: About 30 minutes

Focus

Use *Transparency 25* and *Large Prints 9 Cat* and *10 Child with Puzzle* to discuss how the artists used texture. Ask students to name all the texture words they know. List them on the board.

Teach

Discuss how textures can be made on paper by rubbing the surface with a crayon. Have students use texture rubbings to create a landscape collage.

Reflect

Have students use the four steps of art criticism to evaluate their work. Did they effectively use texture rubbings to create a landscape collage?

Alternate Activity

Materials:
- jumbo crayons (remove the paper)
- 12" × 18" blue construction paper
- 9" × 12" white construction paper
- textured objects for rubbings
- glue
- scissors

1. Demonstrate how to hold a crayon flat against paper and make textures.

2. Direct the students to make at least five different texture rubbings on the white paper.

3. Have students use these textures to make a landscape collage. Students cut or tear the rubbings into a variety of shapes and glue them to a blue background sheet.

4. Then have students use crayons to add details to their collages.
NSAE 1.c

Research in Art Education

"Only through a multifaceted education program that develops divergent as well as convergent thinking—that encourages intuitive as well as rational thought processes—can today's young learner begin to be prepared to cope with the rapidly changing aspects of a technology-oriented world" (Herberholz, Barbara, and Lee Hanson. *Early Childhood Art.* New York: McGraw-Hill, 1994).

Assessment

Use the following rubric to evaluate the artwork students make in the Creative Expression activity and to assess students' understanding of designing with texture.

Have students complete page 61 or 62 in their *Assessment* books.

	Art History and Culture	Aesthetic Perception	Creative Expression	Art Criticism
3 POINTS	The student recognizes that puppetry and toy making are arts that have been around for a long time.	The student describes textures of puppets and toys that he or she has seen in art, in real life, or in the mass media.	The student's puppet has a variety of textures.	The student thoughtfully and honestly evaluates his or her own work using the four steps of art criticism.
2 POINTS	The student shows emerging recognition that puppetry and toy making are arts that have been around for a long time.	The student can sometimes describe textures of puppets and toys that he or she has seen in art, in real life, or in the mass media.	The student's puppet has some texture.	The student attempts to evaluate his or her own work, but shows an incomplete understanding of evaluation criteria.
1 POINT	The student does not recognize that puppetry and toy making are arts that have been around for a long time.	The student cannot describe textures of puppets and toys that he or she has seen in art, in real life, or in the mass media.	The student's puppet does not have texture.	The student makes no attempt to evaluate his or her own artwork.

Assessment, p. 61

Name _____ Date _____ Lesson **3** UNIT 5

Designing with Texture

For the teacher: Use the following prompt for this activity. Using crayons, draw a puppet. Show different textures by drawing yarn hair, furry jackets, or silky shirts.

Level K   Unit 5 • Texture   **61**

Fiber Textures

Lesson 4 introduces fiber textures that come directly from nature, such as straw, leaves, and grass. Students study fine art that shows baskets that were woven from natural fibers.

Objectives

Art History and Culture

To recognize that basketry is an art form

Creative Expression

To create a basket by weaving yarn, ribbon, or raffia into a prepared cup base

Aesthetic Perception

To identify and compare fibers that could be used in weaving

Art Criticism

To evaluate one's own work using the four steps of art criticism

---

Vocabulary ☆ Reading

Review the following vocabulary words with students before beginning the lesson.

fiber fibra—thin, threadlike material generally used to make yarn and woven fabric

See page 179B for additional vocabulary and Spanish vocabulary resources.

· · · · · · · · · · · · · · · · · · · ·

Art Journal: Vocabulary

Have students add this word to the Vocabulary section of their Art Journals.

Lesson Materials
- yarn
- plastic cups (precut with five cuts from the lip to base)
- precut yarn, ribbon, or raffia

Alternate Materials
- berry baskets

Program Resources
- *Reading and Writing Test Prep.*, pp. 60–61
- *Transparency 28*
- *Artist Profiles*, pp. 59, 69
- *Assessment*, pp. 63–64
- *Large Prints 9 Cat* and *10 Child with Puzzle*
- *Art Around the World Collection*

Concept Trace
Fiber Textures
Introduced: Level K, Unit 5, Lesson 4

Reinforced: Level 1, Unit 5, Lesson 5

Lesson 4 Arts Integration

Theatre

Complete Unit 5, Lesson 4 on pages 96–97 of the ***Theatre Arts Connections*** book.

Theatre Arts Connections, p. 96

Music

Sometimes the texture of a composition can have the same texture throughout the complete piece. Listen to "Adagio" from *Quartet #2 in D minor.* There are four string instruments playing continuously.

Movement & Dance

Divide the class into four large groups, and have three groups make the following shapes:

1. A giant fence with spaces between each post
2. A giant tunnel or bridge
3. A large circle (holding hands, standing or sitting)

Have the fourth group explore each shape by traveling in pairs over, under, around, and through each shape.

ocus

Time: About 10 minutes

Activate Prior Knowledge

"Name something you have seen carried in a basket." "Nombren algo que hayan visto que se carga en una cesta".

- Have students name different uses for baskets, such as to display or store food or to hold clothing, toys, or leaves.

Using Literature Reading

- Read *Little Red Riding Hood* by Trina Schart Hyman. Ask students how Little Red Riding Hood uses her basket. What is her basket made of?

Thematic Connection Social Studies

- **Cultural Diversity:** Discuss how some cultures are self-reliant and grow or create all their own necessities, including items like baskets.

Introduce the Art

Look

"The baskets in the photographs could have been used to carry things. The baskets are a form of art." "Las cestas en las fotografías se usaron para cargar cosas. Las cestas son una forma de arte".

Drawing Conclusions Reading

- Ask students to tell what they think might have been carried in the baskets.

Comparing and Contrasting Reading

- Have students describe how the baskets are alike and different.

- Share and discuss information from *Artist Profiles* pages 59 and 69 with students.

Adjectives and Adverbs Language Arts

- List on a chart the adjectives and adverbs students use to describe the fine art.

Art History and Culture

Share information from the Art History and Culture sections with students. Ask students why they think people make baskets.
Possible answers: To hold things or to carry things, or for a decoration.

🖥 Web Connection

Visit **www.arc.gov/index.do?nodeId=2** to learn more about the Appalachian region.

Lesson **4** **Fiber Textures**

◀ **Artist Unknown.** (United States). *Appalachian Basket.* 1988.
....
Split oak. 12 × 12 inches (30.48 × 30.48 cm.). Hudak Private Collection.

Look at the baskets in the pictures. Baskets have texture.

🏺 Art History and Culture

People from all over the world weave baskets. Why do you think people make baskets?

🏺 Art History and Culture

Appalachian Basket

The craft of basket weaving is part of everyday life in many cultures, as baskets are used to store, hold, and carry things. Appalachian people live along the Appalachian mountain range in the eastern part of the United States. Many live a self-reliant life and create or grow all their necessities. Craft skills are often passed down from generation to generation. The Appalachian people are famous for their folk art, music, and dance.

See pages 16–21 and 24–25 for more about subject matter and art history.

Artist Profiles, p. 59

Artist Profile

Appalachian Basket

Creating baskets has become a traditional art form because they have been made by people for so long. Basket makers usually learn to make baskets from their parents or others in their families. Baskets were made to carry things or to gather food grown on farms.

◀ **Artist unknown.** (United States). *Appalachian Basket.* 1988.

Study the basket pictures.

▶ How would each basket feel to touch?

▲ **Artist Unknown.** (Native American, Pomoan). *Gift Basket.* c. 1870–1880.
Sedge, bulrush root, woodpecker tufts. $4\frac{1}{2} \times 9\frac{1}{2}$ inches (11.43 × 24.13 cm). Lowe Art Museum, Miami, Florida.

Aesthetic Perception

Seeing Like an Artist Straw is a fiber. What other fibers could be used to weave a basket?

Art History and Culture

Gift Basket

This gift basket was made by an unidentified Pomo Indian artist from the Northern California coast. The Pomo Indians have long been known for the quality of their handmade baskets. They made many different types of baskets—from simpler styles used to store food, carry items, and catch fish to very ornate and complex gift baskets. For the Pomo, baskets such as the one featured here were special treasures and were often given as gifts. Gift baskets were also burned as offerings to honor the dead.

See pages 16–21 and 24–25 for more about subject matter and art history.

Artist Profiles, p. 69

▶ Artist Profile
Gift Basket
This gift basket was made by an unidentified Pomo Indian artist from the northern California coast. The Pomo people had lived along the California coast for centuries before the area was settled by Russian and European traders. The Pomo lived off the land and the sea by fishing for food and trapping animals for fur. When Russian fur traders established outposts along the California coast they developed a good relationship with the Pomo people, and some even married and later returned to Russia with their Pomo spouses.

▲ **Artist unknown.** (Pomoan, United States).
Gift Basket. c. 1870–1880.
Sedge, bulrush root...

Study

▶ Both baskets would feel rough and scratchy, but *Gift Basket* would probably feel smoother because of its tighter weave. *Appalachian Basket* looks like it would feel bumpy around the bottom and rough and scratchy on the handle.

■ For more examples of art from North America, see the **Art Around the World Collection.**

Art Journal: Concept
Have students draw a picture of a basket.

Aesthetic Perception

Seeing Like an Artist Ask students to name other fibers that could be used to weave a basket. Possible answers: Fibers that could be used to weave a basket include grass, leaves, pine needles, bark, reeds, and thin strips of wood.

Developing Visual Literacy Take students outside to look for textures in the environment. What textures do they see? Could these objects be used as part of an artwork?
NSAE 3.a

Web Connection
Visit **www.nmai.si.edu/exhibitions/ baskets/index.cfm** to learn more about Native American basket weaving.

each

Time: About 30 minutes

"Let's practice weaving with your fingers."
"Vamos a practicar tejer con sus dedos".

Practice

Materials: yarn

- Model weaving for students by placing the yarn between your thumb and second finger. Wrap the yarn *under* the second finger and then *over* the middle finger, and so on. Have students try weaving this way.

Creative Expression

Materials: plastic cups (precut with five cuts from the lip to base), precut yarn, ribbon, or raffia

Alternate Materials: berry baskets

- Distribute the materials and have the students follow the directions on page 171.

- See the Activity Tips on page 245 for visual examples of this lesson's activity.

- Provide each student with a precut plastic drinking cup and let him or her choose the fiber to use for weaving.

- Show students how to put the end of a piece of yarn (or ribbon or raffia) in a slit at the bottom of the cup.

- Model for students how to weave in and out of the slits until the yarn or other fiber is used up. Show them how to add another piece of fiber to finish the weaving process.

- Invite students to tell what they will put in their baskets.

NSAE 1.c

Art Journal: Brainstorming
Show students the plastic cup with slits. Ask students to think about small objects they could put in the cup, such as things they use or collect. Have students draw these objects in their Art Journals.

Using Fiber Textures

Wood, straw, and grass are **fiber textures.**

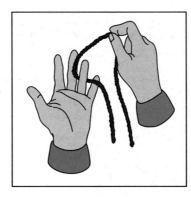

Practice

1. Watch as your teacher shows you how to weave.
2. Practice weaving through your fingers with yarn.

Differentiated Instruction

Reteach
Give a few students each a different textured fiber. Have them hold it up and describe the textures they feel. Encourage other students to help by checking and correcting when necessary.

Special Needs
Students with limited fine motor control may benefit from the use of thicker yarn for this project.

ELL Tips
Display wood, straw, and grass fibers. Label the items and have students say the words with you. Also introduce the term fiber and point to a straw or grass fiber. Explain that fibers from nature can be woven into a basket.

▲ **Olivia Carter.** Age 5.

 Think about the baskets the student made. What kind of fibers did she use to add texture to the baskets?

 **Creative Expression**

What fibers would you use to make a basket?

1. Choose a fiber.
2. Weave the fiber through the slits in the cup.

 Art Criticism

Decide What will you keep in your basket?

Art Across the Curriculum

Use these simple ideas to reinforce art concepts across the curriculum.

★ **Descriptive Writing** List words that students use to describe their baskets. Ask students to choose two words that describe their basket and write them in their Art Journals.

★ **Math** Sort objects into groups, first noting how baskets can be used to sort things.

★ **Science** Identify objects that are made from trees, such as *Appalachian Basket*.

★ **Social Studies** Learn how tools help us do jobs. Discuss the kinds of jobs the baskets in this lesson could help us do.

★ **Technology** Use the tools in a paint program to draw a basket. Visit **SRAonline.com** to print detailed instructions for this activity.

 **Reflect**   Time: About 5 minutes

Review and Assess

"What are some fibers used to weave baskets?" "¿Cuáles son algunas de las fibras que se usan para tejer cestas?"

Think

■ Discuss the student art question. The student artist used yarn to add texture to her baskets.

Informal Assessment

Art Journal: Critical Thinking
Have students answer the Decide question by drawing in their Art Journals.

 Art Criticism

Have students ask themselves the following questions.

Describe ► What fiber did you use to create your basket?

Analyze ► How does the fiber feel to the touch? How does your basket look different from your classmates' baskets?

Interpret ► What do you think is most special about your basket?

Decide ► What will you keep in your basket?

NSAE 2.b; 5.a; 5.c

■ For standardized-format test practice using this lesson's art content, see pages 60–61 in *Reading and Writing Test Preparation*.

Fiber Textures

Extra! For the Art Specialist

Time: About 30 minutes

Focus

Use *Transparency 25* and *Large Prints 9 Cat* and *10 Child with Puzzle* to discuss how the artists used texture. Ask students to explain how the use of texture makes the works of art more exciting.

Teach

Have students feel the texture of their hair and skin. Encourage students to describe how the textures are different. Then have students create a face with textures.

Reflect

Have students use the four steps of art criticism to evaluate their work. Did they effectively use textured materials to create a face?

Alternate Activity

Materials:

- burlap or other textured materials cut in 9" × 12" ovals
- heavy drawing paper or mat board
- glue
- textured materials such as buttons, feather, cotton balls, and yarn

1. Direct the students to select an oval shape cut from burlap or another textured fabric.

2. Have students glue their oval to heavy paper or mat board.

3. Then students use textured materials to make a face.

NSAE 1.c

Research in Art Education

"Children respond to art in a holistic manner; their reactions are immediate, subjective, and rarely go beyond the 'like/don't like' stage . . . . It takes a sensitive teacher to help educate the vision of the child so that appreciation may occur" (Hurwitz, Al, and Stanley Madeja. *The Joyous Vision.* New Jersey: Prentice Hall, 1997).

Assessment

Use the following rubric to evaluate the artwork students make in the Creative Expression activity and to assess students' understanding of fiber textures.

Have students complete page 63 or 64 in their *Assessment* books.

	Art History and Culture	Aesthetic Perception	Creative Expression	Art Criticism
3 POINTS	The student recognizes that basketry is an art form.	The student identifies and compares fibers that could be used in weaving.	The student effectively wove a basket using fiber textures.	The student thoughtfully and honestly evaluates his or her own work using the four steps of art criticism.
2 POINTS	The student shows emerging awareness that basketry is an art form.	The student can sometimes identify and compare fibers that could be used in weaving.	The student's basket shows some use of fiber textures.	The student attempts to evaluate his or her own work, but shows an incomplete understanding of evaluation criteria.
1 POINT	The student does not recognize that basketry is an art form.	The student cannot identify or compare fibers that could be used in weaving.	The student did not weave a basket using fiber textures.	The student makes no attempt to evaluate his or her own artwork.

Assessment, p. 63

Name _____ Date _____

Lesson 4 UNIT 5

Fiber Textures

For the teacher: Use the following prompt for this activity.
Using crayons, draw a picture of baskets. Show straw, yarn, cloth, canvas, or wooden baskets.

Level K   Unit 5 • Texture   **63**

Real Texture on Forms

Lesson 5 focuses on understanding how texture can be created on forms, such as clay. Artists can carve lines or press objects into clay or other materials to create real texture.

Objectives

 Art History and Culture

To recognize that people from different places create textured forms

 Creative Expression

To create textures on a sculptural form by drawing lines and pressing textures into clay

 Aesthetic Perception

To describe the lines used to draw different textures on a sculptural art form

 Art Criticism

To evaluate one's own work using the four steps of art criticism

---

Vocabulary  ★ Reading

Review the following vocabulary words with students before beginning the lesson.

texture *textura*—the element of art that refers to how things feel, or look as if they might feel if touched

real texture *textura real*—texture you can feel

See page 179B for additional vocabulary and Spanish vocabulary resources.

 Art Journal: Vocabulary

Have students add these words to the Vocabulary section of their Art Journals.

Lesson Materials

- clay
- plastic utensils
- pressing objects, such as buttons and thread spools
- clay mats (muslin)
- paper clips

Alternate Materials
- plasticine or modeling clay

Program Resources
- *Reading and Writing Test Prep.,* pp. 62–63
- *Transparency 29*
- *Artist Profiles,* pp. 67, 75
- *Assessment,* pp. 65–66
- *Animals Through History Time Line*
- *Large Print 9* Cat and *10* Child with Puzzle
- *Art Around the World Collection*

Concept Trace
Real Texture on Forms
Introduced: Level K, Unit 5, Lesson 5
Reinforced: Level 1, Unit 5, Lessons 1, 3

Lesson 5 Arts Integration

Theatre

Complete Unit 5, Lesson 5 on pages 98–99 of the *Theatre Arts Connections* book.

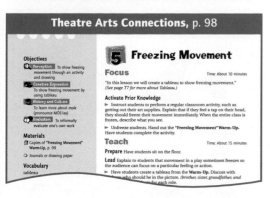
Theatre Arts Connections, p. 98

Music

Listen to "Russian Sailor's Dance" from *The Red Poppy* by Reinhold Gliere. Each time the melody repeats, either more, different, or fewer instruments are used. How does this add to your enjoyment of the piece?

Movement & Dance

Attach elastic loops to one end of small strips of fabric. Have students put one hand through the elastic loops and explore moving with the fabric.

- What happens when you jump? Turn? Stop suddenly?
- Can you create patterns with the fabric? *S* curves, *C* curves, zigzags, spirals?

Focus

Time: About 10 minutes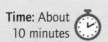

Activate Prior Knowledge

"Have you ever touched a fish? What does a fish feel like?" "Alguna vez han tocado un pez? ¿Cómo se siente el pez?"

- Display a picture of a fish. Encourage students to describe what a fish feels like and to name different parts of a fish.

- Using the *Animals Through History Time Line,* have students name and describe the different parts and textures of other animals.

Using Literature ⭐ Reading

- Read *The Seashore Book* by Charlotte Zolotow. Study the illustrations to find textures. Discuss how the objects in the illustrations would feel if they were real.

Thematic Connection ⭐ Science

- **Ocean Life:** Learn about the kinds of organisms that live in the ocean and discuss how they depend on each other.

Introduce the Art

Look

"Both forms in the photographs have lines carved, or cut, into them to add texture." "Ambas formas en las fotografías tienen líneas talladas, o cortadas, para añadir textura".

Identifying Details ⭐ Reading

- Have students locate the lines on the fish that show the scales, the fins, and the tail.

Making Inferences ⭐ Reading

- Ask students how the artists might have created the lines on the fish and container.

- Share and discuss information from Artist Profiles pages 67 and 75 with students.

🏺 Art History and Culture

Share information from the Art History and Culture sections with students. The Ashanti people are known for their beautiful, handcrafted artwork. Ask students to predict how this fish was used to help tell a story. Answers will vary. Students might say that the storyteller used the fish like a puppet and moved the fish to show the action of the story.

💻 Web Connection

Learn more about the Ashanti people at www.africaguide.com/culture/tribes/ashanti.htm.

Real Texture on Forms

Look at the forms on these pages. The artists added texture to their forms.

▲ **Artist Unknown.** Ashanti people. (Ghana). *Fish, Gold Weight.* Nineteenth–twentieth century.
....
Brass. 3½ inches high (8.89 cm). The Metropolitan Museum of Art, New York, New York.

🏺 Art History and Culture

Long ago the Ashanti people used objects like this fish to weigh their gold. They also used objects like this to help them tell stories.

🏺 Art History and Culture

Ashanti Gold Weights

Ashanti gold weights were made by special artisans who specialized in sculpting and bronze casting. Because almost every Ashanti man owned a set of gold weights, many people in Ghana learned how to make them.

The Ashanti used gold weights beginning in the 1300s to weigh the gold dust. Significantly fewer gold weights have been made since 1889 because in that year the Ashanti stopped using gold as money. The gold weights were also used by storytellers to aid in telling their stories. In addition to fish, gold weights can be shaped like beetles, coins, masks, people, animals, and other forms.

See pages 16–21 and 24–25 for more about subject matter and art history.

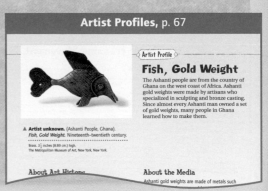

Artist Profiles, p. 67

⟨ Artist Profile ⟩

Fish, Gold Weight

The Ashanti people are from the country of Ghana on the west coast of Africa. Ashanti gold weights were made by artisans who specialized in sculpting and bronze casting. Since almost every Ashanti man owned a set of gold weights, many people in Ghana learned how to make them.

▲ **Artist unknown.** (Ashanti People, Ghana). *Fish, Gold Weight.* Nineteenth-twentieth century. Brass. 3½ inches (8.89 cm) high. The Metropolitan Museum of Art, New York, New York.

About Art History

About the Media

Ashanti gold weights are made of metals such

Study the forms on these pages.

► What do you think the fish would feel like if you touched it?

► Would the container feel the same as the fish?

◄ **Artist Unknown.** (China). *Ritual Wine Container.*
Thirteenth century B.C.
Bronze. $11\frac{7}{8} \times 4\frac{3}{4} \times 4\frac{7}{8}$ inches (30.15 × 12.07 × 12.37 cm).
Arthur M. Sackler Gallery, Smithsonian Institution, Washington, D.C.

Aesthetic Perception

Seeing Like an Artist What kinds of lines would you use to make a clay tiger?

Art History and Culture

Ritual Wine Container

This large, sturdy vessel has a fitted lid and a long, gracefully curving handle attached at both sides. Wine vessels of this kind were known as *Yu* in Shang culture. The exterior of the vessel is etched or carved with intricate designs, symbols, and animal forms. The bronze with which the container is made has developed a beautiful patina resulting from centuries of age, oxidation, and corrosion. Elaborate wine vessels such as this wine container have been found among the treasures buried in the tombs of Shang kings unearthed in northern China. Royalty were usually buried with personal objects and items of value, supporting the Shang belief that royalty would need these things in the afterlife.

See pages 16–21 and 24–25 for more about subject matter and art history.

Artist Profiles, p. 75

Artist Profile
Ritual Wine Container
This ritual wine container was made in China in the thirteenth century B.C. by an unknown artist of the Shang dynasty. The Shang dynasty is considered the beginning of recorded Chinese history by some historians. It was during the Shang dynasty, between the sixteenth and the eleventh centuries B.C. that the Chinese character writing system was developed. Also during this time, China became a thriving agricultural nation, with the development of new farming and animal husbandry techniques and the design of many new types of metal tools and farm implements.

Study

► The long lines on the fish's fins and tail would feel bumpy. The thick lines around the face and eye are smooth but bumpy. The short, crossing lines that create the texture for the fish scales look rather smooth.

► The container looks like it would feel bumpier than the fish because it has more raised lines and detail.

■ For more examples of art from Africa, see the *Art Around the World Collection.*

Art Journal: Concept
Have students draw a picture of a fish that looks like it has texture.

Aesthetic Perception

Seeing Like an Artist Ask students to describe the kinds of lines they would use to make a clay tiger. Possible answers: Since a tiger looks smooth, the lines should be smooth and diagonal or somewhat curved.

Developing Visual Literacy Encourage students to look at home for objects that have real texture. Ask them to describe to the class what they saw or bring in an object to share.

Web Connection
Go to www.asia.si.edu/collections/chineseHome.htm to view more art from China.

 **Teach**

 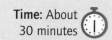

"Let's go on a scavenger hunt for textured surfaces." "Vamos a buscar superficies con textura".

Practice

- Follow the directions on student page 174. Give students five minutes to find one thing that has a raised or carved surface.

- Help students describe the lines used to create each textured surface.

NSAE 3.a; 3.b

Creative Expression

Materials: clay, plastic utensils, pressing objects, such as buttons and thread spools, clay mats (muslin), paper clips

Alternate Materials: plasticine or modeling clay

- Distribute the materials and have the students follow the directions on page 175.

- See the Activity Tips on page 246 for visual examples of this lesson's activity.

- Have students roll a ball of clay and flatten it into a square-, circular-, or rectangular-shaped tile.

- Tell students to press their chosen objects into their tile to create textures in their designs.

- Students can add details with plastic utensils.

- Review the Technique Tips on page 230 for information on working with clay.

NSAE 1.a; 1.c

Art Journal: Brainstorming

Show students a variety of objects they could press into clay. Invite students to choose some objects and think about a design they would like to make with the objects. Have students draw their designs in their Art Journals.

Using Real Texture on Forms

Tools or objects can be used to add **texture** to artwork. The texture that you can feel is called **real texture.**

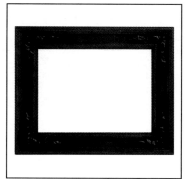

Practice

1. Find something around you that has raised or carved lines.

2. Tell how the lines make texture on the object.

Differentiated Instruction

Reteach
Look around the classroom for a few forms with texture. Have a few students touch them and describe the textures by feel.

Special Needs
Providing students with an array of everyday objects such as combs, old jewelry, and plastic cooking utensils should enable them to think creatively about art materials and processes.

ELL Tips
Review the term *real texture* with students. Let them feel the different fabric swatches to compare textures. Emphasize that texture they can feel is called real texture.

 **Madalyn Kuhn.**
Age 4.
Matthew Ellett.
Age 4.
Bobby Tucker.
Age 5.

Think about the textures on the students' forms. How do you think the students created the textures?

 **Creative Expression**

What objects would you use to show real texture?

1. Roll a ball of clay, and then flatten it.

2. Shape the clay into a circle, square, or rectangle.

3. Press objects into the clay to create texture.

 **Art Criticism**

Describe What objects did you use to create textures in your design?

Art Across the Curriculum

Use these simple ideas to reinforce art concepts across the curriculum.

★ **Narrative Writing** Have students draw an illustration and tell a story about who might have used *Ritual Wine Container* and how the container was used.

★ **Math** Show students a container comparable in size to *Ritual Wine Container*. Fill the container with objects to discover its capacity. Compare and order two or three containers according to capacity.

★ **Science** Discuss the importance of keeping water clean for fish and other animals that need it.

★ **Social Studies** Compare and contrast the environment of a fish to the students' environment. Describe physical characteristics of each environment.

★ **Technology** Use the tools in a paint program to draw a container that has texture on it. Visit **SRAonline.com** to print detailed instructions for this activity.

 **Reflect** 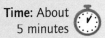 Time: About 5 minutes

Review and Assess

"How can you create real texture on forms?"
"¿Cómo pueden crear la textura real en formas?"

Think

■ Discuss the student art question. The students might have used paper clips or pencils to create the texture on the clay.

Informal Assessment

Art Journal: Critical Thinking
Have students answer the Describe question by drawing a picture in their Art Journals.

Art Criticism

Have students ask themselves the following questions.

Describe ▶ What objects did you use to create textures in your design?

Analyze ▶ What textures did you create in the clay?

Interpret ▶ Name your artwork. Why did you choose that name?

Decide ▶ Do you like the textures in your design?

NSAE 2.b; 5.a; 5.c

■ For standardized-format test practice using this lesson's art content, see pages 62–63 in *Reading and Writing Test Preparation.*

Lesson 5
Wrap-Up

Real Texture on Forms

Extra! For the Art Specialist

Time: About 30 minutes

Focus

Use **Transparency 25** and **Large Prints 9** *Cat* and **10** *Child with Puzzle* to discuss how the artists used texture. Look at the textures in the works of art. What objects in your classroom would have these same textures?

Teach

Discuss with the class how objects can create textures when pressed on soft clay. Hold up several texture tools and have the class describe the marks each one would make. Have students use objects to create real texture on a clay mobile.

Reflect

Have students use the four steps of art criticism to evaluate their work. Did they effectively use objects to create real texture on a clay mobile?

Alternate Activity

Materials:
- earthenware clay
- texture tools
- metal lids or cookie cutters
- drinking straws
- string or heavy fishing line

1. Direct the students to flatten three balls of clay.

2. Have students use jar lids or cookie cutters to make a shape with each ball of clay. Use straws to make a hole at the top and bottom of each shape.

3. Then have students use various objects to press textures into the clay.

4. Fire the clay in a kiln.

5. Use string or heavy fishing line to attach all the clay shapes together. Make a loop at the top for hanging.

NSAE 1.c; 3.a

Research
in Art Education

"It seems without a doubt that children do, indeed, respond to and are able to talk about art in meaningful ways" (Anderson, Tom. "Talking About Art with Children: From Theory to Practice." *Art Education* 39(1). (1986): 5–8).

Assessment

Use the following rubric to evaluate the artwork students make in the Creative Expression activity and to assess students' understanding of texture on forms.

Have students complete page 65 or 66 in their *Assessment* books.

	Art History and Culture	Aesthetic Perception	Creative Expression	Art Criticism
3 POINTS	The student recognizes that people from different places create textured forms.	The student describes the lines used to draw different textures on a sculptural art form.	The student effectively created textures on a sculptural form by drawing lines and pressing textures into clay.	The student thoughtfully and honestly evaluates his or her own work using the four steps of art criticism.
2 POINTS	The student shows emerging awareness that people from different places create textured forms.	The student can sometimes describe the lines used to draw different textures on a sculptural art form.	The student showed emerging ability to create textures on a sculptural form by drawing lines and pressing textures into clay.	The student attempts to evaluate his or her own work, but shows an incomplete understanding of evaluation criteria.
1 POINT	The student does not recognize that people from different places create textured forms.	The student cannot describe the lines used to draw different textures on a sculptural art form.	The student did not create textures on a sculptural form.	The student makes no attempt to evaluate his or her own artwork.

Assessment, p. 65

Name _____ Date _____

Lesson 5 UNIT 5

Real Texture on Forms

1

2

For the teacher: Use the following prompts for this activity.
1. In box 1, use crayons to draw the lines and shapes you used on your clay to show smooth texture.
2. In box 2, draw the lines and shapes you used to show rough texture.

Level K   Unit 5 • Texture   **65**

 **Texture on Shapes**

Lesson 6 focuses on creating real texture by sewing with yarn. Students learn about the art of stitchery in this lesson.

Objectives

 Art History and Culture

To recognize that stitchery is a form of art

 Creative Expression

To sew yarn on burlap to create a stitched artwork

 Aesthetic Perception

To locate and describe textures created by various sewing stitches

 Art Criticism

To evaluate one's own work using the four steps of art criticism

Vocabulary ✩ Reading

Review the following vocabulary word with students before beginning the lesson.

stitchery costura—art made with yarn on cloth

real texture textura real—texture you can feel

See page 179B for additional vocabulary and Spanish vocabulary resources.

 Art Journal: Vocabulary

Have students add this word to the Vocabulary section of their Art Journals.

Lesson Materials
- large, plastic needles
- scraps of burlap
- various yarns (precut)
- 12" × 12" pieces of burlap, taped around the edges
- jumbo crayons

Alternate Materials
- yarn tip dipped in glue and dried overnight

Program Resources
- *Reading and Writing Test Prep.,* pp. 64–65
- *Transparency 30*
- *Artist Profiles,* pp. 35, 66
- *Assessment,* pp. 67–68
- *Animals Through History Time Line*
- *Large Print 9* Cat and *10* Child with Puzzle
- *Art Around the World Collection*

Concept Trace

Texture on Shapes

Introduced: Level K, Unit 5, Lesson 6

Reinforced: Level 2, Unit 5, Lesson 5

Lesson 6 Arts Integration

Theatre

Complete Unit 5, Lesson 6 on pages 100–105 of the *Theatre Arts Connections* book.

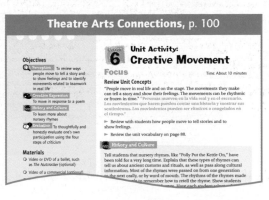

Theatre Arts Connections, p. 100

Music

 A tiny piccolo can change the texture of a song in a big way. Listen to *The Stars and Stripes Forever* by John Philip Sousa. In the last section, a piccolo pierces through the sound of the band with a special melody. This change of texture is so famous, it is traditional for the piccolo player to stand.

Movement & Dance

Just as artists use texture in art, dancers work with contrasting movement qualities and force/energy to express different feelings and ideas. Use words such as boil, melt, quiver, jab, and spring as a stimulus for students to explore different movement qualities.

ocus

Time: About 10 minutes

Activate Prior Knowledge

"Have you ever seen a quilt?" "¿Han visto alguna vez una colcha?"

- Explain that the artwork on student page 176 is a quilt.

Using Literature ⭐ Reading

- Read *The Keeping Quilt* by Patricia Polacco. Point out the pattern and texture in the illustrations.

Thematic Connection ⭐ Social Studies

- **Heritage:** Learn about family customs and traditions. Discuss how skills like quilting are taught from generation to generation.

Introduce the Art

Look

"These artists created texture by sewing lines and shapes on cloth." "Estos artistas crearon las texturas cosiendo líneas y figuras en la tela".

Main Idea and Details ⭐ Reading

- Have students tell a story to explain what is happening on each artwork.

- Ask students to point to the different textures in the works of art and describe them.

- Share and discuss information from Artist Profiles pages 35 and 66 with students.

Adjectives and Adverbs ⭐ Language Arts

- List on a chart the adjectives and adverbs students use to describe the fine art.

🏺 Art History and Culture

Share information from the Art History and Culture sections with students. Quilting has long been popular in China, India, Iran, Egypt, and Africa. Quilting and other needlework such as embroidery have historically been done by women who were not allowed to go to art school to become professional artists. Activities such as quilting provided women with the opportunity to express themselves creatively.

💻 Web Connection

Learn more about Harriet Powers at www.mfa.org/handbook/portrait.asp?id=350.5&s=1.

176 UNIT 5 • Texture

Lesson 6 — Texture on Shapes

◀ **Harriet Powers.** (American). *Bible Quilt, Detail: Dark Day of May 19, 1780.* c. 1897

Pieced and appliquéd cotton embroidered with plain and metallic yarns. 69 × 105 inches overall (175.26 × 266.7 cm). Museum of Fine Arts, Boston, Massachusetts.

Look at the works of art on both pages. The artists added texture to the shapes on each cloth.

🏺 Art History and Culture

Quilting has been a popular art form for a long time. The pictures in quilts often tell a story.

176 Unit 5 • Lesson 6

🏺 Art History and Culture

Harriet Powers

Harriet Powers (här´ē ət pou´ərz) (1837–1911) was born a slave in Athens, Georgia. When she was emancipated, she and her husband bought a small farm on which they raised their children. Powers raised chickens, worked as a seamstress, and made patchwork quilts until she died in 1911. The quilt in this lesson consists of 15 squares of cotton appliqué that are sewn together to tell stories about the Bible and about her own life. Although Powers did not gain recognition in her lifetime as a working quilt artist, her exquisite quilts can now be seen hanging in the Smithsonian Institution.

See pages 16–21 and 24–25 for more about subject matter and art history.

Artist Profiles, p. 35

⬥ Artist Profile ⬥
Harriet Powers
1837–1911

Harriet Powers (ha´ rē ət pou´ ərz) was born in Athens, Georgia. She and her husband bought a small farm where they raised 11 children. Powers earned money by raising chickens, working as a seamstress, and making patchwork quilts until she died in 1911. Although she did not gain fame as a quilt artist in her lifetime (everything she owned at her death was worth a total of $70), her exquisite quilts now are appreciated by visitors to the Smithsonian Institution, and the Museum of Fine Arts in Boston, Massachusetts.

▲ **Harriet Powers.** (American). *Pictorial Quilt.* c. 1895-98.

◄ **Artist Unknown.**
(Hmong).
Embroidered Pillow.
....
Pieced fabrics and embroidery,
15 × 16 inches (38.1 ×
40.64 cm.). Yoshida Private
Collection.

Study the shapes on the works of art.

▶ Point to the shapes the artists created
with yarn on these cloths. This art is
called **stitchery.**

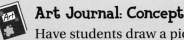 **Aesthetic Perception**

Seeing Like an Artist What shapes did the
artists stitch in the pictures?

Art History and Culture

Hmong Art

Hmong artwork is often an interpretation of the events happening
in the lives and histories of the artists' families. A traditional
Hmong art form is the story cloth, sometimes called a flower cloth.
These textiles are silent storytellers, often serving as the only record
of a journey, battle, or other event experienced by a family or an
entire village. The story cloth is an important part of Hmong
culture, because until the late 1950s, the Hmong language had
no written form.

See pages 16–21 and 24–25
for more about subject
matter and art history.

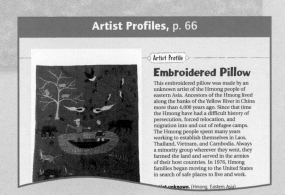

Artist Profiles, p. 66

─ Artist Profile ─

Embroidered Pillow

This embroidered pillow was made by an
unknown artist of the Hmong people of
eastern Asia. Ancestors of the Hmong lived
along the banks of the Yellow River in China
more than 4,000 years ago. Since that time
the Hmong have had a difficult history of
persecution, forced relocation, and
migration into and out of refugee camps.
The Hmong people spent many years
working to establish themselves in Laos,
Thailand, Vietnam, and Cambodia. Always
a minority group wherever they went, they
farmed the land and served in the armies
of their host countries. In 1976, Hmong
families began moving to the United States
in search of safe places to live and work.

...t unknown. (Hmong, Eastern Asia)

Study

▶ Possible answers: Students might point to
the yarn that loops around the sun and
connects to the moon *(Bible Quilt)* or the
plant leaves and stems *(Embroidered
Pillow).*

■ For more examples of art from Asia, see
the ***Art Around the World Collection.***

Art Journal: Concept
Have students draw a picture that
might appear on a quilt.

Aesthetic Perception

Seeing Like an Artist Ask students to identify
the shapes the artists stitched in the fine art.
Possible answers: People, animals, sun,
moon, circles, boat, trees, and flowers.

Developing Visual Literacy Encourage
students to speculate on the event that
inspired the artist to create the scene on
Embroidered Pillow. Who are the people?
Where are they going? Why?

Web Connection
Visit **www.hmong.org/displaycontent.asp?ID=17**
to learn more about the Hmong people.

Teach

Time: About 30 minutes

"Let's practice making some stitches with a needle and some yarn before you sew your own embroidery." "Vamos a hacer algunas puntadas con una aguja y algo de hilo antes de que cosan sus propios bordados".

Review the Technique Tips on page 231 for information on how to sew a running stitch.

Practice

Materials: plastic needles, yarn, scraps of burlap

Alternate Materials: yarn dipped in glue and dried overnight

- Review the Technique Tips on page 231 for information on how to sew a running stitch.

- Model for students how to sew a running stitch. Use a scrap 4-inch square of burlap.

- Provide students with a needle, yarn, and a scrap of burlap, and have them practice sewing some stitches.

Creative Expression

Materials: 12" × 12" pieces of burlap, taped around the edges; large, plastic needles; various yarns (precut); jumbo crayons

Alternate Materials: yarn dipped in glue and dried overnight

- Distribute the materials and have the students follow the directions on page 179.

- See the Activity Tips on page 246 for visual examples of this lesson's activity.

- Have students draw their shape(s) on burlap with crayon.

- Help students with the threading of the needle and the changing of yarn colors. Have students use the running stitch to follow the outlines they have drawn.

NSAE 1.c

Art Journal: Brainstorming

Have students brainstorm some shapes they could sew. Ask students to think of shapes from the classroom, from nature, and so on. Tell students to decide on a shape or shapes and draw it/them in their Art Journals.

NSAE 3.a; 3.b

Using Texture on Shapes

Artists sew yarn to add **real texture** to artwork.

Practice

1. Watch as your teacher shows you how to sew.

2. Practice sewing some stitches.

Differentiated Instruction

Reteach

Fill a box with different textured objects. Have students close their eyes, reach in the box, and take out one object. Ask students to keep their eyes closed as they describe what they feel.

Special Needs

Students with lack of fine motor control or low vision may benefit from larger plastic needles and the use of thicker, more visible thread such as yarn.

ELL Tips

Display samples of stitchery. Introduce the term *stitchery* and write the word on a card. Have students repeat the word with you. Let students touch the yarn or thread and follow the shapes with their fingers. Build a list of words with students to describe how the stitchery feels.

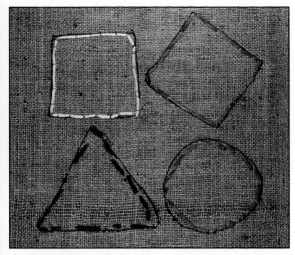

◀ **Rachel Van Amburgh.**
Age 6.

Think about the shapes in the student's artwork. How did the student make texture on the shapes?

 Creative Expression

What kind of designs can you sew on cloth?

1. Think of some shapes you could sew.

2. Draw the shapes on your piece of burlap.

3. Sew along the outlines of your shapes.

 **Art Criticism**

Decide What else might you add to your stitchery?

 **Reflect**   Time: About 5 minutes

Review and Assess

"How do you create textures in stitchery?"
"¿Cómo hacen texturas diferentes en la costura?"

Think

■ Discuss the student art question. The student created texture with yarn.

Informal Assessment

Art Journal: Critical Thinking
Have students answer the Decide question by drawing a picture in their Art Journals.

 Art Criticism

Have students ask themselves the following questions.

Describe ► What shape(s) did you sew on your stitchery?

Analyze ► How do the stitches feel?

Interpret ► What is your stitchery saying about you?

Decide ► What else might you add to your stitchery?

NSAE 2.b; 5.a; 5.c

■ For standardized-format test practice using this lesson's art content, see pages 64–65 in **Reading and Writing Test Preparation.**

● **Art Across the Curriculum** ●

Use these simple ideas to reinforce art concepts across the curriculum.

★ **Narrative Writing** Write a story together about what is happening in the scene on *Embroidered Pillow* or *Bible Quilt*.

★ **Math** Compare lengths of lines, including the yarn lines that create shapes in the students' art.

★ **Science** Identify the living things in the fine art and discuss how they need each other for survival.

★ **Social Studies** Compare and contrast the environment of a fish to the students' environment. Describe physical characteristics of each environment.

★ **Technology** Use the tools in a paint program to draw an object that looks like it has been stitched. Visit **SRAonline.com** to print detailed instructions for this activity.

Texture on Shapes

Extra! For the Art Specialist

Time: About 30 minutes

Focus

Use **Transparency 25** and **Large Prints 9** *Cat* and **10** *Child with Puzzle* to discuss how the artists used texture. Encourage students to think of their favorite textures and name objects that have those textures.

Teach

Ask students to think of their favorite shape. Is it a geometric shape or a free-form shape? Help students learn about textures by creating designs with yarn.

Reflect

Have students use the four steps of art criticism to evaluate their work. Did they create a textured design with yarn?

Alternate Activity

Materials:
- 3"–10" long yarn scraps
- 9" × 12" cardboard
- glue
- scissors

1. Direct students to use a pencil to draw their favorite shape on a piece of cardboard.

2. Have students trace the pencil line with glue and lay the yarn on the glue line.

3. Then students fill the shape with yarn and add various colored yarn scraps to make a design in the background.

NSAE 1.c

Research in Art Education

"Just as culture shapes art, art shapes culture. Our convictions, our technology, and our imagination shape our images, and our images, in turn, shape our perception of the world" (Eisner, Elliot. *The Role of Disciplined-Based Art Education in America's Schools*. The Getty Center for Arts Education in the Arts, 1987).

Assessment
Use the following rubric to evaluate the artwork students make in the Creative Expression activity and to assess students' understanding of texture on shapes.

Have students complete page 67 or 68 in their *Assessment* books.

	Art History and Culture	Aesthetic Perception	Creative Expression	Art Criticism
3 POINTS	The student recognizes that stitchery is a form of art.	The student locates and describes textures created by various sewing stitches.	The student sewed yarn on burlap to create a stitched artwork.	The student thoughtfully and honestly evaluates his or her own work using the four steps of art criticism.
2 POINTS	The student shows emerging awareness that stitchery is a form of art.	The student can sometimes locate and describe textures created by various sewing stitches.	The student showed emerging ability to sew yarn on burlap to create a stitched artwork.	The student attempts to evaluate his or her own work, but shows an incomplete understanding of evaluation criteria.
1 POINT	The student does not recognize that stitchery is a form of art.	The student cannot locate or describe textures created by various sewing stitches.	The student did not sew yarn on burlap to create a stitched artwork.	The student makes no attempt to evaluate his or her own artwork.

Assessment, p. 67

Name _____ Date _____

Lesson **6** UNIT 5

Texture on Shapes

For the teacher: Use the following prompt for this activity.
Using crayons, draw pictures of two things with different kinds of stitching.

Level K

Unit 5 • Texture **67**

Unit 5 Vocabulary Review

collage—bits and pieces of things glued onto paper
collage—trozos y pedazos de cosas pegadas en papel

fiber—thin, threadlike material generally used to make yarn and woven fabric **fibra**—fina, material filiforme usada para coser y tejer

real texture—texture you can feel **textura real**—textura que se palpa

stitchery—art made with yarn on cloth **costura**—el arte hecho con hilo en tela

texture—the element of art that refers to how things feel, or look as if they might feel if touched **textura**—el elemento del arte que se refiere cómo las cosas se sienten o lucen cómo se sienten si son tocadas

visual texture—the way something looks like it might feel if you could touch it **textura visual**—la manera en que un objeto luce como si se pudiera sentir, si se pudiera tocar

Vocabulary Practice

T Display **Transparency 41** to review unit vocabulary words.

Examples ⭐ Vocabulary

Assign vocabulary words to groups of students and ask them to create or find examples of each. Attach the vocabulary word to the example and display each for reference.

Definitions ⭐ Vocabulary

Read the definition of each vocabulary word and have students identify the term you are defining.

Answering Questions ⭐ Vocabulary

Have students practice critical thinking skills by answering questions using unit vocabulary words. For example, "What kind of art is made by gluing many different objects on paper?"

Wrapping Up Unit 5

Texture

Art Criticism

Critical Thinking Art Criticism is an organized system for looking at and talking about art. You can criticize art without being an expert. The purpose of art criticism is to get the viewer involved in a perception process that delays judgment until all aspects of the artwork have been studied.

■ See pages 28–29 for more about art criticism.

Describe

▶ What musical instruments do you see? There is a violin and a trumpet.

▶ What food do you see? We can see two red apples.

▶ What other objects do you see? There are sheets of music and a quilt.

Analyze

▶ What textures do you see? The violin, trumpet, apples, and the paper music sheets look smooth. The trumpet is very shiny. The quilt looks bumpy.

▲ **Peggy Flora Zalucha.** (American). *My Dad's Violin.* 1998.
Watercolor on paper. 20 × 40 inches. (50.8 × 101.6 cm.). Private Collection.

180 Unit 5

Art History and Culture

Peggy Flora Zalucha

Peggy Flora Zalucha (peg′ ē flor′ a zə lōō′ kə) (1948–) was born in Peoria, Illinois. She was raised to appreciate photography and encouraged to take pictures of the world around her. When Zalucha was in college, women were not advised to get studio degrees, so Zalucha got her degree in teaching instead. Her first official job was as an art teacher in a rural Nebraska school. Zalucha has been making and teaching art for more than twenty years.

See pages 16–21 and 24–25 for more about subject matter and art history.

Artist Profiles, p. 57

Artist Profile
Peggy Flora Zalucha
b. 1948
Peggy Flora Zalucha (peg′ ē flor′ a za lōō′ ka) was born in Peoria, Illinois. She was raised to appreciate photography and encouraged to take pictures of the world around her. When Zalucha was in college, women were not advised to get studio degrees, so Zalucha got her degree in teaching instead. Her first official job was as an art teacher in a rural Nebraska school. Zalucha has been making and teaching art for more than 20 years.

 **Art Criticism** **Critical Thinking**

Describe

▶ What musical instruments do you see?

Analyze

▶ What textures do you see?

Interpret

▶ Why are these things together in one painting?

Decide

▶ Does this work look real?

Interpret

▶ Why are these things together in one painting? Answers will vary. Some will say that this is a painting about nice things, or a painting about textures. Some may create a story about how these objects are related or how the instruments may have belonged to one person who liked to sleep with a quilt and liked to eat apples. Encourage their imaginations.

Decide

▶ Does this work look real? Most will agree that everything looks very realistic.
NSAE 5.a; 5.c

> **Art Journal: Writing**
> Have students draw a picture in their Art Journals to answer the Analyze Aesthetic Perception question. Discuss the other questions out loud.

 ## Aesthetic Perception

Critical Thinking Ask students if they have ever seen an instrument.

Describe ▶ What kind of instrument did you see? How did it look and sound?

Analyze ▶ What kinds of textures were on the instrument?

Interpret ▶ What do you think it would be like to play this instrument?

Decide ▶ Did you like this instrument? Why or why not?

"How can you tell the difference between real texture and visual texture?" "Cómo saben la diferencia entre textura real y textura visual?"

T Review unit vocabulary with students using *Transparency 41.*

► Review the different ways texture is portrayed in artwork.

 Art Journal: Writing
Read the questions on page 182 to students. Have students write their answers in their Art Journals or on a separate sheet of paper. 1. B, 2. B, 3. A.

T For further assessment, have students complete the unit test on *Transparency 47.*

LET'S VISIT A MUSEUM
THE NELSON-ATKINS MUSEUM OF ART

Learn About Museums

► The Nelson-Atkins Museum of Art features a permanent collection of European and American paintings, sculptures, prints, and decorative arts, as well as Native American, Oceanic, and pre-Columbian art. The collection is housed in a beautiful 1933 neoclassical building designed by the firm of Wight and Wight of Kansas City, and the grounds are graced by The Kansas City Sculpture Park.

► Encourage students to imagine they are curators of their own museum. Ask them what kinds of exhibits they would like to feature. What would their museum be famous for?

> "The function of a creative artist consists of making laws, not following laws already made."
> —Ferruccio Busoni

Show What You Know

Answer these questions on a separate sheet of paper.

1 Which of these has a bumpy texture?

A.   B.

2 Which of these was made with a fiber?

A.   B.

3 Which of these would you use to add texture on cloth?

A.   B.

The Nelson-Atkins Museum

This museum is in Kansas City, Missouri. It houses art from all over the world.

Unit Assessment Options

Aesthetic Perception

Practice Have students look around the room and identify things that have real texture (clothes, shoes, furniture) and those things with only visual texture (posters, pictures).

Creative Expression   NSAE 5.a; 5.c

Student Portfolio Have students review all the artwork they have created during this unit and select the pieces they wish to put into their portfolios. Have students share their portfolios with classmates and comment constructively about the art.

Art Criticism

Activity Have students select their favorite work of art from the unit. Guide students through study of their selected work using the four steps of art criticism. (See pages 28–29 for more about Art Criticism.)

Texture in Music and Dance

Korean folk music and dance have been around for more than 2,000 years. The songs and dances have been passed on from person to person.

What to Do Create a fan dance.

1. Make a fan and decorate it.

2. Hold the fan in one hand. Find five different ways to move it.

3. Hold the fan in both hands. Find three different ways to move with your fan.

4. Share your fan movements with a partner. Try each other's ideas.

▲ Korean Classical Music and Dance Company. *Korean Classical Music and Dance* and *Toraji Taryong.*

 Art Criticism

 How did you feel as you moved with your fan?

Art History and Culture

Korean Music and Dance

Korean folk music and dance have been around for more than 2,000 years. They have been passed on from person to person. Korean music may sound different than Western music. This is because some songs are made up with only the sounds of the black notes on a piano.

Fans are traditional props used in Korean dances. The fans are usually larger than normal and are decorated in bright colors with feathers. The fans can have patterns, scenes or natural forms drawn on them.

 Texture in Music and Dance

Objective: To create a dance using paper fans as props

Materials: Video, *Korean Classical Music & Dance.* Running Time: 3:08 Audio, *Toraji Taryong.* Running Time: 4:02

Focus
Time: About 10 minutes

■ Read and discuss page 183.

Art History and Culture

■ Share information from the Art History and Culture section with students. Discuss what it means for music and dance to be passed down through the Oral Tradition.

Teach
Time: About 20 minutes

Aesthetic Perception

■ Watch *Korean Classical Music & Dance.* Identify colors and textures on the fans.

Creative Expression

■ Have students make large, accordion-style paper fans and decorate them with colors, patterns, and different textures using items such as feathers, beads, ribbons or raffia.

■ Ask students to create dance movements and poses with their fans.

■ After students have found ways to move, have them pair with a partner. Ask partners to perform for each other.

■ Then select two sets of partners, combine them, and have them perform together.

■ **Informal Assessment** Comment positively as students create movement with their fans.

Reflect
Time: About 5 minutes

 Art Criticism

■ Have students draw in their Art Journals to answer the Interpret question.

Describe Describe the shape, colors, and textures of your fan.

Analyze How did you choose your movements and poses?

Decide Did you like the dances you created?

Unit 6 Planning Guide

	Lesson Title	Suggested Pacing	Creative Expression Activity
Lesson 1	Pattern	45 minutes	Create a drawing of their home using patterns.
Lesson 2	Rhythm and Movement	45 minutes	Create a drawing that shows rhythm and movement.
Lesson 3	Balance	45 minutes	Create a design with even balance.
Lesson 4	Balance in Sculpture	45 minutes	Create a house post that has balance.
Lesson 5	Unity	45 minutes	Create unity in a composition by using lines and shapes.
Lesson 6	Unity in Sculpture	45 minutes	Create a sculpture and arrange it with classmates' sculptures to make one unified work of art.
ART SOURCE ARTSOURCE	Rhythm, Balance, and Unity in Dance	40 minutes	Explore rhythm, balance, and unity through motions made with a partner.

Materials	Program Resources	Fine Art Resources	Literature Resources
12" × 18" white drawing paper, crayons	*Reading and Writing Test Preparation*, pp. 66–67 *Flash Cards*, 10 and 11 *Assessment*, pp. 69–70 *Home and After-School Connections*, pp. 27–30	*Transparency*, 31 *Artist Profiles*, pp. 77, 78 *Large Prints*, 11 and 12 *The National Museum of Women in the Arts Collection*	*This Land Is Your Land* by Woody Guthrie
12" × 18" drawing paper (various colors), oil pastels	*Reading and Writing Test Preparation*, pp. 68–69 *Flash Cards*, 9–11 *Assessment*, pp. 71–72	*Transparency*, 32 *Artist Profiles*, pp. 8, 37 *Large Prints*, 11 and 12 *Art Around the World*	*Tacky the Penguin* by Helen Lester
9" × 12" colored construction paper, scissors	*Reading and Writing Test Preparation*, pp. 70–71 *Flash Cards*, 12 and 14 *Assessment*, pp. 73–74	*Transparency*, 33 *Artist Profiles*, pp. 56, 62 *Animals Through History Time Line* *Large Prints*, 11 and 12 *Women in the Arts Collection*	*Tippy Bear Hunts for Honey* by Coby Hol
cardboard tubes, markers, construction paper scraps, scissors, glue	*Reading and Writing Test Preparation*, pp. 72–73 *Flash Card*, 12 *Assessment*, pp. 75–76	*Transparency*, 34 *Artist Profiles*, pp. 71, 74 *Large Print*, 12 *Art Around the World*	*Babar's Museum of Art* by Laurent de Brunhoff
computer, paint program, printer with paper	*Reading and Writing Test Preparation*, pp. 74–75 *Flash Card*, 18 *Assessment*, pp. 77–78	*Transparency*, 35 *Artist Profiles*, pp. 13, 36 *Large Prints*, 11 and 12 *The National Museum of Women in the Arts Collection*	*Lyle at the Office* by Bernard Waber
4–6 large prints, cardboard tubes of various sizes and lengths, 8" × 10" chipboard, tacky glue, tempera or school acrylics, objects such as beads and yarn, clothespins	*Reading and Writing Test Preparation*, pp. 76–77 *Flash Card*, 18 *Assessment*, pp. 79–80	*Transparency*, 36 *Artist Profiles*, pp. 43, 68 *Animals Through History Time Line* *Large Print*, 12 *Women in the Arts Collection*	*The Great Trash Bash* by Loreen Leedy
"Brother Sun, Sister Moon" by Chuna McIntyre			

6 Principles of Art

Lesson 1: **Pattern** is created by the repetition of lines, shapes, or colors.

Lesson 2: **Rhythm** and **visual movement** are created by the repetition of elements or objects that move the eye through a work of art.

Lesson 3: **Balance** refers to two sides of an artwork having the same shapes, colors, or patterns.

Lesson 4: **Sculptures** can be symmetrical or very similar on opposite sides of an imaginary, central dividing line.

Lesson 5: **Unity** is a feeling of wholeness, or oneness of the artwork.

Lesson 6: **Unity in sculpture** can be achieved by using like colors or forms.

Introduce Unit Concepts

"Artists can use pattern, balance, and rhythm in their art to create interest and a sense of unity." "Los artistas pueden usar patrón, equilibrio y ritmo en sus obras de arte para crear interés y sentido de unidad".

Pattern, Balance, and Rhythm
- Search for repeating forms outside: leaves, tree trunks, grass blades. Identify the shapes that are most often repeated outdoors. Search an interior space and compare the most commonly repeated indoor shapes.

Rhythm and Unity
- Examine the classroom and identify things that belong in a learning classroom. Discuss how these things are unified because of their purpose. Then, reexamine the classroom for objects that belong together because of their shape, color, or size. Discuss this as unity.

Cross-Curricular Projects
- See the *Language Arts and Reading, Mathematics, Science, and Social Studies Art Connections* books for activities that further develop pattern, rhythm, balance, and unity concepts.

Principles of Art

Artists organize art using principles of art.

▲ **Maria Martínez.** (American). *Two Black-on-Black Pots.* 20th century.
....
Ceramic. Courtesy of Maria Martínez, © Jerry Jacka Photography.

Fine Art Prints

Display *Large Prints 11* Ceremonial Cloth and *12 La Danse.* Refer to the prints throughout the unit as students learn about pattern, balance, rhythm, and unity.

Large Print 11

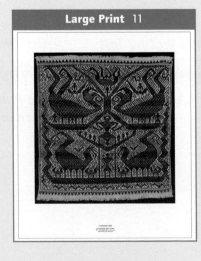

Large Print 12

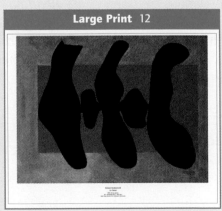

▶ What has the artist repeated on the pottery?

In This Unit you will:
▶ learn about pattern, rhythm, balance, and unity.
▶ see how artists use pattern, rhythm, balance, and unity in their works of art.
▶ use pattern, rhythm, balance, and unity in your artwork.

Maria Martínez
▶ was from New Mexico.
▶ was a Pueblo potter.
▶ had her husband decorate her pottery.

Art History and Culture

Maria Martínez

Maria Martínez (mä rē´ a mär tēn´ ez) (1885–1980) created pots by hand, her husband, Julian Martínez, decorated and fired them. Martínez was an important artist because she and her husband revived a Native American pottery tradition. The technique of smoke firing, for example, was used by the earliest potters in different cultures and regions of the world from Africa to Mexico. Many of the early forms of firing are beginning to be used more and more by contemporary potters.

See pages 16–21 and 24–25 for more about subject matter and art history.

Artist Profiles, p. 26

Artist Profile

Maria Martínez
1881–1980

Maria Martínez (mä rē´ a mär tēn´ ez), of the San Ildefonso Pueblo in New Mexico, was one of the first Native American potters to receive widespread recognition. She learned to make pottery by watching her aunt and her grandmother. In the early years of the twentieth century, Martínez and her husband, Julian, discovered a process for making black pottery similar to that found in nearby excavations. Martínez's skill as a potter was coupled with the design abilities of her husband, who painted the early pots. Later she also worked with her son, Popovi Da, and her daughter-in-law, Santana Martínez.

Examine the Artwork

"Let's search for balance and rhythm in these ceramic pots by the artist Maria Martínez."
"Vamos a buscar el equilibrio y el ritmo en estos vasos de cerámica elaborados por la artista Maria Martínez".

■ Have students study the pots on page 184 and describe what they see.

■ Read the explanations of the principles of art in the Unit Overview. Encourage students to answer these questions: How can you tell these ceramic pots by Maria Martínez are evenly balanced? Possible answer: The works of art are almost exactly the same in the left and right halves. What patterns and lines are repeated to give the artist's pots rhythm? Do your eyes follow the rhythm of the pattern around all sides of the pot? Possible answers: Directional movement is created by repeating lines or patterns. Here we see a stylized leaf shape that is repeated around the top of the pot. Similar shapes create unity by enabling our vision to travel around the entire exterior of the pot.

Unit Pretest

T Display *Transparency 48* as a pretest. Answers: 1. A., 2. B., 3. A.

Home Connection

■ See *Home and After-School Connections* for family newsletters and activities for this unit.

Unit 6 Arts Integration

ILLUSTRATOR PROFILE

Leo Lionni
(1919–1999)

While many of his young classmates were playing soccer in the park, Leo Lionni was busily drawing in an art museum in Amsterdam, Holland, where he was born and raised. Lionni was a self-taught artist who would go on to study business, earning a doctorate degree in economics from the University of Genoa in 1935.

Lionni immigrated to the United States in 1939, where his interest in art and design began to merge with, and eventually overshadow, his business career. Lionni worked for an advertising agency in Philadelphia from 1939 to 1947, then spent two years painting and exhibiting artwork in New York and throughout Europe. Returning to the States, Lionni held the position of art director with *Fortune* magazine for more than a decade before becoming a full-time author and illustrator of children's books.

Lionni was in his late 40s and riding a train with two restless grandchildren when he came up with the idea for his first children's book, *Little Blue and Little Yellow.* Tearing the colorful pages of a magazine into small pieces, Lionni made up a story that kept his grandchildren's attention and later entertained countless other youngsters.

Lionni would go on to produce more than 30 picture books, including the four Caldecott Honor titles *Inch by Inch, Frederick, Swimmy,* and *Alexander and the Wind-Up Mouse.* Themes of kindness and generosity, as well as appealing illustrations, make Lionni's books popular among parents, teachers, and children alike.

While studying Unit 6, share Leo Lionni's illustrations with the class and discuss the principles of art that are evident in his work. What patterns do the students see? Do any objects create rhythm? How did Lionni show balance and unity?

Music

Rhythm in music refers to recurring beats and patterns of long and short notes. Many students can recognize and play some very simple rhythm patterns, especially when they are connected with words in nursery rhymes.

Literature and Art

Watch the video or DVD *The Maestro Plays* by Bill Martin, Jr., to see the difference between musical rhythm and visual rhythm.

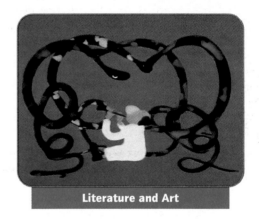

Literature and Art

Performing Arts

 Show *Brother Sun, Sister Moon.* Observe how the dancers show rhythm, balance, and unity.

Artsource®

Pattern

Lesson 1 introduces pattern. Pattern is a surface decoration created by the repetition of lines, shapes, or colors.

Objectives

 Art History and Culture

To recognize that architects are artists who draw designs for homes and other buildings

 Creative Expression

To create a drawing of their home using patterns

 Aesthetic Perception

To locate patterns in fine art and in their environment

 Art Criticism

To evaluate one's own work using the four steps of art criticism

Vocabulary Reading

Review the following vocabulary word with students before beginning the lesson.

pattern patrón—the repetition of lines, shapes, and/or colors

See page 209B for additional vocabulary and Spanish vocabulary resources.

Art Journal: Vocabulary

 Have students add this word to the Vocabulary section of their Art Journals.

Lesson Materials

- 12" × 18" white drawing paper
- crayons

Alternate Materials
- any drawing media

Program Resources

- *Reading and Writing Test Prep.*, pp. 66–67
- *Transparency 31*
- *Flash Cards 10* and *11*
- *Artist Profiles*, pp. 77–78
- *Assessment*, pp. 69–70
- *Large Prints 11* Ceremonial Cloth and *12* La Danse
- *The National Museum of Women in the Arts Collection*

Concept Trace

Pattern

Introduced: Level K, Unit 6, Lesson 1

Reinforced: Level 1, Unit 5, Lesson 4
Level 1, Unit 5, Lesson 6

Lesson 1 Arts Integration

Theatre

Complete Unit 6, Lesson 1, on pages 108–109 of the *Theatre Arts Connections* book.

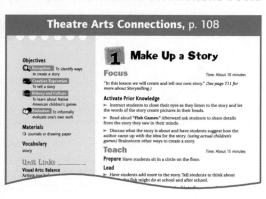

Theatre Arts Connections, p. 108

Music

 The "heartbeat" of music is steady. The rhythm of the words can be quick, long, or uneven. Clap the rhythm of the words to *Twinkle Twinkle, Little Star*. Determine that all four phrases have the same rhythm pattern. Now listen to *Bow Wow Wow*. Which phrase of *Bow Wow* has the same rhythm pattern as *Twinkle*?

Movement & Dance

Dances often contain movement sequences that are repeated. To demonstrate this, lead a sequence based on isolating specific body parts.

- Have students spread out and take 8 counts for each action: rolling head, lifting and dropping shoulders, swinging arms, and stomping feet.
- Take 16 counts to walk to a new place and repeat the sequence.

Activate Prior Knowledge

"Name something that has repeating lines, shapes, or colors on its surface." "Nombre algo que tenga líneas repetidas, figuras o colores en su superficie".

■ Encourage students to think about things they see on highways, or in a store or a school. Discuss what is repeated.

Using Literature ⭐ Reading

■ Read *This Land Is Your Land* by Woody Guthrie. Ask students to identify patterns they see in the illustrations.

Thematic Connection ⭐ Social Studies

■ **Neighborhoods/Communities:** Discuss the types of buildings that are part of the students' community. Ask students to describe physical characteristics of these buildings and explain how they are used by people.

Introduce the Art

Look

"These artists repeated lines, shapes, and colors to make patterns on the buildings." "Estos artistas repetieron líneas, figuras y colores para hacer patrones en los edificios".

■ Ask students to describe the two buildings in the pictures.

Drawing Conclusions ⭐ Reading

■ How do you think these buildings are used? Possible answer: People might live in the *Victorian House*. People might work in offices in the *Wainwright Building*.

■ Share and discuss information from *Artist Profiles* pages 77–78 with students.

Adjectives and Adverbs ⭐ Language Arts

■ List on a chart the adjectives and adverbs students use to describe the fine art.
National Standards for Arts Education in Visual Arts 4.a

 Art History and Culture

Share information from the Art History and Culture sections with students. Explain that architects design and plan how buildings will look, but many additional people are involved in the actual construction.

💻 **Web Connection**

See what it was like to live in a Victorian house by visiting **www.pbs.org/wnet/1900house/**.

186 UNIT 6 • Principles of Art

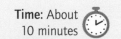
Pattern

◄ **Artist Unknown.** (United States). *Victorian House.* Late 19th century.
Atlanta, Georgia.

Look at these buildings. Artists help create buildings.

 Art History and Culture

These buildings were designed by **architects.** Architects are artists who draw designs for homes and other buildings.

186 Unit 6 • Lesson 1

 Art History and Culture

Victorian Architecture

The Victorian era dates from 1840 to 1900. While architecture from this period was influenced by history and nature, it was also a time of changing technology. Architects had the difficult task of being decorative artists while incorporating the latest technological advancements in their designs.

Victorian houses often served as a status symbol for the owners. Wealthy Victorians spent a large amount of time socializing, and frequently hosting dinner parties that could last for hours, so it was important to them that their house be a showplace of the latest fashion.

See pages 16–21 and 24–25 for more about subject matter and art history.

Artist Profiles, p. 77

┌─ Artist Profile ─┐

Victorian House

This Victorian house was built in Atlanta, Georgia, by an unknown architect and builder. Although the date it was erected is not known, the style and building materials with which it was made indicate that the house was built in the late nineteenth century.

◄ **Artist unknown.** (United States). *Victorian House.* Late nineteenth century.

Louis H. Sullivan.
(United States).
Wainwright Building.
1890–1891.
······························
St. Louis, Missouri.

Study both buildings.

▶ What kinds of lines are repeated?

▶ What kinds of shapes are repeated?

▶ What colors do you see?

Aesthetic Perception

Design Awareness Find lines, shapes, and colors that repeat on your clothes.

Art History and Culture

Wainwright Building

The Wainwright Building was designed by the architectural firm of Adler & Sullivan and was built in St. Louis, Missouri, in 1890–1891. Louis Sullivan was the design partner in the firm. His buildings were known for their beautiful ornamentation. Standing ten stories tall, the Wainwright Building is now shadowed by many taller structures that surround it. However, it is still considered a modern skyscraper because of the technical advances that were used when building it, such as a steel frame to support its height, a ventilation system, and elevators.

See pages 16–21 and 24–25 for more about subject matter and art history.

Artist Profiles, p. 78

Artist Profile

Wainwright Building

The Wainwright Building, located in St. Louis, Missouri, was designed and built by architect Louis H. Sullivan and engineer Dankmar Adler of the architectural firm Adler & Sullivan. Through years of collaboration Adler and Sullivan produced more than 200 buildings. The Wainwright Building was their first attempt at building a multistoried structure. The completion of the building was a major architectural achievement of the late nineteenth century, and Sullivan and Adler received international attention and praise.

◀ **Louis H. Sullivan.** (United States). *Wainwright Building.* 1890–1891.

Study

▶ The *Victorian House* has curved, diagonal, and straight lines that repeat on the blue wood on the front of the house. The *Wainwright Building* has strong vertical lines running down between the columns of windows.

▶ The *Victorian House* has rectangular shingles. The wood trim on the porch has various shapes that repeat, including squares and circles. The *Wainwright Building* has many rectangular windows.

▶ The pink and mauve colors repeat to make a pattern on the *Victorian House*.

■ For more examples of utilitarian art, see **The National Museum of Women in the Arts Collection.**

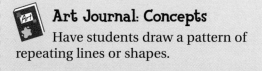

Art Journal: Concepts
Have students draw a pattern of repeating lines or shapes.

Aesthetic Perception

Design Awareness Ask students to find lines, shapes, and colors that repeat on their clothes.

Developing Visual Literacy Ask students if they have ever visited buildings like these. Where were they? How were the buildings used?
NSAE 3.a

Web Connection
To learn more about the Wainwright Building visit http://stlcin.missouri.org/history/structdetail.cfm?Master_ID=1361.

 **Teach**

 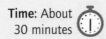

"Let's find patterns inside and outside this room." "Vamos a encontrar patrones adentro y afuera de esta habitación".

Practice

Materials: paper and crayons

- Review geometric shapes. Ask students to draw shapes they remember on their paper.

- Have the students create a pattern on their paper as directed on page 188.

🎨 Creative Expression

Materials: 12" × 18" white drawing paper, crayons

Alternate Materials: any drawing media

- Distribute the materials and have the students follow the directions on page 189.

- Ask students to draw a picture of their home.

- Have students add details to their houses by drawing patterns.

- See the Activity Tips on page 247 for visual examples of this lesson's activity.

- Review the Technique Tips on pages 214–216 for information about drawing.

NSAE 1.a; 1.c

📓 Art Journal: Brainstorming

Encourage students to think about patterns they have seen on houses. Ask students to draw one of these patterns in their Art Journals.

Using Pattern

Repeating lines, shapes, or colors creates **patterns.**

Practice

1. Think about different shapes.

2. Draw a pattern using two different shapes.

Differentiated Instruction

Reteach

Have students look through books and magazines to find plants or animals with patterns, such as the scales on a fish, spots on a leopard, or stripes on a zebra.

Special Needs

To reinforce the concept that shapes form patterns, have pre-cut shapes available that are found in the *Wainwright Building.* Have students place these next to the picture of the building as they identify the shapes.

ELL Tips

Display examples of a shape, a line, and a color pattern. Write the words *shape, line, color,* and *pattern* on cards. As each type of pattern is discussed, introduce the words and have the students say them with you.

▲ Tymber Moss. Age 5.

Think about the patterns you see in the student's drawing.

 **Creative Expression**

Are there any patterns on your home?

1. Draw a picture of your home.
2. Add patterns to your home.

 **Art Criticism**

Analyze Which shapes, lines, or colors did you repeat?

Art Across the Curriculum

Use these simple ideas to reinforce art concepts across the curriculum.

★ **Personal Writing** Have students draw pictures of special buildings they have visited. Ask students to tell the class about these buildings while they share their pictures.

★ **Math** Help students discover that lines, shapes, and colors make patterns in art as well as math. Have students predict what will come next in math patterns.

★ **Science** Study patterns in nature such as the seasons or day and night and predict what will happen next.

★ **Social Studies** Discuss patterns that people follow each day, such as school schedules.

★ **Technology** Use the line and shape tools in a paint program to create patterns. Visit **SRAonline.com** to print detailed instructions for this activity.

Reflect
Time: About 5 minutes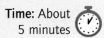

Review and Assess

"Describe a pattern you see." "Describan el patrón que se ve".

Think

Discuss the student art question. The student repeated squares in her picture.

- Identify patterns in **Large Prints 11** *Ceremonial Cloth* and **12** *La Danse*.

Informal Assessment

Art Journal: Critical Thinking
Have students answer the Analyze question by drawing a picture in their Art Journals.

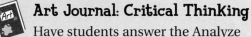 **Art Criticism**

Have students ask themselves the following questions.

Describe ▶ What are you showing in your drawing?

Analyze ▶ Which shapes, lines, or colors did you repeat?

Interpret ▶ Does your pattern remind you of something you have seen before? What was it?

Decide ▶ Do you like how your pattern looks? Why or why not?

NSAE 2.b; 5.a; 5.c

- For standardized-format test practice using this lesson's art content, see pages 66–67 in **Reading and Writing Test Preparation.**

Pattern

Wrap-Up

Extra! For the Art Specialist

Time: About 30 minutes

Focus

Study **Transparency 31** and **Large Prints 11** *Ceremonial Cloth* and **12** *La Danse*. Discuss how the artists used pattern. Ask students to describe the patterns in detail and then invent some new patterns.

Teach

Help students learn about patterns by having them create patterns with beads to make a necklace.

Reflect

Have students use the four steps of art criticism to evaluate their work. Did they effectively create a pattern with the beads?

Alternate Activity

Materials:
- small trays for beads (one per student)
- Pony beads (10–12 per student)
- nylon cording (20" per student)

1. Give each student a tray of beads.

2. Direct them to select 2 or 3 different colors and make a pattern.

3. Have students string the beads on a nylon cord.

4. Help students tie the ends of the cord together to make a necklace.

NSAE 1.c

Research
in Art Education

An ideal arts curriculum would be "one that offers in-depth, carefully sequenced teaching in several art forms for the entire span of young peoples' schooling." It is also beneficial to have extended times of learning in which students may visit museums and concert halls ("Learning in and Through the Arts: Curriculum Implications" in *Champions of Change*, p. 44).

Assessment
Use the following rubric to evaluate the artwork students make in the Creative Expression activity and to assess students' understanding of pattern.

Have students complete page 69 or 70 in their *Assessment* books.

	Art History and Culture	Aesthetic Perception	Creative Expression	Art Criticism
3 POINTS	The student recognizes that architects are artists who draw designs for homes and other buildings.	The student locates patterns in fine art and in his or her environment.	The student's drawing clearly illustrates use of patterns.	The student thoughtfully and honestly evaluates his or her own work using the four steps of art criticism.
2 POINTS	The student shows emerging awareness that architects are artists who draw designs for homes and other buildings.	The student can sometimes locate patterns in fine art and in his or her environment.	The student's drawing shows some use of patterns.	The student attempts to evaluate his or her own work, but shows an incomplete understanding of evaluation criteria.
1 POINT	The student does not recognize that architects are artists who draw designs for homes and other buildings.	The student cannot locate patterns in fine art or in his or her environment	The student's drawing shows no use of patterns.	The student makes no attempt to evaluate his or her own artwork.

Assessment, p. 69

Name _____ Date _____

Lesson 1 UNIT 6

Pattern

For the teacher: Use the following prompt for this activity.
1. Using crayons, draw a repeating pattern with two or three shapes.

Level K   Unit 6 • Principles of Art   **69**

Rhythm and Movement

Lesson 2 introduces rhythm and visual movement, which are created by the repetition of elements or objects that move the eye through a work of art.

Objectives

 Art History and Culture

To identify how Jack Savitsky and Currier and Ives showed rhythm and movement in their art about trains

 Creative Expression

To create a drawing that shows rhythm and movement

 Aesthetic Perception

To explain how rhythm creates the look of movement

 Art Criticism

To evaluate one's own work using the four steps of art criticism

Vocabulary Reading

Review the following vocabulary words with students before beginning the lesson.

rhythm ritmo—the repetition of lines, shapes, and/or colors to create a feeling of movement

movement movimiento—the look of constant motion in a work of art

See page 209B for additional vocabulary and Spanish vocabulary resources.

 Art Journal: Vocabulary

Have students add these words to the Vocabulary section of their Art Journals.

Lesson Materials

- 12" × 18" colored drawing paper
- oil pastels

Alternate Materials

- any drawing media

Program Resources

- *Reading and Writing Test Prep.*, pp. 68–69
- *Transparency 32*
- *Flash Cards 9–11*
- *Artist Profiles*, pp. 8, 37
- *Assessment*, pp. 71–72
- *Large Prints 11 Ceremonial Cloth* and *12 La Danse*
- *Art Around the World Collection*

Concept Trace
Rhythm and Movement
Introduced: Level K, Unit 6, Lesson 2

Reinforced: Level 1, Unit 5, Lesson 6

Lesson 2 Arts Integration

Theatre

Complete Unit 6, Lesson 2, on pages 110–111 of the *Theatre Arts Connections* book.

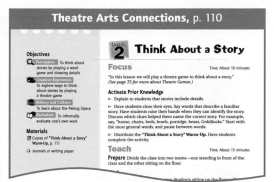

Music

Listen to "Gallop" from *Masquerade Suite*. Before telling the students the title, ask them if swaying, marching, skipping, galloping, or jogging would fit. Have students gallop to the music.

Movement & Dance

Have students identify rhyming words and create movements to interpret those words. For example: hop, pop, drop, stop. Then put two sets of contrasting rhyming words together, such as fast, blast; jiggle, wiggle.

Focus

Time: About 10 minutes

Activate Prior Knowledge

"Make the sound you hear as a train rides on railroad tracks." "Describan el sonido repetido que oyen cuando un tren va sobre los rieles".

■ Encourage students to act out the sound and movement of a railroad train. If necessary, suggest the words "clickety-clack, clickety-clack, clickety-clack." Explain that this repeating sound creates a rhythm and feeling of movement.

Using Literature ★ Reading

■ Read *Tacky the Penguin* by Helen Lester. Ask students to describe examples of rhythm and movement in the illustrations.

Thematic Connection ★ Social Studies

■ **Transportation:** Discuss the types of transportation that students have seen and used. How could we show rhythm and movement when drawing them?

NSAE 3.a; 3.b

Introduce the Art

Look

"These artists repeated lines, shapes, and colors to create a rhythm and feeling of movement." "Estos artistas repetieron líneas, figuras y colores para crear un ritmo y sentido de movimiento".

■ Ask students to describe what they see in each picture.

■ Have students point to shapes that they see repeated.

■ Share and discuss information from *Artist Profiles* pages 8 and 37 with students.

Adjectives and Adverbs ★ Language Arts

■ List on a chart the adjectives and adverbs students use to describe the fine art.

NSAE 4.a

Art History and Culture

Share information from the Art History and Culture sections with students. Encourage students to think about traveling by train. Discuss how this would be different from how they travel today. Would they like it better? Why or why not?

 Web Connection

To learn more about American folk art visit www.folkartmuseum.org/.

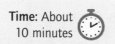

Rhythm and Movement

▲ **Jack Savitsky.** (American). *Train in Coal Town.* 1968.
Oil on fiberboard. 31¼ × 47¾ inches (79.38 × 121.29 cm). Smithsonian American Art Museum, Washington, D.C.

Look at the trains. They look like they are moving.

 ## Art History and Culture

Art can help us learn about life a long time ago. These pictures show us a time when many people used to travel by train.

Art History and Culture

Jack Savitsky

Jack Savitsky (jak sa vit´ skē) (1910–1991) worked in Pennsylvania's coal mines for almost forty years before he was forced to retire in 1959. He dabbled in painting for much of his life, creating signs and murals for businesses. When Savitsky could no longer work in the mines, he returned to painting as a hobby. This painting depicts a coal-fired passenger train bringing miners from Pottsville to the mines of Silver Creek, a mining town where Savitsky grew up and worked. In the distance, a gray building that houses the coal breaker can be seen as well as the company-built employee houses.

See pages 16–21 and 24–25 for more about subject matter and art history.

Artist Profiles, p. 37

▶ Artist Profile ◀

Jack Savitsky
1910–1991

Folk artist Jack Savitsky (jak sa vit´ skē) was born and lived his entire life in the coal-mining region of northeastern Pennsylvania. He began drawing as a boy, and although he never had formal art lessons, his art is in many well-known galleries, collections, and museums. Savitsky left school after sixth grade and went to work in the coal mines, where he was employed for 40 years. Sometimes he even painted on the walls of mines and the sides of mine cars. At other times he painted pictures in exchange for a meal or a couple of gallons of gas. Considered to be one of America's best self-taught painters, "Coal Miner Jack" participated in numerous exhibitions, and his paintings gave a view of the lives of his

▲ **Currier and Ives.** (American).
American Express Train. 1864.
16 × 24⅞ inches (40.64 × 63.20 cm.).
Museum of the City of New York.
New York, New York.

Study both train pictures.

▶ What shapes did the
artists repeat?

Aesthetic Perception

Seeing Like an Artist What shapes would you
repeat to show a car or a boat moving?

Study

▶ In *Train in Coal Town* repetition can be
found in the following: rectangular
windows on the train, circular wheels,
rectangles on the railroad tracks, the
house shapes, and the smoke shapes.

▶ In *American Express Train* repetition can
be found in the following: rectangles on
the railroad tracks, the smoke shapes,
circular wheels, rectangular windows on
the train, and the rectangular shape of the
train cars.

■ For more examples of art from North
America, see the *Art Around the World
Collection.*

Art Journal: Concepts
Have students draw a pattern of
repeating circles to create a sense of
rhythm and movement.

Aesthetic Perception

Seeing Like an Artist Ask students what
shapes they would repeat to show a car or
boat moving.

Developing Visual Literacy Ask students if
they have ever been on a train. Where did
they go? Did they enjoy the ride? Why or why
not?
NSAE 4.a

Art History and Culture

Currier and Ives

The firm of Currier and Ives was in operation as a lithography shop
from 1834–1907. Numerous employees, including artists, colorists,
lithographers, and stone grinders, worked together to produce
more than a million prints of more than 7500 different titles. The
prints were popular in part because of their inexpensive price, but
also because of the variety of subject matter. Prints were available
in nearly any category the public might desire, including sports,
humor, hunting, religion, politics and disaster scenes.

See pages 16–21 and 24–25
for more about subject
matter and art history.

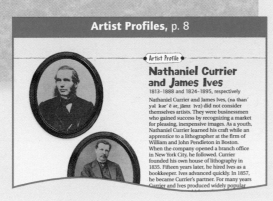

Artist Profiles, p. 8

◆ Artist Profile ◆
**Nathaniel Currier
and James Ives**
1813–1888 and 1824–1895, respectively
Nathaniel Currier and James Ives, (na than´
yal kar´ē ər, jāmz īvz) did not consider
themselves artists. They were businessmen
who gained success by recognizing a market
for pleasing, inexpensive images. As a youth,
Nathaniel Currier learned his craft while an
apprentice to a lithographer at the firm of
William and John Pendleton in Boston.
When the company opened a branch office
in New York City, he followed. Currier
founded his own house of lithography in
1835. Fifteen years later, he hired Ives as a
bookkeeper. Ives advanced quickly. In 1857,
he became Currier's partner. For many years
Currier and Ives produced widely popular

Web Connection
To learn more about printmaking, visit
www.moma.org/whatisaprint/flash.html.

Teach

Time: About 30 minutes

"Let's role-play again the movement and rhythm of a train." "Vamos a representar nuevamente el movimiento y el ritmo de un tren".

Practice

- Have students turn their arms like a train's wheels moving along a track as directed on page 192.

Creative Expression

Materials: 12" × 18" drawing paper (various colors), oil pastels

Alternate Materials: any drawing media

- Distribute the materials and have the students follow the directions on page 193.

- Have students begin drawing their train tracks by drawing two parallel lines that wander around their paper. Then have them add the ties to hold the tracks together. The repetition of the tracks will create visual rhythm and visual movement on the paper.

- Then have students draw a train on their tracks.

- See the Activity Tips on page 247 for visual examples of this lesson's activity.

- Review the Technique Tips on page 216 for information about using oil pastels.

NSAE 1.a; 1.c

Art Journal: Brainstorming

Discuss the parts of a train. Have students draw these parts in their Art Journals.

Using Rhythm and Movement

Repeated shapes will create a sense of **rhythm** and **movement.**

Practice

1. Think about a train's wheels.
2. Move your arms like a train's wheels moving on a track.

Differentiated Instruction

Reteach
Have students raise their hands in succession. Reinforce the idea that their eyes are forced to move in order to follow the rhythm of the hands.

Special Needs
Lesson material, when presented in a variety of ways, is more likely to be retained by students. The use of comic strips that show movement may provide an additional means of reinforcing the concepts of this lesson.

ELL Tips
Draw a simple picture of a car, a boat, and a train. Add dashed lines for the car, waves for the boat, and railroad tracks for the train. Explain that the repeating dashed lines, waves, and tracks create a rhythm and feeling of movement.

▲ **Kyle Farren.** Age 5.

Think about the rhythm you see in the student's drawing. How did the student make the trains look like they are moving?

 Creative Expression

How can you show movement in your drawing?

1. Draw train tracks on your paper.
2. Draw a train on your tracks.

 **Art Criticism**

Decide Does your train create a sense of rhythm and movement? Is there anything else you might add to show more movement?

Art Across the Curriculum

Use these simple ideas to reinforce art concepts across the curriculum.

★ **Descriptive Writing** Help students compile a list of words that describe how a train sounds when it is moving, such as clickety-clack or chugga chugga. Stand in a line to form a train of people and repeat the words together as you move around the room.

★ **Math** Look at how Savitsky painted houses in a row. Count the houses out loud.

★ **Science** Study how people use heat from a fire, such as the train engines in the fine art.

★ **Social Studies** Discuss how machines, like a train, can help us travel to places too far to walk.

★ **Technology** Use a paint program to draw a train that looks like it is moving. Visit **SRAonline.com** to print detailed instructions for this activity.

 **R**eflect Time: About 5 minutes

Review and Assess

"How do you create a sense of rhythm and movement in an artwork?" "¿Cómo crean una sensación de ritmo y movimiento en una obra de arte?"

Think

Discuss the student art question. The student repeated lines on the train track and circles for the wheels. The curved line of the smoke also gives the feeling of movement.

■ Identify patterns in *Large Prints 11 Ceremonial Cloth* and *12 La Danse.*

Informal Assessment

Art Journal: Critical Thinking
Have students answer the Decide question by drawing a picture in their Art Journals.

 **Art Criticism**

Have students ask themselves the following questions.

Describe ▸ What shapes, colors, and lines did you use for your train?

Analyze ▸ What shapes, colors, and lines did you repeat to show a feeling of movement?

Interpret ▸ Where is your train going? Is it going fast or slow?

Decide ▸ Does your train create a sense of rhythm and movement? Is there anything else you might add to show more movement?

NSAE 2.b; 5.a; 5.c

■ For standardized-format test practice using this lesson's art content, see pages 68–69 in *Reading and Writing Test Preparation.*

Rhythm and Movement

 Extra! For the Art Specialist

Time: About 30 minutes

Focus

Study *Transparency 32* and *Large Prints 11 Ceremonial Cloth* and *12 La Danse*. Discuss how the artists used rhythm. How does the use of rhythm create movement? Trace the movement across the work of art with your finger.

Teach

Help students learn about rhythm and movement by printing a repeated shape design.

Reflect

Have students use the four steps of art criticism to evaluate their work. Did they effectively show rhythm and movement in their repeated shape designs?

Alternate Activity

Materials:
- 9" × 18" paper in assorted colors
- shaped sponges
- tempera paint

1. Play a selection of music that has a steady beat. Tell students that the beat of the music creates a rhythm. When shapes or colors are repeated in a work of art it also creates a rhythm.

2. Direct the students to select a shaped sponge.

3. Have students use one color to print the shape in a straight line across their papers.

4. Then have students continue printing shapes in lines across the paper until they fill the paper.

NSAE 1.c

Research in Art Education

"I argue that many of the most complex and subtle forms of thinking take place when students have an opportunity either to work meaningfully on the creation of images— whether visual, choreographic, musical, literary, or poetic— or to scrutinize them appreciatively" (Eisner, Elliot W. *The Arts and the Creation of Mind*. New Haven: Yale Univ. Press, 2002).

Assessment

Use the following rubric to evaluate the artwork students make in the Creative Expression activity and to assess students' understanding of rhythm and movement.

Have students complete page 71 or 72 in their *Assessment* books.

	Art History and Culture	Aesthetic Perception	Creative Expression	Art Criticism
3 POINTS	The student identifies how Savitsky and Currier and Ives showed rhythm and movement in the fine art in this lesson.	The student can explain how rhythm creates the look of movement.	The student's drawing clearly illustrates rhythm and movement.	The student thoughtfully and honestly evaluates his or her own work using the four steps of art criticism.
2 POINTS	The student shows emerging awareness of how Savitsky and Currier and Ives showed rhythm and movement in the fine art in this lesson.	The student can give some explanation of how rhythm creates the look of movement.	The student's drawing shows some rhythm and movement.	The student attempts to evaluate his or her own work, but shows an incomplete understanding of evaluation criteria.
1 POINT	The student cannot identify how Savitsky or Currier and Ives showed rhythm and movement in the fine art in this lesson.	The student cannot explain how rhythm creates the look of movement.	The student's drawing shows no rhythm or movement.	The student makes no attempt to evaluate his or her own artwork.

Assessment, p. 71

Name _____ Date _____ Lesson 2 UNIT 6

Rhythm and Movement

| 1 | 2 |

For the teacher: Use the following prompts for this activity.
1. Using crayons, draw circles in box 1 that show quick movement.
2. Draw circles in box 2 that show slow movement.

Level K   Unit 6 • Principals of Art **71**

Balance

Lesson 3 introduces balance. Balance refers to two sides of an artwork having the same shapes, colors, or patterns. If an artwork is divided in half and both halves are exactly the same, we say they are equal in balance, or have even balance. Balance in animals is introduced in this lesson.

Objectives

 Art History and Culture

To recognize that artists from different cultures use even balance in their designs

 Creative Expression

To create a design with even balance

Aesthetic Perception

To locate even balance in an object and verbally describe how the object is balanced

Art Criticism

To evaluate one's own work using the four steps of art criticism

Vocabulary ⭐ Reading

Review the following vocabulary word with students before beginning the lesson.

even balance equilibrio simétrico—both halves are equal. The left side and right side are the same.

See page 209B for additional vocabulary and Spanish vocabulary resources.

 Art Journal: Vocabulary

Have students add this word to the Vocabulary section of their Art Journals.

Lesson Materials

- 9" × 12" colored construction paper
- scissors

Alternate Materials
- a variety of papers such as wallpaper or giftwrap

Program Resources

- *Reading and Writing Test Prep.*, pp. 70–71
- *Transparency 33*
- *Flash Cards 12, 14*
- *Artist Profiles,* pp. 56, 62
- *Animals Through History Time Line*
- *Assessment,* pp. 73–74
- *Large Prints 11* Ceremonial Cloth and 12 La Danse
- *The National Museum of Women in the Arts Collection*

Concept Trace

Balance

Introduced: Level K, Unit 6, Lesson 3

Reinforced: Level 1, Unit 6, Lesson 1
Level 1, Unit 6, Lesson 2

Lesson 3 Arts Integration

Theatre

Complete Unit 6, Lesson 3, on pages 112–113 of the *Theatre Arts Connections* book.

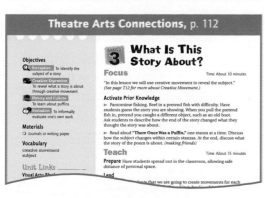

Theatre Arts Connections, p. 112

Music

 Balance in music happens when you can hear all parts evenly. If someone sings loudly so another person's soft voice cannot be heard, the balance is off. Drums have to be careful not to drown out the smaller instruments. Listen to *Symphony No. 73 in D major, Movement 4* "La Chasse" by Franz Joseph Haydn. Is any part overly exaggerated?

Movement & Dance

Explore ways to balance on different parts of the body. Balance on tip toes. Balance standing on one leg. Sit down, tilt your body to one side, and balance on one hip. What professions require good balance? Possible answers: Firefighter, tightrope walker, gymnast, dancer, and construction worker.

Focus

Time: About 10 minutes

Activate Prior Knowledge

"Imagine a line down the middle of a duck. What parts of the duck are the same on each half?" "Imaginense una línea por la mitad de un pato. ¿Qué partes del pato son iguales en cada mitad?"

- Display the *Animals Through History Time Line* and encourage students to describe what makes other animals evenly balanced.

Using Literature ⭐ Reading

- Read *Tippy Bear Hunts for Honey* by Coby Hol. Ask students to identify examples of even balance in the illustrations.

Thematic Connection ⭐ Science

- **Dinosaurs:** While studying dinosaurs discuss how each dinosaur has even balance. Which body parts are the same on each half?

Introduce the Art

Look

"Ducks and other animals are balanced." "Los patos y otros animales están equilibrados".

- Explain that one half of the animal has the same parts as the other half. This is called *even balance*. People and some objects have even balance too.

Main Idea and Details ⭐ Reading

- Have students first study *Butterfly* and describe what they see.

Drawing Conclusions ⭐ Reading

- Then have students imagine folding the image in half vertically. Ask students to study the left and right sides of the image. Does it have balance?

- Have students repeat this procedure with *Button Robe–Orca Whale Design*.

NSAE 4.a

🏺 Art History and Culture

Share information from the Art History and Culture sections with students. Designs like *Butterfly* are created with simple tools, such as a knife or scissors and paper. This old art form is still one of the most popular arts of Chinese village people today.

💻 Web Connection

To learn more about Chinese paper cutting, visit **www.travelchinaguide.com/intro/arts/paper_cut. htm.**

Balance

Look at the butterfly. One half looks the same as the other half.

▲ **Artist Unknown.** (China). *Butterfly.* c. 1950.
Cut paper. $8\frac{1}{2} \times 15\frac{1}{8}$ inches (21.59 × 38.41 cm.). Museum of International Folk Art, Santa Fe, New Mexico.

🏺 Art History and Culture

Artists have been making cut paper designs in many countries for many years. The designs are often used as decorations for celebrations.

🏺 Art History and Culture

Chinese Paper Cutting

The origins of paper cutting as a craft lie deep in history. Paper was invented during the Han dynasty in China (206 B.C.–A.D. 220). Very few examples of early paper cutting exist. Those that have survived suggest that the craft was developed concurrently with the invention of paper. Some of the earliest examples of paper cutting were found in a tomb near Turfan.

See pages 16–21 and 24–25 for more about subject matter and art history.

Artist Profiles, p. 62

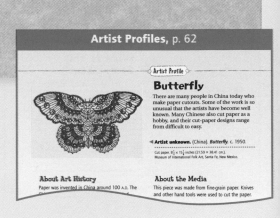

🖎 Artist Profile

Butterfly

There are many people in China today who make paper cutouts. Some of the work is so unusual that the artists have become well known. Many Chinese also cut paper as a hobby, and their cut-paper designs range from difficult to easy.

◄ **Artist unknown.** (China). *Butterfly.* c. 1950.
Cut paper. $8\frac{1}{2} \times 15\frac{1}{8}$ inches (21.59 × 38.41 cm.).
Museum of International Folk Art, Santa Fe, New Mexico.

About Art History
Paper was invented in China around 100 A.D. The

About the Media
This piece was made from fine-grain paper. Knives and other hand tools were used to cut the paper.

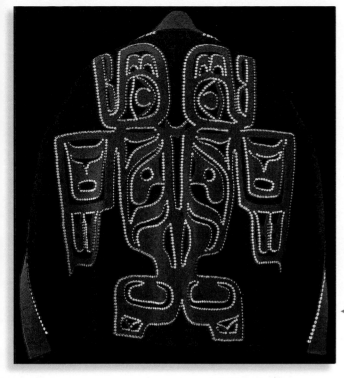

◀ **John Yeiltatzie.** (Haida).
***Button Robe–Orca Whale
Design.*** c. 1890.
....
54 × 70 inches (137.16 × 177.8 cm.).
Seattle Art Museum, Seattle, Washington.

Study both pictures.

▶ Describe the parts of the butterfly that
are the same on each half.

▶ Describe the parts of the whale design
that are the same on each half.

 Aesthetic Perception

Seeing Like an Artist What other animals can
you name that have even balance?

Art History and Culture

John Yeiltatzie

John Yeiltatzie (jän yēl tat′ shē) (c. 1850) was a Kaigani Haida artist
during the late 1800s and early 1900s. Kaigani Haida is a Native
American group from British Columbia on the northwest Canadian
coast. Today Haida artists receive commissions from around the
world. Many are represented in national and international
museums and in collections such as the Hauberg Collection at the
Seattle Art Museum.

See pages 16–21 and 24–25
for more about subject
matter and art history.

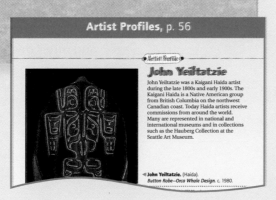

Artist Profiles, p. 56

Study

Ask students to point to and describe the
parts that are the same on each half of the
butterfly and then whale design.

▶ In *Butterfly* the size of each half of the
butterfly is the same. The wing shapes,
patterns, and lines on each half are the
same.

▶ In *Button Robe–Orca Whale Design* the
patterns, shapes, and lines are the same
on each half. The size of the shapes is the
same on each half.

■ For more examples of utilitarian art, see
***The National Museum of Women in the
Arts Collection.***

Art Journal: Concepts
Have students draw a picture of an
insect that has even balance.

Aesthetic Perception

Seeing Like an Artist Ask students to name
animals that have even balance.

Developing Visual Literacy Have students
look around them to find objects that have
even balance. Does everything have even
balance?   NSAE 3.a; 3.b

Web Connection
To learn more the Haida people, visit
www.tlingit-haida.org/.

Teach

Time: About 30 minutes

"Let's move like an animal and identify the animal parts that create even balance."

"Vamos a movernos como un animal e identificar las partes del animal que crean equilibrio simétrico".

Practice

- Have students stand in an open space and flap their arms like wings. (See student page 196.)

- Identify the body parts that give birds even balance. You may wish to display a picture of a bird or draw one on the board.

Creative Expression

Materials: 9" × 12" construction paper (various colors), scissors

Alternate Materials: a variety of papers like wallpaper or giftwrap

- Distribute the materials and have the students follow the directions on page 197.

- Show students how to fold their paper in half vertically.

- See the Activity Tips on page 248 for visual examples of this lesson's activity.

- Review the Technique Tips on page 221 for information on using scissors.

- Have students cut shapes into the unfolded edge of their paper to create a balanced design.

NSAE 1.c

Art Journal: Brainstorming

Ask students to think about shapes they would like to use in their designs. Have students draw these shapes in their Art Journals.

Using Balance

An animal has **even balance.** The left half and the right half of an animal are the same.

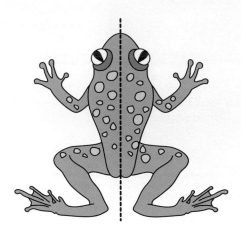

Practice

1. Pretend you are a bird.
2. Move your arms like a bird's wings flapping.
3. What body parts give the bird balance?

Differentiated Instruction

Reteach
Use animal toys or dolls to demonstrate even balance to students.

Special Needs
Many students with disabilities excel in creative activity. Provide a challenging and age-appropriate extension for this lesson by asking students to transform their cut-out into a fantasy animal, complete with colors and other details.

ELL Tips
Display pictures of animals, people, and objects that are facing frontward. Draw a line down the middle of each one. On cards write *left half, right half,* and *even balance.* Use the cards as you point out the features on each half of an image and discuss how each opposite half has the same features.

◄ **Rachel Perkins.** Age 5.

Think about the balance you
see in the student's design.

 **Creative Expression**

How can you make a balanced
design with paper and scissors?

1. Fold your paper in half the
   long way.
2. Cut shapes into the unfolded
   edge.

 **Art Criticism**

Analyze Does your
design have balance?
Why or why not?

Art Across the Curriculum

Use these simple ideas to reinforce art concepts across the curriculum.

★ **Narrative Writing** Write a story together about the *Button Robe–Orca Whale Design* and who wore it. Have students draw a picture of the person wearing the robe, showing even balance.

★ **Math** Draw a line down the middle of shapes, noting how an imaginary line was drawn down the middle of the butterfly and robe in the lesson. Look for even balance in the shapes.

★ **Science** Help students record observations about parts of animals including wings, feet, heads, and tails. Identify examples of even balance on animals and name the parts that create the balance.

★ **Social Studies** Study pictures of numerous butterflies. Have students vote for their favorite butterfly and then determine which butterfly the class likes best.

★ **Technology** Use a paint program to draw an insect that has even balance. Visit **SRAonline.com** to print detailed instructions for this activity.

 **Time:** About 5 minutes

Review and Assess

"What is even balance?" "¿Qué es equilibrio simétrico?"

Think

Discuss the student art question. The shapes are the same on each half of the design.

■ Identify even balance in *Large Prints 11 Ceremonial Cloth* and *12 La Danse.*

Informal Assessment

Art Journal: Critical Thinking
Write *Yes* and *No* on the board. Have students answer the Analyze question by writing *Yes* or *No* in their Art Journals. Then discuss *why* or *why not* out loud.

 **Art Criticism**

Have students ask themselves the following questions.

Describe ► What shapes did you cut into your design?

Analyze ► Does your design have balance? Why or why not?

Interpret ► How could you use your cut paper design?

Decide ► Is there anything you would like to add to your paper design?

NSAE 2.b; 5.a; 5.c

■ For standardized-format test practice using this lesson's art content, see pages 70–71 in *Reading and Writing Test Preparation.*

Lesson 3 Wrap-Up
Balance

Extra! For the Art Specialist

Time: About 30 minutes

Focus

Study **Transparency 33** and **Large Prints 11** *Ceremonial Cloth* and **12** *La Danse*. Discuss how the artists used balance. How do the works of art make you feel when you look at them? Are they calm and relaxed? Explain.

Teach

Help students learn about balance by creating a butterfly design.

Reflect

Have students use the four steps of art criticism to evaluate their work. Did they effectively show even balance in their butterfly design?

Alternate Activity

Materials:
- 9" × 12" white drawing paper
- crayons
- scissors
- pencils
- watercolors

1. Have students create a design using a butterfly shape. Start by having students fold a piece of construction paper in half.

2. Next have students draw a wing shape on one side of the paper starting and ending on the folded line.

3. Then have students cut the wing shape and open the paper.

4. Have students draw matching shapes on both sides of the wings and then use crayons to color the shapes.

5. When finished students can paint over their drawings with watercolors.

NSAE 1.a; 1.c

Research in Art Education

Artistically talented students engage in more self-regulatory behavior in classes with arts integration than in classes without arts integration ("Using Art Processes to Enhance Academic Self-Regulation" in *Critical Links*, p. 64). These self-regulatory behaviors included paying attention, problem solving, asking questions, taking risks and being prepared.

Assessment

Use the following rubric to evaluate the artwork students make in the Creative Expression activity and to assess students' understanding of balance.

Have students complete page 73 or 74 in their **Assessment** books.

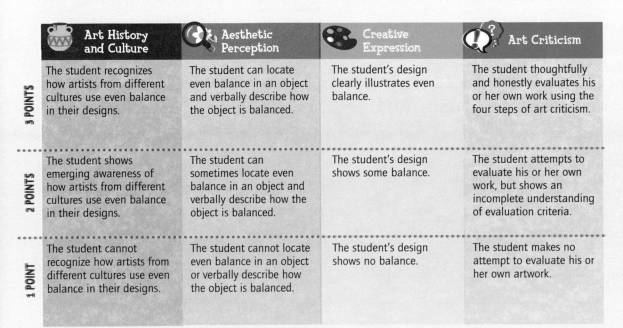

	Art History and Culture	Aesthetic Perception	Creative Expression	Art Criticism
3 POINTS	The student recognizes how artists from different cultures use even balance in their designs.	The student can locate even balance in an object and verbally describe how the object is balanced.	The student's design clearly illustrates even balance.	The student thoughtfully and honestly evaluates his or her own work using the four steps of art criticism.
2 POINTS	The student shows emerging awareness of how artists from different cultures use even balance in their designs.	The student can sometimes locate even balance in an object and verbally describe how the object is balanced.	The student's design shows some balance.	The student attempts to evaluate his or her own work, but shows an incomplete understanding of evaluation criteria.
1 POINT	The student cannot recognize how artists from different cultures use even balance in their designs.	The student cannot locate even balance in an object or verbally describe how the object is balanced.	The student's design shows no balance.	The student makes no attempt to evaluate his or her own artwork.

Assessment, p. 73

Name _____ Date _____

Balance

Lesson 3 UNIT 6

1

2

For the teacher: Use the following prompts for this activity.
1. Using crayons, draw a shape in box 1.
2. Draw the same shape in box 2 to create balance.
3. Repeat this activity with a different set of shapes.

Level K

Unit 6 • Principals of Art   73

Balance in Sculpture

Lesson 4 introduces balance in sculpture. Sculptures can be symmetrical or very similar on opposite sides of an imaginary, central dividing line.

Objectives

 Art History and Culture

To recognize that artists from different cultures use balance in their sculptures

 Creative Expression

To create a house post that has balance

 Aesthetic Perception

To recognize that sculptures have balance when both halves are the same

 Art Criticism

To evaluate one's own work using the four steps of art criticism

Vocabulary Reading

Review the following vocabulary word with students before beginning the lesson.

even balance **equilibrio simétrico**—both halves are equal. The left side and right side are the same.

See page 209B for additional vocabulary and Spanish vocabulary resources.

 ### Art Journal: Vocabulary

Have students add this word to the Vocabulary section of their Art Journals.

Lesson Materials

- cardboard tubes (paper towel or toilet paper rolls, or roll and staple 10" square pieces of posterboard)
- markers
- construction paper scraps
- scissors
- glue

Alternate Materials

- 9" × 12" construction paper for rolling into a tube
- glue or tape for holding tube closed

Program Resources

- *Reading and Writing Test Prep.*, pp. 72–73
- *Transparency 34*
- *Flash Card 12*
- *Artist Profiles*, pp. 71, 74
- *Assessment*, pp. 75–76
- *Large Print 12* La Danse
- *Art Around the World Collection*

Concept Trace

Balance in Sculpture

Introduced: Level K, Unit 6, Lesson 4

Reinforced: Level 1, Unit 6, Lesson 2

Lesson 4 Arts Integration

Theatre

Complete Unit 6, Lesson 4, on pages 114–115 of the *Theatre Arts Connections* book.

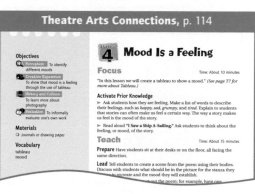

Theatre Arts Connections, p. 114

Music

Balance in the form of a composition is most readily apparent in the ABA form. Listen to "Minuet" from *Eine Keine Nachtmusic* by Wolfgang Amadeus Mozart. Have students raise their hands when they hear the entrance of the B section and then again at the return of A.

Movement & Dance

The human body is like a living, breathing sculpture. It can take many different postures and do many actions. Ask students to create a sculpture that opens upward and outward with their bodies. Then ask them to create a sculpture that is closed inward. Try another that reaches out into the space. Ask students to describe how their balance changes when going from one type of sculpture to another.

Focus

Time: About 10 minutes

Activate Prior Knowledge

"Do all objects look the same on both halves?" "¿Parecen igual todos los objetos en ambas mitades?"

- Show the students two forms, one that is symmetrical and one that is not (perhaps a water pitcher and a sugar bowl).

- Help students conclude that some objects have balance and some do not.

Using Literature ⭐ Reading

- Read *Babar's Museum of Art* by Laurent de Brunhoff. Ask students to identify examples of balance in sculpture in the illustrations.

Thematic Connection ⭐ Social Studies

- **America:** Show students pictures of famous sculptures in America such as the Statue of Liberty and Lincoln Memorial. Discuss whether these sculptures have balance.

Introduce the Art

Look

"Let's look closely at these sculptures." "Vamos a observar detalladamente estas esculturas".

- Ask students to study the sculptures and describe what they see.

Drawing Conclusions ⭐ Reading

- Explain to students that long ago these works of art were used by people. Ask students how they think these items might have been used.

Adjectives and Adverbs ⭐ Language Arts

- List on a chart the adjectives and adverbs students use to describe the fine art.

NSAE 4.a

🏺 Art History and Culture

Share information from the Art History and Culture sections with students. Explain to students that when visitors would come to a house the owner of the house would tell his guests what the various carvings on the post represented.

💻 Web Connection

Visit the Smithsonian Arthur M. Sackler Gallery online at **www.asia.si.edu/collections/chineseHome.htm** to learn more about Chinese art.

Balance in Sculpture

Look at these sculptures. Do they have balance?

◀ **Artist Unknown.** (China). *Ritual Bell.* 12th century B.C.
Bronze. 12 7/16 × 9 3/4 × 6 inches (30.96 × 24.77 × 15.24 cm.). Arthur M. Sackler Gallery, Smithsonian Institution, Washington, D.C.

🏺 Art History and Culture

House posts like the one on the next page are carved by the owner of the house. The pictures on the post tell a story about the family who lives in the house.

🏺 Art History and Culture

Ritual Bell

The *Ritual Bell* was made in China in the twelfth century, B.C., by an unknown artist of the Shang Dynasty. The Shang Dynasty is considered by some historians to have been the beginning of Chinese history. The *Ritual Bell* is a large, heavy, spectacularly adorned bell used for ceremonial purposes. Objects such as the *Ritual Bell* have been found among the treasures buried in the tombs of Shang kings.

See pages 16–21 and 24–25 for more about subject matter and art history.

Study both pictures.

► Describe the parts of the bell that are the same on each half.

► Describe the parts of the house post that are the same on each half.

◄ **Artist Unknown.** (North America). *House Post.* 19th century.
....
111½ × 38³⁄₁₆ inches (283.21 × 97 cm.). Seattle Art Museum, Seattle, Washington.

 Aesthetic Perception

Design Awareness Look around you. What forms do you see that have balance?

Art History and Culture

House Post

House Post was made by an unidentified artist of the Bella Bella people of British Columbia, Canada, probably sometime during the nineteenth century. The Bella Bella people are a subgroup of the Kwakiutl peoples of the northwestern coastal region of North America. Posts like this one are the most historically important art forms to the Kwakiutl and other northwestern coastal peoples in North America. *House Post* shows a large image of some sort of supernatural bird, possibly a thunderbird from Kwakiutl mythology.

See pages 16–21 and 24–25 for more about subject matter and art history.

Artist Profiles, p. 71

> **Artist Profile**
> **House Post**
> An unidentified artist of the Bella Bella people of British Columbia, Canada, made this house post. The Bella Bella people are a subgroup of the Kwakiutl of the northwestern coastal region of North America. The term *Kwakiutl* refers collectively to approximately 5,500 tribes of the Canadian First Nations. This house post was made sometime during the nineteenth century.
>
> ◄ **Artist unknown.** (Canada).

Study

► *Ritual Bell* is symmetrical. The shapes, patterns, and lines on each half are the same.

► *House Post* also has the same patterns, shapes, and lines on each half. Features like eyes, ears, arms, and legs are the same on each half.

■ For more examples of art from Asia, see the *Art Around the World Collection.*

Art Journal: Concepts
Have students draw a picture of a totem pole that has even balance.

Aesthetic Perception

Design Awareness Ask students to look around them and name forms they see that have even balance.

Developing Visual Literacy Have students study *House Post.* Ask students to explain who they think the two characters are on the post and why the artist chose to show them. NSAE 3.a; 5.a; 5.c

Web Connection
Visit the Seattle Art Museum at www.seattleartmuseum.org/.

Teach

Time: About 30 minutes

"Let's try to create a live sculpture." "*Vamos a tratar de crear una escultura en vivo*".

Practice

- Organize students into groups of five. (See *Student Edition* page 200.)

- Ask each group to try to create a balanced live sculpture. Let each group show its symmetrical pose to the class.

Creative Expression

Materials: cardboard tubes, markers, construction paper scraps, scissors, glue

Alternate Materials: 9" × 12" construction paper for rolling into a tube, glue or tape for holding tube closed

- Distribute the materials and have the students follow the directions on page 201.

- Direct students to cut shapes for the face, arms, and legs of the house post creature.

- Have students arrange and glue these parts on the cardboard tube so that they are balanced.

- Students can use markers to add more color and detail to their house posts.

- See the Activity Tips on page 248 for visual examples of this lesson's activity.

- Review the Technique Tips on page 222 for tips on using glue.

- Have students exhibit their work and express ideas about each other's work.

NSAE 1.a; 1.c; 5.a; 5.c

Art Journal: Brainstorming

Ask students to think about what kind of house post they would like outside their house. What kind of eyes, ears, and mouth would it have? How many limbs will it have? Have students draw these shapes in their Art Journals.

Using Balance

Sculptures can have **balance**. Sometimes parts on the left half and the right half are the same.

Practice

1. Form a group of five.
2. Arrange your bodies to create a balanced live sculpture.

Differentiated Instruction

Reteach
Hold up symmetrical and asymmetrical objects. Have students tell you which ones are evenly balanced and why.

Special Needs
Ensure success in this project by helping students recognize the visual clues the artist of *House Post* left for the viewer that give information about the family.

ELL Tips
Define *even balance*. Bring a two-handled cup to class and ask students if both halves are exactly alike. Does the cup have even balance? Have students draw the cup.

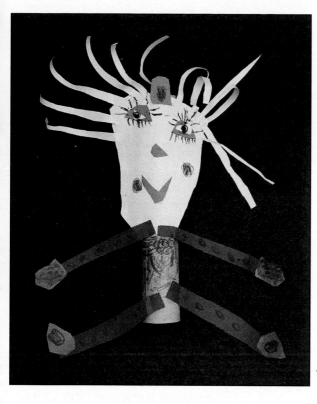

Think about how the student used balance in her house post.

◀ Lorayna Hinton.
Age 5.

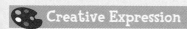
Creative Expression

What kind of house post would you make for your house?

1. Cut shapes for the face, arms, and legs of the creature.
2. Glue them to the tube so they are balanced.

Art Criticism

Interpret What story does your house post tell?

Art Across the Curriculum

Use these simple ideas to reinforce art concepts across the curriculum.

★ **Expository Writing** Write directions together for how to make a house post.

★ **Math** Sort objects by those that have balance and those that do not. Compare and order two or three objects according to length, capacity, and weight.

★ **Science** Discuss ways that rocks can be useful, including being used for sculpture. Show students pictures of sculptures carved from a variety of stones such as alabaster, marble, sandstone, and limestone.

★ **Social Studies** Discuss family customs and traditions, pointing out that creating a house post was custom for the Bella Bella people. Ask students if their families have any customs or traditions they follow.

★ **Technology** Use a paint program to draw a house post that has even balance. Visit **SRAonline.com** to print detailed instructions for this activity.

Reflect
Time: About 5 minutes

Review and Assess

"What makes a sculpture have balance?"
"¿Qué hace una escultura tener equilibrio simétrico?"

Think

Discuss the student art question. The eyes, arms, legs, hands, and feet give this house post balance.

▪ Review balance using *Large Print 12 La Danse.*

Informal Assessment

Art Journal: Critical Thinking
Have students answer the Interpret question by drawing a picture in their Art Journals. Allow students to share their stories out loud.

Art Criticism

Have students ask themselves the following questions.

Describe ▶ What are the names of the lines, shapes, and colors you used?

Analyze ▶ How do the lines, shapes, and colors create balance on your house post?

Interpret ▶ What story does your house post tell?

Decide ▶ What part of your house post do you like best?

NSAE 2.b; 5.a; 5.c

▪ For standardized-format test practice using this lesson's art content, see pages 72–73 in *Reading and Writing Test Preparation.*

Balance in Sculpture

Extra! For the Art Specialist

Time: About 30 minutes

Focus

Study **Transparency 34** and **Large Print 12** *La Danse*. Discuss how the artists used balance. How did the artists make both sides look equal?

Teach

Discuss with students how balance makes things feel restful. Point out that faces are balanced because they are the same on both sides. Help students learn about balance by creating a mask.

Reflect

Have students use the four steps of art criticism to evaluate their work. Did they effectively show even balance in their mask design?

Alternate Activity

Materials:
- 9" × 12" paper (assorted colors)
- glue
- scissors
- feathers
- shape stickers
- craft sticks

1. Have students fold a sheet of paper in half two times.

2. Next have students cut a shape for eyes near one end of the double fold. Open the paper so it is still folded once.

3. On the center fold, have students cut a shape for the nose and mouth. Students might want to trim the edges of the rectangle to make a more interesting shape.

4. Have students open the paper and decorate it with feathers, markers, and shape stickers.

5. Use glue to attach a large craft stick for a handle on the mask.

NSAE 1.c

Research in Art Education

"There is more to learning about art than learning to do it. Most people will not actually seek to make art in their lifetime, but all of us have daily contact with visual stimuli that deliberately (in package design, fashion, or good building) or accidentally (a pattern of leaves on snow or an unexpected bright color against a faded doorway) appeal to our aesthetic sense and offer a bit of visual order in the bustle of the everyday" (Elizabeth Vallance. "Criticism as Subject Matter in Schools and in Art Museums." *Journal of Aesthetic Education* 22 (4). (1988): 69–81).

Assessment

Use the following rubric to evaluate the artwork students make in the Creative Expression activity and to assess students' understanding of balance in sculpture.

Have students complete page 75 or 76 in their **Assessment** books.

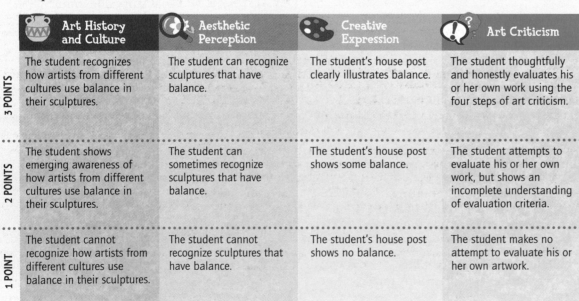

	Art History and Culture	Aesthetic Perception	Creative Expression	Art Criticism
3 POINTS	The student recognizes how artists from different cultures use balance in their sculptures.	The student can recognize sculptures that have balance.	The student's house post clearly illustrates balance.	The student thoughtfully and honestly evaluates his or her own work using the four steps of art criticism.
2 POINTS	The student shows emerging awareness of how artists from different cultures use balance in their sculptures.	The student can sometimes recognize sculptures that have balance.	The student's house post shows some balance.	The student attempts to evaluate his or her own work, but shows an incomplete understanding of evaluation criteria.
1 POINT	The student cannot recognize how artists from different cultures use balance in their sculptures.	The student cannot recognize sculptures that have balance.	The student's house post shows no balance.	The student makes no attempt to evaluate his or her own artwork.

Assessment, p. 75

Name _____ Date _____

Balance in Sculpture

Lesson **4** UNIT 6

For the teacher: Use the following prompt for this activity.
Using crayons, draw a creature that has balance.

Level K · Unit 6 • Principals of Art **75**

Lesson 5 Unity

Lesson 5 introduces unity. Unity is a feeling of wholeness, or oneness of the artwork. It is a sense of belonging to a group or part of a whole.

Objectives

Art History and Culture

To recognize that artists from similar cultures have different styles of painting

Creative Expression

To create unity in a composition by using lines and shapes

Aesthetic Perception

To recognize unity in fine art and verbally describe why the artwork has unity

Art Criticism

To evaluate one's own work using the four steps of art criticism

Vocabulary  Reading

Review the following vocabulary word with students before beginning the lesson.

unity *unidad*—the feeling of wholeness or oneness that is accomplished by properly using the elements and principles of art

See page 209B for additional vocabulary and Spanish vocabulary resources.

Art Journal: Vocabulary

Have students add this word to the Vocabulary section of their Art Journals.

Lesson Materials

- computer paint program
- printer with paper
- assorted objects, some that share a common theme or purpose and others that do not (for example: pencil, chalk, crayon, marker, candy, shoe)

Alternate Materials

- crayons or markers on white or light-colored paper

Program Resources

- *Reading and Writing Test Prep.*, pp. 74–75
- *Transparency 35*
- *Flash Card 18*
- *Artist Profiles*, pp. 13, 36
- *Assessment*, pp. 77–78
- *Large Prints 11* Ceremonial Cloth and *12* La Danse
- *The National Museum of Women in the Arts Collection*

Concept Trace

Unity

Introduced: Level K, Unit 6, Lesson 5

Reinforced: Level K, Unit 6, Lesson 6
Level 1, Unit 6, Lesson 5

Lesson 5 Arts Integration

Theatre

Complete Unit 6, Lesson 5, on pages 116–117 of the *Theatre Arts Connections* book.

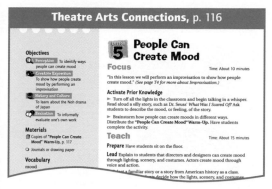

Theatre Arts Connections, p. 116

Music

A song will have unity by having patterns that repeat. Sing *Miss Mary Mack*. How many phrases have an upward melodic line? How many phrases have the same rhythm pattern?

Movement & Dance

When dancers move at the same time together, doing the same movement, it is called moving in unison. Lead the class in a unison circle dance. Students form a circle holding hands:

- Walk 8 counts to the center and 8 counts back.
- Walk 8 counts to the right and 8 counts to the left.
- Clap, stomp, turn around, and shake for 8 counts each. Repeat dance.

 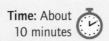

Focus

Time: About 10 minutes

Activate Prior Knowledge

"Have you ever been to a dance?" "¿Han estado alguna vez en un baile?"

- Ask students to share their experiences with dancing. Where were they? Was it a special occasion? Who danced?

Using Literature ⭐ Reading

- Read *Lyle at the Office* by Bernard Waber. Ask students to identify job duties in the story. Point out how the employees work together to get the work done. Look for examples of unity in the illustrations.

Thematic Connection ⭐ Social Studies

- **Jobs/Work:** Discuss types of jobs and why people work. Explore how unity is in the workplace (people work together toward a common goal, coworkers might have similar duties, and workers have similar training for their job).

Introduce the Art

Look

"Let's look at these paintings." "Vamos a observar estas pinturas".

Main Idea and Details ⭐ Reading

- Ask students to describe what is happening in each picture.

Compare and Contrast ⭐ Reading

- Discuss how the pictures are alike and different.

- Share and discuss information from *Artist Profiles* pages 13 and 36 with students.

Adjectives and Adverbs ⭐ Language Arts

- List on a chart the adjectives and adverbs students use to describe the fine art.
NSAE 4.a

🏺 Art History and Culture

Share information from the Art History and Culture sections with students. Explain that Diego Rivera was Mexican and Carmen Lomas Garza is an American of Mexican descent. Although they experienced some similar cultural events like dances, their artistic styles make the paintings look very different.

💻 Web Connection

To learn more about Diego Rivera, visit www.diegorivera.com/index.php.

Lesson 5 · Unity

Look at these paintings. What is happening in each picture?

▲ **Diego Rivera.** (Mexican). *Zandunga Tehuantepec Dance.* c. 1935.
Charcoal and watercolor. 19 × 24 inches (48.1 × 60.6 cm.). Los Angeles County Museum of Art, Los Angeles, California.

🏺 Art History and Culture

These artists are from similar cultures, but their style of painting is very different.

🏺 Art History and Culture

Diego Rivera

Diego Rivera (dē ā´ gō rē vā´ rä) (1886–1957) was best known for the murals he painted. He was a highly productive artist and painted many murals in Mexico and the United States. Rivera wanted to create art that could be understood and enjoyed by ordinary people. Public murals were ideal for him because many people could see his work.

See pages 16–21 and 24–25 for more about subject matter and art history.

Artist Profiles, p. 36

Artist Profile
Diego Rivera
1886-1957

Diego Rivera (dē ā´ gō rē bā´ rä) was one of the most productive Mexican artists. He attended art school in Mexico but did not stay long. His first exhibition of paintings in 1907 won him a scholarship to Europe. There he studied the work of modern artists. After returning from a second trip to Europe in 1911, he became Mexico's leading mural painter. Rivera was a large man with strong opinions. His great love for his people and his country showed in his art. Crowds gathered to watch him paint his large murals on public walls. His third wife was the famous painter Frida Kahlo. They often fought and separated, but they always supported each other's artistic efforts.

▲ **Carmen Lomas Garza.** (American). *Dance at El Jardin.* 1995.

Alkyds and oils on canvas. 24 × 32 inches (60.96 × 81.28 cm.). Private Collection.

Study both pictures.

▶ Name the objects you see in the first picture. Do they belong together?

▶ Name the objects you see in the second picture. Do they belong together?

Aesthetic Perception

Seeing Like an Artist What objects could you draw in a picture about school?

Art History and Culture

Carmen Lomas Garza

Carmen Lomas Garza (kär´ män loō´ mäs gär´ sä) (1948–   ) is a contemporary Hispanic artist from south Texas. Garza's inspiration for her art is often her childhood memories of the experiences of the Mexican-Americans in her family and community. Her goal is to produce works of art that portray the beauty of Hispanic culture.

See pages 16–21 and 24–25 for more about subject matter and art history.

Artist Profiles, p. 13

Study

▶ *Zandunga Tehuantepec Dance:* men and women standing, women sitting, trees that have been decorated, a room, a wide door. The objects belong together because the men and women are dancing together and the women sitting look as if they are waiting to dance.

▶ *Dance at El Jardin:* men, women, boys, girls, musicians, instruments, poles with strings of lights, bushes, a dance floor, and stage for the band. The objects belong together because the people are dancing together, the band is playing music for the dancers, and the lights are lighting up their outside dance.

■ For more examples of genre art, see *The National Museum of Women in the Arts Collection.*

Art Journal: Concepts

Have students draw a group of objects that have something in common.

Aesthetic Perception

Seeing Like an Artist Ask students to name objects they would include in a picture about school.

Developing Visual Literacy Ask students how these paintings make them feel and how they think the artists feel about dancing.
NSAE 3.a; 3.b; 5.a; 5.c

Web Connection
To learn more about Carmen Lomas Garza and study her portfolio, visit **www.carmenlomasgarza.com/**.
NSAE 5.a; 5.c

Teach

Time: About 30 minutes

"Let's group objects that belong together."
"Vamos agrupar los objetos que pertenecen juntos".

Practice

Materials: assorted objects (several that share a common theme, such as writing tools, and a few that do not fit the theme)

- Display a group of assorted objects for students. Several of the objects should share a common theme or "belong together."

- Ask students to identify the objects that belong together and explain why they belong together.

Creative Expression

Materials: computer, paint program, printer with paper

Alternate Materials: crayons or markers on white or light-colored paper

- Help students open a paint program on the computer.

- Ask students to use the line and shape tools to draw pairs of people dancing together.

- Then have students use the pencil tool with a wide line to create colorful clothes for the people.

- Have students use the fill tools to add color to the drawing.

- See the Activity Tips on page 249 for visual examples of this lesson's activity.

NSAE 1.a; 1.c

Art Journal: Brainstorming

Ask students to imagine a dance. Have students draw some things they would see at a dance in their Art Journals.

Using Unity

When a work of art has **unity,** it looks like everything belongs together.

Practice

1. Look at the objects your teacher shows you.

2. Which objects belong together?

Differentiated Instruction

Reteach
Show students two or three different kinds of fruit. Ask them what other objects belong in this group.

Special Needs
Some students may find it helpful to work with a partner for this computer activity. Carefully pair students and set working guidelines so that each student has equal input and responsibility.

ELL Tips
Give students a variety of geometric and free-form shapes. Have them group shapes that are alike. Explain that each shape group has unity because the shapes are alike. Write *group* and *unity* on the board. Have students say the words with you.

◀ **Paul Hulett.**
Age 5.

Think about how the student showed unity in his drawing.

Creative Expression

How can you show unity in your drawing?

1. Use the shape tool and line tool to show couples dancing.
2. Draw clothes and other details on your picture.

Art Criticism

Analyze What did you do to help your drawing have unity?

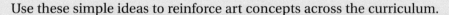

Art Across the Curriculum

Use these simple ideas to reinforce art concepts across the curriculum.

★ **Personal Writing** Ask students to tell about a time when they danced or saw others dance. Have them draw a picture to illustrate their descriptions of this event.

★ **Math** Count the people in each painting. Use manipulatives to represent these numbers. Identify which painting has more people. How many more does it have?

★ **Science** Group organisms and objects as living and nonliving, including the objects in the fine art.

★ **Social Studies** Understand how classroom rules help everyone work together, just as objects in a work of art work together to create unity.

★ **Technology** Use a paint program to draw a picture of something special you do with your family. Be sure to show unity by drawing objects that belong together. Visit **SRAonline.com** to print detailed instructions for this activity.

Reflect   Time: About 5 minutes

Review and Assess

"What helps create a feeling of unity in an artwork?" "¿Qué ayuda a crear una sensación de unidad en una obra de arte?"

Think

Discuss the student art question. There is unity because the people belong together. They are all dancing and are in the same place.

■ Identify unity in **Large Prints 11 Ceremonial Cloth** and **12 La Danse**.

Informal Assessment

Art Journal: Critical Thinking
Have students answer the Analyze question by drawing a picture in their Art Journals. Discuss their answers out loud.

Art Criticism

Have students ask themselves the following questions.

Describe ▶ How many different things are in your drawing?

Analyze ▶ What did you do to help your drawing have unity?

Interpret ▶ How does your drawing make you feel?

Decide ▶ Is there anything you could add to give your drawing a greater feeling of unity?

NSAE 2.b; 5.a; 5.c

■ For standardized-format test practice using this lesson's art content, see pages 74–75 in **Reading and Writing Test Preparation**.

 **Lesson 5**
Wrap-Up

Unity

 Extra! **For the Art Specialist**

Time: About 30 minutes

Focus

Study *Transparency 35* and *Large Prints 11 Ceremonial Cloth* and *12 La Danse.* Discuss how the artists used unity. How do the shapes create unity?

Teach

Help students learn about unity by creating designs from a pair of shapes.

Reflect

Have students use the four steps of art criticism to evaluate their work. Did they effectively show unity in their artwork?

Alternate Activity

Materials:
- 9" × 12" construction paper (assorted colors)
- glue
- scissors
- pencils
- markers

1. Direct the students to think of a person or animal shape.

2. Have them draw the shape on a folded sheet of paper and then cut it out. They will have two identical shapes.

3. Next have students glue the two identical shapes on another piece of paper.

4. Encourage students to use markers to add details to the picture.

NSAE 1.c

Research
in Art Education

There is a link between "arts education and creative thinking, academic self-concept, and school climate" ("Learning In and Through the Arts: The Question of Transfer" in *Critical Links,* p. 66). Students in schools with quality arts programs tend to use more creativity, take more risks, and view themselves as academically competent.

Assessment
Use the following rubric to evaluate the artwork students make in the Creative Expression activity and to assess students' understanding of unity.

Have students complete page 77 or 78 in their *Assessment* books.

	Art History and Culture	Aesthetic Perception	Creative Expression	Art Criticism
3 POINTS	The student recognizes that artists from similar cultures have different styles of painting.	The student can recognize unity in fine art and verbally describe why the artwork has unity.	The student's composition clearly illustrates unity.	The student thoughtfully and honestly evaluates his or her own work using the four steps of art criticism.
2 POINTS	The student shows emerging awareness of how artists from similar cultures have different styles of painting.	The student can sometimes recognize unity in fine art and verbally describe why the artwork has unity.	The student's composition shows emerging awareness of unity.	The student attempts to evaluate his or her own work, but shows an incomplete understanding of evaluation criteria.
1 POINT	The student cannot recognize how artists from similar cultures have different styles of painting.	The student cannot recognize unity in fine art or verbally describe why the artwork has unity.	The student's composition shows no unity.	The student makes no attempt to evaluate his or her own artwork.

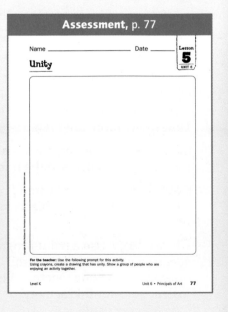

Assessment, p. 77

Name _____ Date _____ Lesson **5** UNIT 6

Unity

For the teacher: Use the following prompt for this activity.
Using crayons, create a drawing that has unity. Show a group of people who are enjoying an activity together.

Level K   Unit 6 • Principles of Art   **77**

Lesson 6 Overview

Unity in Sculpture

Lesson 6 introduces unity in sculpture. Unity in sculpture can be achieved by using like colors or forms in a sculpture to give it a feeling of wholeness or oneness.

Objectives

 ### Art History and Culture

To recognize that artists from different cultures show different activities in their art

 ### Creative Expression

To create a sculpture and arrange it with classmates' sculptures to make one unified work of art

 ### Aesthetic Perception

To recognize unity in sculpture and verbally describe why a sculpture has unity

Art Criticism

To evaluate one's own work using the four steps of art criticism

Vocabulary Reading

Review the following vocabulary words with students before beginning the lesson.

unity unidad—the feeling of wholeness or oneness that is accomplished by properly using the elements and principles of art

sculpture escultura—a three-dimensional work of art

See page 209B for additional vocabulary and Spanish vocabulary resources.

Art Journal: Vocabulary

Have students add these words to the Vocabulary section of their Art Journals.

Lesson Materials

- 4–6 large prints
- cardboard tubes of various sizes and lengths (toilet paper, paper towels, gift wrap)
- 8" × 10" chipboard for bases
- tacky glue
- tempera or school acrylics
- found objects such as beads, feathers, yarn, and buttons
- clothespins for holding things together temporarily
- assorted magazines
- scissors

Alternate Materials
- roll and staple 10" square pieces of posterboard

Program Resources
- *Reading and Writing Test Prep.*, pp. 76–77
- *Transparency 36*
- *Flash Card 18*
- *Artist Profiles*, pp. 43, 68
- *Animals Through History Time Line*
- *Assessment*, pp. 79–80
- *Large Print 12 La Danse*
- *The National Museum of Women in the Arts Collection*

Concept Trace
Unity in Sculpture
Introduced: Level K, Unit 6, Lesson 6
Reinforced: Level 1, Unit 6, Lesson 6

Lesson 6 Arts Integration

Theatre

Complete Unit 6, Lesson 6, on pages 118 123 of the *Theatre Arts Connections* book.

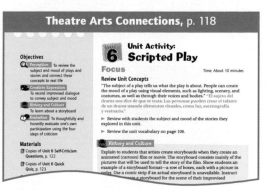

Theatre Arts Connections, p. 118

Music

 Listen to "Tuileries" from *Pictures at an Exhibition*. The instrumental sounds stay high and light throughout the piece. There is a contrasting middle section where the melody smoothes out. Why does the total piece have a feeling of unity even with the contrasting section in the middle?

Movement & Dance

Have a small group of students demonstrate unity by making a live group sculpture in which each person adds to the shape in a thoughtful way. Then ask a different group of students to use their bodies to combine shapes in a disjointed way so no one builds onto or attaches their shape to any of the ones before. Ask which sculpture looked and felt as if the pieces went together to make a whole.

 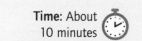**ocus**

Time: About 🕐
10 minutes

Activate Prior Knowledge

- "Where do you see groups of animals that are similar?" "¿Dónde ven grupos de animales que son parecidos?"

- Ask students if they have seen related groups of animals at a zoo or farm.

Using Literature ⭐ Reading

- Read *The Great Trash Bash* by Loreen Leedy. Talk about cooperation in the story. Study the illustrations and ask students to explain why an illustration has unity.

Thematic Connection ⭐ Social Studies

- **Cooperation:** Discuss ways in which we cooperate each day with our families and friends. Ask why cooperation is important.

Introduce the Art

Look

"Let's study these works of art." "Vamos a estudiar estas obras de arte".

Main Idea and Details ⭐ Reading

- Ask students to describe what they see in each picture.

- These are *installations*, works of art that are made for a specific space, usually indoors but sometimes outdoors. Installations are often temporary, so artists photograph them. Some installations like Sandy Skoglund's are made from many pieces and materials, so artist assistants are used to help create the installation.

Adjectives and Adverbs ⭐ Language Arts

- List on a chart the adjectives and adverbs students use to describe the fine art.

NSAE 4.a

 Art History and Culture

Share information from the Art History and Culture sections with students. Sandy Skoglund created each dog as an individual sculpture. She later arranged them in the installation *The Green House*, took photographs, and then made prints.

 Web Connection

To learn more about Sandy Skoglund, visit www.sandyskoglund.com/.

Unity in Sculpture

Look at these works of art.
Do they have unity?

▲ **Sandy Skoglund.** (American). *The Green House.* 1990.
Cibachrome color print. $46\frac{1}{4} \times 63$ inches (117.48 × 160.02 cm).

 Art History and Culture

Sandy Skoglund used clay to create all the dogs in this work of art.

 Art History and Culture

Sandy Skoglund

Sandy Skoglund (san´ dē skōg lund´) (1946–) spent the first part of her childhood near Boston and then moved around the United States with her family. She had polio when she was young, and the time she spent indoors cultivated her passion for drawing. Her drawings often depicted fantasy lands and environments. These early imaginations have filtered into her work today with installations that create entirely new environments with fantastic elements, such as walls of jam and floors of eggshells. Skoglund believes an artist should make use of a wide range of materials that explore color and texture. Her work involves the viewer's sense of smell, taste, and familiarity with fabric textures.

See pages 16–21 and 24–25 for more about subject matter and art history.

Artist Profiles, p. 43

◀ Artist Profile ▶

Sandy Skoglund
b. 1946

Sandy Skoglund (san´ dē skōg lund´) spent the first part of her childhood near Boston and then moved around the United States with her family. She had polio when she was young, and the time she spent indoors cultivated her passion for drawing. Her drawings often depicted fantasy lands and environments. These early imaginations have filtered into her work today with installations that create entirely new environments with fantastic elements, such as walls of jam and floors of eggshells. Skoglund has been an undergraduate professor at Rutgers University and credits her students with keeping her in touch with the world outside the New York art scene.

▲ **Artist Unknown.** (China). *Four Ladies of the Court Playing Polo.* 8th century.
••••••••••••••••••••••••••
Painted terra cotta. 10 inches high (25.4 cm.). Nelson-Atkins Museum of Art, Kansas City, Missouri.

Study both pictures.

▶ Why do you think the artist made most of the dogs blue?

▶ How are the sculptures alike in the second picture?

Aesthetic Perception

Design Awareness What objects are repeated in your classroom?

Unit 6 • Lesson 6 **207**

Study

▶ Sandy Skoglund might have made most of the dogs blue so we would see them as a group. Our eyes are drawn to them because they share the same bright color. Making most of the dogs the same color gives the artwork unity.

▶ The sculptures in *Four Ladies of the Court Playing Polo* look alike because each sculpture is a horse with a woman riding on it. All of the women are looking down. Each horse is supported by pedestals under the horse's belly. The sculptures are all made of the same material (terra cotta).

■ For more examples of genre art, see *The National Museum of Women in the Arts Collection.*

Art Journal: Concepts
Have students draw a group of objects that have something in common.

Aesthetic Perception

Design Awareness Ask students to name objects that are repeated in the classroom, such as chairs, tables, or closets.

Developing Visual Literacy Ask students to explain why they think the artists chose to show the particular items that are in *The Green House* and *Four Ladies of the Court Playing Polo.*
NSAE 3.a; 3.b; 5.a; 5.c

Art History and Culture

Tang Dynasty

The Tang Dynasty (618–907 A.D.) was a time of growth and creativity in many different art forms in China. Due in part to a prosperous economy, the Tang Dynasty saw tremendous advances in science and technology, and its creative minds were prolific in the creation of brilliant art, music, painting, pottery, and literature. Some historians view the Tang Dynasty as the golden age of arts and sciences in Chinese history. The art of ceramics has a long and rich history in China, and various styles of pottery and sculpture were developed and perfected during the Tang Dynasty. New types of ceramic glazes and glazing techniques also were invented by Tang Dynasty artists.

See pages 16–21 and 24–25 for more about subject matter and art history.

Artist Profiles, p. 68

Artist Profile

Four Ladies of the Court Playing Polo

An unidentified Chinese artist of the Tang dynasty created *Four Ladies of the Court Playing Polo* between 618 and 906.

◀ **Artist Unknown.** (China). *Four Ladies of the Court Playing Polo.* Eighth century.
••••••••••••••••••••
Painted terra-cotta. 10 inches (25.4 cm.) high. Nelson-Atkins Museum of Art, Kansas City, Missouri.

About Art History
The Tang dynasty was a time of growth and ... ...ing. The

camels, acrobats, polo players, and court ladies as their subjects. San cai statuettes have been found in large numbers in the tombs of wealthy Tang dynasty nobles.

Web Connection
Visit the Nelson-Atkins Museum of Art online at **www.nelson-atkins.org/**.

LESSON 6 • Unity in Sculpture **207**

 **Teach** Time: About 30 minutes

"What kinds of things can you find in a magazine?" "¿Qué tipos de cosas se pueden encontrar en una revista?"

Practice

Materials: assorted magazines, scissors

■ Ask students to look in magazines for objects that would create unity if used together in a work of art. The objects might share a common purpose or be alike because of color or form.

■ Have students cut out these pictures and explain how they could create unity in a work of art.

Creative Expression

Materials: 4-6 large prints, cardboard tubes of various sizes and lengths, 8" × 10" chipboard, tacky glue, tempera or school acrylics, objects such as beads and yarn, clothespins

Alternate Materials: roll and staple 10" square pieces of posterboard

■ Have students experiment with the tube shapes and try to organize them into an animal form.

■ Once students have arranged their forms have them glue the sections together. Tell the students to count to ten while holding two pieces together so that the glue holds well.

■ Next have students paint their animals.

■ After the paint dries have students glue their animals to a chipboard base.

■ Encourage students to add optional materials as decorations.

■ When finished have students create a unified installation by grouping all the animals together on a colored paper-covered table top.

■ See the Activity Tips on page 249 for visual examples of this lesson's activity.

NSAE 1.a; 1.c

Art Journal: Brainstorming
Ask students to think about some of their favorite animals. Have students draw an animal in their Art Journals that they would like to create as a sculpture.

Using Unity in Sculpture

Colors and forms that are alike help create **unity** in sculpture.

Practice

1. Look at pictures in magazines.

2. Cut out pictures that would create unity in a work of art.

Differentiated Instruction

Reteach
Have students observe features of the school that are the same and give it unity, such as doors, doorknobs, windows, and furniture.

Special Needs
For this group learning experience, model norms of cooperation by asking for the input of all students and verbally recognizing the accomplishments of each group member.

ELL Tips
Display a few forms that are alike. Ask students if they look as if they belong together and why. Explain that forms that are alike create a sense of unity. Define *unity* for students. Use the word in a sentence. Have students select some colors and forms in the room that together create a feeling of unity.

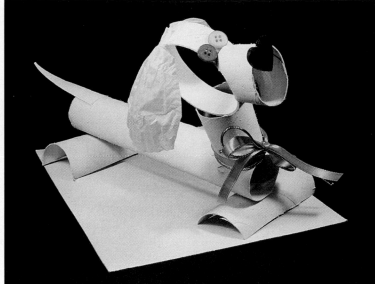

◀ Alec Coleman.
Age 5.

Think about what makes unity in this work of art.

How can you show unity with sculpture?

1. Use cardboard tubes to make an animal sculpture.

2. Arrange your sculpture with your classmates' sculptures to make one work of art.

 **Art Criticism**

Analyze Does the arrangement of sculptures have unity? Why or why not?

Art Across the Curriculum

Use these simple ideas to reinforce art concepts across the curriculum.

★ **Narrative Writing** Write a story together about the animals in the installation the class made.

★ **Math** Have students use geometric shape to create a design with unity.

★ **Science** Discuss how repetition can create unity. Have students identify parts that are repeated in living things.

★ **Social Studies** Have students draw a symbol of an important person, event, or thing. Encourage students to show unity in their work.

★ **Technology** Use a paint program to draw a picture of your family on vacation. Visit **SRAonline.com** to print detailed instructions for this activity.

Reflect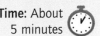
Time: About 5 minutes

Review and Assess

"How do sculptors create unity in their works of art?" "¿Cómo crean unidad los escultores en sus obras de arte?"

Think

Discuss the student art question. There is unity because the artist repeated shapes and colors.

■ Identify unity in **Large Print 12** *La Danse.*

Informal Assessment

Art Journal: Critical Thinking
Write *Yes* and *No* on the board. Have students answer the Analyze question in their Art Journals. Discuss their answers.

 **Art Criticism**

Have students ask themselves the following questions.

Describe ▸ What shapes and colors did you use in your sculpture?

Analyze ▸ Does the arrangement of sculptures have unity? Why or why not?

Interpret ▸ Does the class arrangement represent anything in particular?

Decide ▸ Does your sculpture add to the unity of the class arrangement?

NSAE 2.b; 5.a; 5.c

■ For standardized-format test practice using this lesson's art content, see pages 76–77 in *Reading and Writing Test Preparation.*

Unity in Sculpture

Extra! ## For the Art Specialist

Time: About 30 minutes

Focus

Study **Transparency 36** and **Large Print 12** *La Danse*. Discuss how the artists used unity. Point to the objects that belong together in the works of art.

Teach

Explain how artists use color, shape, and texture to unify objects in a work of art.

Reflect

Have students use the four steps of art criticism to evaluate their work. Did they effectively show unity in their artwork?

Alternate Activity

Materials:
- 9″ × 12″ drawing paper
- markers

1. Ask students to think of an animal or creature and draw it at least three times on their paper.

2. Have students color the animals one color to make them more unified.

3. Then ask students to think of where the animals live and draw their environment.

NSAE 1.c

Research in Art Education

"If perception is basic to all learning, if selective viewing is a desirable kind of behavior, and if conceptualization comes after sensory experiences, then it becomes imperative that teachers provide paths for numerous visual and tactile explorations so as to keep all of the child's senses alive and active" (Herberholz, Barbara, and Lee Hanson. *Early Childhood Art*. New York: McGraw-Hill, 1994).

Assessment

Use the following rubric to evaluate the artwork students make in the Creative Expression activity and to assess students' understanding of unity in sculpture.

Have students complete page 79 or 80 in their **Assessment** books.

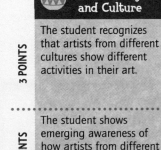

	Art History and Culture	Aesthetic Perception	Creative Expression	Art Criticism
3 POINTS	The student recognizes that artists from different cultures show different activities in their art.	The student can recognize unity in sculpture and verbally describe why a sculpture has unity.	The student's sculpture clearly illustrates unity and is an effective part of a unified installation.	The student thoughtfully and honestly evaluates his or her own work using the four steps of art criticism.
2 POINTS	The student shows emerging awareness of how artists from different cultures show different activities in their art.	The student can sometimes recognize unity in sculpture and verbally describe why a sculpture has unity.	The student's sculpture shows emerging awareness of unity and is somewhat effective as part of a unified installation.	The student attempts to evaluate his or her own work, but shows an incomplete understanding of evaluation criteria.
1 POINT	The student cannot recognize how artists from different cultures show different activities in their art.	The student cannot recognize unity in sculpture or verbally describe why a sculpture has unity.	The student's sculpture shows no unity and is not an effective part of a unified installation.	The student makes no attempt to evaluate his or her own artwork.

Assessment, p. 79

Name _____ Date _____ Lesson **6** UNIT 6

Unity in Sculpture

For the teacher: Use the following prompt for this activity.
Using crayons, create a drawing that has unity. Show of a set of animals in your drawing.

Level K   Unit 6 • Principals of Art   **79**

Unit 6 Vocabulary Review

even balance—both halves are equal. The left side and right side are the same. **equilibrio simétrico**—ambas mitades son iguales. El lado izquierdo y derecho son iguales.

movement—the look of constant motion in a work of art **movimiento**—la apariencia de una moción constante en una obra de arte

pattern—the repetition of lines, shapes, and/or colors **patrón**—la repetición de líneas, figuras y/o colores

rhythm—the repetition of lines, shapes, and/or colors to create a feeling of movement **ritmo**—la repetición de líneas, figuras y/o colores para crear una sensación de movimiento

sculpture—a three-dimensional work of art **escultura**—una obra de arte tridimensional

unity—the feeling of wholeness or oneness that is accomplished by properly using the elements and principles of art **unidad**—una sensación de integridad que se encuentra usando propiamente los elementos y principios artísticos

Vocabulary Practice

T Display *Transparency 42* to review unit vocabulary words.

Silly Words and Sentences ⭐ Vocabulary
Ask students questions in the form of riddles using the vocabulary words. Encourage students to use the vocabulary words in their answers.

Examples ⭐ Vocabulary
Display pictures to help illustrate the meanings of new vocabulary words.

Visualization Strategies ⭐ Vocabulary
Label objects in the classroom that demonstrate the meaning of the vocabulary words.

Wrapping Up Unit 6
Principles of Art

 Art Criticism

Critical Thinking is an organized system for looking at and talking about art. You can criticize art without being an expert. The purpose of art criticism is to get the viewer involved in a perception process that delays judgment until all aspects of the artwork have been studied.

- See pages 28–29 for more about art criticism.

Describe

▶ Ask students to describe what they see in this painting. Possible answers: At the bottom there is a row of blue circles with yellow dots in the center. Above each one is a green or blue-green triangle. Above the triangles there is a black silhouette of a bridge and a city at night, with the lights on in the buildings. The sky behind them is blue with black lines. Above the city there is a curved black line.

On the left side of the painting there is a black area with an opening shaped like a pointed arch with a lot of geometric shapes and building shapes in it. There are two blue curving lines, one short and one long. At the left edge, there are straight yellow lines. There are also straight black lines and slanted black lines. The right side is very similar to the left.

In the center there is a long blue shape. It comes to a white point at the bottom.

Analyze

▶ Ask students where they see a pattern of repeated shapes. Possible answers: The white dots at the top form a pattern. At the very bottom the triangles form a pattern. The lights on the buildings are a random pattern of yellow shapes.

▲ **Joseph Stella.** (Italian-American). *The Brooklyn Bridge: Variations on an Old Theme.* 1939.

Oil on canvas. 70 × 42 inches (177.8 × 106.68 cm.). Whitney Museum of American Art, New York, New York.

 Art History and Culture

Joseph Stella

Joseph Stella (jō´ sef ste´ lə) (1877–1946) was born in Italy. He came to the United States as a young man and began painting portraits of immigrants living in New York City. A group that was concerned about immigrants was impressed with Stella's work and sent him to coal mines and industrial regions of Pennsylvania and West Virginia. Stella painted the workers there so that others would understand the terrible working conditions they faced. He was impressed by the power and creativity of the American Industrial age. In time, he turned from painting the workers to painting symbolic pictures of technology and machines.

See pages 16–21 and 24–25 for more about subject matter and art history.

Artist Profiles, p. 45

‹ Artist Profile ›

Joseph Stella
1877–1946

Joseph Stella (jō´ sef ste´ lə) was born in Italy. He came to the United States as a young man and began painting portraits of immigrants living in New York City. A group that was concerned about immigrants was impressed with Stella's work. The group sent him to the coal mines and industrial regions of Pennsylvania and West Virginia. Stella painted the workers there so others would understand the terrible working conditions they faced. Stella saw how the growth of industry and the use of machines was affecting human lives. However, he was also impressed by the power and creativity of the American industrial age. In time, he turned from painting workers to painting symbolic pictures of technology and machines.

 **Art Criticism** Critical Thinking

Describe

▶ What do you see in the painting?

Analyze

▶ Where do you see a pattern of repeated shapes?

Interpret

▶ What do you think this painting is about?

Decide

▶ Does this painting make you think?

Interpret

▶ Encourage students to explain what they think this painting is about. Answers will vary. Many will recognize that this is about a bridge and a city.

▶ Ask students to explain how the top and bottom parts of the painting belong together. Possible answers: Some will realize that the bridge on the bottom left has the same arches as the two pointed arches in the rest of the painting. They may realize that this is different views of the same bridge.

Decide

▶ Ask students if this painting makes them think. Answers will vary.

NSAE 5.a; 5.c

> **Art Journal: Writing**
> Have students draw a picture in their Art Journals to answer the Interpret Aesthetic Perception question. Discuss the other questions out loud.

 Aesthetic Perception

Critical Thinking Ask students if they have ever crossed a bridge.

Describe ▶ How did you cross the bridge? By car, bus, walking?

Analyze ▶ What did you see on the bridge that repeated and created rhythm?

Interpret ▶ How did you feel when you were on the bridge?

Decide ▶ Do you like crossing bridges? Why or why not?

"How do artists create unity in an artwork?"
"¿Cómo los artistas crean unidad en un obra de arte?"

T Review unit vocabulary with students using *Transparency 42.*

- Review pattern, rhythm, and balance in art.

- Remind students that pattern, rhythm, and balance are used to create a feeling of unity in an artwork.

- Encourage students to find patterns that are repeated in the room and create a rhythm. Have them name a few things they see every day that have balance.

Art Journal: Writing

Read the questions on page 212 to students. Have students write their answers in their Art Journals or on a separate sheet of paper. 1. A, 2. B, 3. B

T For further assessment, have students complete the unit test on *Transparency 48.*

CAREERS IN ART

Artists

► Encourage students to imagine that they are professional artists. Ask them what kinds of art they would like to exhibit at a show such as sculpture, landscape, portraits, and photography.

"Works of art, in my
opinion, are the only
objects in the material
universe to possess
internal order, and that
is why, though I don't
believe that only art
matters, I do believe in
art for art's sake."

—E.M. Forster

Show What You Know

Answer these questions on a separate sheet of paper.

❶ Which of these shows a pattern?

A.   B.

❷ Which of these has even balance?

A.   B.

❸ Which group of objects has unity?

A.   B.

Unit Assessment Options

Aesthetic Perception

Practice Ask students to identify examples of pattern and balance in the classroom.

Creative Expression

Student Portfolio Have students review all the artwork they have created during this unit and select the pieces they wish to put into their portfolios. Have students share their portfolios with classmates and comment constructively about the art.
NSAE 5.a; 5.c

Art Criticism

Activity Have students select their favorite work of art from the unit. Guide students through study of their selected work using the four steps of art criticism. (See pages 28–29 for more about Art Criticism.)

CAREERS IN ART

Artists

Some artists earn a living by selling their art. Making art is their job.

Painters use paint to create pictures on flat surfaces, such as paper, canvas, or silk.

Sculptors are artists who make sculptures. A sculpture is a form that we can look at from every side.

▲ **Painter**

Rhythm, Balance, and Unity in Dance

Chuna McIntyre is a Yup'ik Eskimo. When he was young, his grandmother told him stories. In these stories the sun, moon, and animals sang and danced.

What to Do Mirror simple movements with a partner.

1. Find a partner. Decide who will be the leader and who will be the mirror.

2. The leader should start by slowly moving his or her arms. The mirror should imitate the leader.

3. Add more slow movements with other body parts. Then add strong movements.

4. Take turns being the leader and the mirror.

▲ Chuna McIntyre. *Brother Sun, Sister Moon.*

 **Art Criticism**

Analyze What made it possible for you and your partner to move together?

Unit 6 **213**

 Art History and Culture

Yup'ik Dance

The Yup'ik Eskimos of Alaska perform dance movements and gestures that are symmetrical. When one side of the body does a movement, the other mirrors it. Movements always begin on the right side of the body, and then the left side of the body creates a movement that is symmetrical or balances the original movement. Sometimes the sides move together, such as lifting both arms at the same time.

 # Rhythm, Balance, and Unity in Dance

Objective: To explore rhythm, balance, and unity through motions made with a partner

Materials: Chuna McIntyre, *Brother Sun, Sister Moon.* Running Time: 6:54

 Focus   Time: About 10 minutes

- Read the information on page 213.

- Have students identify rhythm, balance, and unity in *Brother Sun, Sister Moon.*

Art History and Culture

- Find and discuss information about rhythm, balance, and unity in basket weaving by Yup'ik Eskimos.

 Teach   Time: About 20 minutes

Aesthetic Perception

- Ask students to identify objects in the classroom that have even balance.

Creative Expression

- Have students stand in an open space and follow the steps on student page 213.

- **Informal Assessment** Comment positively on the students' ability to mirror each other's movements.

 Reflect   Time: About 10 minutes

 **Art Criticism**

- Have students draw in their Art Journals to answer the Analyze question. Discuss the following Art Criticism questions out loud.

Describe ▶ Describe some of your movements.

Interpret ▶ What feelings or ideas came to mind as you moved?

Decide ▶ How well do you think you and your partner did in this mirroring activity?

Drawing

It is important to allow the students to experiment with the drawing media. Use gentle guidance to show them how to properly hold the drawing media. Prior to use, demonstrate the techniques as they are illustrated here. Proper handling and use will increase success and establish good habits for the future. It will also make the media last longer.

Pencil

- Primary pencils with medium-soft lead should be used.

- When making thin lines, the students should hold the pencil as in writing.

- For thick lines, hold the pencil on its side near the point between the thumb and fingertips.

Crayon

- Thin lines and small dots can be created with the sharpened end of the crayon.

- Thick lines and large dots can be made with the flat end. Large areas can be colored in with the side of an unwrapped crayon.

- Students may become concerned over broken crayons. Reassure them that these pieces are still useful for drawing and coloring areas.

Drawing

Pencil

Thin lines

Thick lines

Crayon

Thin lines

Thick lines

Large spaces

Small dots

Large dots

Technique Tips

Crayon Rubbing

Rub away from your holding hand.

Marker

Use the tip.

Use the side of the tip.

Put on the cap.

Crayon Rubbing

- When rubbing textures, have the student hold the uncovered crayon so that he or she is rubbing with the side of the crayon, not the tip.

- With one hand, hold the paper and the edges of the material being rubbed. Then rub away from the holding hand for every stroke. If the student rubs back and forth, the paper will wrinkle up and a smooth rubbing will not be made.

- Rubbings can be made with an uncovered wax crayon, an uncovered oil pastel, or the side of a pencil point.

- It is better to use dark colors to make the rubbing so that the texture impression shows up. Red, green, blue, and violet are good colors to use.

- Some materials that make good rubbings are burlap, lace, weeds, shoe bottoms, and commercial rubbing plates.

Marker

- To avoid damage, students should not press hard on the marker tip. Tell them to handle the marker gently for better control.

- For thin lines and dots, a conical-tipped marker can be used.

- The side of the tip can be used to make wider lines and to color areas.

- Remind students to replace the cap to prevent drying.

Oil Pastels

- Oil pastels are pigments that are mixed with oil and compressed into sticks. They are used like crayons. By pressing with gentle force and coloring over an area several times, students can create the effect of paint.

- Students can create lines by drawing with the tip. Textures can be created by making marks such as dots and lines. Textures can also be made by layering colors and scratching though with a paper clip that has been straightened.

- Colors can be mixed or blended by smearing them with a paper towel wrapped around a finger.

- Oil pastels break easily. Reassure the students that these pieces can still be used like new ones. If the oil pastels become dirty from use, instruct the students to mark on a paper towel until the colors are clean again.

Colored Chalk

- Colored chalks are used to make colorful, soft designs. The use of dustless chalk is recommended for elementary classrooms. The tip of the chalk is used much like an oil pastel to make lines. To fill a space or shape with solid color, use gentle force and color over an area more than once.

- Colors can be mixed or blended by smearing them together with a paper towel wrapped around a finger.

- Like oil pastels, colored chalks break easily. Reassure the students that these pieces can still be used like new ones. Colored chalks also become dirty from use. Instruct students to mark on a paper towel until the colors are clean.

Technique Tips

Oil Pastel

Lines

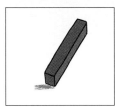
Color in large spaces.

Blend colors.

Colored Chalk

Lines

Color in large spaces.

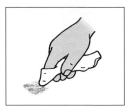
Blend colors.

Painting

Taking Care of Your Paintbrush

Rinse and blot to change colors.

Technique Tips

Taking Care of Your Paintbrush

Clean your brush when you are done.

1. Rinse.

2. Wash with soap.

3. Rinse again.

4. Shape.

5. Store.

Painting

Taking Care of Your Paintbrush

- Taking proper care of a paintbrush will increase its time in use. By teaching students the rules for proper care, good habits will be established in the beginning.

- Students should always thoroughly rinse the brush tips after switching to a new color of paint. Next, they should gently blot the brush on a paper towel to test for missed paint. If paint appears on the towel, the brush should be rinsed and tested again. Sometimes paint gets deep inside the bristles and the brush needs more rinsing.

- To properly wash and store the brush when finished, students should:

    1. Rinse the brush under gently flowing water. Do not use hot water.

    2. Place a small amount of soap in the palm of one hand. Gently rub the bristles of the brush in their soapy palms. This will remove stubborn paint from deep inside the bristles.

    3. Rinse the brush under gently running water to remove all of the soap.

    4. Reshape the bristles into a point.

    5. Store the brushes in a container with the bristles up so the shape will be kept when the brush dries.

- When these habits are established early in the school year, the students will be more likely to respect the importance of proper care of the art media and tools.

Tempera

- For best results, it is recommended that quality liquid tempera paint is used. Powdered tempera paints seldom mix with water thoroughly. Tempera paint of a lesser quality is usually not opaque with one application. Also, the colors of cheaper temperas don't mix as well.

- Students should have the opportunity to experiment with a variety of brush sizes when using tempera.

- Demonstrate the following steps:

  1. In general, students should hold the brush as they would a pencil, but farther back on the handle.

  2. When getting ready to paint, dip the brush into water to moisten the bristles. To remove excess water from the brush, gently wipe the end of the brush on the inside edge of the container. This will allow the water to run back into the container. Discourage the students from tapping their brushes on the rim of the container. This will prevent paint splatters.

  3. Dip the brush into the paint and brush paint over the area that is to be covered, using only as much paint as needed. Remind students not to scrub the brush.

  4. To change colors, review the steps on page 217.

  5. When mixing paints on a palette, always mix the darker color into the lighter color a little at a time until the desired color is reached. This reduces wasted paint. Paper plates work well as palettes and reduce cleanup.

  6. To paint rough textures, use a dry brush with a small amount of paint.

  7. To create smooth textures, use a moist brush with a normal amount of paint.

Technique Tips

Tempera

Wipe the brush.

Mix the paint on a palette.

Use a wide brush for large spaces.

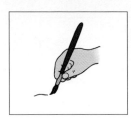

Use a thin, pointed brush for details.

Technique Tips

Watercolor

Put water on each color.

Dip the brush in the paint.

Mix on a palette.

Press firmly for thick lines.

Press lightly for thin lines.

Watercolor Resist

Crayons and oil pastels show through.

Watercolor

- School watercolors come in semimoist cakes. Moisten each cake that is going to be used by dripping a little water from the brush onto the cake and gently stirring the water on the surface of the paint.

- Create thick lines by gently pressing down on the brush.

- Create thin lines by lightly touching the surface of the paper with the tip of the brush.

Watercolor Resist

- By drawing on the paper first with crayons and/or oil pastels, students can achieve a resist effect. Because of their waxy or oily compositions, crayons and oil pastels show through watercolors. Best results are achieved when cool-colored drawings are painted over with warm colors, or vice versa.

Painting Texture with Watercolor

■ To create textures such as stipple (dots) or lines, demonstrate this technique for students.

1. Wet a round, soft-bristled watercolor brush.

2. Hold the brush over the container of water and gently squeeze the excess water from the bristles. Stress that this is a squeeze and not a pull or the bristles may pull out from the brush.

3. Gently divide the bristles into spikes.

4. Carefully touch the moistened paint cake with the bristle tips so that some paint is absorbed by the bristles. Gently touch the paper with the separated bristles.

5. When finished, rinse, clean, and reshape the brush.

■ This technique will take some practice. Gentle taps will create irregular dots for bushes, treetops, and other textures. Gentle, upward strokes will create irregular lines for grass, fur, and other textures.

Technique Tips

Painting Rough Texture with Watercolor

1. Dip the brush in water.

2. Hold the brush over a container. Squeeze water out.

3. Divide the bristles into spikes.

4. Dip the brush in paint. Lightly touch the brush to paper.

5. Rinse. Shape the bristles into a point.

Technique Tips

Collage

Using Scissors

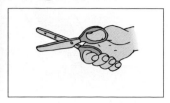

Hold scissors this way.

Hold the paper by its edge with your other hand.

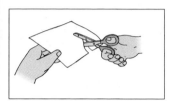

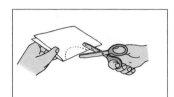

Always cut away from your body.

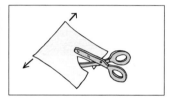

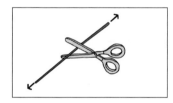

Have a friend stretch cloth as you cut.

Do the same with yarn.

Collage

Scissors

- It is important to teach students safety when they use scissors. They should always cut away from their bodies. Of course they should never point their scissors at others, spin them on the table, or walk around the room with them.

- There are scissors specially made to spring open for students with physical disabilities, or who are not yet developmentally ready to use standard school scissors. Many scissors on the market today can be used with the right or left hand. If these are not available, keep a supply of "lefty" scissors for students who need them.

- To cut thick yarn or fabric, encourage students to work in pairs. While one cuts, the other can stretch the yarn or fabric. This makes cutting easier and encourages cooperation.

Glue

Below are a few tips to share with the students to prevent waste, mess, and wrinkling of paper.

- To attach two pieces of fabric or paper, use only a few drops of glue and smooth them with the tip of the bottle.

- When finished, students should close the top first, then clean the bottle and store upright.

Technique Tips

Using Glue

Use only a few glue dots on one paper.

Smooth with the tip of the glue bottle.

Press the papers together.

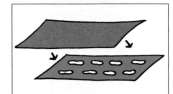

Close the bottle and clean the top.

Technique Tips

Arranging a Design

Tear shapes.

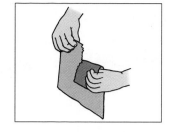

Tear strips.

Cut shapes.

Use found objects.

Make a design.

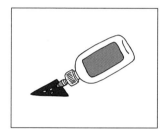

Glue the pieces
into place.

Arranging a Design

- Provide a variety of textured and colored papers, yarns, fabrics, and found objects for students to use. Hard-to-cut materials should be precut for students.

- When using paper, students may choose to tear and/or cut their shapes.

- Encourage students to arrange the design first. They should pay as much attention to the negative spaces as the positive ones.

- Glue only after the final colors, shapes, and textures have been chosen and arranged. White glue will attach most porous items to the background surface.

Paper Sculpture

Making Strip Forms

Paper strips can be folded, curved, twisted, and then glued to create many different forms. A few basic forms are described here. Students will create many more.

1. Prepare by precutting enough paper strips for class use. This can be done on a paper cutter. The strips should be one to three inches wide in a variety of lengths.

2. Make a circle by curving the strip around to its beginning and gluing the ends together.

3. Make a box by folding a strip into four equal sections, leaving a small section for a tab. Bend the tab over its matching end and glue.

4. Make a triangle form by folding a strip into three sections plus a tab. Glue together.

5. Make a cone by cutting out a circle, cutting along its radius, overlapping the side of the cut, and gluing into a cone shape.

Building with Forms

- To join two cardboard forms, it is best to put the tape on one piece and then place it against the second piece before pressing the tape firmly in place.

- Tacky glue can also be used to join two forms. Apply a small amount of tacky glue to one surface, spread it thin with the bottle tip, and then gently press the two pieces together and hold them for a count of ten.

Paper Sculpture

Making Strip Forms

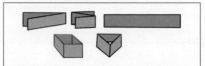

Use paper strips to make stairs, stars, tunnels, and other things.

Cones

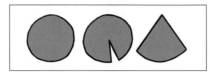

Building with Forms

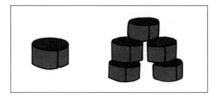

Technique Tips

Weaving

Making a Paper Loom

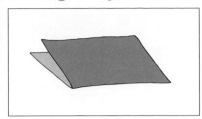

1. Fold paper in half.

2. Cut wide strips from the folded edge. Don't cut to the other edge.

3. Open the paper.

....

Weaving on a Paper Loom

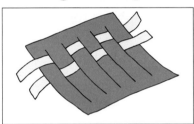

Over and under.

Weaving

Making a Paper Loom

- To make a paper loom, instruct the students to:
  1. Fold a rectangular piece of construction paper in half.
  2. Begin cutting lines from the folded edge, but don't cut all the way to the other end.
- The students can find the stopping point by locating a point three to four finger widths from the open end of the paper. Another method for finding the stopping point is to use a ruler to draw lines for the students to cut along. Draw a thicker line across the stopping point. If you have access to a copy machine that accepts heavy paper, pre-draw one loom and make copies to distribute to students.

Weaving on a Paper Loom

- Precut enough paper strips for each loom. These can be different widths, but the length should be at least the width of the loom.
- To ensure success, have students practice weaving a single strip over and under until they understand the concept.
- Next, students should practice alternating the beginning of each new strip over and under. When this concept has been grasped, they can continue weaving until completion.
- Use a dot of glue to fasten the ends of the strips to the loom.

Printmaking

- Oil-based modeling clay can be used to make a stamp. This is done by drawing or sculpting a design on a flat piece of modeling clay. There are a variety of tools manufactured for carving clay. Some classroom items that will work just as well include plastic eating utensils, craft sticks, and paper clips. The straightened end of a paper clip can be used to draw in the clay. The rounded end can be used as a gouge to carve clay away. To create a raised stamp, simply add pieces of clay to the bottom of the clay stamp.

Using a Brayer

- Below is the procedure for using a brayer, which is a soft roller, to make prints.

  1. Pour a small amount of water-based printing ink or paint onto a flat, solid surface. Roll the brayer in the ink or paint until there is an even coating on the surface and brayer.

  2. Roll the brayer over the top of the stamp. The ink should cover the stamp evenly without getting into the grooves of the design.

  3. Apply the stamp carefully to the paper, rubbing the back of the stamp with the side of the fist.

  4. Peel the paper and stamp apart.

  5. Reink the stamp as needed if you wish to make more than one print.

  6. When finished, wash the brayer, surface, and stamp.

- Another method for making prints calls for a paintbrush to apply the ink or paint. This method works better than the brayer with a raised stamp that the brayer would flatten out. Brush the ink or paint onto the stamping surface. Then follow the steps above, ending with thoroughly cleaning the brush.

Technique Tips

Printmaking

Making a Stamp Print

  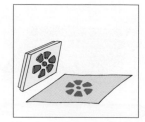

1. Paint the stamp.

   Or, press the stamp into a paint-filled sponge.

2. Press the stamp onto paper and lift.

Using a Brayer

  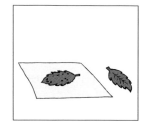

1. Roll the brayer through the ink.

2. Roll the brayer over a leaf.

3. Press the leaf onto paper and lift.

Technique Tips

Printmaking

Making a Sponge Print

Use a different sponge for each color. Dip a sponge in paint. Press it onto paper.

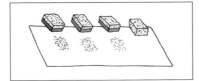

Making a Stencil

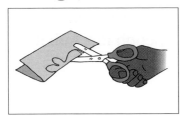 

Cut a shape from folded paper.

Sponge Printing with a Stencil

Hold the stencil in place. Press paint into the stencil with a sponge.

Making a Sponge Print

- If students wish to cut a sponge into a specific shape, use thin sponges. Draw the shape on the sponge with a marker and use scissors to cut it out.

- Dispense colors onto individual palettes, or spread out on a surface large enough to avoid mixing. Lightly press the sponge into the paint, being careful not to get too much paint on it. Lift the sponge and lightly press it into place on the paper. The sponge should be thoroughly rinsed between colors.

Making a Stencil

Have students use the following procedure for making a stencil.

1. Fold a 6″ × 9″ piece of stiff paper in half.

2. Begin cutting on the folded edge, and cut out half the shape. Make sure to finish cutting the shape back on the folded edge. This will result in a solid shape to unfold and a matching negative shape.

3. If the shape cannot be cut from a fold, just cut the shape from the middle of the paper. Save both the positive and the negative shapes. Both can be used as stencils.

Sponge Printing with Stencils

Have students use the following procedure for sponge painting with stencils.

1. Have a sponge for each color.

2. Hold the stencil firmly in place. Don't let it slip. Tape it if necessary.

3. Dip the sponge into the paint.

4. Press the sponge *into* the negative stencil. Press the sponge *around* the positive stencil.

Technique Tips

Printmaking

Monoprint

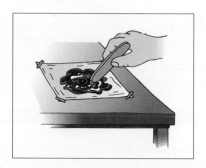 

1. Make a design in paint.

2. Lay paper on top. Rub the back.

3. Peel away the paper.

Technique Tips

Transfer Print

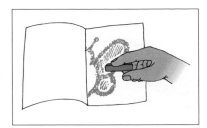

1. Fold paper in half. Unfold and draw on one half.

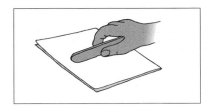

2. Refold the paper and rub.

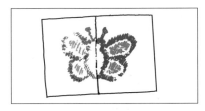

3. Open the paper.

Sculpting

Working with Clay

- Always protect the work area with a cloth or newspaper. Clay dust is messy. Always wash the tables after working with clay.

- To help prevent earth clay from drying and cracking, students should not overhandle the clay. Keep damp paper towels nearby for students to keep their hands moist.

- Clay is often sold in 25-pound bags. The bags are usually strong enough to keep the clay damp, but be sure to close the bag tightly with a twist tie or some other device to keep it sealed. It is a good idea to place the bag inside a second bag, like a heavy duty garbage bag, for long-time storage.

- The following steps are for modeling a person or animal from clay:

  1. Roll the piece of clay into an oval-shaped form. **Describe this to the students as a "potato" shape.**

  2. Pinch a head shape on one end.

  3. Pinch and pull out arms and legs.

  4. Leave some, but not too much, clay for the body.

  5. Squeeze the head, arms, legs, and body into the desired shapes.

- Because students at this level are not developmentally ready to grasp the idea of proportion, arms and legs may be skinny. The concept is to identify and sculpt the major body parts. Details can be added by pinching, pulling, squeezing, or by using carving techniques.

Carving Clay

There are a variety of tools manufactured for carving clay. Some classroom items that will work just as well are plastic eating utensils, craft sticks, and paper clips. The straightened end of a paper clip can be used to draw in the clay. The rounded end can be used as a gouge to carve clay away.

Sculpting
Working with Clay

Squeeze, pull, and shape the clay to make it soft. Form clay into an oval shape.

Squeeze and pinch.

Pinch and pull.

Adding Texture to Clay

Carve the clay. Use a pointed tool.

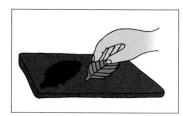

Press an object that has texture into the clay.

Technique Tips

Sculpting

Joining Clay

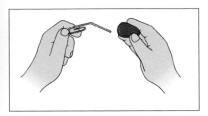

Score the edge.

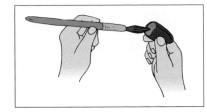

Apply slip.

Squeeze and smooth.

Stitchery

The Running Stitch

Thread a needle.

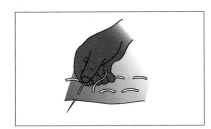

Use a running stitch.

Joining Clay

- Clay is joined by using **slip,** a creamy mixture of clay and water. Slip can be made by putting a few dry pieces of clay in a container and covering them with water. When the clay dissolves, stir to achieve a creamy consistency.

- Joining clay also requires a scoring tool such as a straightened paper clip. The steps below are called the four S's—score, slip, squeeze, and smooth. You have to put the surfaces together before you can smooth the seam.

  1. **Score** the two pieces to be joined.

  2. Apply **slip** to one of the surfaces.

  3. **Squeeze** the two surfaces together.

  4. **Smooth** the seam.

Stitchery

- Large tapestry needles purchased at fabric stores, craft shops, or from art supply catalogs are appropriate for embroidery. They have blunt points and large eyes for easier threading.

- When threading the needle, discourage students from moistening the end of the yarn or thread. It doesn't work and spreads germs. Below are two alternate methods. Either of them will require some patience to master.

  1. Demonstrate twisting the end of the yarn or thread to make a point. Then push it through the eye of the needle.

  2. Another method is to bend the end of the yarn or thread back against itself and then push the looped end through the eye of the needle. This method keeps the frayed end from blocking the opening of the eye of the needle.

- Pull about one fourth of the length of the yarn or thread through the needle. The students can grasp this in their stitching hand as they embroider to keep the yarn or thread from pulling out of the needle. Do not encourage them to tie knots.

- The **running stitch** is made by simply pulling the needle and yarn or thread up through the fabric and pushing it back through the front in a path. When finished, let the loose ends hang out the back. Trim them.

Activity Tips

Line

 **Creative Expression**

1. Think about thick and thin lines.
2. Create a blanket for yourself with different lines.

 **Lines Can Make Calm Pictures**

Unit 1 · Lesson 2

 Creative Expression

1. Tear the paper into short and long pieces.
2. Place the pieces on the page to make a calm landscape.
3. Glue the pieces to the page.

Activity Tips

Unit 1 · Lesson 3   Lines Can Make Busy Pictures

 **Creative Expression**

1. Use the shape and pencil tools to draw a clown.

2. Make the hair by drawing zigzag lines.

3. Decorate the costume with diagonal lines.

Unit 1 · Lesson 4   Curved Lines

 **Creative Expression**

1. Think of your favorite game to play on the playground.

2. Draw a picture of yourself playing.

3. Use curved and diagonal lines to show things moving.

Activity Tips

Unit 1 · Lesson 5 — Smooth and Rough Lines

 **Creative Expression**

1. Think about different types of pets.
2. Draw a pet using smooth and rough lines.

Unit 1 · Lesson 6 — Broken Lines

 Creative Expression

1. Cut paper strips into small squares.
2. Glue them to the paper to form an outline of an animal.

Activity Tips

Shape

🎨 **Creative Expression**

1. Think about the different imaginary creatures you have seen in books.

2. Draw an imaginary creature of your own.

. . . .

Geometric Shapes

🎨 **Creative Expression**

1. Cut out some shapes.

2. Choose the ones you like best and glue them on the paper.

Activity Tips

Unit 2 · Lesson 3 **Free-Form Shapes**

 **Creative Expression**

1. Roll ink onto leaves.
2. Press the leaves on your paper.

Unit 2 · Lesson 4 **More About Shapes**

 Creative Expression

1. Draw a picture of your house. Use geometric shapes.
2. Draw the background with free-form shapes from nature.

Activity Tips

Body Shapes

 **Creative Expression**

1. Draw a big picture of yourself. Fill the entire sheet of paper.
2. Show how you look today. Draw the clothes you are wearing.

The Shape of People

 Creative Expression

1. Think about the size of people in your family.
2. Cut out different-size shapes to show the people in your family.
3. Arrange the shapes on your paper.

Activity Tips **237**

Activity Tips

Unit 3 · Lesson 1   A Garden of Colors

🎨 Creative Expression

1. Think about the types of flowers you like best.
2. Draw your own flower garden.

Unit 3 · Lesson 2   Recognizing Objects by Color

🎨 Creative Expression

1. Choose paper that matches the fruit colors.
2. Cut shapes and make a collage.

Activity Tips

Looking at Colors

🎨 **Creative Expression**

1. Create a collage using the color your teacher gives you.

2. Find that color in magazine pictures. Cut out pieces of that color to make your collage.

Primary Colors

🎨 **Creative Expression**

1. Find an object you like.

2. Use red, yellow, and blue markers only. Draw and color a picture of your object.

Activity Tips

Colors Show Feelings

 **Creative Expression**

1. Choose bright or dull colors for your portrait.

2. Draw your face and body. Then add details.

Unit 3 · Lesson 6 **Light and Dark Colors**

 Creative Expression

1. Create a sea picture with light and dark colors.

2. Add details like fish, waves, and plants.

Activity Tips

Unit 4 · Lesson 1   ## Space in Art

 **Creative Expression**

1. Draw a landscape with trees or houses.
2. Color the sky.

Unit 4 · Lesson 2   ## Form

 **Creative Expression**

1. Make a clay form of yourself.
2. Use a pencil to add a face and clothing.

Activity Tips

Space and Form

 **Creative Expression**

1. Practice holding and moving your paper-towel tube.

2. Use the tube to make a puppet.

A Building Is a Form

 **Creative Expression**

1. Fill the paper bag with newspaper. Staple a folded piece of paper to the top so it looks like a roof.

2. Decorate your house with doors and windows.

242 Activity Tips

Activity Tips

An Animal Is a Form

 **Creative Expression**

1. Make an animal with four legs out of clay.
2. Use a pencil to add eyes and other details.

Forms Can Be Used

 Creative Expression

1. Pinch your clay ball to form a pot.
2. Use a pencil to make a design on your pot.

Activity Tips **243**

Activity Tips

Unit 5 · Lesson 1　Texture You Can Touch

🎨 Creative Expression

1. Think about the shapes you see in a landscape.
2. Cut out the shapes.
3. Use the shapes to make a landscape with textures.

Unit 5 · Lesson 2　Texture You Can See

🎨 Creative Expression

1. Design a hat that has different textures.
2. Make crayon rubbings to create different textures.

Activity Tips

Unit 5 · Lesson 3 Designing with Texture

🎨 Creative Expression

1. Think about a puppet you would like to make.
2. Choose textured materials for your puppet.
3. Glue the materials on your paper bag.

Unit 5 · Lesson 4 Fiber Textures

🎨 Creative Expression

1. Choose a fiber.
2. Weave the fiber through the slits in the cup.

Activity Tips

Real Texture on Forms

🎨 Creative Expression

1. Roll a ball of clay, and then flatten it.
2. Shape the clay into a circle, square, or rectangle.
3. Press objects into the clay to create texture.

Texture on Shapes

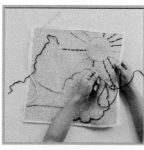

🎨 Creative Expression

1. Think of some shapes you could sew.
2. Draw the shapes on your piece of burlap.
3. Sew along the outlines of your shapes.

246 Activity Tips

Activity Tips

Unit 6 · Lesson 1 — Pattern

 Creative Expression

1. Draw a picture of your home.
2. Add patterns to your home.

Unit 6 · Lesson 2 — Rhythm and Movement

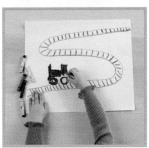

 Creative Expression

1. Draw train tracks on your paper.
2. Draw a train on your tracks.

Activity Tips

Unit 6 · Lesson 3 — Balance

 **Creative Expression**

1. Fold your paper in half the long way.
2. Cut shapes into the unfolded edge.

Unit 6 · Lesson 4 — Balance in Sculpture

 Creative Expression

1. Cut shapes for the face, arms, and legs of the creature.
2. Glue them to the tube so they are balanced.

Activity Tips

Unit 6 · Lesson 5 — Unity

Creative Expression

1. Use the shape tool and line tool to show couples dancing.

2. Draw clothes and other details on your picture.

Unit 6 · Lesson 6 — Unity in Sculpture

Creative Expression

1. Use cardboard tubes to make an animal sculpture.

2. Arrange your sculpture with your classmates' sculptures to make one work of art.

Visual Index

Artist Unknown
Painted Storage Jar
c. 2500–1700 B.C.
(page 146)

Artist Unknown
*Ancient Egyptian Hippo
"William"*
1991–1786 B.C. (page 143)

Artist Unknown
Ritual Wine Container
13th century B.C. (page 173)

Artist Unknown
Ritual Bell
12th century B.C.
(page 198)

Artist Unknown
Camillus
A.D. 41–54. (page 131)

Artist Unknown
*Four Ladies of the Court
Playing Polo*
618–906. (page 207)

Artist Unknown
*Bactrian Camel with
Packsaddle*
700–750. (page 142)

Artist Unknown
Taj Mahal
1638–1648. (page 139)

Jean-Étienne Liotard
*Portrait of Marthe
Marie Tronchin*
c. 1758–1761.
(page 161)

Katsushika Hokusai
Boy Juggling Shells
c. 19th century.
(page 49)

Artist Unknown
House Post
19th century.
(page 199)

Artist Unknown
Fish, Gold Weight
19th–20th century. (page 172)

Artist Unknown
Bowl
c. 1800. (page 147)

William Blake
The Fly from *Songs of Innocence and Experience*
c. 1825. (page 48)

Katsushika Hokusai
The Great Wave Off Kanagawa
1831–1833. (page 34)

Katsushika Hokusai
Kirifuri Waterfall on Mt. Kurokami in Shimotsuke Province
c. 1832–1834.
(page 117)

Currier and Ives
American Express Train
1864. (page 191)

Currier and Ives
My Little White Kittens into Mischief
1865. (page 53)

Artist Unknown
Gift Basket
c. 1870–1880. (page 169)

Artist Unknown
*Classic Serape Style
Wearing Blanket*
1875. (page 36)

W. H. Brown
Bareback Riders
1886. (page 44)

Artist Unknown
Octopus Bag
c. 1890. (page 109)

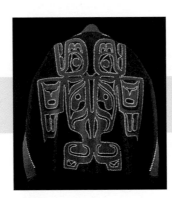

John Yeiltatzie
*Button Robe—Orca
Whale Design*
c. 1890. (page 195)

Louis H. Sullivan
Wainwright Building
1890–1891. (page 187)

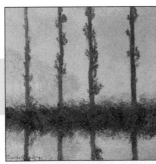

Claude Monet
The Four Trees
1891. (page 40)

John Henry Twachtman
Waterfall Blue Brook
c. 1895–1900.
(page 116)

Harriet Powers
*Bible Quilt, Detail:
Dark Day of May 19, 1780*
c. 1897. (page 176)

Artist Unknown
Hand Puppets
late 19th century.
(page 164)

Artist Unknown
Victorian House
late 19th century.
(page 186)

Felipa Trujillo
Man
early 20th century.
(page 130)

Artist Unknown
Embroidered Pillow
20th century. (page 177)

Maria Martinez
Two Black-on-Black Pots
20th century. (page 184)

Pablo Picasso
The Tragedy
1903. (page 113)

Raoul Dufy
*Le Pantheon et Saint-
Étienne-du-Mont*
c. 1903–1906.
(page 126)

Louis Comfort Tiffany
*Garden Landscape and
Fountain*
c. 1905–1915. (page 56)

**A. Schoenhut Co.
American Toymakers**
*Schoenhut's Humpty
Dumpty Circus*
c. 1905–1935. (page 45)

Henri-Charles Manguin
Port Saint Tropez, le 14 Juillet
1905. (page 60)

Frank Lloyd Wright
Stockman House
1908. (page 138)

Theophile-Alexandre Steinlen
L'Hiver, Chat sur un Coussin
(Winter: Cat on a Cushion)
1909. (page 52)

Marc Chagall
I and the Village
1911. (page 105)

Gabriele Münter
Child with Ball
c. 1916. (page 160)

Georgia O'Keeffe
Autumn Leaves,
Lake George, N.Y.
1924. (page 75)

Edward Hopper
The Lighthouse at Two Lights
1929. (page 127)

Grant Wood
American Gothic
1930. (page 64)

Artist Unknown
Conchero Pull Toys
1930s. (page 165)

Diego Rivera
*Zandunga Tehuantepec
Dance*
c. 1935. (page 202)

Allan Rohan Crite
School's Out
1936. (page 78)

Henri Matisse
Woman in a Purple Coat
1937. (page 94)

Edouard Vuillard
*Morning in the Garden
at Vaucresson*
1937. (page 97)

Henri Matisse
La Musique (Music)
1939. (page 108)

Joseph Stella
*The Brooklyn Bridge:
Variations on an Old Theme*
1939. (page 210)

Henry Moore
Reclining Figure
1939. (page 134)

Visual Index   **255**

Jacob Lawrence
Harriet Tubman Series #4
1939–1940. (page 83)

William H. Johnson
Li'l Sis
1944. (page 82)

Ben Shahn
World's Greatest Comics
1946. (page 79)

Artist Unknown
Butterfly
c. 1950. (page 194)

Auguste Herbin
Composition on the Word "Vie" 2
1950. (page 70)

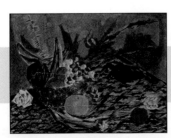

Jacob Lawrence
Still Life with Grapes and Roses
1954. (page 101)

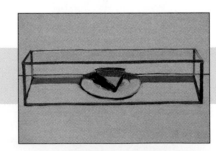

Wayne Thiebaud
Caged Pie
1962. (page 71)

Maurice Sendak
Where the Wild Things Are
1963. (page 66)

Wayne Thiebaud
Three Machines
1963. (page 104)

George Segal
The Diner
1964–1966. (page 150)

David Hockney
American Collectors
1968. (page 41)

Mercer Mayer
There's a Nightmare in My Closet
1976. (page 67)

Jack Savitsky
Train in Coal Town
1968. (page 190)

Marc Chagall
The Four Seasons
1974. (page 57)

Allan Houser
Earth Song
1978. (page 124)

Betty Parsons
Winged Frog
1978. (page 156)

Visual Index   **257**

Audrey Flack
Energy Apples
1980. (page 100)

Rodney Alan Greenblat
Control Chair
1986. (page 120)

John Hoover
Eagle and Salmon
1987. (page 157)

Artist Unknown
Appalachian Basket
1988. (page 168)

Romare Bearden
Family
1988. (page 87)

Janet Fish
Feeding Caitlin
1988. (page 112)

David Wiesner
Free Fall
1988. (page 74)

Sandy Skoglund
The Green House
1990. (page 206)

Sylvia Long
Illustration from *Ten Little Rabbits*
1991. (page 37)

Leo Twiggs
Big Blues Man II
1993. (page 90)

Peggy Flora Zalucha
Sprinkler Garden
1994. (page 96)

Duane Hanson
Old Couple on a Bench
1994–1995. (page 135)

Carmen Lomas Garza
Dance at El Jardin
1996. (page 203)

Miriam Schapiro
Father and Daughter
1997. (page 86)

Peggy Flora Zalucha
My Dad's Violin
1998. (page 180)

Beau Dick
Urban Raven/Urban Indian Transformation Mask
2002. (page 154)

Glossary

art form
A type of art

black

blue

bright colors

broken line

brown

circle

collage
Bits and pieces of things
glued onto paper

color

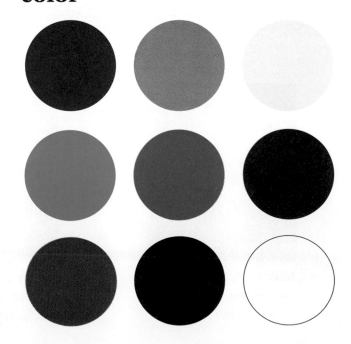

curved lines

darker

diagonal line

dull colors

even balance

Both halves are equal. Left side and right side are the same.

fiber

A material used to make baskets and cloth. Grass, yarn, and straw are kinds of fibers.

form

free-form shapes

geometric shapes

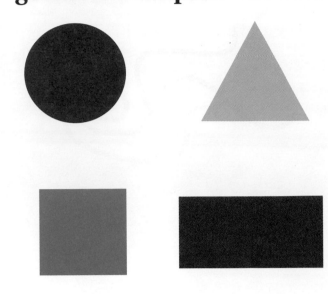

green

horizontal lines

lighter

Mixing a color with white
makes it lighter.

line

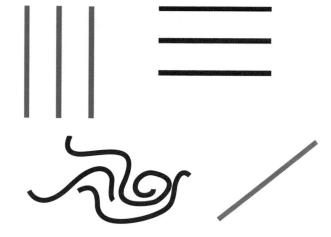

movement

mural

A painting done on a wall

orange

outline

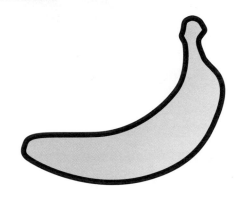

painting

An art form using paint on a
flat surface

pattern

primary colors

Red, yellow, and blue

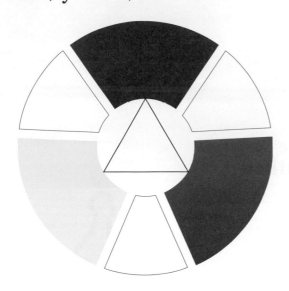

printing

Pressing a shape from one thing to another many times

real texture

Texture you can feel

rectangle

red

rough line

rhythm

sculpture

A kind of art that can be seen from all sides

shape

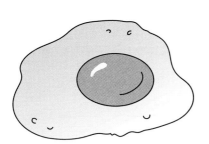

smooth line

---

solid line

A continuous line

space

The empty places around and between shapes.

square

stitchery

Art made with yarn on cloth

texture

How something feels

thick line

thin line

---

triangle

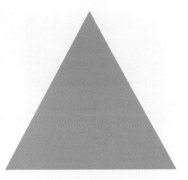

unity

A feeling of belonging together

vertical lines

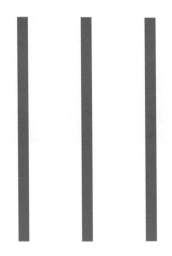

violet

visual texture

Texture you can see, but cannot touch

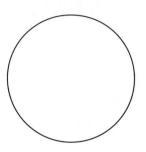

white

yellow

zigzag line

Index

storytelling, 48
style, 96
Sullivan, Louis H., 187

T

Taj Mahal (Unknown), 139
Ten Little Rabbits (Long), 37
texture
    in dance, 183
    defined, 154–155
    and design, 164–167
    and fibers, 168–171
    and form, 172–175
    in music, 183
    real, 158–159, 172–175
    and shape, 176–179
    and touch, 156–159
    visual, 162–163
There's a Nightmare in My Closet
    (Mayer), 67
Thiebaud, Wayne, 71, 104
Three Machines (Thiebaud), 104
Tiffany, Louis Comfort, 56
The Tragedy (Picasso), 113
Train in Coal Town (Savitsky), 190
trains, 190–193
triangle, 72
Trujillo, Felipa, 130
Twachtman, John Henry, 116
Twiggs, Leo, 90
Two Black-on-Black Pots
    (Martínez), 184

U

unity, 202–209

Urban Raven/Urban Indian
    Transformation Mask (Dick),
    154

V

van Gogh, Vincent, 63
Victorian House (Unknown), 186
visual texture, 162–163
Vuillard, Edouard, 97

W

Wainwright Building (Sullivan),
    187
Waterfall Blue Brook
    (Twachtman), 116
weaving, 170
Where the Wild Things Are
    (Sendak), 66
Wiesner, David, 74
Winged Frog (Parsons), 156
Woman in a Purple Coat
    (Matisse), 94
Wood, Grant, 64, 65
World's Greatest Comics (Shahn),
    79
Wright, Frank Lloyd, 138

Y

The Yale University Gallery, 122
Yeiltatzie, John, 195

Z

Zalucha, Peggy Flora, 96, 180
Zandunga Tehuantepec Dance
    (Rivera), 202

Acknowledgments

Grateful acknowledgment is given to the following publishers and copyright owners for permissions granted to reprint selections from their publications. All possible care has been taken to trace ownership and secure permission for each selection included. In case of any errors or omissions, the Publisher will be pleased to make suitable acknowledgments in future editions.

Reprinted with the permission of Simon & Schuster Books For Young Readers, an imprint of Simon & Schuster Children's Publishing Division, From THE CHICK AND THE DUCKLING by Mirra Ginsburg, pictures by Jose & Arianne Aruego. Cover illustration, Copyright © 1972 by Jose Aruego. All rights reserved.

Reprinted with the permission of Simon & Schuster Books For Young Readers, an imprint of Simon & Schuster Children's Publishing Division, from 1 IS ONE by Tasha Tudor. Copyright © 1956 by Oxford University Press. Copyright © renewed 1984 by Corgi Cottage Industries, L.L.C. All rights reserved.

THE STORY OF LIGHTNING AND THUNDER. Copyright © Ashley Bryan (1993). Used by permission of the author.

From TIMOTHY GOES TO SCHOOL by Rosemary Wells, copyright © 1981 by Rosemary Wells. Used by permission of Dial Books for Young Readers, A Division of Penguin Young Readers Group, A Member of Penguin Group (USA) Inc., 345 Hudson Street, New York, NY 10014. All rights reserved.

From OX-CART MAN by Donald Hall, copyright © 1979 by Donald Hall, text. Used by permission of Viking Penguin, A Division of Penguin Young Readers Group, A Member of Penguin Group (USA) Inc., 345 Hudson Street, New York, NY 10014. All rights reserved.

From THE VERY HUNGRY CATERPILLAR by Eric Carle, copyright © 1969 and 1987 by Eric Carle. Used by permission of Philomel Books, A Division of Penguin Young Readers Group, A Member of Penguin Group (USA) Inc., 345 Hudson Street, New York, NY 10014

Photo Credits

Table of Contents

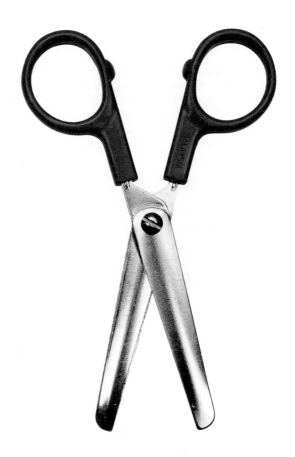

The Elementary Art Curriculum

Rosalind Ragans, Ph.D., Associate Professor Emerita, Georgia Southern University

Art education is for all students. It provides learning opportunities for the artistically talented few, as well as the many students who may never produce art outside the classroom.

A strong elementary visual arts curriculum teaches students that they can communicate a variety of ideas and emotions in many different ways. Students learn that some problems have many different solutions, and they will not be afraid to use divergent-thinking strategies. They will learn concepts and techniques that will give them control of the visual images they produce.

A strong elementary art curriculum also enables students to expand their perceptive, interpretive, and analytical abilities. They learn to find meaning in visual images, and they learn to identify aesthetic qualities in a variety of works of art and in the environment. They begin to develop the ability to make aesthetic judgments.

The visual arts have always been an integral component in the history of humanity, and through the study of art history, students will develop a better understanding of beliefs and ideas that are different from their own.

The four components of a quality art program are Aesthetic Perception, Art Criticism, Art History and Culture, and Art Production and Creative Expression.

Aesthetic Perception

Aesthetics is a branch of philosophy. In visual art, aesthetics becomes the study of the nature of beauty and art. Aesthetics is concerned with the question "What is art?" In the past, aesthetics was defined as the study of beauty because the creation of beauty was thought to be the purpose of art. Today, some aestheticians still believe that the purpose of art is to create beauty or beautifully organized arrangements of the elements of art. Some believe that art must imitate reality. Others think of art as a strong means to communicate ideas and emotions.

Aesthetic concepts are the core of the *Art Connections* curriculum. They are the framework upon which all aspects of art learning are constructed. The **About Aesthetic Perception** section in the *Student Edition* and *Teacher Edition* offers concrete methods for introducing students to aesthetics.

Art Criticism

Works of art are the focus of every lesson. Art criticism is the sequential process used in this textbook to guide students through the procedures needed to learn from these works of art. Art criticism enables students to learn from works of art that have been created by artists from many cultures and time periods. Art criticism also provides a procedure that students can use to objectively study their own art products.

The four-step process of art criticism will help students expand their perceptive, analytical, interpretive, and aesthetic valuing abilities. The sequential steps of art criticism are similar to those used in the scientific method. During the first two steps, **Describe** and **Analyze,** students are asked to collect data objectively. During the third step, **Interpret,** students speculate about the meaning of the work based on the data collected: they make a hypothesis abut the idea, emotion, or mood expressed by the artist. During the fourth step, **Decide,** or aesthetic judgment, the students offer their conclusions about the work of art.

Art criticism helps students study a work of art before making an aesthetic judgment. Too often, beginners look at a work of art briefly and immediately make a value judgment. The sequential procedures in art criticism force the students to postpone judgment while becoming immersed in the image.

In this program art criticism is used as a higher-level method of thinking about the concepts taught in each unit. One work of art has been selected that emphasizes the elements or principles that were the focus of the lesson. Art criticism is also used to help students make a personal assessment of the artwork produced during the Creative Expression activities. The questions offered are neutral and avoid judgments involving likes and dislikes. This avoids embarrassing moments when discussing works in front of peers.

Art History and Culture

Art Connections is not an art history text, but any study of art should begin with learning something about the history of world art and the people who created it. Information about art history related to the featured work of art in each lesson is provided for the students throughout the text. The **About Art History and Culture** section provides an overview of how to include art history information in classroom instruction. Additional information is provided for the teacher in each lesson and in ancillary materials such as the *Artist Profiles* books and on the backs of the *Large Prints.* The *Art Around the World* collection and *The National Museum of Women in the Arts Collection* contain works of art from many countries and provide additional historical and cultural information.

Art Production and  Creative Expression

Each lesson includes an art production activity identified as **Practice** and **Creative Expression** in the *Student Edition.* This is the place for each student to creatively explore the lesson concept. Hands-on activities are often the most enjoyable aspect of art learning. The student integrates and internalizes the verbal and visual concepts of the lesson during the creative manipulation of art materials. While every component in the art program is equally important, every component does not need equal time. Art production requires the longest amount of time.

Do not skip the self-assessment section of the lesson. Most students would be embarrassed to offer subjective statements about their own work or the work of classmates. The four steps of art criticism offer an objective procedure for thinking about the concepts and technical procedures used during the creation of art.

Art Magazine Resources for Teachers

American Artist	*ARTnews*	*Crayola Kids*
Art Education	*Arts and Activities*	*Scholastic Art*
Art to Zoo	*Arts Education Policy Review*	*School Arts*

About Aesthetic Perception

Richard W. Burrows , Executive Director, Institute for Arts Education, San Diego, California

The Association of Institutes for Aesthetic Education promotes and fosters aesthetic education principles and practices through professional and institutional development. The Association provides policy and program leadership to the arts and education field at the national, state, and local levels.

Aesthetics has been defined as the branch of philosophy that focuses on the nature of beauty, the nature and value of art, and the inquiry processes and human responses associated with those topics.

Aesthetic perception can be most simply defined as an educational approach designed to enhance understanding of artistic expression. Aesthetic perception requires two primary elements to exist: a work of art and a viewer to perceive it. An aesthetic perception approach to viewing works of art is predicated on the belief that the arts can be studied in an active, experiential way. The focus is on developing skills of perception by using works of art as a "textbook" or a focus for study. The instruction delivered by teachers is in partnership with the work of art.

Aesthetic perception provides opportunities to heighten perception and understanding through direct encounters with a broad spectrum of works of art. Students and teachers become actively involved with the artwork—observing, listening to and discussing works of art, and exploring their perceptions of these works through participatory activities. The focus is on developing skills of perception through greater understanding of art forms, of how artists make aesthetic choices, and of how these understandings relate to other aspects of life.

Misconceptions About Aesthetic Perception

As aesthetic perception approaches have become more widely used, a number of misconceptions have developed about the purpose of aesthetic perception education in the understanding of works of art.

Multidisciplinary Versus Interdisciplinary

The purpose of aesthetic perception is not to explore the commonalities among works of art. Each work of art must be studied separately first; connections should be made after an in-depth understanding of that particular work. Every work of art has a separate intention and

different meaning. If aesthetic perception is to develop a thinking- or meaning-based understanding of the work of art, then activities must reflect that point of view.

You Cannot Teach What You Do Not Like

A strong "personal" negative reaction to a work of art does not invalidate it as an object of study for students.

Arts Integration

While arts experiences must integrate with all other areas of the curriculum, it is important to understand the separate language that the arts have and acknowledge the connections with other cross-curricular areas as they arise.

The Therapeutic Value of Aesthetic Perception

Very often students and teachers will comment on the therapeutic value of aesthetic perception—it seems separate from the actual art-making processes. This is often a side effect of active engagement in artistic creation and perception. This is not the purpose of aesthetic perception, which should be seen as an alternative way of viewing the work of art and the world in which it is created.

Using Aesthetic Perception

Below are some guidelines for using an aesthetic-perception approach to education.

Deciding What to Teach

It would not be appropriate to teach the same elements over and over in connection with each work of art. Instead, knowledge of all of the elements within a given art discipline should provide the background knowledge for making a decision about what aesthetic perception experiences to design. These decisions should be based on the most predominant elements in the work of art—the responses and the backgrounds of the students.

Creating a Safe Space and Adopting a Critical Stance

It is important to create a working and learning environment with both students and teachers in which they feel comfortable taking risks and trying out new ideas. This does not mean, however, that everything that occurs in aesthetic perception has to be met with uncritical approval. Instead, experiences can be structured so that participants receive feedback on their aesthetic choices and are given an opportunity to revise and improve their solutions to problems.

Documenting the Experience

Various types of documentation serve as a way of recording the aesthetic perception events as they occur or are revisited. This documentation should include written observations, interviews, journals, and student projects. It is important in any case to record this work in order to be able to see the "habits of mind" that reveal themselves in this complex and rich way of thinking and knowing.

Aesthetic perception is a long-term undertaking and requires a patient conviction that the arts and aesthetic perception should be a part of the learning experience of young people. It requires flexibility, stamina, ingenuity, and perseverance. The rewards are astronomical in terms of student response, content understanding, and classroom relationships.

Introduction to Art History

Gene A. Mittler, Ph.D., Professor Emeritus, Texas Tech University

> *"The art of the Greeks, of the Egyptians, of the great painters who lived in other times, is not an art of the past; perhaps it is more alive today than it ever was. Art does not evolve by itself; the ideas of people change and with them their mode of expression."* —Pablo Picasso

One of the primary goals of education in the visual arts is to prepare students to make and support intelligent and sensitive decisions about works of art. In order to make those kinds of decisions students can employ two ways of examining and responding knowledgeably to visual art forms. One of these ways, art criticism, involves them in learning *from* works of art. Another approach is art history, which enables students to learn *about* works of art and the artists who created them.

The Art History Approach to Learning about Art and Artists

Art historians contend that no work of art can be fully understood unless it is viewed in relation to the circumstances in which it was created. Every artwork is created in a particular place at a particular time in history and to some degree is bound to reflect the prevailing conditions of that time and place. For example, an art history approach to the study of a painting by Rembrandt would include an examination of seventeenth century Holland—the time and place in which that particular artist lived and worked. Adhering to this approach would require that students focus attention on the social, religious, and economic conditions that existed in the republic at that time in history before focusing attention on the painter and his work. All these conditions would have impacted Rembrandt's choice of subject matter, medium, his way of handling materials, and the visual language he chose to use in expressing his ideas and feelings.

Art history, then, involves a study of the visual arts in relation to the times and places from which they sprang. This study will provide students with a richer, broader, and deeper understanding of the specific art objects selected for study and the world as it existed when those art objects were created. However, to determine the significance of the place of a particular work, such as a picture by Rembrandt, involves more than just an examination of the world conditions at the time that artist lived. It also requires a study of what went on in the world *before* and *after* Rembrandt painted his picture. A study of this kind will show students that Rembrandt, like all artists, took into account the works of other artists, selecting some ideas and techniques to use in his own painting while rejecting other ideas and techniques. This is a valuable lesson that students can apply to their own efforts to create art.

Consequently, a historical examination of a painting by Rembrandt would include the identification of any artists who may have influenced his style of painting. The most important of these artists was the Italian painter Caravaggio, whose paintings Rembrandt never saw, but without which his own work would not have taken on certain stylistic innovations. However, to understand Caravaggio, students would have to become acquainted with the artists *he* admired as well as the ones he rejected while arriving at his own revolutionary painting style. Thus, students adhering to an art history approach will find themselves involved in a fascinating learning process not unlike a game of dominoes, in which an entire row of game pieces is seen to collapse by upsetting the first domino in that row. The very last "domino" to fall in this comparison of art history to dominoes would be the very first visual image ever created—perhaps an image scratched on the rough wall of a cave by the very first prehistoric artist.

The Use of Historical Periods

For convenience, art historians divide the history of art into more or less artificial periods such as Medieval, Renaissance, Baroque, and Rococo. Doing so does no harm as long as students are reminded that the changes in art history identified by these labels, like changes of the seasons, are gradual. Each historical period passes into the next as smoothly as spring passes into summer.

If it can be assumed that an understanding of the present can be illuminated by a study of the past, then a chronological ordering of art history periods can be most helpful. By beginning at the beginning and observing the changes in art created from one year, decade, or century to the next, students will find it easier to understand how the art produced today has its roots in the art produced in the past. If students are to gain an understanding of art history, they should be afforded opportunities to see and learn about art examples from every corner of the world representing every historical period, not just those created by Western artists.

In every art history period students will encounter artists whose works preserve the traditional values of earlier artists, artists who chose to build upon current art trends, and still other artists who opted to explore revolutionary ways of expressing themselves through their art. Art history is filled with the stories of artists who accepted or rejected, endorsed or protested, conformed or reformed, contrasted or destroyed, dreamed of the past or conjured up visions of the future—but every one of those artists did so from the springboard of his or her own time and place, be that tenth-century China or twentieth-century America.

Art History as a Means of Understanding Each Other

Through art history students learn that a painting, a statue, or a temple is a consequence of how imaginative, sensitive members of any given society viewed and responded to the world around them. Art history also encourages students to regard works of art as more than objects that are pleasing to the eye, more than splendid and original products of human skill and inventiveness. Works of art also represent springboards for learning, revealing how differently people thought and acted at different times and in different geographical locations throughout the long history of humankind. A work of art reveals not only the customs, social habits, architecture, and technical achievements of its time and place; it also reflects the prevailing fears, beliefs, superstitions, desires, and values of people living in different ages at different geographic locations. Art history, then, is a vital part of the history of the human race.

Art History and Changing Tastes

As they study art history, students will discover that, over time, works of art do not always look the same to the people viewing them. This happens because people from different times and places look at art from different points of view. Cultures vary and change and so do tastes. Take any great artist or any great work of art from a bygone era and note how there have been periods in which that artist or work has been highly regarded, treated with indifference, or even ridiculed. For example, few today would venture a negative judgment of a painting created by Rembrandt, who is universally regarded as one of the greatest artists of all time. Yet, over the years, this Dutch master has not always been understood or appreciated. Indeed, when Italian artists first viewed a painting by Rembrandt they were puzzled and disappointed. They failed to understand why this artist was so highly regarded. His style, they concluded, was most peculiar because it made use of large areas of dark values and made no use of outlines favored by Italian artists.

Students must learn that art is a two-way process involving *both* artist and viewer. If students are to grasp more than the superficial appearance of a work of art, they must be prepared to learn its purpose, its *contemporary* meaning within the society in which it was produced, and its place in the historical process. No work of art is created in a vacuum. If students are to share in the ideas and feelings that contributed to the creation of a work of art, they must recognize the concepts, desires, and expectations of the person expressing those ideas and feelings at a particular point in time. This will result in a richer, broader, deeper understanding of both the artwork and the culture that witnessed its creation.

The Art History Operations

The study of art history is made easier for students if a plan of action is offered. One such plan makes use of four steps, or operations, that bear the same labels used to describe the four steps used in art criticism. These operations are description, analysis, interpretation, and decision. However, while these operations enable students to gain information from works of art during art criticism, they also are used to help students gather information about those works during art history. Briefly, the four art history operations are:

Description During this first operation, students seek to discover when, where, and by whom the work was created. In other words, they determine the period in which the work was created, the place where the artist lived, and, assuming it is known, the name of the artist.

Analysis This operation requires students to identify the unique features in a work of art that determine its artistic style. In the visual arts, style has come to mean the personal and unique way in which the artist uses the elements and principles of art to express ideas and feelings. For example, one artist may choose to delineate shapes in his painting by surrounding them with a heavy dark outline. Another painter might ignore the use of an outline and suggest shapes by creating areas of bright hues that contrast with the dull hues surrounding them.

> "Art historians contend that no work of art can be fully understood unless it is viewed in relation to the circumstances in which it was created."

Interpretation When interpreting a work of art, students take into account the impact of time and place upon the artist. It is during this operation that they learn that pictures of the same subject painted at the same time but in different geographic locations typically differ in appearance because they reflect different traditions and values. A landscape painted in fifteenth-century Italy will differ dramatically from a landscape painted at the same time in Japan. Moreover, a work of art created in the same country but at different times may also bear few stylistic similarities. A landscape painted by a French artist living and working in the late nineteenth century would have little in common with a landscape done by a French artist living and working at the beginning of the same century.

In an effort to express themselves in visual terms, artists make use of the materials and processes placed in their hands by the circumstances of time and place. Thus, a nineteenth-century African artist might have carved a figure from a piece of wood to serve as a dwelling place for a departed spirit, while a seventeenth-century artist applied his brush to canvas to paint a lifelike portrait of his king. In the spotlight of history, the efforts of both artists are magnified or diminished, honored or dismissed by forces that neither could predict or control but that had little to do with the values the artists sought to express in their work. It is the desire to discover those values that motivates students when interpreting artists' works.

Decision The final art history operation requires that students make a decision about the historical importance of a work of art. They will discover that some works are more important than others because they were the first examples of a new, revolutionary style. Others are found to be significant because they are the most accomplished and successful examples of a particular style. As their knowledge and understanding of art grows, students will find themselves liking a great many more works of art than they thought possible at the start. Gradually they will gain confidence in their historical judgments and exercise skill in defending those judgments.

Art history is a fascinating, provocative learning experience affording students the opportunity to travel through time and space. It provides them with access to the inner lives of many kinds of people and offers clues to where we come from and who we are. Finally, art history reveals that artists and their art have succeeded in helping people communicate with each other in a manner we cannot express in any other way.

elopment **T5**

Art Criticism

Rosalind Ragans, Ph.D., Associate Professor Emerita, Georgia Southern University

Art criticism is organized discussion about art. The art criticism procedures used in this program were developed by Edmund B. Feldman based on his analysis of the writings of professional art critics. He organized the elaborate procedures followed by critics and summarized them into four steps. The purpose of these four steps is to delay impulse judgments of visual images and to involve the viewer in a complex interaction with the image that can result in a truly aesthetic experience.

Art criticism involves the use of high-level thinking skills. The viewer translates the visual language of the image created by an artist into everyday words. To have a truly aesthetic experience the viewer must go beyond simple identification and recognition to the types of thinking required to analyze, interpret, and judge visual clues.

Anyone can do art criticism. All that is needed are eyes to see the image and a brain to think about what is seen. Art criticism gives a viewer of any age the confidence to discuss a work of art without worrying about what other people have said about it. One does not need to know anything about the artist, the style, or the time when the work was made to get involved with the work. After the steps of art criticism have been followed in a school setting, students are usually so interested in the art that they want to know more about the who, what, where, when, and how of the work. In other words, the students are ready to learn about art history and culture.

Description

The first step of art criticism is a clue-collecting step. The purpose of this step is to get to know the work as intimately and deeply as one can. All the information from the credit line should be noted. It is important for the viewer to know whether the artwork is 20 × 30 inches or 20 × 30 feet. The medium with which the work is made is also important. Whether a piece of sculpture is modeled with clay or carved from stone affects the viewer's impression. Then the observer names everything that is seen in the image. During description the observer must remain objective. All the descriptive terms must be neutral, value-free words.

Analysis

This is an advanced form of description. It is also an objective, clue-collecting step. During this stage the viewer studies the elements of art and the principles that have been used to organize those elements. It is during this step that the viewer begins to discover how the artist has organized the formal qualities of the work to create the content or meaning. In this program you will see how the art criticism lesson at the end of each unit is used to reinforce the concepts taught during each unit. Works of art have been selected that will help the student comprehend the artist's use of the specific elements or principles that were introduced in that unit.

Interpretation

This is the most important part of art criticism. It is during this step that the viewer pulls together all the descriptive and analytical observations to make sense of the work. The viewer makes inferences about the mood, meaning, or message being conveyed by the work. This step goes beyond narration to a generalization about life. The viewer makes guesses, but these ideas must be supported by the clues collected during the first two steps. This can be the most difficult step because it requires imagination and courage. Every interpretation can be different because each is based on the feelings and life experiences of the viewer. No one individual has done or seen exactly the same things as the next person. The viewer may see ideas in a work of art that were never dreamed of by the artist. That is not wrong. It simply means that the work is so powerful that it carries special meanings for everyone.

A good interpretation goes beyond answering "What is happening?" to answering "What does it mean?"

Decision (Judgment)

This is the step where a professional critic will decide the quality of a work. Is this as good as the rest of the works by this artist? How does it measure up to the works of other artists in the same group? The students who are using this program do not have enough experience to make that level of decision, so the works of art in *Art Connections* have been selected because they have already been judged to be outstanding examples of art.

The students are asked to make personal decisions. There are two levels of judgment to be made. The first is "Do you like the work?" This opinion may be embarrassing for students to share in front of classmates, and it is best left unspoken. No one can ever tell someone else what they should like or dislike.

The second level of judgment is also subjective. We ask the student to decide why the work is successful, and we use aesthetic theories to help each individual make decisions about the work. The three aesthetic theories that we employ are the most common theories: imitationalism/realism, formalism/composition, and emotionalism/expressionism. More than one theory can be used to judge a work of art.

- Some critics think the most important thing about a work of art is the realistic presentations of the subject matter. People with this point of view think that an artwork should imitate life. This theory, called **imitationalism** or **realism,** focuses on realistic representation.
- Other critics think that composition is the most important factor in a work of art. This aesthetic theory, called **formalism** or **composition,** places emphasis on the design qualities, the arrangement of the elements of art using the principles of art.
- **Emotionalism** or **expressionism** is the theory concerned with the content or meaning of the work. This theory requires that a work of art convey a message. It must arouse a response of feelings, moods, or emotions in the viewer.

In this program we provide leading questions to help the teacher and student delve into a work of art by using the steps of art criticism. These are not all the questions that can be addressed in viewing a work, and teachers are encouraged to go beyond what is presented on the pages of these books.

Meeting National and State Standards for Art Education

Nan Yoshida

Art Connections has been carefully designed to help educators meet the standards of state and national art curriculum guidelines.

The *National Standards for Arts Education* are part of Goals 2000, the overarching plan for improving American education. Approved by the United States Congress in 1994, the standards describe what every young American student should know and be able to do in the arts.

In addition to the national standards, individual states have curriculum documents that set forth guidelines and requirements in subject areas. For example, both the *Texas Essential Knowledge and Skills for Art* and the *Visual and Performing Arts Framework for California Public Schools, Kindergarten through Grade Twelve* discuss four components of visual arts education common to most other state guidelines.

Placing the national standards side by side with the Texas and California standards, one can readily see that the documents match in their expectations of what students should know and be able to do in the visual arts.

Art Connections has been developed with these national and state expectations in mind. Every lesson in the program was designed to address the components of art education in Aesthetic Perception, Art History and Culture, Creative Expression, and Art Criticism.

Aesthetic Perception
(Artistic Perception)

Each lesson begins with Activate Prior Knowledge, which asks students to recall and visualize an image from personal experience that will help them take a purposeful look at the artwork.

Introduce the Art focuses students' attention on specific attributes of the artwork, design elements and principles, underlying structures, and functions. As students answer the questions about the work of art, they develop critical *observation* skills.

Aesthetic Perception directs students to extend their artistic perception to their environment and objects in the environment. The transition is made to use keen visual and tactile perception of formal art objects in everyday life (lifelong learning).

> "In *Art Connections* students are exposed to a variety of types and styles of art from many cultures and historical periods."

Art History and Culture
(Cultural Context)

In *Art Connections* students are exposed to a variety of types and styles of art from many cultures and historical periods. Students study art from Africa; Asia; Australia; Europe; and North, Central, and South America. They learn about the role of the artist in societies. They develop appreciation for paintings, drawings, prints, photographs, sculptures, textiles, and architecture. They relate to folk, decorative, functional, and formal arts.

While information about the works of art and the artist is necessarily brief in the *Student Edition,* teachers are encouraged to use the Art History and Culture feature of the *Teacher Edition* and the *Artist Profiles* books to provide students with enriching information about the artists, the periods of art history, and cultural perspectives.

Creative Expression
(Art Production)

Creative expression is fundamental to every art lesson. The Practice activity provides a structure for students to apply lesson concepts in meaningful practice. In the Creative Expression activity, students refine their new knowledge and skills by producing original artwork based on their personal visions. The lessons throughout the program introduce a variety of art media and techniques.

Art Criticism
(Aesthetic Valuing)

Reflection and self-assessment are inherent in the art-making process. Upon completion of the Creative Expression activity, students evaluate their own work using the four steps of art criticism: Describe, Analyze, Interpret, and Decide. These four steps of art criticism are a method for making an informed critique of others' artwork as well.

Arts Integration

In addition to the high priority placed on teaching the visual arts as a unique discipline, both national and state standards recommend the appropriate integration or interrelation of the visual arts with the other arts disciplines of music, dance, and theatre. Toward this goal, every unit in *Art Connections* culminates with a lesson integrating one of these performing arts. In addition, connections are made to music and movement/dance in every lesson of the *Teacher Edition.*

Curriculum Integration

The *Teacher Edition* has an Art Across the Curriculum section that ties art concepts to other curriculum areas. Every lesson has a connection to Reading/Language Arts, Math, Science, Social Studies, and Technology.

> ### National Standards for Arts Education © 1994
>
> 1. Understand and apply media, techniques, and processes.
> 2. Use knowledge of structures and functions.
> 3. Choose and evaluate a range of subject matter, symbols, and ideas.
> 4. Understand the visual arts in relation to history and cultures.
> 5. Reflect upon and assess the characteristics and merits of their work and the work of others.
> 6. Make connections between the visual arts and other disciplines.

Displaying Students' Art

Jackie Ellett

"My picture is hanging in the hall!" exclaims an excited second-grader. Yes, having one's work displayed is exciting. When you display a child's artwork, you are communicating two things to that child: you value what he or she has created *and* you value the child.

Why Display Students' Art?

Students are intrigued by the work their peers produce and are eager to join in any discussion that arises from the shared experiences of the work. They often compare what they have created to the work made by their peers. A natural aesthetic experience occurs, and questions and comparisons arise. These are either verbalized or internalized, depending on the circumstance of the viewing. "Why did Erin paint that flower large and the others small?" "I like the details of the seeds that Galvin added to his painting; I'll do more details next time." These are examples of questions, comments, or thoughts that may arise when students are viewing a display. Not only do displays allow students to appreciate their completed projects, but they also allow students to aspire to better art endeavors.

A class display allows students the opportunity to stand back and critique their work. A teacher-led critique is best. Students are able to evaluate their work, gain insight into things they may not have thought about, and may learn a new solution to a problem they have encountered. Discussing their works as you would a fine-art print validates the importance of what they have created. Art is so personal that a discussion can become quite insightful.

Preschool and early elementary-aged students are eager to take their works of art home to show their parents what they have created. You should ask permission of all students to display their work. By asking permission you are showing respect for their work, and for those students as individuals.

Displays are also a good way to show administrators, parents, and the community what students are learning.

Where to Display Students' Art

Many art educators believe that the farther away from the classroom the display, the more selective the images need to be. In the classroom, every student's art may be displayed.

This area can be controlled by the teacher, students, or both. Students can be allowed to change their own work when they decide to.

Outside of the classroom there is usually an assigned area for each class to display its work. Bulletin boards made of composition board are the most desirable of all surfaces for two-dimensional art. Artwork is easily attached using staples, and the walls are protected from any damage.

Setting up a school gallery of permanent or rotating student art is wonderful for promoting the art program within a school. This should be housed in a high-traffic area where parents, administrators, and visitors can view students' art. In "Leadership and the Elementary Art Specialist: Twenty Ways to Improve Your Program's Position in the Educational System," Phillip Dunn recommends establishing a "Principal's Permanent Art Collection." Having a gallery within the school with professionally matted and framed student art communicates that students' works and the art program are valued. In an era where budget cuts are customary, promoting the work of students is very important to the survival of art programs.

Displays in local businesses, civic centers, or art centers help educate the public about the work being done within their schools. These exhibits contain a mix of student art that has gone through a selection process. Depending on the guidelines and formality of the display, the works can be mounted, matted, or framed, with three-dimensional works displayed in sculpture cases or on sculpture stands.

How to Display Students' Art

Student art can be displayed in a variety of ways. Some teachers take digital photos of their students in the process of creating a work of art and critiquing their work, and then take a photo of the finished art itself. These images can be posted on a school Web site with descriptions of the activity. Digital images are sometimes used as screen savers on the school's computer system and highlighted on closed-circuit TVs in the classrooms. The most common method of display, however, is the bulletin board. These have evolved from simple displays to elaborate descriptions of the process and documentation of student learning. Teacher-focused bulletin boards have given way to student-focused displays that often include student reflections

and interpretations. Including descriptions of the process and background information adds to better understanding of the learning that has taken place.

Two-dimensional works of art should be mounted on larger contrasting or neutral-toned paper. The top and sides are usually of equal width with the bottom larger, unless the work is square, in which case all four sides are equal in width. When matting art, a two- to three-inch mat is standard, with the bottom being an inch wider than the top and sides. The mat acts as a resting place, so when arranging mounted or matted art, the works should not overlap.

A sheet of butcher paper or bulletin-board paper can be attached to a wall to define a display area and unify the works of art. Poster board or construction paper cut wider on all sides than the largest paper used by a class can be attached to the wall as an area for mounting individual students' work. Glue a clothespin to the top of the mounted paper so students can easily change their artwork. The background papers are usually in neutral colors, although primary colors may be used in classrooms for younger children. Each background paper is individually identified by placing the child's name in large print on a label.

Three-dimensional works look best in sculpture cases or on sculpture stands. Not every school can afford these. Arranging sturdy boxes of varying heights and covering them with complementary cloths allow sculptures to be equally viewed. If sculptures are of varying sizes, the largest should always be placed toward the back and the small works in front. Arranging works in odd numbers creates interest as well.

Mobiles and kites are best displayed from the ceiling. Make certain that all materials are well attached and that the items hung from the ceiling are secure so they do not fall or set off sensor alarms. As with all displays, it is important to know your school's policies about the types of adhesives allowed. Hot glue has a tendency to peel paint, low-temperature glue guns may not work on some surfaces, and double-sided tape can leave a residue. Humidity and the wall's surface both affect what will and will not work. Reusable tacky putty sticks to most surfaces and leaves few marks.

Displays do much to enhance and rejuvenate students' spirits and allow students to communicate in a way that is neither mathematical nor verbal. The art that students make is very personal and deserves careful attention when being displayed.

Art Assessments

Assessment in art can be problematic for a variety of reasons. Many educators are reluctant to evaluate a student's creative expression as good or bad. Because there are often no right or wrong answers, students and their parents could challenge a teacher's subjective opinion of a work if it is reflected in a letter grade. Furthermore, many teachers without a strong art background do not feel qualified to grade student artwork. In addition, teachers do not want to discourage creative expression by giving a low grade or an undeserved grade. Many people also often feel that talented students have the advantage in art class and that students should not be evaluated on how talented they are, but rather on how much effort they put into their work and how much progress they make.

All of these assessment difficulties stem from the focus on art production in the art classroom, rather than a reflection of art history and culture, aesthetics, or art criticism. A broader focus in the art classroom and a variety of assessment options may help in more effective art assessment.

Assessment of Lesson Objectives

Instead of subjective opinions of whether or not one likes a student's artwork, students can be evaluated on whether or not they meet the art lesson objectives or demonstrate the knowledge and skills introduced in the lesson. In a quality art program, there are objectives for aesthetic perception, art history, and art criticism, as well as for demonstrating understanding of the elements and principles of art in art production.

In *Art Connections,* every lesson has four clear, measurable objectives. At the end of each lesson, a rubric provides evaluation criteria for each objective.

Art Production: Evaluating Student Artwork

Art teachers frequently evaluate student artwork on the basis of how well it reflects the elements and principles of art that are being stressed in the lesson and how well the student meets the criteria for the artwork. Some teachers can construct rubrics or standards for the artwork beforehand and tell students how their work will be evaluated at the time it is assigned. Other teachers use

written or mental checklists of their standards as they look at student artwork. Teachers may use this form of evaluation as an opportunity to discuss the work with a student and find out whether the student thought he or she met the objectives for the artwork.

In *Art Connections,* teachers can also use the Assessment Masters in the *Assessment* book to get an idea of whether a student understands the elements or principle of art for a lesson.

Art Criticism and Aesthetic Perception: Self- and Peer-Assessment

The four-step process of art criticism (Describe, Analyze, Interpret, Decide) provides a procedure that students can use to objectively study their own art products, as well as the works of others. The sequential steps of art criticism are similar to those used in the scientific method. During the first two steps, Describe and Analyze, students are asked to collect data objectively. During the third step, Interpret, students speculate about the meaning of the work based on the data collected: they make a hypothesis about the idea, emotion, or mood expressed by the artist. During the fourth step, Decide, students offer their aesthetic judgment about the work of art. The sequential procedures in art criticism force students to postpone judgment while becoming immersed in the image. It forces them to have a fully funded visual experience before drawing conclusions about a work.

Art Connections includes art criticism questions for every Creative Expression activity. Additionally, the Aesthetic Perception feature in every lesson of the *Student Edition* provides students with an opportunity to evaluate their developing aesthetic perception.

Art History and Culture

Art is a visual record of history and diverse cultures. The goals for elementary art education are that students understand and appreciate different historical periods, cultures, and artistic styles and develop respect for the traditions and contributions of diverse societies.

In *Art Connections* every lesson introduces a work of art from a particular culture, time, and style. In the Introduce the Art strategies, teachers are encouraged to compare, contrast,

and share the Art History and Culture information as well as the information provided in *Artist Profiles* to help students develop an understanding of the visual arts in relation to history and cultures. Through discussion and elements in students' own artwork, teachers can evaluate students' awareness in this area.

Portfolio Assessment

Art educators could claim to have inspired the growing use of portfolio assessment in other subject areas. Many art teachers collect the best examples of a student's work and look at the progress over time. They display it and discuss it with students and parents. Student art journals with ideas, drawings, and sketches also provide an opportunity for portfolio assessment.

In *Art Connections* students are encouraged to keep their best work in a Student Portfolio and to maintain an Art Journal. Reminders of these types of portfolio assessments appear in the *Teacher Edition.*

Performance Assessment

Unlike other subject areas, art education has a long tradition of performance assessment. In art class students make things to demonstrate what they can do. In quality art programs, teachers use performance descriptions not only for art production, but also for art criticism, art history and culture, and aesthetic perception to aid them in evaluating student demonstrations of their knowledge and skills in art.

In *Art Connections,* every work of art a student produces can be considered for performance assessment of the lesson concept. Performance assessments can also involve discussions about the works of art to introduce the lesson concept and art criticism questions.

Art not only enables teachers to evaluate student knowledge and skills in art each year, but it also provides a wonderful opportunity to assess students' growth and development over time. Students and parents are often reluctant to discard artwork and fondly review it from time to time to see how children's ideas and skills have changed. Schools often keep examples of student artwork in student portfolios from year to year.

A thoughtful and fair art assessment program enables teachers to really see how much their students are capable of accomplishing.

Art and Cross-Curricular Connections

Tina Farrell

The study and production of artwork enhances learning in all areas of the curriculum. When teachers and students connect art to other subjects, learning occurs in the natural and interrelated way that it exists in the real world. We know from experience that learning is most meaningful when it is interconnected, not isolated. Therefore, making the natural connections that exist within each discipline of study, art including, enhances total understanding and brings meaning to fragmented information.

Below are a few of the ways that art education can impact the study of other subjects.

Reading/Language Arts In the viewing and analysis of a work of art, students develop oral and written communication skills. Teachers can enhance the language process by writing art terms and concepts on the board, having students generate lists of adjectives and adverbs to describe works of art, encouraging reflective inquiry into art, having students read about art and artists, and having students use works of art as stimuli for all forms of writing.

Mathematics Mathematics concepts are enhanced through art. When math concepts are presented or expressed in a visual or manipulative manner, students can more easily grasp them. The comparison and development of shapes and forms, visual-spatial relationships, measurement, proportion, estimation, and grids and graphs, for example, all are best explained through art.

> "We know from experience that learning is most meaningful when it is interconnected—not isolated."

Science In the art-making process, children learn that multiple ways to solve problems exist. They learn to discover, imagine, try new materials and techniques, experiment, develop and test hypotheses, and observe and record visual data. These are many of the skills, objectives, and habits of mind taught in science.

Social Studies The history of the world is reflected in the functional and aesthetic works of art produced by the peoples of the world. Children can gain great insights about near and distant cultures through the study of art, artifacts, and architecture.

The Arts The arts all complement each other in the skills, elements, principles, and beliefs that are emphasized in each one. Each discipline presents a unique way to express ideas and transform emotions into song, dance, interactions, words, or images. Visual artists research, develop rough drafts (sketches), plan, develop ideas, produce completed visual ideas, and sign and title their works. These are the processes that authors, writers, dancers, composers, actors, and poets also employ.

Life Skills In art, children develop craftsmanship, self-discipline, dedication to a task, skills for working both individually and cooperatively, and pride in one's work. These skills are necessary for success in all areas of their lives.

Critical-Thinking Skills Studying the visual arts develops higher-level thinking skills as studenst analyze, compare, interpret, synthesize, and make inferences and judgments about works of art.

Art is a great integrating subject because art, first and foremost, is a form of human communication. Art is one of the first forms of communication for children. Children often express complex ideas through visual symbols that represent their beginning language systems. Art is a vehicle for children to learn about the world around them and to organize the information in a comprehensive format. As young children draw, they take textures, shapes, and colors from a complex world and form them into coherent visual images. This visual cognition, a powerful way for children to process information, is the basis for learning in and through art.

A Sampling of Art Program Resources for Schools

The California Arts Project
   (http://www.ucop.edu/tcap/aeol.html)
Getty Education Institute for the Arts
   (http://www.artsednet.getty.edu)
The Kennedy Center ArtsEdge
   (http://artsedge.kennedy-center.org)

The Metropolitan Museum of Art
   (http://www.metmuseum.org/explore/index.asp)
The Educator's Reference Desk
   (http://www.eduref.org/cgi-bin/res.cgi/Subjects/Arts)

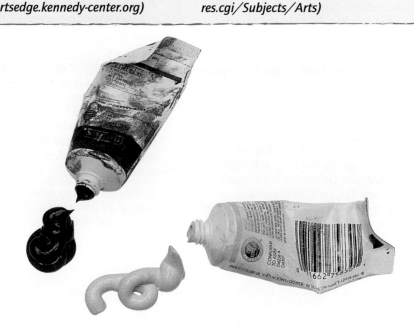

Integrating the Four Art Forms

Susan Cambigue-Tracey, Education Division, The Music Center of Los Angeles County

Albert Einstein said, "Imagination is more important than knowledge." Without exercising the imagination, knowledge is stored in the individual containers of the mind, but connections are not made. When students are taught to use the elements, skills, and content of the visual and performing arts the possibilities for synthesizing and applying what they know are multiplied. Teachers need to ensure that imagination and creativity are always nourishing the roots of learning.

The importance of artistic activity for all students goes beyond the intrinsic value of each art form in itself. Real arts investigation requires the rigor of being able to focus, make decisions, develop discipline, promote originality, and undertake research, study, and practice. Helping students to experience new ways of thinking and seeing allows them to construct personal meaning from what they experience and to build confidence and motivation.

Each art form is a discrete discipline with its own elements, vocabulary, and strategies. However, it is interesting to see connections among them where there are fundamental concepts shared across the arts and other subjects. For example, lines in art are the marks used to create images. Line in dance is the path of gestures and traveling movements, as well as body design. Line in music is a melody and also the lyrics of a song, while lines in theatre are the words that the actors speak.

A common core of knowledge is built through the arts. The principles of visual art, such as emphasis, variety, harmony, unity, and contrast, are the underlying principles used to creating anything—an architectural structure, a musical composition, a piece of literature, a dance, or a play.

It is easy to find ways to integrate one or more of the art forms and still make connections that are viable and authentic. For example, when viewing and discussing a work of art from a particular time period or culture, select music from that same time period or culture. Aztec art will have more relevance when Aztec-inspired music is played or students can view an Aztec dance and see the colors and design of the costumes. A style of music might also inspire art. Matisse did a jazz series that begs for jazz music and dance. Students can then see and hear the structural and improvisational aspects of this style in three different art forms.

When viewing or painting family scenes in art, challenge students to think of family activities that can be portrayed in a tableau, or live, frozen picture. When viewing or creating sculpture, pair students and have one person become the "clay" and the other the "sculptor" who shapes the clay with respect and cooperation. This can extend into dance by directing the sculpted person (clay) to develop a movement idea lasting eight counts that starts and ends with the sculpted pose or form. Two people in contrasting sculptural poses can have eight counts to slowly transform from one into the other.

Three-dimensional forms in art can inspire counterbalanced (push, pull, leaning) designs made by small groups. A story, such as "The Two Skyscrapers Who Wanted to Have a Child" by Carl Sandburg, could be retold using story theatre or be portrayed in tableaux or as dramatized scenes. Students could also research musical selections to accompany their work.

> "Imagination is more important than knowledge."
> –Albert Einstein

Students will be better able to express emotions in their visual artwork if they first work with them through drama, music, and dance. Students can begin by showing a variety of emotions in the face, hands, and feet and then move toward portraying these emotions in postures such as sitting, standing, and walking. Everyday activities such as cooking or brushing teeth can be done with different emotional motivations. Students can also create short musical pieces depicting an emotion or mood or find music that expresses specific feelings or moods.

All four performing arts can become a powerful component of integrated learning. For example, during a fifth-grade project focused on the Lewis and Clark expedition, students did research in books and on the Internet to collect historical, scientific, geographical, and cultural content. This information served as the basis for group projects in music, dance, theatre, visual arts, technology, and language.

Challenged by well-designed tasks, students discussed what they knew and selected different aspects to explore through dance, music, theatre, and visual art. They learned songs of the times, listened to traditional fiddle music, and learned a rhythmic chant that was used to measure the depth of rivers. In dances, they captured the sense of traveling through "boundless space"; portrayed animals encountered during the expedition; created weather conditions such as storms; and showed the struggles in navigating rivers, waterfalls, and mountains. In theatre, students drew upon the historical characters, interpreted various scenarios, and read journal entries of Lewis and Clark. Visual art classes focused on observation drawings of plants and wild animals.

Students also created journals in which they recorded their feelings, observations, sketches, and discoveries. They were able to make connections between their own journeys and that of the Corps of Discovery. Finally, the students shared what they had learned about this epic journey in a multi-arts culmination.

The arts bring accessibility and vitality to learning, empowering students to construct meaning that has relevance for their lives. When children learn to draw, they learn to see. When children learn to act, they learn how it feels to be in different roles, cultures, and circumstances. When children learn to dance, they learn to feel comfortable in their bodies and to use movement expressively. When children learn to play an instrument, they learn perseverance and the rewards of expression through music. When children learn to sing, they release their voices and are empowered to harmonize. When children learn to write a play, they learn to observe life by thinking, reflecting, and writing. When creativity and imagination are nurtured, children learn how to use all of their resources to solve problems, to dream, and build on the ideas of others.

The Creative Process and Problem Solving

Bunyan Morris, Art Teacher, Effingham County School System, Georgia

There is great reward in watching the artistic growth of a child. Simply providing the media and the time for creating is not enough. The student's natural curiosity and desire to create must be nurtured, encouraged, and challenged. Even the brightest and most talented students need a teacher's guidance in developing the critical-thinking skills necessary for creative problem solving. The intention of this article is to provide ideas and methods for fostering creativity by developing and encouraging divergent problem solving and critical-thinking skills in elementary school art students.

Classroom Management

Fostering creativity in the art classroom is possibly an art teacher's most important skill. In order to encourage creativity, a teacher must be able to relate to students at their thinking level and then guide them to a higher level of cognitive reasoning. Classroom and behavior management are essential. There cannot be an atmosphere of creativity in a room with chaos. That is not to say that one must be a firm authoritarian. A good art teacher will learn how to walk the fine line between maintaining order and maximizing creative energy among students. Although some may not admit it, all students prefer an educational environment that is free from annoying distractions created by other students. Therefore, good behavior management is a must for maintaining a creative environment.

Visual References

Introducing a lesson with a work of art and going through the art criticism process is a tried and true method of encouraging creativity. It is important to discuss works of art that are related to the objectives of the lesson. Working strictly from imagination and memory is usually not effective. Students must have visual references from which to gather ideas.

Picture files, reference books, and the Internet are just a few sources for visual images. Photographs of people and various natural and humanmade objects provide ideas and references for drawing. Images can be collected from magazines and calendars or unwanted photographs. The image file should be organized according to subject matter or theme.

Reference books filled with images related to the lesson should be available to students. They may be checked out of the media center and kept in the room, or they may belong to the classroom. Some media specialists are willing to search for and reserve books that a teacher may need for an upcoming lesson.

An image search on the Internet is one method to help students access a visual reference that may not be available in the classroom's image file, reference books, or the school's media center.

Art Journals

Students who keep art journals maintain handy reference tools. An art journal is the best way to record ideas through sketching and writing. If art journals and writing tools are kept handy, students can jot down ideas or make sketches to save for future use. Ideas can come to mind any place or any time such as in the cafeteria, on the playground, or at the bus stop. The method or tool doesn't really matter that much. It is just important that students have a way of practicing and recording creative ideas.

Exercising the Brain

Reading should be encouraged. Students who like to read perform better in all subjects. Descriptive language stimulates the imagination. Reading a passage about the beauty of a tree or the sound of a waterfall creates a visual image in the brain. This visual image can be stored in the sketchbook and later rendered as a sculpture, painting, or drawing. Encouraging reading encourages creativity. Teachers and schools should encourage parents to limit their children's time watching television because this takes away from reading and creative play time.

Resting the Brain

Teachers should be tolerant of students taking small breaks. Sometimes students need down time to regenerate their mental energy. This down time can take the form of daydreaming or play. Both are important to the creative process. Common sense and good judgment is used to determine when a student is using time for thinking as opposed to just wasting time. Students should be reminded to get a

> "Fostering creativity in the art classroom is possibly an art teacher's most important skill."

good night's sleep every night. This is not something teachers can control, but it should be encouraged. We all know that brains function better after a good night's rest.

Enriching Observation Skills

Enriched observation skills lead to more focused experimentation in art. Artists are naturally observant, but teachers know that most students are not born with natural talent. Through practice, all students can enrich their observation and critical-thinking skills. It is important to get students to slow down and see what they might not otherwise observe. One way to do this is to play an observation game. With the students' help, the teacher can set up a still life in the room. A fun game similar to "I Spy" can be played once the still life is ready. The students describe textures, lines, shapes, colors, and other elements and principles of art found within the real-life objects. The teacher writes the observations and descriptions on the board. Once the game is over and students move to the project portion of the lesson, they will be better equipped with enriched observation skills and more focused critical-thinking skills as they create.

In order to gain more focused and creative experimentation from students, an important goal of every art teacher should be to encourage creativity and divergent problem solving and critical thinking. Hopefully, teachers will find value in the ideas shared in this article and combine them with their own ideas to encourage creativity in their students.

Using Writing to Enhance Your Art Curriculum

Mary Lazzari, Ed.S., Elementary Art Teacher, Clarke County School District, Athens, Georgia

In recent decades, art teachers have expanded their area of expertise from art production to lessons that include art criticism, art history, and aesthetics. Art is being used as a vehicle not only for increasing creativity but also for developing thinking skills. One way to broaden the art experience and enhance these skills is through guided, interactive writing techniques. Writing about art is an essential component of a well-rounded art curriculum because it provides students with the opportunity to transform thoughts and feelings into words and images. It can also provide the art teacher a more personalized format for communicating with a large student population and assist art teachers in meeting the increased demand to qualify and quantify their students' learning.

> "Art is being used as a vehicle not only for increasing creativity but also for developing thinking skills."

A visual arts curriculum rich in written language activities can facilitate the development of higher-order thinking skills, such as the ability to analyze, defend, and interpret. The use of written statements can help students slow down and refine their thoughts about their own art and the art of others. Words can become the voice for a shy or inarticulate student. With writing as a means of self-expression, art educators can be more in tune with their students' inner thoughts. Some art teachers may be reluctant to incorporate writing into their curriculum because they fear a less than enthusiastic response from their students. Here are a variety of suggestions that can help motivate elementary students to write about art.

Journals

Whether it is a few sheets of paper stapled together or a spiral notebook, students enjoy having a place to write their private thoughts and feelings. Journals can be used to record the thought process from the beginning to the end of a project. It can also be a place to brainstorm ideas or vent frustrations. Art teachers can give written feedback and encouragement to each student in his or her journal.

Titles

Materials: Selected works of art, pencil and paper

At the completion of a project, students can write descriptive titles for their works of art. A title can inform, challenge, or even surprise a viewer. Younger children or students with a language deficit can dictate the title as the teacher writes. Include the student's title when displaying the artwork. Students can also think of a new title for a famous work of art. Compare it to the artist's original title and discuss the similarities and differences.

Acrostic Poems

Materials: Selected works of art, pencil and paper (for individual writings), or dry/wipe board (for group writing)

Select an artist's name or art topic and write the letters vertically. Instruct students to think of words that describe the artist or topic. Students should think of a decriptive word for each letter in the artist's name or art topic. Descriptive words can start, end, or have the letter anywhere in the selected word. Display acrostic poems with the art work that inspired them.

Venn Diagrams

Materials: Individual sheets of Venn diagrams (or draw a large diagram on the board for a whole group discussion); a set of art postcards

Place an image in each of the two outer circles of the Venn diagram. Students describe qualities they see in each of the two works of art. Qualities that are unique to each image are written in the circle that contains the image. Qualities that they have in common are written in the center of the diagram where the two circles overlap. Invite individuals or groups to share their observations. Mount and display Venn diagrams with student artwork.

Artist Statements

Materials: Pencil and paper

Direct students to write three to five sentences about their artwork. Have the students consider these questions: What did I study? What did I create? What did I learn? Display the artist statements with the completed artwork.

Writing Buddies

If you have students who are reluctant or unmotivated to write during art class, have them work in groups. Ask for a student volunteer to be the group secretary. This student is responsible for writing down the group's thoughts and ideas. Students who are not strong in written expression will still feel success in sharing their ideas and opinions.

Brainstorming Ideas

Incorporate writing at the beginning of a lesson by having students use writing devices such as webs. The main topic is placed on the center of the page and ideas that support or expand it are written on the sides.

Vocabulary

Incorporate vocabulary into the art room. Post the "Word of the Day" on a chart or bulletin board display. Build a "Word Wall" with art vocabulary that is added throughout the year. Use word labels on art materials and equipment around the room. Create art flash cards with art words or concepts printed on them. Use the flash cards to find elements such as line, shape, and color in works of art or to review these concepts at the beginning or end of a lesson.

Try writing yourself!

Post statements about projects when displaying your students' works of art. Describe the learning objects and concepts in your statement. Use the display to inform parents, teachers and administrators about the rich and interesting learning that is taking place in your art class. Include articles about lessons, projects, and student achievements in your school or district newsletter.

Writing is an important means of creative expression. It is as valid and essential to the art curriculum as drawing or painting. Using writing to augment the art curriculum not only improves the students' ability to express ideas, it helps the art teacher communicate more effectively with every student. When art teachers integrate art instruction and writing about art, the entire curriculum is enhanced. By pairing art production, a realization of students' thoughts and ideas, with writing, a reflective way to understand and validate their opinions and feelings, art teachers can broaden the scope of the art experience. At the same time, the art teacher will develop a critical means to record and assess student learning.

The Importance of Cultural Diversity Through Art in the Elementary Classroom

Jane Rhoades Hudak, Ph.D., Professor of Art, Georgia Southern University

Culture is learned. People acquire information about the world and how to deal with it as members of a society. Individuals do not learn about their culture by themselves. Children learn about the art of their own culture and other cultures through family and friends, through the mass media, and through the Internet. The information learned this way is often valuable, but it cannot be relied upon to always give adequate and correct information. Schools are often the most effective place for giving students the opportunity to learn about the art of their culture and other cultures.

Our view of the nature of the world and our place in it is expressed and communicated culturally. Every society has institutions that teach culture—family and school are two of the best examples in our society. All societies have religions, which are bodies of cultural knowledge and practices. We also have rituals for birth and death. All cultures have objects that are used for everyday living. We express our world and views through dance, drama, music, and art. We decorate our world and our bodies. We paint our faces and the walls of our houses. We make music with instruments and our voices. All this activity is shaped by our participation in a cultural tradition.

A quality elementary art program provides a wonderful opportunity for teachers to expose students to a variety of cultures as well as their own and to help them to become culturally aware. Following are several of the areas such a program can enhance.

Art Promotes Intracultural Understanding

Through a culturally diverse art program, students begin to understand the role and function that art and artists play in society. Through learning about the art of other cultures, they have the opportunity to identify similarities and differences among their culture and others. They learn that art reflects the religion, politics, economics, and other aspects of a culture.

Through a quality art program, students can address issues of ethnocentrism, bias, stereotyping, prejudice, discrimination, and racism. Students can learn that no one racial, cultural, or national group is superior to another and that no one group's art is better than another.

Art Teaches Self-Esteem Through Diversity

Through a quality art program, students learn to recognize, acknowledge, and celebrate racial and cultural diversity through art within their own society. A good program helps promote the enhancement and affirmation of their self-esteem and encourages pride in their heritage. Personal expression is encouraged, and the result is often a statement in visual form that is both inventive and filled with personal meaning.

Art Teaches Effective Communication

When a quality art program is implemented, students are encouraged to increase their visual literacy skills. Students begin to understand that artists transmit information that cannot be disclosed through other modes of communication. Students learn visual literacy by looking, understanding, talking, writing, and making images. They learn that each society has its own way of communicating through image. Through a culturally sensitive art program, students will be able to discuss and compare art from other societies.

Art Teaches about the Past

Through a quality art program, students develop sensitivity and understanding for the history of humankind. For many periods in history, it is only through visual remains or material culture that societies' cultures can be pieced together. Experiences that students have with these art objects from the past teach them respect for others, challenge their minds, and stimulate not only their intellect but also their imagination.

Art Teaches Critical Thinking

A culturally sensitive art program encourages a variety of critical thinking skills. When students look at art from other cultures, they make critical judgments and develop their own opinions. Students are asked to identify and recall information; to organize selected facts and ideas; to use particular facts, rules, and principles; to figure out component parts or to classify; and to combine ideas and form a new whole.

Art Teaches Perceptual Sensitivity and Aesthetic Awareness

As a result of a quality art program, students develop a keen sense of awareness and an appreciation for beauty. They learn that each culture has its own criteria for beauty. Art experiences help cultivate an aesthetic sensitivity and respect for the natural and humanmade environment. Art classes are the only place in the school curriculum where students learn about what constitutes quality visual design—about harmony, order, organization, and specific design qualities such as balance, movement, and unity.

Art Teaches Creativity

When a culturally sensitive art program is implemented, creativity in all students is stimulated and nurtured. Students learn to solve problems creatively. They learn that every society has some form of creative expression. In some societies, no one special person is called an artist—everyone in the culture makes "art" objects.

Teachers can help prevent students from having a simplistic view of other cultures and help them understand the cultural context of how and why works of art are created. *Art Connections* has been carefully constructed so that students will be exposed to works of art that represent a wide variety of cultures. Questions and strategies are designed to help teachers put art in a cultural context for students. The Art History and Culture feature in the *Teacher Edition* and the *Artist Profiles* book provide additional information about the works of art and the artists.

As a teacher, you are a cultural transmitter. A quality art program taught by a culturally sensitive teacher benefits every student. When educators teach in a systematic, meaningful way, students acquire knowledge about art and cultures that will benefit them throughout their lives.

Museum Education

Marilyn J.S. Goodman, Director of Education, Solomon R. Guggenheim Museum

Museums are truly magnificent places. In recent years, these bastions of culture have taken tremendous strides toward making their collections accessible to a broader audience. Museum educators are usually eager to share new information and ideas and are delighted to assist school educators with programs and materials that can easily be incorporated into the classroom. Museums contain a wealth of treasures that offer extraordinary resources for teachers and students, and which will undoubtedly enrich the overall classroom experience.

Getting acquainted with museums in your region can be a real eye-opener. Museums collect objects that document human achievement, both in our own and in other cultures. A local historical society or farm museum might contain a variety of clothing and tools that can bring history to life. A science museum may offer interactive exhibits about phenomena in the natural or physical sciences, sensory perception, new technologies, or space exploration. A children's museum will offer hands-on displays specially designed to motivate young children to learn by doing. Art museums contain visually stunning works that reflect the diversity of human thought and experience.

Museums do not supplant classroom instruction. They enhance and reinforce what is taught by providing raw materials in the forms of objects, artifacts, and exhibits. Museums give students the chance to see and sometimes handle the real thing. It is one thing to talk about Egypt's role in the history of civilization; it is another thing entirely to see the wrappings on a cat mummy, discover hieroglyphs on a sarcophagus, or be overwhelmed by the power and grandeur of large stone sculptures of kings and queens.

When students have the chance to look at portraits, still lifes, landscapes, genre scenes, furniture, clothing, and artifacts, they learn more than by just seeing a picture of a person, place, or thing. They learn how to "read" a culture. Perhaps more importantly, they learn to develop their own process of investigation and critical inquiry. What was this person's life really like? What can one learn about the class structure of this society? What can we tell about craftspeople, available materials, or the objects this society valued? What does the clothing tell us about the climate of the region? What can we learn about the geography, topography, and vegetation? What did people eat? How did they spend leisure time? What were their

religious beliefs? Is there any evidence of trade and communication with other regions? What scientific inventions were present at the time? Can one tell if they communicated through language or by writing? Because children are naturally curious, objects will motivate them to think, research, and learn.

> "A visit to a museum will make the curriculum come alive as students begin to explore objects and learn about their meanings."

A visit to a museum will make the curriculum come alive as students begin to explore objects and learn about their meanings. Museum objects give us information in a way that is very different from reading about the objects. Students must think critically to determine both the questions and answers for themselves. A first-hand, visual investigation of an object's style, material, subject matter, and physical characteristics offers preliminary clues to deciphering its meaning. When the exploration is combined with other knowledge, such as the geography and natural resources of a region; the historical context; the social, political, and economic structure of a culture; or even advances in science and technology, students can be engaged in a type of learning that is truly multidisciplinary and may lead them into other areas of study. Moreover, methods for gathering information go far beyond what people see. Exploring objects and works of art allows students to use all of their senses, combining intellect with intuition. The

opportunity for experiential, emotional, and intellectual learning is always present.

Museum objects present different historical and cultural perspectives. Students can gather information about people, culture, belief systems, values, and the ways people lived in the past. Museum visits encourage students to see things from broader global and intellectual points of view, developing respect for the work, lives, and points of view of others. Students are encouraged to respond in a variety of ways and on different levels. Most importantly, students are invited to formulate and express their ideas and then discuss them with others.

To learn about museum resources, teachers can contact the education departments of museums in their region. If teachers explain the level of their students, the subjects they are studying, and the specific aspects of the curriculum they would like to supplement, the museum's education department can help to tailor the resources to the class. In addition to guided tours and workshops, the museum education department may offer materials for loan, including slides, pamphlets, posters, postcards, kits, and other printed materials. Some museums have teacher resource rooms filled with books, films, videos, CD-ROMs, and computer databases geared toward educators. Trained staff is available to answer questions or to help teachers develop a complete learning unit that can integrate museum objects with classroom studies.

Using museums is an excellent way to enrich and enliven the classroom experience. Educators can take the first step by learning all they can about the rich and diverse resources available to them and their students.

U.S. Museum Resources

Alabama

1 Birmingham Museum of Art
*2000 8th Avenue North,
Birmingham*
http://www.ARTSbma.org

2 Mobile Museum of Art
4850 Museum Drive, Mobile
http://www.mobilemuseum
ofart.com

3 Montgomery Museum
of Fine Arts
1 Museum Drive, Montgomery
http://www.mmfa.org

Alaska

4 Alaska State Museum
395 Whittier Street, Juneau
http://www.museums.
state.ak.us/asmhome.html

5 Anchorage Heritage Library
Museum
*301 West Northern Lights
Boulevard, Anchorage*
http://www.wellsfargohistory.
com/museums/alaska.ht

6 Anchorage Museum
of History and Art
*121 West 7th Avenue,
Anchorage*
http://www.anchorage
museum.org

Arizona

7 Heard Museum
2301 N Central Avenue, Phoenix
http://www.heard.org/

8 Phoenix Art Museum
*1625 North Central Avenue,
Phoenix*
http://www.phxart.org

9 Scottsdale Museum
of Contemporary Art - (SMOCA)
7380 E 2nd St, Scottsdale
http://www.scottsdalearts.org

Arkansas

10 Arkansas State
University Museum
Jonesboro, AR 72467
http://museumastate.edu

11 Historic Arkansas Museum
*200 East 3rd Street,
Little Rock*
http://www.arkansashistory.
com/

12 Old State House Museum
*300 West Markham Street,
Little Rock*
http://www.oldstatehouse.com

California

13 Asian Art Museum
of San Francisco
Golden Gate Park, San Francisco
http://www.asianart.org

14 Berkeley Art Museum
and Pacific Film Archive
2625 Durant Avenue, Berkeley
http://www.bampfa.berkeley.
edu

15 El Museo Mexicano -
Mexican Museum
*Fort Mason Center,
Building D, San Francisco*
http://www.mexican
museum.org

16 J Paul Getty
Center Museum
*1200 Getty Center Drive,
Los Angeles, CA*
http://www.getty.edu

17 Japanese American
National Museum
*369 East 1st Street,
Los Angeles*
http://www.janm.org

18 Korean American Museum
*3780 Wilshire Boulevard
220, Los Angeles*
http://www.kamuseum.org

19 L A County Museum
of Art
*5905 Wilshire Boulevard,
Los Angeles*
http://www.lacma.org

20 San Francisco Museum
of Modern Art
*151 3rd Street Building A,
San Francisco*
http://www.sfmoma.org/

21 Santa Barbara
Museum of Art
1130 State Street, Santa Barbara
http://www.sbmuseart.org

22 Southwest Museum
234 Museum Drive, Los Angeles
http://www.southwest
museum.org/

Colorado

23 Aspen Art Museum
590 North Mill Street, Aspen
http://www.aspenart
museum.org

24 Boulder Museum
of Contemporary Art
1750 Thirteenth Street, Boulder
http://www.bmoca.org/

25 Denver Art Museum
100 West 14th Avenue, Denver
http://www.denverart
museum.org

Connecticut

26 New Britain Museum
of American Art
*56 Lexington Street,
New Britain*
http://www.nbmaa.org

27 Norwalk Museum
41 North Main Street, Norwalk
http://www.norwalkct.org/
norwalkmuseum/index.htm

28 Wadsworth Atheneum
Museum of Art
600 Main Street, Hartford
http://www.wadsworth
atheneum.org/

Delaware

29 Delaware Art Museum
*800 S Madison Street
Suite B, Wilmington*
http://www.delart.org

30 Sewell C Biggs Museum
of American Art
406 Federal Street, Dover
http://www.biggsmuseum.
org

31 Winterthur Museum
Route 52, Winterthur
http://www.winterthur.org/

Florida

32 Bass Museum of Art
2121 Park Ave, Miami
http://www.bassmuseum.org/

33 Key West Art and
Historical Society
281 Front Street, Key West
http://www.kwahs.com

34 Lowe Art Museum
1301 Stanford Drive, Miami
http://www.lowemuseum.
com/

35 Miami Art Museum
101 West Flagler Street, Miami
http://www.miamiart
museum.org/

36 Museum of Fine Arts,
St Petersburg
*255 Beach Drive Northeast, St
Petersburg*
http://www.fine-arts.org

37 Salvador Dali Museum
*1000 3rd Street South,
St Petersburg*
http://www.salvadordali
museum.org

Georgia

38 Albany Museum of Art
311 Meadowlark Drive, Albany
http://www.albany
museum.com/

39 High Museum of Art
*1280 Peachtree Street
Northeast, Atlanta, GA*
http://www.high.org

40 Morris Museum of Art
1 10th Street, Augusta
http://www.themorris.org

Hawaii

41 Contemporary Museum,
Honolulu
*2411 Makiki Heights Drive,
Honolulu*
http://www.tcmhi.org

42 Kauai Museum
4428 Rice Street, Lihue
http://www.kauaimuseum.org

43 University of Hawaii
at Manoa Art Gallery
*University of Hawaii at Manoa,
Honolulu*
http://www.hawaii.edu/
artgallery

Idaho

44 Boise Art Museum
670 Julia Davis Drive, Boise
http://www.boiseart
museum.org

45 Eagle Rock Art Museum
and Education Center, Inc.
*300 S Capital Avenue,
Idaho Falls*
http://www.eaglerockart
museum.org

Illinois

46 Art Institute of Chicago
*111 South Michigan Avenue,
Chicago*
http://www.artic.edu/aic/

47 Krannert Art Museum
*500 East Peabody Drive,
Champaign*
http://www.kam.uiuc.edu

48 Martin D'Arcy
Museum of Art
*6525 N Sheridan Road,
Chicago*
http://darcy.luc.edu

49 Mitchell Museum
of the American Indian
*2600 Central Park Ave,
Evanston*
http://www.mitchell
museum.org/

50 Museum of
Contemporary Art
*220 East Chicago Avenue,
Chicago*
http://www.mcachicago.org

51 Smart Museum of Art
*5550 South Greenwood Avenue,
Chicago*
http://smartmuseum.
uchicago.edu/

Indiana

52 Brauer Museum of Art
*Valparaiso University Center
for the Arts, Valparaiso*
http://wwwstage.valpo.edu/
artmuseum/index.html

53 Eiteljorg Museum
of American Indian
and Western Art
*500 West Washington Street,
Indianapolis*
http://www.eiteljorg.org

54 Indianapolis
Museum of Art
*1200 West 38th Street,
Indianapolis*
http://www.ima-art.org

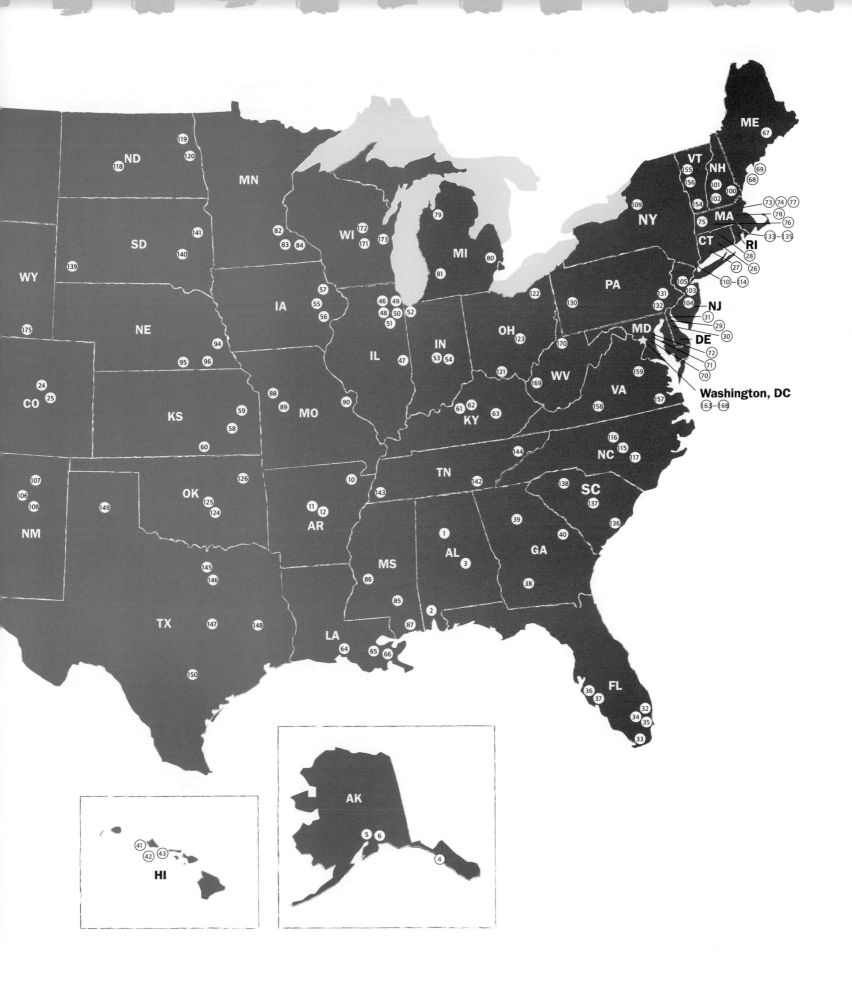

U.S. Museum Resources (continued)

Iowa

55 Cedar Rapids
Museum of Art
*410 3rd Avenue Southeast,
Cedar Rapids*
http://www.crma.org

56 Davenport Museum of Art
*1737 West 12th Street,
Davenport*
http://www.art-dma.org

57 Dubuque Museum of Art
36 East 8th Street, Dubuque
http://www.dbqart.com

Kansas

58 Coutts Memorial Museum
*110 North Main Street,
El Dorado*
http://skyways.lib.ks.us/
kansas/museums/coutts/ind

59 Spencer Museum of Art
*1301 Mississippi Street,
Lawrence*
http://www.ukans.edu/~sma/

60 Wichita Art Museum
*West Museum Boulevard,
Wichita*
http://www.wichitaart
museum.org

Kentucky

61 Kentucky Museum
of Arts + Design
609 West Main Street, Louisville
http://www.kentuckycrafts.org

62 Speed Art Museum, the
2035 South Third St., Louisville
http://www.speedmuseum.org

63 University of Kentucky
Art Museum
*Rose and Euclid Avenue,
Lexington*
http://www.uky.edu/Art
Museum/

Louisiana

64 African-American Museum
*125 New Market Street,
St Martinville*
http://stmartinparish-
la.org/tourism_africanmuseum

65 Louisiana State Museum
751 Chartres Street, New Orleans
http://lsm.crt.state.la.us/

66 New Orleans
Museum of Art
*City Park 1 Collins Diboll Circle,
New Orleans*
http://www.noma.org

Maine

67 Farnsworth Art Museum
*352 Main Street, Box 466,
Rockland*
http://farnsworthmuseum.org/

68 Ogunquit Museum
of American Art
Shore Road, Ogunquit
http://www.ogunquit
museum.org

69 Portland
Museum of Art
7 Congress Square, Portland
http://www.portlandmuseum.
org

Maryland

70 African Art
Museum of Maryland
*5430 Vantage Point Road,
Columbia*
http://www.Africanart
museum.org

71 Baltimore
Museum of Art
10 Art Museum Drive, Baltimore
http://www.artbma.org/

72 Walters Art Museum
*600 North Charles Street,
Baltimore*
http://www.thewalters.org

Massachusetts

73 Harvard University
Art Museums
32 Quincy Street, Cambridge
http://www.artmuseums.
harvard.edu/

74 Institute of Contemporary
Art
955 Boylston Street, Boston
http://www.icaboston.org

75 MASS MoCA -
Massachusetts Museum
of Contemporary Art
87 Marshall Street, North Adams
http://www.massmoca.org

76 Mead Art Museum
*Amherst College, PO Box 5000,
Amherst*
http://www.amherst.edu/
~mead/

77 Museum of Fine Arts
Boston
465 Huntington Avenue, Boston
http://www.mfa.org/

78 Worcester Art Museum
55 Salisbury Street, Worcester
http://www.worcesterart.org

Michigan

79 Cranbrook Art Museum
*39221 Woodward Avenue,
PO Box 801, Bloomfield Hills*
http://www.cranbrook.
edu/art/museum/

80 Detroit Institute of Arts
*5200 Woodward Avenue,
Detroit*
http://www.dia.org

81 Grand Rapids
Art Museum
55 Division Ave N, Grand Rapids
http://www.gramonline.org

Minnesota

82 Frederick R Weisman
Art Museum
*333 East River Road # 200,
Minneapolis*
http://hudson.acad.umn.edu/

83 Minnesota Museum
of American Art
*Landmark Center 75 West 5th
Street West, St Paul*
http://www.mmaa.org

84 Walker Art Center
*725 Vineland Place,
Minneapolis*
http://www.walkerart.org

Mississippi

85 Lauren Rogers
Museum of Art
*5th Avenue and 7th Street,
Laurel*
http://www.lrma.org/

86 Mississippi Museum
of Art
*201 E Pascagoula St
Ste 103, Jackson*
http://www.msmuseumart.
org/

87 Walter Anderson
Museum of Art
*510 Washington Avenue,
Ocean Springs*
http://www.walteranderson
museum.org/

Missouri

88 Albrecht-Kemper Art Museum
2818 Frederick Avenue, St Joseph
http://www.albrecht-
kemper.org/

89 Nelson-Atkins
Museum of Art
4525 Oak Street, Kansas City
http://www.nelson-
atkins.org/

90 St Louis Art Museum
1 Fine Arts Drive, St Louis
http://www.slam.org

Montana

91 Art Museum of Missoula
*335 North Pattee Street,
Missoula*
http://www.artmissoula.org/

92 Hockaday Museum
of Art
*2nd Avenue East at
Third Street, Kalispell*
http://www.hockadayart
museum.org/

93 Montana Museum
of Art and Culture
University of Montana, Missoula
http://www.umt.edu/partv/
famus/

Nebraska

94 Joslyn Art Museum
2200 Dodge St., Omaha
http://www.joslyn.org

95 Museum of Nebraska Art
(MONA)
2401 Central Avenue, Kearney
http://monet.unk.edu/mona/

96 Sheldon Memorial
Art Gallery and
Sculpture Garden
*University of Nebraska-Lincoln,
12th and R Streets, Lincoln*
http://sheldon.unl.edu/

Nevada

97 Las Vegas Art Museum
*9600 West Sahara Avenue,
Las Vegas*
http://www.lvam.com

98 Nevada Museum of Art
160 West Liberty Street, Reno
http://www.nevadaart.org

99 Walker African-American
Museum and Research Center
*705 W Van Buren Ave,
Las Vegas*
http://members.aol.com/
Bigbrwnsis/

New Hampshire

100 Currier Museum of Art
201 Myrtle Way, Manchester
http://www.currier.org

101 Hood Museum of Art
Wheelock Street, Hanover
http://web.dartmouth.
edu/~hood/

102 Mariposa Museum
26 Main Street, Peterborough
http://www.mariposa
museum.org

New Jersey

103 Jane Voorhees
Zimmerli Art Museum
*71 Hamilton St, Rutgers
University, New Brunswick*
http://www.zimmerlimuseum.
rutgers.edu

104 Jersey City Museum
*350 Montgomery Street,
Jersey City*
http://www.jerseycity
museum.org/

105 Princeton University
Art Museum
Princeton University, Princeton
http://www.princetonart
museum.org/

New Mexico

106 Georgia O'Keeffe Museum
217 Johnson Street, Santa Fe
http://www.okeeffe
museum.org

107 Harwood Museum of Art
*238 Ledoux Street, 4080
NDCBU, Taos*
http://www.harwood
museum.org

108 Institute of American
Indian Arts Museum
Cathedral Place, Santa Fe
http://www.iaiancad.org

New York

109 Albright-Knox
Art Gallery
1285 Elmwood Avenue, Buffalo
http://www.albrightknox.org

110 Metropolitan Museum
of Art
*6626 Metropolitan Avenue
FL 2, Flushing*
http://www.Metmuseum.org/

111 Museum of Modern Art
MoMA
11 West 53 Street , New York
http://www.moma.org/

112 New Museum
of Contemporary Art
583 Broadway, New York
http://www.newmuseum.org/

113 Solomon R Guggenheim
Museum, New York
1071 5th Ave at 89th, New York
http://www.guggenheim.org
/new_york_index.html

114 Whitney Museum
of American Art
*945 Madison Avenue FL 5,
New York*
http://www.whitney.org

North Carolina

115 Ackland Art Museum
*Columbia and Franklin Street,
Chapel Hill*
http://www.ackland.org

116 Duke University
Museum of Art
*Buchanan Blvd-Trinity Avenue,
Durham*
http://www.duke.edu/web/
duma/

117 North Carolina Museum
of Art
2110 Blue Ridge Road, Raleigh
http://www.ncartmuseum.org/

North Dakota

118 North Heritage Center of
the State Historical Society of
North Dakota, Bismarck
http://www.state.nd.us/hist/
index.html

119 North Dakota
Museum of Art
Centennial Drive, Grand Forks
http://www.ndmoa.com

120 Plains Art Museum
219 7th Street South, Fargo
http://www.plainsart.org/

Ohio

121 Cincinnati Art Museum
953 Eden Park Drive, Cincinnati
http://www.cincinnatiart
museum.com/

122 Cleveland Museum of Art
11150 East Boulevard, Cleveland
http://www.clemusart.com/

123 Columbus Museum of Art
480 East Broad Street, Columbus
http://www.columbusmuseum.
org

Oklahoma

124 Fred Jones Jr
Museum of Art
410 West Boyd Street,
University of Oklahoma, Norman
http://www.ou.edu/fjjma/

125 Oklahoma City
Art Museum
3113 Pershing Boulevard,
Oklahoma City
http://www.okcartmuseum.
com/

126 Philbrook Museum of Art
2727 South Rockford Road,
Tulsa, OK
http://www.philbrook.org/

Oregon

127 Coos Art Museum
235 Anderson Avenue, Coos Bay
http://www.coosart.org

128 Portland Art Museum
1219 SW Park Ave., Portland
http://www.pam.org

129 University of Oregon
Museum of Art
1223 University of Oregon,
Eugene
http://uoma.uoregon.edu/

Pennsylvania

130 The Andy Warhol
Museum
117 Sandusky Street, Pittsburgh
http://www.clpgh.org/warhol/

131 The Palmer
Museum of Art
Curtin Rd, The Pennsylvania
State University, University Park
http://www.psu.edu/dept/
palmermuseum/

132 Philadelphia
Museum of Art
26th Street and the Benjamin
Franklin Parkway, Philadelphia
http://pma.libertynet.org/

Rhode Island

133 Museum of Art,
Rhode Island School of Design
224 Benefit Street, Providence
http://www.risd.edu/

134 Museum Of Primitive
Art & Culture
1058 Kingstown Road,
South Kingstown

135 National Museum
of American Illustration
Vernon Court 492 Bellevue
Avenue , Newport
http://www.american
illustration.org

South Carolina

136 Gibbes Museum of Art
135 Meeting Street, Charleston
http://www.gibbes.com/

137 Columbia Museum of Art
Main and Hampton Streets,
Columbia
http://www.colmusart.org/

138 The Spartanburg County
Museum of Art
385 S Spring St., Spartanburg
http://www.sparklenet.com/
museumofart

South Dakota

139 Journey Museum
222 New York Street, Rapid City
http://www.journeymuseum.org

140 Oscar Howe Art Center
and Middle Border Museum
1300 E University Street P.O
Box 1071 Mitchell
http://www.oscarhowe.com/
index.htm

141 South Dakota Art Museum
P.O Box 2250, Brookings
http://web.sdstate.edu/sites/
artmuseum/

Tennessee

142 Hunter Museum of Art
10 Bluff View, Chattanooga
http://www.huntermuseum.
org/

143 Institute of Egyptian
Art and Archaeology
The University of Memphis,
Memphis
http://www.memst.edu/
egypt/about.html

144 Knoxville Museum of Art
1050 Worlds Fair Park Drive,
Knoxville
http://www.knoxart.org

Texas

145 Dallas Museum of Art
1717 North Harwood, Dallas
http://dm-art.org/

146 Kimbell Art Museum
3333 Camp Bowie Blvd.,
Fort Worth
http://kimbellart.org/

147 Mexic-Arte Museum
419 Congress Avenue, Austin
http://www.mexic-arte
museum.org

148 The Museum of Fine Arts
1001 Bissonnet, Houston
http://mfah.org/

149 Panhandle-Plains
Historical Museum,
West Texas A&M University
2401 4th Ave., Canyon
http://www.wtamu.edu/
museum/

150 San Antonio Museum
of Art
200 West Jones Avenue,
San Antonio
http://www.sa-museum.org

Utah

151 BYU Museum of Art
Brigham Young University,
Provo
http://www.byu.edu/moa/

152 St George Art Museum
175 East 200 North, St George
http://www.ci.st-george.ut.us/
arts/artmuseum.php

153 Utah Museum of Fine
Arts, University of Utah
370 South 1530 East
University of Utah , Salt Lake City
http://www.utah.edu/umfa/

Vermont

154 The Bennington Museum
West Main St., Bennington
http://www.bennington
museum.com

155 Robert Hull
Fleming Museum
Colchester Avenue, Burlington
http://www.uvm.edu/
~fleming/home/

156 Shelburne Museum
US Route 7, PO Box 10,
Shelburne
http://www.shelburne
museum.org

Virginia

157 Chrysler Museum of Art
245 West Olney Rd., Norfolk
http://www.chrysler.org/

158 Maier Museum of Art
2500 Rivermont Avenue,
Lynchburg
http://www.rmwc.edu/
Maier/

159 Virginia Museum
of Fine Arts
2800 Grove Ave., Richmond
http://www.vmfa.state.va.us/

Washington

160 Frye Art Museum
704 Terry Ave., Seattle
http://fryeart.org/

161 Jundt Art Museum
502 East Boone Avenue,
Spokane
http://www.gonzaga.edu/
Campus+Resources/Museums
+an

162 Seattle Art Museum
100 University St., Seattle
http://seattleartmuseum.
org/

Washington, D.C.

163 Arthur M Sackler Gallery
and the Freer Gallery of Art
1050 Independence Avenue, SW
http://www.asia.si.edu/
default.htm

164 Corcoran Gallery of Art
500 17th Street Northwest
http://www.corcoran.org/

165 Hirshhorn Museum
and Sculpture Garden
Independence Avenue
and 7th Street Southwest
http://hirshhorn.si.edu/

166 National Gallery of Art
http://www.nga.gov/

167 The National Museum
of Women in the Arts
1250 New York Ave., NW
http://www.nmwa.org/

168 Smithsonian Museums
Smithsonian Institution
http://www.si.edu/

West Virginia

169 Huntington Museum
of Art
2033 McCoy Rd., Huntington
http://www.hmoa.org/

170 Oglebay Institute:
Mansion Museum and
Glass Museum
Burton Center, Wheeling
http://www.oionline.com/

Wisconsin

171 Elvehjem Museum of Art
800 University Avenue,
Madison
http://www.lvm.wisc.edu

172 Leigh Yawkey Woodson
Art Museum
700 North Twelfth St, Wausau
http://www.lywam.org/

173 Milwaukee Art Museum
750 North Lincoln Memorial
Dr., Milwaukee
http://www.mam.org/

Wyoming

174 National Museum
of Wildlife Art
2820 Rungius Road, Jackson
http://www.wildlifeart.org

175 University of Wyoming
Art Museum
2111 Willett Dr., Laramie
http://uwadmnweb.uwyo.
edu/artmuseum/

World Museum Resources

Argentina

1 Fundacion Federico Klemm
Buenos Aires, Argentina
www.fundacionfjklemm.org

Australia

2 Art Gallery of New South Wales
Sydney, Australia
www.artgallery.nsw.gov.au/

3 Australian National Art Gallery
Canberra, Australia
www.nga.gov.au/Home/index.cfm

4 Museum of Contemporary Art
Sydney, Australia
www.mca.com.au/

Austria

5 Kunsthistorisches Museum Wien
Vienna, Austria
www.khm.at/

Bahrain

6 Al Hayat Museum
Manama, Bahrain
www.beitalquran.com/

Brazil

7 Museu Historico Nacional
Rio de Janeiro, Brazil
www.museuhistoriconacional.com.br/ingles/index.htm

Canada

8 Art Gallery of Calgary
Calgary, Canada
www.artgallerycalgary.com/

9 Morris and Helen Belkin Art Gallery, University of British Columbia
Vancouver, Canada
www.belkin-gallery.ubc.ca/

10 Art Gallery of Newfoundland and Labrador
St. Johns, Canada
www.mun.ca/agnl/main.html

11 Art Gallery of Nova Scotia
Halifax, Canada
www.agns.gov.ns.ca/

12 Art Gallery of Ontario
Toronto, Canada
www.ago.net/navigation/flash/index.cfm

13 National Gallery of Canada
Ottawa, Canada
www.national.gallery.ca/

14 The Montreal Museum of Fine Arts
Quebec, Canada
www.mmfa.qc.ca/en/index.html

15 McMichael Canadian Art Collection
Toronto, Canada
www.mcmichael.com/

16 Winnipeg Art Gallery
Winnipeg, Canada
www.wag.mb.ca/

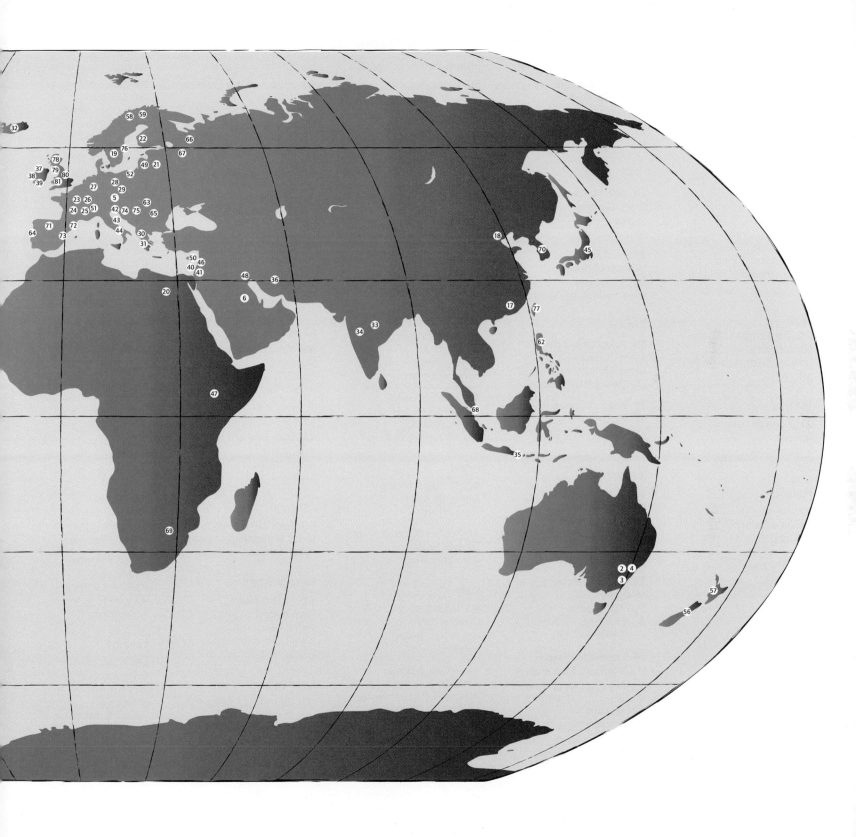

World Museum Resources

China

17 Hong Kong Museum of Art
Hong Kong, China
www.lcsd.gov.hk/CE/Museum/Arts/english/intro/eintro.html

18 Palace Museum
Beijing, China
www.dpm.org.cn/

Denmark

19 National Museum
Copenhagen, Denmark
www.natmus.dk/sw1413.asp

Egypt

20 The Egyptian Museum
Cairo, Egypt
www.egyptianmuseum.gov.eg/

Estonia

21 Estonian National Museum
Tartu, Estonia
www.erm.ee/?lang=ENG

Finland

22 The Finnish National Gallery
Helsinki, Finland
www.fng.fi/fng/rootnew/en/vtm/etusivu.htm

France

23 The Louvre
Paris, France
www.louvre.fr/louvrea.htm

24 Musee d'Orsay,
Paris, France
www.musee-orsay.fr/

25 Centre Georges Pompidou
Paris, France
www.cnac-gp.fr/Pompidou/Accueil.nsf/tunnel?OpenForm

Germany

26 Neues Museum
Nuremberg, Germany
www.nmn.de/

27 Hamburg Kunsthalle
Hamburg, Germany
www.hamburger-kunsthalle.de/

28 Alte National Galerie
Berlin, Germany
www.alte-nationalgalerie.de/

29 Bauhaus Archiv Museum of Design
Berlin, Germany
www.bauhaus.de/english/

Greece

30 Acropolis Museum
Athens, Greece
www.culture.gr/2/21/211/21101m/e211am01.html

31 Benaki Museum
Athens, Greece
www.benaki.gr/index-en.htm

Iceland

32 Living Art Museum
Reykjavik, Iceland
www.nylo.is/English/index.html

India

33 National Museum of India
New Delhi, India
www.nationalmuseumindia.org/index.html

34 Chhatrapati Shivaji Maharaj Vastu Sangrahalaya
(Formerly the Prince of Wales Museum of Western India)
Mumbai (Bombay), India
www.bombaymuseum.org/

Indonesia

35 Agung Rai Museum of Art
Ubud, Bali, Indonesia
www.nusantara.com/arma/

Iran

36 National Museum of Iran
Tehran, Iran
www.nationalmuseumofiran.com/

Ireland

37 Hunt Museum
Limerick, Ireland
www.huntmuseum.com/

38 Irish Museum of Modern Art
Dublin, Ireland
www.modernart.ie/

39 National Gallery of Ireland
Dublin, Ireland
www.nationalgallery.ie/

Israel

40 The Israel Museum
Jerusalem, Israel
www.imj.org.il/

41 Tel Aviv Museum of Art
Tel Aviv, Israel
www.tamuseum.com/

Italy

42 Uffizi Gallery
Florence, Italy
www.uffizi.firenze.it/welcomeE.html

43 Museo di Roma
Rome, Italy
www.museodiroma.comune.roma.it/PalazzoBraschi/inizio.mostra

44 Vatican Museum
Vatican City
http://mv.vatican.va/3_EN/pages/MV_Home.html

Japan

45 Kyoto National Museum
Tokyo, Japan
www.kyohaku.go.jp/index e.htm

Jordan

46 Darat al Funun Home for the Arts
Amman, Jordan
www.daratalfunun.org/

Kenya

47 National Museum of Kenya
Nairobi, Kenya
www.museums.or.ke/

Kuwait

48 Kuwait National Museum
Kuwait City, Kuwait
www.kmia.org.kw

Latvia

49 State Museum of Art
Riga, Latvia
www.vmm.lv/en/muzejs.html

Lebanon

50 American University of Beirut Archaeology Museum
Beirut, Lebanon

Liechtenstein

51 Kunstmuseum Liechtenstein
Vaduz, Liechtenstein
www.kunstmuseum.li/web2306e/index.html

Lithuania

52 Lithuanian Art Museum
Vilnius, Lithuania
www.ldm.lt/ldm_en.htm

Mexico

53 Museo de Arte Moderno
Mexico City, Mexico
www.arts-history.mx/museos/mam/home2.html

54 National Museum of Anthropology
Mexico City, Mexico
www.mna.inah.gob.mx/

55 Museo de Arte Contemporaneo de Oaxaca
Oaxaca, Mexico
www.arts-history.mx/museos/maco/home.html

New Zealand

56 Centre of Contemporary Art
Christchurch, New Zealand
www.coca.org.nz/

57 Auckland Art Gallery
Auckland, New Zealand
www.aucklandartgallery.govt.nz/

Norway

58 National Gallery of Norway
Oslo, Norway
www.museumsnett.no/nasjonalgalleriet/flash_versjon_engelsk/

59 Lillehammer Art Museum
Lillehammer, Norway
www.lillehammerartmuseum.com/

Panama

60 Museo de Arte Contemporaneo de Panama
Panama, Republic of Panama
www.macpanama.org/

Peru

61 Museo Arqueologico
Rafael Larco Herrera
Lima, Peru
museolarco.perucultural.
org.pe/

Philippines

62 Philippine National
Museum
Manila, Philippines
http://nmuseum.tripod.
com/

Poland

63 Polish National Museum
Warsaw, Poland
www.mnw.art.pl/

Portugal

64 Museu Calouste
Gulbenkian
Lisbon, Portugal
www.gulbenkian.pt/

Romania

65 The National Museum
of Art of Romania
Bucharest, Romania
http://art.museum.ro/
museum.html

Russia

66 The State Hermitage
Museum
St. Petersburg, Russia
www.hermitagemuseum.
org/

67 Pushkin Museum
of Fine Arts
Moscow, Russia
www.museum.ru/gmii/

Singapore

68 Singapore Art Museum
*Singapore, Republic of
Singapore*
www.nhb.gov.sg/SAM/
sam.shtml

South Africa

69 Pretoria Art Museum
Pretoria, South Africa
www.pretoriaartmuseum.
co.za/

South Korea

70 Seoul Metropolitan
Museum of Art
Seoul, South Korea
www.metro.seoul.kr/
muse/eng/

Spain

71 Guggenheim
Bilbao Museum
Bilbao, Spain
www.guggenheim-
bilbao.es/idioma.htm

72 Museu d'Art
Contemporani
Barcelona, Spain
www.macba.es/home.php

73 Valencian Institute
of Modern Art
Valencia, Spain
www.ivam.es/

Switzerland

74 Kunstmuseum Basel
Basel, Switzerland
www.kunstmuseumbasel.
ch/de/

75 Kunsthaus
Zurich, Switzerland
www.kunsthaus.ch/

Sweden

76 National Museum
Stockholm, Sweden
www.nationalmuseum.se/

Taiwan

77 National Palace Museum
T'aipei, Taiwan
www.npm.gov.tw/english/
index-e.htm

United Kingdom

78 National Gallery
of London
London, England
www.nationalgallery.
org.uk/

79 British Museum
London, England
www.thebritishmuseum.
ac.uk/

80 Tate Gallery
London, England
www.tate.org.uk/home/
default.htm

81 Victoria and
Albert Museum
London, England
www.vam.ac.uk/

Uruguay

82 Museo Nacianal
de Artes Visuales
Montevideo, Uruguay
www.mnav.gub.uy/

Elements and Principles of Art

Scope and Sequence

Elements of Art	Level K						Level 1						Level 2						Level 3					
	U1	U2	U3	U4	U5	U6	U1	U2	U3	U4	U5	U6	U1	U2	U3	U4	U5	U6	U1	U2	U3	U4	U5	U6
Line	1-6						1-6	1					1-4						1-2					
Shape		1-6		6				1-6	1				5-6					2, 4	3-6					
Color			1-6						1-6						1-3			1, 3		1-6				
Value															4-6							1		
Space			1, 3							2, 5, 6				5-6							1-3			
Form			2-6	5					1-4	4			1-4					2, 4	4-6					
Texture					1-6				1-3								5-6						5-6	

Principles of Art	Level K						Level 1						Level 2						Level 3					
	U1	U2	U3	U4	U5	U6	U1	U2	U3	U4	U5	U6	U1	U2	U3	U4	U5	U6	U1	U2	U3	U4	U5	U6
Pattern						1					4-5				1-2								1-3	
Rhythm						2						6			3-6								4-6	
Balance					3-4						1-2					1-2						1-4		
Proportion																								
Emphasis										3-4						3-4								3-4
Variety																3-4								2
Harmony																	1-2							1
Unity						5-6						5-6						5-6						5-6

*Numbers indicate lesson numbers within a given unit.

Table 1

Level 4 U1	U2	U3	U4	U5	U6	Level 5 U1	U2	U3	U4	U5	U6	Level 6 U1	U2	U3	U4	U5	U6	Level 7 Exploring Art	Level 8 Understanding Art
1–6						1–2						1						Chapter 2, 6, 7, 8, 9, 10, 11	Chapter 2, 6, 8, 9, 12, 15, 16
	1–2					3	1						2					Chapter 2, 6, 8, 9, 10, 11	Chapter 2, 3, 5, 8, 9, 13, 14, 16, 17
		1–4						1–4						1–4				Chapter 2, 4, 8, 9, 11, 13	Chapter 2, 3, 4, 8, 11, 12, 14–17
		5–6					4–6						2–3					Chapter 14	Chapter 13, 14, 15
		1–3					1–3								5–6			Chapter 2, 4, 10, 12	Chapter 6, 7, 13, 15
		1–3					4–6								3–4			Chapter 2, 6, 11, 12, 13	Chapter 6, 14, 15
			4–5							1					5–6			Chapter 2, 14	Chapter 3, 5, 6, 11–16

Table 2

Level 4 U1	U2	U3	U4	U5	U6	Level 5 U1	U2	U3	U4	U5	U6	Level 6 U1	U2	U3	U4	U5	U6	Level 7 Exploring Art	Level 8 Understanding Art
	3							5–6					1–3					Chapter 3, 6	Chapter 7, 8, 10, 15, 17
	4–6								2–3				4–6					Chapter 3, 4, 7	
			1–3							4–6					1–4			Chapter 3, 11, 12	Chapter 5, 7, 9, 10, 11, 13
		4–6							1–6							1–6		Chapter 3, 11, 14	Chapter 5, 11, 12
		6		5						3–4					5–6			Chapter 3, 11	Chapter 5, 10, 11, 12, 16
				5						2							1–2	Chapter 3, 6, 13	Chapter 3, 4, 5, 10, 15
				4						1							3–4	Chapter 3, 6, 7	Chapter 4, 5, 7, 12, 16
					6					5–6							5–6	Chapter 3	Chapter 7

Media

Scope and Sequence

Media	Level K						Level 1						Level 2						Level 3					
	U1	U2	U3	U4	U5	U6	U1	U2	U3	U4	U5	U6	U1	U2	U3	U4	U5	U6	U1	U2	U3	U4	U5	U6
Collage	6	2	2, 3		1	3	3		5			3, 4	5	5						4				
Drawing	2, 4, 5	4, 5	1, 4, 5	1	2	1, 2	1	1–3, 5	1, 4		2, 6	1, 5				2, 3	2–4, 6	4	1, 2, 5, 6	3	1	1	3, 5	6
Fiber Arts				4, 6							5						5					6		2
Mixed Media		6		3, 4	3				5			5	1	2	2, 6	2	2, 3	6			6	4, 6		4
Painting	1		6					1, 2, 4	4	3, 6	6			3, 4	6	1, 4–6			1, 3	3	2	2, 3, 5	4	
Photography																								
Printmaking		3								4					1					1			1	
Three-Dimensional Forms				2, 5, 6	5	4, 6			1–4	3		6	1	1, 3, 4		4	1	5		4, 5		2, 3	4, 6	1, 5
Technology	3	1				5	6	6	2								5	2, 6				5	2	3

*Numbers indicate lesson numbers within a given unit.

Level 4						Level 5						Level 6						Level 7	Level 8
U1	U2	U3	U4	U5	U6	U1	U2	U3	U4	U5	U6	U1	U2	U3	U4	U5	U6	Exploring Art	Understanding Art
	6	3				1		4	2			5	6				1	Chapter 1, 6, 10	Chapter 10
1–6	3, 4	2		1, 2, 4, 5		2, 4, 5	1, 4	1, 5	1, 4	3	2	1	3	1, 2, 4	3–5	1, 2, 5		Chapter 2, 7, 11, 14	Chapter 3, 15, 16
					3, 6						2	4	2				3, 5	Chapter 1, 2, 3, 13	Chapter 7, 8, 10, 12
	1, 5		4, 5			1, 4				1			6			6	4	Chapter 5, 13	Chapter 2, 3
		4–6		2, 5			2, 3	3	3	4, 5	1	5	1, 2, 4	5	1			Chapter 2, 3, 4, 5, 6, 9, 11, 14	Chapter 1–8, 10, 11, 13–17
			3			6											2	Chapter 10	Chapter 1, 17
										3								Chapter 3, 4, 8	Chapter 1, 3, 6, 8, 14–17
			1–3				5, 6	6	5, 6		6	3, 4		3, 6	6	3	6	Chapter 2, 3, 4, 5, 7, 12, 13	Chapter 1, 2, 3, 5–13, 15–17
	2	1		6	6	3		2			6		5			2	4	Chapter 4, 11, 15	Chapter 3, 17

Program Glossary

A

active lines *noun* Lines that show action and add energy and movement to a work of art. Diagonal, zigzag, and curved lines are examples of active lines.

additive sculpture *noun* When something is added to either relief or freestanding sculpture

alternating pattern *noun* Can repeat a motif, but change position; alter spacing between motifs or add a second motif

analogous color scheme *noun* Uses colors that are side by side on the color wheel and have a common color

analogous colors *noun* Colors that sit side by side on the color wheel and have a common hue. Violet, blue-violet, blue, blue-green are examples of analogous colors.

angle *noun* A shape formed when two lines extend in different directions from the same point

animal forms *noun* A three-dimensional representation of an animal

ant's view *noun* Viewers feel they are looking up, toward an object or figure.

appliqué *noun* An art form in which cutout fabrics are attached to a larger surface

approximate symmetry *noun* A special kind of formal balance where both sides of a design are almost exactly the same. One example is the human face: each side is almost the same as the other.

arc *noun* Any portion of a curved line from a circle

architects *noun* Artists who design buildings, cities, and bridges using three-dimensional forms

architecture *noun* The art of designing and planning buildings, cities, and bridges

armature *noun* A framework for supporting material used in sculpting

art form *noun* A type of art

assemblage *noun* A sculpture technique in which a variety of objects is assembled to create one complete piece

asymmetrical balance *noun* Another name for informal balance

asymmetry *noun* Another name for informal balance. Something asymmetrical looks balanced even if it is not the same on both sides.

atmospheric perspective *noun* The effects air and light have on how we perceive an object

axis *noun* A real or imaginary line across the center of a work of art

B

background *noun* The area of the picture plane farthest from the viewer

balance *noun* The principle of design that deals with visual weight in an artwork

bird's-eye view *noun* Or aerial view; viewers feel they are looking down on a scene.

black ■

blending *noun* A shading technique that creates a gradual change from light to dark or dark to light

blind contour drawing *noun* A drawing that is made by looking at the object being drawn, not at the paper.

blob *noun* A type of free-form shape

body forms *noun* Three-dimensional representations of a person

body proportions *noun* The size relationship of one part of the body to another

brass *noun* A metal made by combining copper and zinc

bright colors *noun* colors that appear to reflect light

broken (line) *noun* A line that is made of a series of dashes, not solid

building *noun* a structure where we live, work, meet, or play

C

calm lines *noun* Lines that give a work of art a quiet and peaceful mood. Horizontal and vertical lines are calm lines.

carving *noun* Art made by cutting into the surface of the medium.

central axis *noun* A real or imaginary dividing line that can run in two directions, vertically and horizontally

circle *noun* A round, geometric shape made when all points are placed the same distance from a center point.

close-up view *noun* Viewers feel they are right next to an object, or are a part of the action in a picture.

coil *noun* A long roll of clay joined into a circle or spiral. Clay coils are used to make pottery.

collage *noun* A two-dimensional work of art made up of pieces of paper and/or fabric to create the image.

collograph *noun* A printmaking technique where cut papers or thin boards are arranged to create an image on a stiff printing plate.

color *noun* 1. The art element that is created from reflected light; 2. In balance: a brighter color has more visual weight than a dull color; 3. In perspective: bright-colored objects seem closer, while dull or pale objects appear farther away.

color intensity *noun* The brightness or dullness of a color

color scheme *noun* A plan for organizing the colors used in an artwork

color spectrum *noun* The effect that occurs when light passes through a prism and separates into a band of colors in the order of red, orange, yellow, green, blue, and violet.

color wheel *noun* Shows the color spectrum bent into a circle

column *noun* A supporting pillar on a building

complementary color scheme *noun* Uses one set of complementary colors; for example, red and green, blue and orange, and yellow and violet

complementary colors *noun* Colors that are opposite each other on the color wheel

complex geometric shapes *noun* Shapes made by combining simple geometric shapes such as triangles, squares, and rectangles. Some examples of complex geometric shapes are diamonds, pentagons, trapezoids, hexagons, parallelograms, and octagons.

contour *noun* The edges and surface ridges of an object

contour hatching *noun* A shading technique that follows the form of an object

contour lines *noun* Continuous, unbroken lines that show the edges and surface ridges of an object or figure

contrast *noun* 1. A technique for creating a focal point or area of interest in a work of art using differences in elements; 2. In emphasis: contrast occurs when one element stands out from the rest of the work; 3. showing differences between things

converging *adj.* (*verb*) Coming together at one point or place

converging lines *noun* One of the six perspective techniques. Parallel lines seem to converge or move toward the same point as they move away from you.

cool colors *noun* Green, violet, and blue. They suggest coolness and move away from the viewer.

cool hues *noun* Blue, green, and violet. Cool hues are associated with cool things like snow, water, and grass.

cross-hatching *noun* A shading technique created when sets of parallel lines cross or intersect

culture *noun* Another word for custom

curling *verb* Hold one end of a long strip of paper. Grip the middle of the paper strip next to the side of a pencil. With a quick motion, pull the strip firmly across the pencil.

curved *adj.* Lines that bend and change gradually or turn inward to form spirals

curved (line) *noun* A line that changes directions slowly and bends in arcs

curving movement *verb* Using curved lines to move the viewer's eyes through a work of art and make the viewer feel that objects in the work of art are moving along curves

D

dark lines *noun* Created by using less water for watercolor paints

dark value *noun* A value that has more black added to it

decorative *adj.* Serving to make more beautiful; to adorn with ornaments

depth *noun* 1. The appearance of distance; 2. How far something extends toward or away from the viewer.

detail *noun* One of the six perspective techniques. Objects with fuzzy, blurred edges appear farther away than those with clear sharp edges.

diagonal *noun* (*adj.*) Lines that are slanted. They look as if they are falling or rising. They make things look active.

diagonal movement *verb* Using diagonal lines to move the viewer's eyes through a work of art and make the viewer feel that objects in the work of art are moving along diagonals

dimension *noun* A measurement of the amount of space an object takes up in one direction

diorama *noun* A display of a scene using sculpted, miniature figurines

directional lines *noun* How a line moves: diagonally, vertically, or horizontally

distortion *noun* A deviation from normal or expected proportions

dominant *noun* (*adj.*) The part of the work of art that seems more important to the viewer. Dominant elements have been emphasized.

dominant element *noun* The element in a work of art that is noticed first.

dull colors Colors that are not bright

E

earthenware *noun* Ceramics made out of clay and fired at a low heat

elongate *verb* To stretch out or make long

embroidery *noun* The art of decorating designs with needle and thread

emphasis *noun* The principle of design that stresses one area in an art work over another area

even balance *adj.* Both halves are equal. Left side and right side are the same.

exaggerate *verb* To make much larger than actual size

exaggeration *noun* To increase or enlarge beyond what is expected or normal

F

facial proportions *noun* The relationship of one feature of a face to another feature

faraway view *noun* Or eye-level view; viewers feel they are standing far away from the scene.

fiber *noun* A material used to make baskets and cloth. Grass, yarn, and straw are kinds of fibers.

flowing lines *noun* Create a feeling of calm and gracefulness. Flowing lines are fluid; they change direction and size.

flowing rhythm *noun* Created when curved lines or shapes are repeated

focal point *noun* The point where the receding lines meet. It is the first part of a composition to attract the viewer's attention.

foreground *noun* The area of the picture plane that is closest to the viewer

form *noun* A three-dimensional object that is measured by height, width, and depth

formal balance *noun* Occurs when equal or similar elements are placed on opposite sides of a central axis

Program Glossary (continued)

free-form forms *noun* Three-dimensional forms with irregular edges often found in nature

free-form shapes *noun* Two-dimensional images made of straight or curved lines or a combination of both

freestanding *noun* Forms that can be seen from all around

freestanding sculpture *noun* A three-dimensional work of art that can be viewed on all sides because it is surrounded by space

fringing *verb* Make parallel straight cuts along the edge of a piece of paper to create a ruffled look.

frontal proportions *noun* A front view of the head that is divided by three horizontal lines across the central axis

futurists *noun* A group of Italian artists during the early twentieth-century who repeated and overlapped shapes and lines to create the illusion of movement

G

geometric forms *noun* Mathematically precise forms based on geometric shapes

geometric shapes *noun* Mathematically precise shapes: circle, square, and triangle

gesture *noun* An expressive movement

gesture drawings *noun* Quick drawings used to capture the position or pose of the body

gesture lines *noun* Lines drawn to capture the movement of a person, an animal, or an object in a painting or drawing

gesture sketch *noun* Quick drawings used to capture the position or movement of the body

guide lines *noun* Lines used by artists to create both full-face and profile portraits more accurately

H

hand tools *noun* Simple instruments for carving or sculpting

harmony *noun* The principle of art that creates unity by stressing similarities of separate but related parts

hatching *noun* A shading technique that looks like a series of parallel lines

height *noun* A vertical measurement, or how tall something is

high-intensity color *noun* A pure hue such as red

highlights *noun* Small areas of white or light value to show the brightest spots

horizon line *noun* The point at which the earth and sky meet. The horizon line is always at the viewer's eye level.

horizontal *noun* (*adj.*) A line that moves from side to side

hues *noun* The spectral colors, or colors of the rainbow. Hues do not include black or white. Hues are red, orange, yellow, green, blue, and violet.

I

informal balance *noun* A way of organizing parts of a design so that unlike objects have equal visual weight

installation *noun* An artwork that was created for a specific place, such as a gallery or outdoor location

intensity *noun* The brightness or dullness of a color

interior designers *noun* Artists who decorate the inside of a building

intermediate colors *noun* Colors made by mixing a primary color and a secondary color. There are six intermediate colors— red-orange, yellow-orange, yellow-green, blue-green, blue-violet, and red-violet.

intermediate hues *noun* Yellow-green, red-orange, blue-green, made by combining a primary hue with either of the secondary hues that are adjacent on the color wheel

invented texture *noun* Created when an artist uses lines or other elements to make a textural look without any specific texture in mind

irregular *adj.* Does not follow a rule or pattern

isolation *noun* An object is emphasized by its placement apart from other objects.

J

jeweler *noun* An artist who designs and makes jewelry

jewelry *noun* Three-dimensional artwork that is made for people to wear

K

kinetic movement *noun* Actual or real movement

kinetic sculpture *noun* A three-dimensional form that actually moves in space

L

landscape *noun* a picture of the outdoors

light lines *noun* Created by adding more water to watercolor paints

light value *noun* A value that has more white added to it

line *noun* A mark drawn by a tool such as a pencil, pen, or paintbrush as it moves across a surface

line variety *noun* The different possibilities in the character of lines. For example, lines can be long or short, thick or thin, rough or smooth, and broken or solid.

linear perspective *noun* A system used to create the illusion of depth on a flat surface

lines *noun* One of the six perspective techniques. Parallel lines seem to converge or move toward the same point as they move away from the viewer.

location *noun* Artists can emphasize an object by placing it closer to the center of the piece.

low-intensity color *noun* A dull hue made by mixing a color with its complement

M

mandala *noun* A radial design divided into sections or wedges, each of which contains a different image

maquette *noun* A small model for a larger sculpture

mask *noun* A three-dimensional art form of sculpted faces

matte *noun* A dull, sometimes rough finish

medium *noun* The supply an artist uses to create art. Some media are clay, paint, or wood.

middle ground *noun* The area of the picture plane that is usually toward the center

minimal details *noun* Used in gesture sketches to complete the drawing

mix a neutral color *verb* Mix a neutral color with another color to change its value

mixed-media *noun* An art object that has been created from an assortment of media or materials

mobile *noun* A moving sculpture in which shapes are balanced and arranged on wire arms and suspended from the ceiling to move freely in the air currents

monochromatic *adj.* A color scheme that is made up of one color and the tints and shade of that color

monochromatic color scheme *noun* Uses only one color and the values of that color

monotonous *adj.* Lack of variety; boring

monumental sculptures *noun* Sculptures that are larger than human forms

motif *noun* A unit that is made up of objects or art elements that can be repeated

movement *noun* The principle of art that leads a viewer's eyes throughout a work of art

mural *noun* A painting done on a wall

N

negative space *noun* The empty space that surrounds objects, shapes, and forms

neon *noun* A special kind of light that can be made to be many bright colors

neutral color scheme *noun* Uses black, white, and a variety of grays

neutral colors *noun* Black, white, and gray; give hues a range of values

nonobjective *adj.* Art that has no recognizable subject matter

O

one-point linear perspective *noun* A system used to create the illusion of depth on a flat surface where all receding lines meet at one point

opaque *adj.* Does not let light through

outline *noun* a line drawn around the edge of an object

overlap *verb* To place one object on top of another object and partially cover the first object up

overlapping *noun* 1. One object covers a portion of another object. 2. In perspective: one of the six perspective techniques; the object covering another will appear closer to the viewer, creating a feeling of depth.

P

painting *noun* An art form using paint on a flat surface

paper sculpting techniques *noun* Six different techniques used to create paper sculptures: scoring a straight line, scoring a curve, pleating, curling, fringing, tab and slot.

parallel lines *noun* Lines that move in the same direction and always stay the same distance apart

pattern *noun* A repeated surface decoration

perception drawing *verb* Looking at something carefully and thinking deeply about what you see as you draw

perspective *noun* The method used to create the illusion of depth in two-dimensional art: overlapping, size, placement, detail, color, converging lines

perspective techniques *noun* The six techniques an artist uses to create the illusion of depth in two-dimensional art: overlapping, size, placement, detail, color, converging lines

photograph *noun* A picture taken using light-sensitive film and a camera

picture plane *noun* The surface of a drawing or painting

placement *noun* One of the six perspective techniques. Objects placed lower in the picture appear to be closer than those placed near eye level. There are three areas on a picture plane: foreground, middle ground, and background.

pleating *verb* Fold piece of paper from edge to edge. Then fold the same amount of paper in the other direction. Continue folding the paper back and forth in this manner.

point of view *noun* The angle at which the viewer sees an object

portrait *noun* A two- or three-dimensional artwork created in the image of a person or animal

posed *verb* Arranged in a special way

position *noun* In balance: a larger, positive shape and a small, negative space can be balanced by a small, positive shape and a large, negative space.

positive space *noun* Refers to any object, shape, or form in two- and three-dimensional art

primary colors *noun* Red, yellow, and blue. They cannot be made by mixing colors.

primary hues *noun* Red, yellow, and blue, used to mix the other hues on the color wheel

print *noun* An image created by using a stamp or printing plate. When artists make prints, they can make many identical images.

printing *verb* Pressing a shape from one thing to another many times

printing plate *noun* A plate that holds the image that will be used to create a print

prism *noun* A wedge-shaped piece of glass that bends light as it passes through

profile *noun* A side view of a person or animal

profile proportions *noun* A side view of the head that is divided by three horizontal lines

proportion *noun* The principle of art that is concerned with the size relationship of one part to another

Program Glossary (continued)

R

radial balance *noun* A type of balance that occurs when the art elements come out, or radiate, from a central point

rainbow *noun* An arc of spectral colors, usually identified as red, orange, yellow, green, blue, indigo, and violet, that appears in the sky opposite the sun

random pattern *noun* Occurs when the motif is repeated in no apparent order

ratio *noun* A comparison of size between two things

real texture *noun* Texture you can feel

realistic scale *noun* When an artist creates a work of art where everything fits together and makes sense in size relation

rectangle *noun* A four-sided geometric shape made of all right angles and whose opposite sides are equal in length.

regular pattern *noun* Occurs when identical motifs are repeated with an equal amount of space between them

relief *noun* A type of sculpture where forms project from a flat background

relief sculpture *noun* A sculpture in which objects stick out from a flat surface

repeated lines *noun* Used to give the feeling of movement or motion in a gesture drawing

repetition *noun* Lines, shapes, colors, or textures that are repeated throughout an artwork

rest *noun* The negative space between repetitions of the motif

rhythm *noun* The principle of design that organizes the elements in a work of art by repeating elements and/or objects

rough *noun* (*adj.*) A surface that has ridges; not smooth

rough (line) *noun* A line that has jagged, uneven edges

S

sail *noun* A type of free-form shape

scale *noun* Size as measured against a standard reference

score *verb* The repeated scratching of the clay surface at the area that another scored piece will be attached

scoring a curve *verb* Gradually cut bending curves in the paper with the point of the scissors

scoring a straight line *verb* Hold a ruler in the center of a piece of paper. Run the point of the scissors along the edge of the ruler to cut the paper in a straight line.

sculpture *noun* Three-dimensional art

sculpture model *noun* The study or detailed example of what the sculpture will look like when completed

secondary colors *noun* Orange, green, and violet. These colors are made by mixing two primary colors.

secondary hues *noun* Orange, green, and violet; the result of mixing two primary hues

self-portrait *noun* A two- or three-dimensional artwork that an artist makes of him or herself

sets of complementary colors *noun* There are three sets on the color wheel: red and green, blue and orange, and yellow and violet.

shade *noun* Any hue blended with black

shading *noun* A technique for creating dark values or darkening an area by repeating marks such as lines or dots

shadows *noun* Shaded areas in a painting or drawing

shape *noun* A two-dimensional area that is measured by height and width

shape reversal *noun* Occurs when an object, shape, or form is positive space in one image and then in another image becomes negative space

shiny *noun* Bright from reflected light

silhouette *noun* The shape of a shadow

simulated texture *noun* Imitates real texture, see also visual texture

size *noun* 1. in perspective: objects that are closer look larger than objects that are farther away; 2. In balance: a large shape or form will appear to be heavier than a small shape, and several small shapes can balance one large shape.

slip *noun* A mixture of clay and water that is creamy to the touch and is used to attach two scored pieces of clay together

smooth *noun* A surface free from roughness; even

smooth (line) *noun* A line that has even edges

solid (line) *noun* A line that has no breaks, gaps, or holes

space *noun* The art element that refers to the areas above, below, between, within, and around an object

spectral color scheme *noun* Uses all the colors of the rainbow: red, orange, yellow, green, blue, and violet

spectral colors *noun* The colors of the light spectrum: red, orange, yellow, green, blue, and violet

spectrum *noun* The range of colors that it is possible to see; the rainbow

splash *noun* A type of free-form shape

square *noun* A four-sided geometric shape where all sides are the same length and all angles are right angles

statue *noun* Three-dimensional art that is a body form

still life *noun* The arrangement of common inanimate objects from which artists draw or paint

stippling *noun* A shading technique using dots to show value

stitchery *noun* Art made with yarn on cloth

storyteller doll *noun* A Native American sculpture that shows one person relating the history of the culture to many children

style *noun* A unique quality of an object

subordinate *noun* The parts of the artwork that seem less important. Subordinate objects are not emphasized.

subtractive sculpture *noun* When an artist carves pieces away from a form

surrealism *noun* An art movement that emphasized art in which dreams, fantasy, and the subconscious served as inspiration for artists

symmetrical When two sides of a work of art are mirror images of each other

symmetry *noun* A type of formal balance in which two halves of a balanced artwork are identical, mirror images of each other

T

tactile texture *noun* The texture that can be felt

texture *noun* 1. The art element that refers to the way something feels; 2. In balance: a rough texture has an uneven pattern of highlights and shadows. For this reason, a rough surface attracts the viewer's eyes more easily than a smooth, even surface.

thick (line) *adj.* Wide

thick line *noun* Created by beginning with a thin line and gradually pressing the brush down

thin (line) *adj.* Narrow

thin line *noun* Created when a brush is held vertically to paper and touched lightly with the tip of the brush

three-dimensional *adj.* Has measurements in three directions: height, width, and depth

three-dimensional patterns *noun* Patterns that have depth and are formed on the surface of a sculptural form

three-dimensional rhythm *noun* A principle of design that indicates movement by the repetition of elements in a form

tint *noun* Any hue blended with white

transparent *adj.* Allows light to pass through so objects on the other side can be seen

triangle *noun* A three-sided geometric shape

two-dimensional *adj.* Shapes that are flat and can be measured by length and width

two-dimensional decoration *noun* Flat decoration produced on the surface of a work of art

U

unity *noun* The feeling of wholeness in a work of art. Artists use repetition and grouping to show that different parts of a work belong together.

unrealistic scale *noun* When an artist makes size relationships that do not make sense

V

value *noun* The lightness or darkness of a hue

value contrast *noun* The lightness or darkness stands out from the value that surrounds it

vanishing point *noun* The point on the horizon line where all parallel receding lines meet

variety *noun* The principle of art which is concerned with difference or contrast

vertical *noun* (*adj.*) Lines that move straight up and down. They make things look tall, steady, and calm.

visual movement *noun* Occurs when the eye is pulled through a work of art by a rhythm of beats and rests

visual rhythm *noun* The feeling of movement created when artists repeat colors, shapes, lines, and textures to lead the viewer's eyes through a work of art

visual texture *noun* Or simulated texture, imitates real texture. It is the illusion of a three-dimensional surface.

visual weight *noun* cannot be measured on a scale; it is measured by which objects the viewer's eyes see first.

W

warm colors *noun* Red, yellow, and orange. They suggest warmth and come toward the viewer.

warm hues *noun* Red, orange, and yellow. Warm hues are associated with warm things such as fire or sunshine.

weave *verb* To interlace or interweave strips or strands of material

width *noun* A horizontal measurement, or how long across something is

Z

zigzag *noun* (*adj.*) A line that is made by joining diagonal lines

Program Index

Program Index (continued)

Program Index (continued)

Program Index (continued)

Program Index (continued)